Contract Law and International Trade Regulation

Contract law and international trade are two significant and distinct areas of legal practice that often intersect. While rooted in the standard contract law syllabus, this comprehensive advanced textbook seeks to examine the interaction between contract law rules and international trade regulation. It blends in-depth discussion of the most important traditional legal concepts in both these areas of the law with a careful analysis of emerging issues and more contemporary topics, such as digital contracting, trade in services, and the Europeanisation of contract law at the level of the European Union.

Facilitating engagement with the subject matter in a way that bridges foundational legal principles and contemporary debates, the authors provide a rigorous intellectual analysis of the law, where both precedents and applicable legislation are discussed critically. A comparative analysis is offered between English common law, which is used as the constant yardstick, and its EU counterpart. Focusing on key themes such as globalisation, IT and digitalisation, ESG and sustainability, the Covid-19 pandemic, Brexit and human rights, this book allows readers to deepen their knowledge and understanding of contract law and international trade regulation while developing an appreciation of the contemporary relevance of these areas of the law and their challenges.

Contract Law and International Trade Regulation will be a valuable text for advanced undergraduate and postgraduate law students.

Pierre de Gioia Carabellese (PhD, JD, LLM, PGCAP, CMI, CMgr, MA, LLB & Diploma Legal Practice – Scotland) is Kozminski Professor of Business Law at Kozminski University. He is Solicitor (UK), Notary Public (Edinburgh), CILEX Legal Executive (England and Wales), and Avvocato (Rome). Also, he has been Professor of Law in England since 2017 (Huddersfield Advance HE).

Camilla Della Giustina (PhD, JD, TEAP (University of Glasgow and Surrey)) is a member of Ciarb and Avvocato in Rome (fully qualified lawyer in Italy). Her areas of expertise are business law, drones' law and cryonics.

Contract Law and International Trade Regulation

Contemporary Issues and Challenges

Pierre de Gioia Carabellese and Camilla Della Giustina

Routledge
Taylor & Francis Group
LONDON AND NEW YORK

Designed cover image: smagilov/Getty Images ®

First published 2026
by Routledge
4 Park Square, Milton Park, Abingdon, Oxon OX14 4RN

and by Routledge
605 Third Avenue, New York, NY 10158

Routledge is an imprint of the Taylor & Francis Group, an informa business

British Library Cataloguing-in-Publication Data
A catalogue record for this book is available from the British Library

ISBN: 978-1-041-08555-3 (hbk)
ISBN: 978-1-041-08545-4 (pbk)
ISBN: 978-1-003-64594-8 (ebk)

DOI: 10.4324/9781003645948

Typeset in Times New Roman
by Apex CoVantage, LLC

To those who inspired each of us, the authors.

Contents

Table of cases

Table of statutes

UK

EU

US

International

1 Introduction and legal theory

Chapter Overview

1. Introduction

Contract, which is one of the core disciplines of business law, governs both agreements and transactions between two or more parties, outlining their rights and obligations. Contracts can be of many forms: from the simple handshake agreement to lengthy and more complex documentation. Although this is true, all contracts share common characteristics and must adhere to the principles of contract law.

From a terminological perspective, in the scholars' debate, sometimes it is possible to find both "the law of contracts" and "the law of contract".[1] This dual definition represents a consequence of the "contractualism phenomena":[2] the contractualisation of the relationship between the individual and the State, as well as the impact of the IT evolution also in the area of contract law (business to business contract, for example). Therefore, it seems to be more appropriate to adopt the following terminology: general principles in the contract law matter.

From a legal theory perspective too, in England and Wales there were two different legal system, each of them based on its own cases in contract:

- Common law.
- Equity: The latter developed – and still develops – its own principles, consideration and remedies, to contractual problems. Further, it supplements common

1 (O'Sullivan and Hiliard 2020).
2 (Hillman 2012).

DOI: 10.4324/9781003645948-1

law where the latter is deficient. More in general, equity interventions in a contractual problem are based on the conscience of the parties. Consequently, equitable relief is discretionary and may be more flexible.

It is also important to mention that English law of contract can be found in the decisions of the courts, albeit supplemented by a number – indeed small – of statutory measures. A part of the statute in this area derives from European directives. The only common law jurisdictions in Europe are England and Wales, Cyprus and Ireland; Scotland constitutes a mix-legal system (a common law with significant Roman roots and civil law influences).

As from October 2000 the Human Rights Act 1998, incorporating the European Convention on Human Rights, has become enforceable under domestic law. The main rights recognised by ECHR are protection of property; right to life; prohibition of torture; the right to liberty/security; right to a fair trial and hearing as well as to no punishment without lawfully authority; respect for private/family life, home and correspondence; freedom of thought; conscience and religion; freedom of expression; freedom of assembly/association; freedom to marry; and prohibition of discrimination.

Important pieces of legislation in the English contract law are the Sale of Goods Act 1979, the Unfair Contract Terms Act 1977 and the Consumer Rights Act 2015.

2. The history of contract law

Before the Norman Conquest, the law of contracts was rudimentary and merely aimed to protect the honest buyer against possible claims made by some third person alleging that the beasts were stolen from him. Anglo-Saxon society knew what a credit was, although there had never been any opportunity, nor any need, for regulating contracts.

Germanic ancestors did not have an *ad hoc* general notion relating to the concept of promise or agreement as a source of civil obligations. More precisely, and under a purely Roman law terminology, early Germanic law recognised only formal and real contracts: sale was a real, not consensual, transaction.

While these legal systems share the same ancient roots, the difference is on how they developed principles around contract law. For instance, in Italy, where the Roman tradition never faded away, the Roman contract law principles has been fully implemented. By contrast, in England and Wales, the King's judges developed a more business-oriented contract law: the need for this was to provide a practical solution to controversies, rather than to develop a written legal framework, the "code", *codice*. Moreover, terms *mutuum*, *commadutum*, *locatum*, *conductum*, were used by a clerical reader rather than that King's lawyer.

In a nutshell, in the early common law there was not any general theory of contract or, better, it was not any theory suitable to satisfied certain legal tests, promises or agreements. The system was based on writs designed to protect rights coming from a few transactions giving rise to what parties generally described as contract.

The turning point took place since fourteenth, fifteenth and sixteenth centuries during which the King's courts of common law were developing new and more general remedies for breaches of contracts. The most important novelty was the "action on the case" principle: the latter covered instances of non-feasance when a writ became available against a promisor who had made a binding promise and never performed it. This approach became the normal remedy for breaches of contract. However, it evolved as a method of redressing the damage suffered by a promisee who had been disappointed by the failure of his promisor to redeem his promise.

Beside the common law courts evolution, the ecclesiastical courts and the Court of Chancery had tried to fill the gap in the law, particularly in common law. For instance, where a promisor had pledged his faith to perform his promise (i.e., he had made a promise), but it failed to fulfil that promise or agreement, his failure constituted an ecclesiastical offence.

From another perspective, the King's courts seemed to enforce only contracts ratified under such pledge of faith. Thus, the Constitution of Clarendon (1164) discouraged the ecclesiastical courts from attempting to enforce them. Despite this prohibition, the ecclesiastical courts continued to exercise jurisdiction over persons who had pledged their faith to perform contractual obligations and then failed to honour what they have said/wrote. In this respect, the trite statement was the following one:

> The Church very early took a strong view of the sanctity of contractual relationships, insisting that in conscience the obligation of a contract was completely independent of writings, forms and ceremonies, and tried so far as she could to translate this moral theory into terms of law.[3]

During medieval period, in English law cannon lawyers used to insist on the fact that it was a religious duty to keep faith. Furthermore, during the same medieval *interregnum*, in the absence of an adequate common law remedy for breach of contract, the Court of Chancery, as well as the ecclesiastical courts, was approached by petitioners seeking to redress breaches of contracts. As the great majority of the medieval chancellors were ecclesiastics, it was natural for them to follow, as much as possible, the same lines as the Church courts. They offered remedies in cases where good faith and honest dealing demanded enforcement of promises.

Throughout the seventeenth and eighteenth centuries, when it was recognised a general remedy for the breach of an agreement, and before the doctrine of consideration had been fully defined as workable criterion for determining what agreements should be legally enforceable, a discussion among judges about the duty to enforce moral obligations started flourishing. A best example of this is *Dutton v Poole*.[4] It constitutes a landmark case before the Court of Chancery relating to the

3 (Plucknett 2001).
4 (1677) 2 Lev. 210, 211–12.

privity of contract coupled with lack of consideration. These two elements, joint together, preclude third-party suit for breach of a contract and an exception to the rule in appropriate close family relationships.

The factual background was concerned with a contract, signed by a son with his father for his father to not cut down an oak woodland. Under the consideration point of view, the son would make a payment for his sister of £1000 once she had married. The money gained from the woodland would have been paid to the sister. However, the father died before the sister was married; consequently, the son refused to pay his sister money as previously agreed, at the time of marriage. Thus, the sister sued her brother for the amount that was originally promised between the father and son.

This decision represents a crucial judicial case because the concept of privity of contract had not been fully established at this stage. The court needed to ascertain whether the daughter could be privy to a contract between the father and son regarding payment. In other words, it was vital for the court to establish whether the daughter had given consideration for the promise that was made by the son to his father to pay the daughter the sum of money upon her marriage.

The court found in favour for the sister on the basis that the relationship between the father and the daughter had made the sister party to the agreement. It was true even if she was not included at the time when the contract was agreed. Again, a relationship between father and daughter was found to extend that there was a consideration given by the father in the promise to the children.

More in general, the theory of contract existing in the common law must be found in the history of the common law actions, given the link between contract and action. Thus, the theory of the common law stresses that the purpose of the action is to enforce the obligation to account. From this a question arises, and it relates to the nature of the obligation; however, the answer should not be found in contract law. Thus, if and where a bond was conditioned to render an account, the action could be used only if the conditions which created the obligation to account would exist.

There was no such thing as the action before 1232. According to the theory of the common law, the action existed for one purpose only: to enforce the obligation to account.

Again, from a historical perspective, the word "contract" raises two distinct problems:

- How did contracts become actionable at all?
- How did consideration become the test of the enforceability of such contracts?

The answer to the first question is to be found in the history of *Assumpsit*, an action with a *delictual* origin that, at the end, support the enforcement of contract. Although the origin of *Assumpsit* was not clear, it became settled that no promise was enforceable unless it were made upon a valid consideration.[5]

5 (Barbour 1914).

3. Contract law: a definition

As said previously, contract law constitutes one of the main topics of business law: contract law encompasses legal rules binding agreements between persons in society. Moreover, contract law plays a vital role also to business organisation: the latter performs most of its own business by making contracts, with customers, suppliers or employees.

A contract is based on agreement, but it is not so simple to define what an agreement is. In this respect, a lot of qualifications must be considered:

- The objective appearance rather than the fact of agreement.
- The element of voluntary transactions or not.
- The imposition of terms by law.
- The interrelationship of the law of contract and tort.
- The form of the contract.
- The enforcement of contractual obligations.

Additionally, in the contract law matter, the concept of relational contracts too exists. This approach shows that trust, cooperation, and obligations constitute central element of contract. Although it is true, to perfectly understand contracts it is quintessential to analyse the context and all relational elements linked with the social background. In this respect, contracts shall be considered elements of power, solidarity, reciprocity and harmonisation with the social matrix. Consequently, every claim shall be read under the relational theory. During this line of reasoning, the "reasonable expectation" of the parties shall be based on interpretation of different factors, such as conventions, business practices, and objectives standards. The consequence of this is that contract law shall be interpretated and read in the light of the factual context.

Furthermore, what is explained recall the notion of implicit dimension of contract. Again, also this approach emphasises the strict connection between social dimension and the agreement itself. For instance, the ethnic identity of contractual parties may determine the scope of contractual trust, cooperation and often, also, parties' expectations. Not only does contract law reflect culture, but also, it mirrors broader political, economic and social choices.[6]

One of the main characteristics of the contract law in the UK is the freedom of contract principle.[7] This was established in *Prime Sight Ltd. v Lavarello*[8] where Lord

6 (Valle 2004).
7 (Moellers 2018).
8 [2013] UKPC 22. M assigned a long lease to Prime Sight, the company, which was controlled by him. The deed of assignment acknowledges the payment and receipt of the consideration. No consideration had been paid. M's trustee in bankruptcy sought payment of the consideration. When this was not forthcoming, L petitioned for the winding up of the company. The company sought to have the petition struck out on grounds that the debt was disputed on substantial grounds. The question was whether the company could rely on this acknowledgment when both parties knew it to be untrue.

Toulson stated the following: "Parties are ordinarily free to contract on whatever terms they choose, and the court's role is to enforce them". To elaborate, this includes also the freedom to include clauses or potentially harsh terms if freely accepted by the other party. The consequences of this approach are two. The first one is the underlying philosophy: the liberal *laissez-faire* market conception of a contract. The second one relates to the protection: it was achieved by two main rules:

- Using the *contra proferentem* interpretation rule: in this respect, it is mandatory to refer to *Houghton v Trafalgar Ins*,[9] which discusses the meaning of the word "load" in the exclusion clause and if it could apply to carrying too many passengers. The claimant and defendant (the insurer) had entered an insurance contract that included an exemption clause. The latter prescribed that the defendant was not liable to pay out where the claimant's vehicle had an excess load at the time of an accident. The specific wording was that the coverage was excluded for "loss, damages and or liability caused or arising whilst the car is conveying any load in excess of that for which it was constructed". The claimant suffered a car accident and attempted to claim on his policy. At the time of the accident there were six people in the vehicles, but the vehicle was designed to seat only five. It was held that the meaning was ambiguous, and in such cases the meaning would be interpreted in the interest of the insured, that is, *contra proferentem*.
- Finding that unfair terms had not been incorporated. In *Chapelton v Barry Urban Dist. Council*[10] the controversy was about the interaction between an acceptance and exclusion clauses. It was stated that a display of goods could be an offer and a whole offer, rather than an invitation to treat. It constitutes an example for how onerous exclusion clauses can be deemed to not be incorporated in a contract. More in depth, a deckchair ticket constituted a "mere voucher or receipt", not a contractual document.

4. The influence of the European Union in UK contract law

UK joined in the European Union in 1973, a historic moment in which the consumer protection was starting to be recognised as an important social policy with an ad hoc regulation. From a UK legal system perspective, the consumer protection was adopted in 1974 with Consumer Credit Act. It may be defined as a patchwork of laws with a nascent and evolving consumer protection.

In the EU legal system, by contrast, the EU legislation covered every aspect of consumer law.

This is an example to the approach of UK legal system to the contract law area. The approach to common law may be defined as conservative based on contractual fairness; however, in the area of consumer protection English law has been very open.

9 [1954] 1 OB 247.
10 [1940] 1 KB 532.

On the other hand, the European Union approach seems to be focused on the conflict existing between business and consumer interests or, better, between those who favour an ethic of self-interest/self-reliance and those who advocate a more protective ethic. In other words, for the European Union the most important divides may be based on interests: the interest of consumer, on one hand, and the interest of traders, on the other hand.

Another proof of this the fact that the Consumer Rights Act 2015 goes beyond the protection afforded by the directive relating to unfair terms.[11]

5. European Union contract law

European Union contract law encapsulates two forms: hard law and soft law. The first one comprises regulations, directives that member states have the duty to implement to achieve the *acquis communautaire*. Soft law refers to sets of principles, restatements of the rules that the compilers think are common to different laws of contract.[12]

Soft-law statements of principles of contract law does not constitute only a European phenomenon. In 1980 the International Institute for the Unification of Private Law (UNIDROIT) began work on the Principles of International Commercial Contracts. The purpose is to encourage international trade between parties in different countries with different laws of contract as "neutral international principles". Therefore, these principles shall be applied by a court or an arbitrator if parties have agreed that their contracts should be under the "generally accepted principles". In this case, the contract must be subject to:

- National law.
- International private principles.

If the internal market constitutes the milestone of the European Union, the same conclusions cannot be drawn f from contract law: the latter does not represent an objective of the EU. Nevertheless, among jurist the attention is focused more on European Union legislation rather than the national legislation. This approach is known as "Europanisation of private law",[13] and it epitomises a paradox: on one hand contract law does not focus on the European Union piece of legislation, on the other hand scholars stress more EU legislature rather than the national one. Further, it emphasised the need to regard the Constitution of Contract Law, even if from a comparative perspective.

As a result of this, the European Commission decided to turn its legislative attention to European contract law. One output was Commission's proposal for a

11 (Howells 2017).
12 (Antonioli and Iamiceli 2024).
13 (Reimann and Zimmermann 2019).

regulation of a Common European Sales Law. Despite this, the proposal was withdrawn in 2014 due to lack of technical support in the Council.

As a result of this, contract law remains a national law matter; however, among scholars, the opportunity to shape a European legal framework has been circulating for a while; this would be aimed to harmonise the different legal systems. There are at least two ways to justify this:

- To strengthen the single market.
- To enhance the consumer protection and safety.

Although it is true, EU law has exerted an influence on contract law in the individual member states. The influence derives from a long list of directives that are designed to ensure that laws of member states afford a substantially harmonised minimum level of consumer protection. National contract law, indeed, are not uniform even if the area of directives applies. A reason of that is the different implementation made by different national laws.[14]

Also, it is worth stressing that contract law is subject to the pressure of fundamental rights: after the end of the Second World War, scholars' attention has been turned to the protection of human rights. In this respect, the first interaction between contract law and human rights may be traced back to the judgment of the German Federal Courts. More precisely, the *Bundesarbeitsgericht* recognised an immediate effect of several basic constitutional rights on employment contract.[15] The reference goes to the famous *Lüth*-judgment. In this case, the German Federal Court (*Bundesverfassungsgericht*) developed the horizontal application of fundamental rights in Germany. More in detail, it was held that the German basic law erected an "objective system of values" in its sections rights. This case law is vital because with "*Lüth*" a new globally conception of constitutional rights was born. These rights, the constitutional rights, are not primarily concerned with the limitation of the power of the State rather with the adequate protection of the right-holders' personal autonomy.

By contrast, in *DeShaney v Winnebago County*,[16] the Supreme Court of the United States held that a state government agency's failure to prevent child abuse by a custodial parent did not violate the child's right to liberty under the purposes of the Fourteenth Amendment to the United States Constitution.

One of the main questions is concerned with the debate around effects of fundamental rights in contract law and, specifically, if these rights are directly binding also on private parties. In other words, the burning question refers to the roles of legislator judges and private parties to give effect to fundamental rights in contract law. To elaborate, in the past the question was how fundamental rights should be integrated in contract law; by contrast, in recent times, the question is why fundamental rights should be given effect also in contract law.

14 (Kötz 2017).
15 BVerfG, January 15, 1958.
16 489 U.S. 189.

This demonstrates the tension between party autonomy, on one side, and the protection of weaker contract parties, on the other side. The result of this consists in the power of both judges and courts. The latter are adapting traditional contract law instruments to the contemporary democratic and social values. Therefore, from a European perspective, the two opposite pole-values are constituted by the principle of solidarity and the principle of autonomy.

The underlying doctrine is constituted by the so-called *Drittwirkung* theory, or horizontal effect theory. Strictly linked with this topic is another one, that is, the distinction between "horizontal effect" and "vertical effect".[17]

Drittwirkung means, literally, "third party effect"; it lays its roots in the idea that fundamental rights shall govern the State-citizens relationship. The consequence of this is that fundamental rights reverberate also outside the State-citizens relationship; the latter shall bind third parties too.

It is important to distinguish *Drittwirkung* effect from the terminology used in private law to the extent of a contract to a third party, therefore a party that is not party to the contractual relationship, the right/power to invoke the provisions of agreement against the contracting parties.[18]

Moreover, it is crucial to distinguish the concept of direct/indirect effect between the human rights matter and this concept in the contract law/private law area.

In human rights it is possible to affirm the following:

- Direct effect means that a State may be liable if this State violated certain human rights.
- Indirect effect occurs when a positive obligation is imposed on a State to make its law comply with Treaty rights.[19]

By contrast, in contract law:[20]

- Direct effect refers to the application of fundamental rights in contract law in the way in which they have been formulated on the constitutional level.
- Indirect effect indicates the protection of human rights through the interpretation of provision of private law or contract law. For instance, the reference is to general clauses, such as good faith and/or good morals.[21]

6. Legal theory, contract law and platform economy

Businesses have been affected and are still affected by platform business model arisen among different sectors, from retail (Ebay, Amazon Marketplace), travel (Airbnb), food home-delivery services (Deliveroo Hero), transportation (Uber,

17 (Caro De Sousa 2013).
18 (Beyleveld and Pattinson 2002).
19 *Marleasing SA v La Commercial Internacionale de Alimencation SA* [1990] E.C.R. I-4135.
20 (Gareth 2012).
21 (Mar 2008).

Blabla car) and banking (Zopa). This phenomenon is perfectly coupled with the digitalisation of products, services and business processes. Due to this increasing digitalisation, contract law too is affected by this new trend and scenario, able to change the traditional and even more ancient existing rules.[22]

In this respect, it should be noted that, whilst the underlying idea of platform business model does not represent a novelty, it is also true that the IT development changed the quantitative and qualitative dimension of contracts signed through online platform.

From a terminological perspective, a frequent expression is "disruptive technology":[23] The latter alludes to the impact of IT development on business model. New challenges arise from this: for example, contract law is informed to the notion of freedom of contract whose corollary is the exercise of private autonomy. Yet one consequence of the digital revolution is the rise of automated contracting where an individual interacts with one or more computers with the purpose to arrange a transaction. Therefore, one question is if it is required to change the basic principle for treating a binding obligation as a contract to accomplish autonomation.[24]

References

Antonioli, Luisa, and Paola Iamiceli. 2024. *The Making of European Private Law: Changes and Challenges*. Università degli Studi di Trento.

Barbour, Willard Titus. 1914. "The History of Contract in Early English Equity." In *Oxford Studies in Social and Legal History*, edited by Paul Vinogradoff. Oxford: Clarendon Press.

Beyleveld, Deryck, and Shaun D. Pattinson. 2002. "Horizontal Applicability and Horizontal Effect." *Law Quarterly Review* 118 (3): 623–46.

Bush, Christoph, Hans Schulte-Nölke, Aneta Wiewiórowska-Domagalska, and Fryderyk Zoll. 2016. "The Rise of the Platform Economy: A New Challenge for EU Consumer Law?" *Journal of European Consumer and Market Law* 5 (1): 3–10.

Caro De Sousa, Pedro. 2013. "Horizontal Expressions of Vertical Desires: Horizontal Effect and the Scope of the EU Fundamental Freedoms." *Cambridge Journal of International and Comparative Law* 3 (2): 479–505.

Christensen, Clayton M. 1997. *The Innovator's Dilemma – When New Technology Causes Great Firms to Fail*. Boston: Harvard Business Review.

Gareth, Davies. 2012. "Freedom of Movement, Horizontal Effect and Freedom of Contract." *European Review of Private Law* 20 (3): 805–27.

Hillman, Robert A. 2012. *The Richness of Contract Law: An Analysis and Critique of Contemporary Theories of Contract Law*. Springer Science & Business Media.

Howells, Geraint G. 2017. "The European Union's Influence on English Consumer Contract Law." *George Washington Law Review* 85 (6): 1904–52.

Kötz, Hein. 2017. *European Contract Law*. Oxford: Oxford University Press.

Mar, Chantal. 2008. *Fundamental Rights in European Contract Law: A Comparison of the Impact of Fundamental Rights on Contractual Relationship in Germany, Netherlands, Italy and England*. Kluwer Law International.

22 (Bush et al. 2016).
23 (Christensen 1997)
24 (Twigg-Flesner 2016).

Moellers, Thomas M.J. 2018. "Working with Legal Principles – Demonstrated Using Private Autonomy and Freedom of Contract as Examples." *European Review of Contract Law* 14 (2): 101–37.
O'Sullivan, Janet, and Jonathan Hiliard. 2020. *The Law of Contract*. Oxford: Oxford University Press.
Plucknett, Theodore Frank Thomas. 2001. *A Concise History of the Common Law*. The Lawbook Exchange, Ltd.
Reimann, Mathias, and Reinhard Zimmermann. 2019. *The Oxford Handbook of Comparative Law*. Oxford: Oxford Academic.
Twigg-Flesner, Christian. 2016. "Disruptive Technology – Disrupted Law? How the Digital Revolution Affects (Contract) Law." In *European Contract Law and the Digital Single Market: The Implications of the Digital Revolution*, edited by Alberto De Franceschi, 21–48. Intersentia.
Valle, Alberto Salazar. 2004. "The Complex Context of Contract Law." *Osgoode Hall Law Journal* 42 (3): 515–32.

2 Contracts and agreements

Chapter Overview

1. The definition of a contract

The law of contracts defines the perimeter of circumstances where a promise or promises are enforceable, although not all promises may be enforced by the Court. A promise may be enforceable as a contract, only if certain elements are present. These are as follows:

- An agreement where offer and acceptance are met.
- A consideration, which means the value recognised by the law of mutual exchange.
- An intention to create legal relations.

A contract needs all these three conditions to be met.

A gentlemen's agreement constitutes a less rigid and formal type of contract: it is an understanding – seemingly less than an agreement – between two or more parties, often referred to "handshake agreements".

Agreements, albeit merely verbal, are also binding. In the UK, exceptions to this rule are those relating to property purchases, or rental agreements, consumer credit contracts and intellectual property rights.

By contrast, in the US a verbal agreement is not binding when it involves the following:

- The sale or transfer of an interest in land o real estate.

DOI: 10.4324/9781003645948-2

- Terms that outlast the lifetime of one of the parties, for example copyright.
- Selling goods valued greater than $500.
- Marriage or divorce agreements.
- Terms that will take longer than one year to carry out.
- Someone's promise to pay someone else's debt.

It should be noted that agreements have some benefits. They are quick and simple, informal and flexible in nature. Different from agreements, contracts are written documents from which arise duties, responsibilities and commitments both parties must adhere to. Normally, contracts are formal and legally binding agreements: the entities involved can use them as supporting evidence when and if one of them fails to comply with the rules. In other words, if one party breaches the contracts or fails to properly perform their end of the deal, the other party can take a legal action.

A written contract possesses a lot of benefits, such as the following ones: (1) it is legally enforceable; (2) it is a tangible proof of its binding nature; (3) it minimises risk and disputes; (4) it is based on online template; (5) it benefits from transparency of terms and responsibilities.

Moreover, a contract is legally binding if the following requirements are present, such as the following:

- Offer and acceptance.
- Consideration.
- Legality.
- Capacity.
- Mutual assent.

Consequently, a contract constitutes a legally binding agreement where parties are generally free to agree. To decide whether a contract exists, courts have developed a test: the latter is named objective test. This test suggests that a court is entitled to give effect to an agreement if, based on words and conducts of the parties, it is possible to infer that a reasonable man would conclude a contract.

The objective test is aimed at testing and assessing the intention of the parties: the essential question is whether, objectively, parties have entered an agreement despite claims from the parties to the contrary.[1]

This was explained in *Smith v Hughes*:[2] Mr Hughes was a racehorse trainer. Because of a mistake, he bought a quantity of oats that were the same as a sample he had been shown. In other words, Mr Hughes had misidentified the kind of oats. Because of this his horses could not eat them; therefore, he refused to pay for oats. The main problem was that he needed old oats as this was the only one suitable for the horses he owned and their ad hoc diet; however, the oats sent were green, the same type as the initial sample. Mr Smith's view on the matter was totally different: he argued

1 (Smits 2017).
2 (1871) LR 6 QB 597.

that Mr Hughes had entered the contract, therefore the counterparty was at fault for not paying the future delivery of oats of the kind originally ordered. To summarise, the burning issue was whether the contract could be voided by Mr Hughes. The court, to decide this case, applied the objective test. Based on this, the court held that:

- There was a contract, and it would not be voided.
- An objective test revealed that a reasonable person would expect the sale of good quality oats in a similar contract since there was not any express discussion about old oats.
- It was also an example of *caveat emptor* or buyer beware: the latter was constituted by the sample that was given to Mr Hughes to inspect the oats.

Another important case is *RTS Flexible Systems Ltd v Molkerei Alois Müller*.[3] The claimant was a supplier of automated machines and agreed to manufacture an automated system in the defendant's factory. Work began based on a letter of intent with a long form contract to follow; the letter of intent expired whilst negotiations on the long form contract continued. A dispute arose as to whether the defendant's performance requirements were satisfied by the machines delivered by the claimants.

The High Court held that, if that the letter of intent expired and a new contract was concluded, the latter had a retrospectively application. In the case under analysis, the Court of Appel did not recognise the existence of the 'second' contract. By contract, the Supreme Court provided with a different interpretation, based on the communication – encompassed both words and conducts – between parties. Furthermore, the conclusion was that an honest, sensible businessman, in the same position as the parties in the controversy, as well as from an objective assessment, would have intended to enter legally binding relations. If a contract is negotiated "subject to contract" and works before the execution of the final contract, it is not possible to affirm that always it would be a contract on the terms that were agreed "subject to contract". Any waiver of a subject to contract clause may be inferred from communication and conduct too.

In the specific case, the conduct of the parties was unequivocal: the conclusion was that parties had made a binding agreement to waive the "subject contract" provision. Additionally, the substantial performance had already occurred; the essential terms (e.g., price) were agreed upon, and negotiations were in advantages stage.

Contract may be defined also as an agreement giving rise to obligations which are enforced or recognised by law. In common law there are three basic essential features required to engender a contract: (1) agreement, (2) contractual intention, (3) consideration.

2. Contract law and tort law

A legal point needs to be clarified from the outset. Contract law constitutes part of private law. The latter encapsulates both contract law and tort law, or delict in

3 [2010] UKSC 14.

Scottish legal system.[4] The English law of obligations is traditionally divided into two categories: tort and obligations in contract.

From a historical perspective, both contract and tort derive from the action of trespass on the case seeking compensation by way of damages. Originally, in one of the first controversies, a claim was based on a breach of King's peace.[5] The Judicature Act 1873 introduced a new code of civil procedure; the practice and further legislation, arising from it, shaped differences in procedures based on the nature of the action. This legislation, *de facto*, created new differences in procedures, depending on the nature of the action: a consequence of this was the segregation of contract law from tort.

In tort law, obligations were imposed not on parties, rather based on a general rule. By contrast in contract law obligations arise because of the voluntary obligations assumed by parties.

"Tort" possesses a French origin; it derives from the Latin word "*tortura*", i.e., "to twist". Therefore, tort is relating to those acts which are twisted, not correct or straight. Moreover, tort constitutes a civil wrong: an individual who commits a tort breaches a duty imposed by law to public, whereas the injured party has the right to compensation.

It is crucial to clarify that tort does not represent a breach of contract or a breach of trust or any other similar obligation. Further, tort is a wrong, independent of a contract. In fact, while contract and the breach of contract are concepts defined in a specific and clear manner, tort is left to a certain degree of uncertainty.

Additionally, tort constitutes a civil wrong that imposes a duty to act reasonably, a duty of care.[6] The latter is based on a what a reasonable person, in the same circumstances it would do so. This constitutes a legal fiction based on an objective test. To elaborate, the mentioned test is focused not on what a person honestly thought was the right thing to do but what the person should have done based on what a reasonable person would have done in the same or similar circumstance. Another standard is the Good Samaritan Laws: if a person does not have a particular relationship with another person (doctors and patient relationship, for instance), a person is not legally responsible to help someone who is in need. In other words, a law does not force people to make moral decisions to help others.[7]

In English common law, a leading case in tort law is *Bolton v Stone*:[8] the claimant was injured after a ball from a neighbouring cricket pitch flew into her outside home. The cricket field had been built and arranged so that it would be protected by a 17-foot gap between the ground and the top of the surrounding fence. However, it has been well-known that balls got over the fence and landed in people's yards. Although this was rare and the strike was exceptional, the claimant sued the cricket club in the tort of negligence for her injuries.

4 (Reid 2022).
5 (Maitland 1936).
6 See *Donoghue v Stevenson* [1932] AC 562.
7 (Martín-Casals 2019).
8 [1951] AC 850.

The main issue was what factors were relevant to determine how the reasonable person would have behaved; consequently, it was crucial to establish when the defendant was in breach of their duty of care. It was held, by the House of Lords, that the cricket club was not in breach of their duty. To establish if defendant was in breach of their duty of care, some factors should be considered. These factors may be summarised as follows:

- The likelihood of harm.
- The precautions adopted by defendant in terms of costs and efforts.
- If the defendant provided a socially useful service.

In a nutshell, it was established that a reasonable cricket club would not have behaved in a different way.

It should be noted further that two cases have had an impact in tort law and, more precisely, medical tort law: (1) *Montgomery v Lanarkshire Health Board*;[9] (2) *McCulloch v Forth Valley Health Board.*[10]

In *Montgomery v Lanarkshire Health Board* not only did the Court overrule the earlier *Sidaway v Board of Governors of the Bethlem Royal Hospital* but also it changed the Bolam test. More accurately, in *Montgomery v Lanarkshire Health Board* it was stressed that the requirement of informed consent or informed choice by patient in a medical treatment possesses a fundamental role on the duty of disclosure by medical practitioners. In essence, the Court did not adhere to "a model of the relationship between doctor and patient based upon medical paternalism".[11]

With *McCulloch v Forth Valley Health Board* the attention turned on information about reasonable alternative treatments. In a nutshell, the court holds that, if a doctor concludes that a particular treatment is reasonable, he is bound to discuss it with the patient even if he/she would advise following a different approach.[12]

From a comparative common law perspective, the difference existing between tort and contract is well defined in *Central Trust Co v Rafuse*,[13] a leading case of the Supreme Court of Canada about liability of solicitors, negligence and breach of contract. Two solicitors (Mr Rafuse and Cordon) had been hired by a company which had purchased the shares of Stonehouse Motel and Restaurant Ltd. The agreement of sale required the purchase to take out a mortgage on the property and used as part of the purchase price of shares. These two solicitors had been retained to complete mortgage transaction. The creditor tried to prevent the foreclosure by claiming that the mortgage was invalid. The case *Central and Eastern Trust Co v Irving Oil Ltd*[14] was under the Supreme Court of Canada scrutiny; it stated that the mortgage was invalid. As a result of this, Central Trust brought an action against the lawyers for negligence and breach of contract.

9 [2015] UKSC 11.
10 [2023] UK SC 26; 2023 SLT 725.
11 [2015] UKSC 11.
12 (MacLeod 2024).
13 [1986] 2 SCR 147.
14 [1980] 2 SCR 29.

The two solicitors claimed that:

- Their liability, if in existence, was in contract, not in tort.
- Their conduct was not negligent.
- The Nova Scotia Trust Company had contributory negligence.
- The contract signed by Nova Scotia Trust Company and the respondents was illegal due to the illegality of the objects.
- The appellant's action was barred by the statute of limitations.

The court stated that:

- The duty in tort and contract were two entirely separate duties and can be held currently by a defendant.
- The plaintiff, two solicitors, were not statute-barred from commencing an action: the commencement of the limitation period was postponed by the common law "discovered principle". Based on it, "A cause of action arises for purposes of a limitation period when the material facts on which it is based have been discovered or ought to have been discoverability by the plaintiff by the exercise of reasonable diligence".

3. The offer

A contract is an agreement, typically between two persons, giving rise to obligation on the part of both persons which are enforced or recognised by law. These parties shall be named as offeror and offeree: the first one, offeror, is the party that makes an offer to offeree.[15]

The offer may be defined as an expression of willingness to contract on certain terms: this expression is made with the intention that it shall become binding as soon as it is accepted by the offeree. The latter, again, is the person to whom it is addressed.

In the area of contract, an important distinction is between unilateral and bilateral contract. The first one, unilateral contract, constitutes an exchange or a promise of an act. More precisely, unilateral contract involves a promise by one party only it follows that it generates an obligation for one party only; a typical unilateral contract is the offer of a reward for the return of lost property.

The main difference exists between unilateral and bilateral contracts is based on the parties that share promise. In bilateral contracts, promises are made between two parties; on the opposite side in unilateral contract only the promisor makes a promise. Furthermore, in unilateral contract:

- The promise made by promisor is addressed to an individual or a group or the world at large.
- Acceptance occurs when another party performs the promisors' request.

15 (Stone and James 2019).

To summarise, an offer is a definite promise by the offeror to be bound, without more, if the offeree agrees to the offer terms.

A leading case is *Carlill v Carbolic Smoke Ball Company*[16] where, on one hand, it was stressed the significance of offer and acceptance, and on the other hand, it was distinguished between offers and invitations to treat. Carbolic Smoke Ball, the defendant, placed an advertisement in a newspaper for their products: it stated that any person who purchased and used their product but still contracted influenza despite properly following the instructions would be entitled to a £100 reward. Further, the advert stated that the company had demonstrated its sincerity by placing £1,000 in a bank account to act as the reward. The claimant, Mrs Carlill, purchased some smoke balls and, despite proper use, contracted influenza. Consequently, she attempted to claim the £100 reward from the defendant. The latter argued that he was not bound by the advert because the advert did constitute an offer, but more precisely, it was an invitation to treat. The defendant's position was based on the following circumstances:

- The advert was a mere "puff" and lacking a true intent.
- The offer could not be made to the entire world.
- The claimant did not provide acceptance in a technical manner.
- The words used in the advert were not sufficiently precise.
- There was a lack of consideration.

The issue concerned the possibility to qualify an advert as an offer or an invitation to treat. The Court of Appeal found that:

- The claimant was binding by a unilateral contract because the advert amounted to the offer.
- Mrs Carlill provided acceptance due to completing the conditions stipulated by the advert.
- The fact that the company claimed to have deposited £1,000 at the Alliance Bank was proof of the serious intent to be legally bound.
- Consideration was identifiable in the use of the balls.

The principle was that the advertisement was an offer, and an offer does not have to be made to a specific person; it can be made to the whole world.

There is a further significant case where the difference between an offer of sale and the invitation to treat is discussed: *Partridge v Crittenden.*[17] The defendant advertised for a sale of number of Bramblefinch cooks and hens, stating that the price was to be 25 shillings for each. Under the *Protection of Birds Act 1954*, it was unlawful to offer for sale any wild live bird. The Royal Society for the Prevention of Cruelty to Animals (RSPCA) brought a prosecution against the defendant under

16 [1893] 1 QB 256.
17 [1968] 2 All ER 421.

the Act. At this trial, the defendant was found guilty of the offence by the magistrates; he appealed this conviction.

The issues were two: (1) if the advertisement was either an offer of sale or an invitation to treat;[18] (2) if the phrase "offer for sale" had the same meaning in contract law and criminal law. The court held that the advertisement was not an offer but an invitation to treat. Consequently, the defendant was not guilty. Further, the court emphasised that it did not adopt a stricter interpretation of the concept "offer for sale" in criminal context compared with the contractual one. Otherwise, the court would usurp the legislative function.

Another important case that should be mentioned is *Gibson v Manchester City Council*:[19] the defendant, City Council, had adopted a policy of selling council houses to its tenants. The claimant was a tenant of such council house who had applied for details of the house he was renting and applicable mortgage terms using the printed form designated and supplied by the defendant for this purpose. In February 1971 the City treasurer responded to this application stating that "the [council] may be prepared to sell you the house at the purchase price"; in addition it provided details of a mortgage as well as invited the claimant to make a formal application using an enclosed form. In March 1971 the claimant returned the completed form to the defendant. The House of Lords did not recognise this letter as an offer since the letter did not contain any reference to the price. Consequently, a contract was not concluded, and the letter constituted an invitation to treat.

From this it is possible to infer that the terms of the offer must be certain. This was stressed in two cases: *Loftus v Roberts*[20] and *G Scammell and Nephew v HC&JG Ouston*.[21]

In the first one, *Loftus v Roberts*, it was held that, when a contract of employment is made, all the key terms must be identifiable; otherwise, the agreement will not be enforceable. One of the main terms is the remuneration wage.

In *G Scammell and Nephew v HC&JG Ouston* the court held that the clause regarding the hire-purchase terms was so vague that there could not be a precise meaning inferable from it. Consequently, an enforceable contract did not exist between parties.

4. The invitation to treat

An invitation to treat is a statement made by one person (A) suggesting to another (B) to make A an offer. More precisely, an invitation to treat requires that a person (A) makes a declaration that she will consider offers made to her, then she is only making an invitation to treat.

18 In the first case the defendant was guilty; in the second no offence was committed.
19 [1979] 1 WLR 294.
20 [1902] 18 TLR CA.
21 [1941] AC 251.

By contrast, if a proposition is made by one person with the intention that if the other party accepts that proposition, there will then be a contract between them.[22] The proposition constitutes an offer.

Harvey v Facey[23] is a contract law case decided by the United Kingdom Judicial Committee of the Privy on the appeal from the Supreme Court of Judicature of Jamaica. This case is important since it explains the difference that exists between an offer and supply information. As far as the factual background is concerned, the topic was a negotiation over a property in Jamaica, at that time British: the defendant, Mr Lm Facey, had been carrying out negotiations with the mayor and Council of Kingston to sell a piece of property to Kingston City. On 7th October 1983, Facey was traveling on a train between Kingston and Porus. The appellant, Harvey, who wanted the property to be sold to him rather than to the City, sent a telegram. The correspondence, encapsulated into the telegram, was as follows: "Will you sell us Bumper Hall Pen? Telegraph lowest cash price-answer paid". The reply to this was: "Lowest price for Bumper Hall Pen £900". As result of this, Harvey replied: "We agree to buy Bumper Hall Pen for the sum of nine hundred pounds asked by you. Please send us your title deed in order that we may get early possession".

Facey refused to sell at that price, to which Harvey sued. While his action was dismissed in the first stage, his claim was victorious before the Court of Appeal. The latter recognised that a binding agreement had been proved. Further, the appellants obtained by the Supreme Court of Judicature in Jamaica to appeal to the Queen in Council, the Privy Council, which reversed the appeal court's opinion. More in detail, the Privy Council held in favour of the defendant; it was stressed that the first telegram did not constitute an offer because it was a request of information. The defendant's consequent response was not an offer but merely the provision of information. Finally, the claimant's final telegram was an offer, but the defendant did not accept it. Thus, there was no contract.

This case represents a milestone because it clarifies that:

- Asking for information about a potential contract does not normally constitute an offer.
- Responding with information is not an offer.
- The silence is not sufficient to accept an offer.

In *Pharpaceutical Society of Great Britain v Boots Cash Chemists*[24] the main question was whether the contract of sale was concluded when the customer selected the product from the shelves or when the items were paid for. The defendant ran a self-service shop in which non-prescription drugs and medicines – many of which were listed in the Poisons List provided in the Pharmacy and Poisons Act 1933 – were sold. These items were displayed in open shelves from which they

22 See (Li, Yi, and Li 2014).
23 1893 AC 552 (1893).
24 [1953] 1 QB 401.

could be selected by the customer, placed in shopping baskets and taken to the till where they would be paid for; the till was operated by a registered pharmacist. The claimant argued that the defendant was in breach of Section 18(1), Pharmacy and Poisons Act 1933, which required the supervision of a registered pharmacist for the sale. The Court of Appeal stated that the defendant was not in breach of the contract due to the fact that the contract was completed under the supervision of the pharmacist. The underlying reason is that the display of goods on the shelves does not constitute an offer which was accepted when the customer selected the item. The correct legal construction was that the costumer made an offer to the cashier upon arriving at the till, which was accepted when payment was taken.

Strictly linked with this decision is *Fisher v Bell*[25]: the issue was whether the display of the knife constituted an offer for sale or an invitation to treat. The defendant shopkeeper displayed in his shop window a flick knife accompanied by a price ticket displayed just behind it; he was charged with offering for sale a flick knife, in contrast with Section 1(1), Restriction of Offensive Weapons Act 1959.

The court held that, in accordance with the general principle of contract law, the display of the knife was not an offer of sale but merely an invitation to treat, and as such the defendant had not offered the knife for sale within the meaning of Section 1(1) of the piece of legislation just cited. In legal terms, the position in the window was inviting customers to offer to buy it. The statute ought to be construed in accordance with the legal meaning. Thanks to this case, it was established that, in contract law, the display of an item in a shop window represents an invitation to potential customers to treat. The defendant was not guilty of the offence with which he had been charged.

To summarise, an invitation to treat consists of a statement or act made by one person (A) inviting the other (B) to make A an offer. By contrast, an offer is a proposition put by one person to another person made with the intention that it shall become legally binding as soon as it is accepted by the other person.

5. Other typologies of invitation to treat

Invitation to treat encapsulates also other different typologies, such as the following:

- TV Advertisement: the rule a newspaper advertisement is an invitation to treat. In *Partirdge v Crittenden*[26] the Court held that the advertisement was not an offer but an invitation to treat.
- Requests for bids or tenders: the general rule is that, when a company invites tenders, this is only treated as an invitation to treat and not an offer. In *Spencer v Harding*[27] it was stated that an offer inviting tenders to be submitted for the purchase of stock did not amount to an offer capable of acceptance to sell that

25 [1961] QB 394.
26 [1968] 1 WLR 1204.
27 (1870) LR 5 CP 561.

stock, rather it amounted to an invitation to treat. More in depth, the circular did not constitute an offer but an invitation to gather tenders. Moreover, in *Harris v Nickerson,*[28] it was established that an advertisement that goods will be put up for auction does not constitute an offer to any person that the goods will be put up. Therefore, the advertiser is free to withdraw the goods from the auction at any time prior to the auction. In a nutshell, the advertisement did not constitute an offer, but it was a mere declaration of intent.

- The sale of a house, see *Gibson v Manchester City Council*, just discussed previously.
- Retailers' website.

It is important to focus on auctions: the general rule is that an auction, by inviting bids to be made, makes an invitation to treat. The offer is made by bidder which is accepted when the auctioneer strikes the table with his hammer.[29] The advertisement of an auction sale is generally only an invitation to treat. Occasionally, it is possible that auction lots will not have a reserve price, therefore, the auction sale may be advertised as being "without reserve". A reserve price is a price agreed between the auctioneer and the seller as being the lowest price which the auctioneer may accept for the lot. If the bidding does not reach the reserve price, the lot will be withdrawn from the sale. In this scenario, the most important case is *Barry v Davies (t/a Healthcare Ball & Co)*:[30] two machines being sold at an auction were advertised by auctioneer as being "sold without reserve", and no one else entered any bids. The defendant's auctioneer – acting as the defendant's agent – decided that the machines were worth far more than £200 each, being worth around £14,000 each. He withdrew them from the auction before the hammer fell. The claimant sued the defendant, alleging that there was no contract between the parties because of the following:

- The bidder in an auction does not provide any consideration with his bid.
- The auctioneer acts as an agent for the owner of the goods.

Therefore, the issue was if there was an enforceable contract between the bidder and the defendant. The Court of Appeal held in favour of the claimant: a collateral contract existed between the auctioneer and the claimant. This contract clarified that the defendant had to accept the claimant's bid if it was the highest bid. The defendant had breached this contract by withdrawing the machines from the auction instead of selling the machines to the claimant.

Consequently, the conclusions are as follows:

- When goods are sold by auction without a reserve price, there is a collateral contract between the auctioneer and the participants that the auctioneer will sell to

28 (1873) LR 8 QB 286.
29 *British Car Auctions Ltd v Wright* [1972] 1 WLR 1519.
30 [2000] 1 WLR 1962, CA.

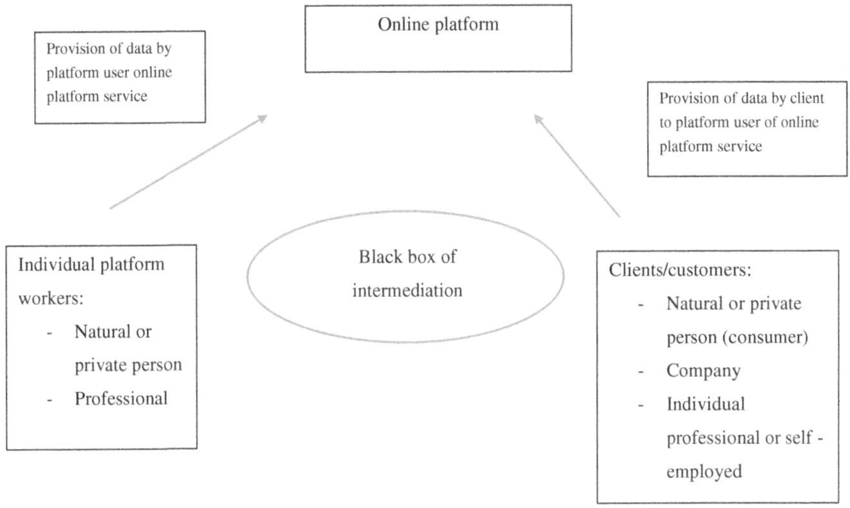

Figure 2.1 Contracts in platform economy

the highest bidder. Nevertheless, the buyer may withdraw their bid at any time before the auctioneer's hammer falls.

- Where goods are auctioned with a reserve price, the collateral contract only requires the auctioneer to accept the highest bid if it exceeds that reserve price.

6. Contracts and agreement in platform economy

As said in the previous chapter, technological development has a strong influence on contract law relations too. More in detail, the purchase of digital goods and services with a "click" action. From the latter, four different kinds of online – international or national – transactions originate: (1) business-to-business (B2B); (2) business-to-consumer (B2C); (3) platform-to-business (P2B); (4) platform-to-consumer relationships (P2C).[31]

In the platform economy both clients/consumers and individual platform workers belong to the platform; moreover, the individual platform workers provide client/consumers with a provision of services online or on-location.

The notion of platform encompasses different categories: social media or massively multiplayer online games; for contract law it is vital the concept of market makers, matchmakers or marketplaces.[32]

From this, it appears clear that platforms emerged at a point of fortuitous technological convergence: new techniques for customer tracking, immersive social design and data analysis. Platform business model converged with demands of

31 (Picker 2001).
32 (Evans 2003; Evans and Schmalensee 2016).

capital markets imposing a new imperative design which demand continued evolution of the networked information environment toward a pervasive intermediation and "datafication".

Furthermore, platforms are infrastructure-based strategies for introducing functions into networks. The latter is a mode of organisation in which hubs and nodes structure the flows of transactions and interactions. Thus, a network organisation is not a unique property of digital information and communications networks, rather a connection of human activities relies on communication and interconnection. Additionally, platform adopt technical protocols and centralised control to define networked spaces in which users can conduct heterogeneous activities and structure those spaces for ease use. Therefore, protocol-based control enables intermediation to facilitating legibility.[33]

Because of this, contracts and contract law are under an increasing pressure: digital platforms use contracts and standard terms in a different manner entering contracts with various type of costumers in multi-sided markets. In the latter on one side there is end users of social media services and on the other side app users and app developers. In both these markets, terms of contracts are rarely negotiated since platforms use standard terms, unilaterally regardless of where a customer lives or is established. Moreover, much of interpretation and application of these rules is administered by the digital platform itself to enforce compliance with its private regulatory regime. The platform is in charge too of the control of contents of the contract between end-user and the business offering the goods or services.[34]

From a descriptive perspective, online platforms are virtual spaces allowing meeting of two or more groups connected by each other by indirect network effects. Moreover, there are three main elements:

- The existence of two separate groups of users that use the platform as an intermediary.
- The existence of indirect networks effects which means that the value one user derives from the use of the platform increases according to the number of users in the other group.
- The non-neutrality of the price structure: platform can influence the volume of transactions by increasing the usage price of the platform for one group and decreasing the usage price for the other group.

References

Cohen, Julie E. 2017. "Law for the Platform Economy." *Georgetown Law Faculty Publications and Other Works* 51 (2): 133–204.

Evans, David S. 2003. "The Antitrust Economics of Multi-Sided Platform Markets." *Yale Journal on Regulation* 20: 334.

33 (Cohen 2017).

34 (Rutgers and Sauter 2021).

Evans, David S., and Richard Schmalensee. 2016. *Matchmakers: The New Economics of Multisided Platforms*. Harvard Business Review Press.
Li, Rita Yi Man, Lut Li Yi, and Rita Yi Man Li. 2014. *An Offer, an Invitation to Treat and Transaction Costs. Law, Economics and Finance of the Real Estate Market: A Perspective of Hong Kong and Singapore*. Springer.
MacLeod, John. 2024. "Double Duty: McCulloch v Forth Valley Health Board." *Edinburgh Law Review* 28 (1): 130–33.
Maitland, Frederic W. 1936. *The Forms of Action at Common Law: A Course of Lectures*. Cambridge: Cambridge University Press.
Martín-Casals, Miquel. 2019. *The Borderlines of Tort Law: Interactions with Contract Law*. London: Intersentia.
Picker, Colin B. 2001. "A View from 40,000 Feet: International Law and the Invisible Hand of Technology." *Cardozo Law Review* 23 (1): 149–220.
Reid, Elspeth. 2022. *The Law of Delict in Scotland*. Edinburgh: Edinburgh University Press.
Rutgers, Jacobien, and Wolf Sauter. 2021. "Promoting Fair Private Governance in the Platform Economy: EU Competition and Contract Law Applied to Standard Terms." *Cambridge Yearbook of European Legal Studies* 23 (11): 343–81.
Smits, Jan M. 2017. *Contract Law: A Comparative Introduction*. Edward Elgar Publishing.
Stone, Richard, and Devenney James. 2019. *The Modern Law of Contract*. Routledge.

3 The acceptance of an offer

Chapter Overview

1. Introduction

The two main and necessary elements that should exist to form a contract are the acceptance and the offer. To explain the relationship existing between the acceptance and the offer, it was said that the acceptance should be a "mirror image" of the offer.

Consequently, if a communication fails short of this, it will merely constitute a manifestation of gratitude; however, it would not be an acceptance. In *Arcadis Consulting v AMEC*,[1] the Hight Court held that parties did enter a contract, based on a simple letter of intent where the liability of Hyder was not limited.

This conclusion would have been true, even if every version of the terms of the formal contract under discussion had included a limit of liability of Hyder for breach of its professional duty. Furthermore, also an acceptance of a draft agreement by

1 (BSC) [2016] EWHC 2509 (TCC)). Hyder was engaged by Buchan to carry out design works on two projects including a multi-story car park. These two works were carried out under a letter of intent in anticipation of a wider agreement, which did not materialise. Buchan alleged that there were defects in the multi-story car park, and it may need to be demolished and rebuilt. Buchan claimed that the cost of rectifying the defects totalled £40 million and sought to recover this amount from Hyder. The latter argued that if they were liable for these defects, their liability was capped to £610,515, a figure which Hyder argued had been incorporated into the agreement.

DOI: 10.4324/9781003645948-3

subsequent conduct indicated assent to its terms, even if the draft stated that it was binding only when signed.[2]

It is crucial to establish, objectively, the existence of a contractual acceptance, as it occurs to define the existence of a contractual offer. To elaborate, acceptance occurs when the offeree's words, or conduct, give rise to the objective inference that the offeree assented to the offeror's terms. The acceptance can be either by words or by conduct.

In *Brogden v Metropolitan Railway Company*,[3] the House of Lords held that also the conduct of the parties may constitute an acceptance. In the specific case, it was recognised the existence of a valid contract between parties: the draft of the contract was amended, and this change was accepted by the conduct of the parties.

It is quintessential to distinguish two other concepts: the counteroffer and queries.

The first one, counteroffer, materialises when the offeree adds news terms while accepting the offer. More in details, a counteroffer implies a rejection of the original offer. A leading case in English law is represented by *Hyde v Wrench*.[4] The court held that a counteroffer implies a replacement of the original offer; because of this, the original offer becomes no longer available.

As far as the enquiry is concerned, it is possible to affirm that an enquiry is a query about offer, to obtain more information. More precisely, an enquiry relates to whether the offeror would be prepared to vary the offer and the original offer stands.

To understand this, it is crucial to explain *Stevenson Jaques & Co. v McLean* case.[5] The defendant, Mclean, offered to sell iron to the claimant, Stevenson Jaques & Co., for the price of 40s; the offer would remain open until the following Monday. Stevenson sent a telegram to Mclean, asking whether he would accept a payment of 40 over a two-month period, or what his longest limit would be for payment. Mclean did not respond to this, although they sold the iron to another party, without informing Stevenson Jacques of this action. On Monday morning, Stevenson Jacques sent a telegram to accept the offer, unaware that it had been sold.

The issue was whether there was a binding contract between the parties and if the telegram sent by the complainant was an enquiry for information or a counteroffer.

The court held that the claimant had made an enquiry for more information about where the terms of the offer could be changed. Therefore, it was not a specific

2 In this respect, see *Reveille Independent LLC v Anotech International (UK) Ltd* [2016] EWCA Civ 443.

3 (1877) 2 App Cas 666. Between parties did not exist a written contract and they decided to sign a formal written contract for their future business dealings. Meanwhile, parties send and receive, reciprocally, a draft of contract with minor amendments, however nobody communicated officially their acceptance. During this time, their business continued to run.

4 (1840) 49 ER 132: Mr Wrench offered to sell the farm he owned to Mr Hyde; Mr Wrench offered to sell property to £1,200 but this was declined by Mr Hyde. Further, Mr Wrench offered the farm for £1,000, and it said that this constituted the final offer; Mr Hyde offered £950 that was refused by Mr Wrench. After Mr Hyde confirmed to buy for £1,000, the sum offered by Mr Wrench, however Mr Wrench refused to sell. As a result of this, Mr Hyde brought an action for specific performance due to breach of the contract.

5 (1880) 5 QBD 346.

wording to indicate that it was either a counteroffer or rejection. To elaborate it is possible to affirm the following principles:

- The court decision seems to contrast with *Hyde v Wrench.*
- It means, in a nutshell, that the offer made by the defendant was still valid and the second telegram by the complainant formed a binding contract.
- If the promise of the offer was expected to remain open until Monday, it would not be self-binding; thus, the offeror could revoke this at any time.
- This *decisum* does not recognise the existence of a revocation, unless communicated to the claimant.

To summarise, an acceptance shall be acceptance, in an unconditional way, of an offer. Should the acceptance encompass any reservations and/or variations to the terms, it does not constitute acceptance. Therefore, the acceptance, for it to be valid, shall be

- Absolute.
- Unqualified.
- Communicated.
- Writer or by conduct.

2. The communication of the acceptance

The general existing rule is that acceptance is not effective until it is communicated to the offeror. A consequence of this is that acceptance cannot be made merely via silence. In this respect, the leading case is *Felthouse v Bindley.*[6] Paul Felthouse, the claimant, had a conversation with his nephew, John, relating to buy a horse; after their discussion, the uncle replied by letter. In this letter it was written that, if Paul Felthouse did not hear anymore from John as regards the horse, he would consider acceptance of the order done and he would own the horse; John did not reply and was busy at auctions. Mr Bindley ran the auction, and John advised him not to sell the horse; however, by accident, the horse was sold to someone else. Paul sued Mr Bindley in tort of conversion with it necessary to shoe that the horse was his property, to prove that there was a valid contract. By contrast, Mr Bindley argued that there was not a valid contract since John did not communicate his acceptance of the complainant's offer. In a nutshell, the question was whether a silence or a failure to reject an offer constitutes acceptance. It was held that a contract did not exist between Paul and John: an acceptance of offer did not occur, consequently, silence did not constitute acceptance, and an obligation cannot be imposed by another. To summarise, John, the nephew, failed to respond to the complainant.

Although it is correct, the appropriate answer to the question – if silence constitutes or not acceptance – may be the following one: silence will not constitute

6 (1862) 11 Cb (NS) 869.

acceptance when to do so would involve forcing a contract on an unwilling party. As a result of this, silence can constitute acceptance when this does not involve forcing a contract upon an unwilling party. In *Rust v Abbey Life*[7] it was accepted the statement of the "silence as acceptance rule", albeit in limited circumstances. The question the court needed to deal with was whether a binding contract had been concluded between an applicant for an investment in property bonds and the insurance company offering such bonds. The circumstance was that, in response to an application, a form was submitted by the applicant, accompanied by a cheque in the appropriate amount; the insurance company allocated this amount of money to units of the relevant fund, in the name of the investor: they also sent her a policy of insurance. Brandon LJ states as follows:

> While it may well be that in many cases silence or inactivity is not evidence of acceptance, having regard to the facts of this case and the history of the transaction between the parties as previously set out, it seems to me to be an inevitable inference from the conduct of the plaintiff in doing and saying nothing for seven months that she accepted the policy as a valid contract between herself and the first defendant.

A burning question concerns the timing of communication when it is received by a machine and outside the usual office hours; this was discussed in *Tenax Steamship Co v Owners of the Motor Vessel Brimnes (The Brimnes)*.[8] *Brimmes* was the name of the ship belonging to the defendant, owners of the Motor Vessel Brimnes. An agreement between the defendant and the claimant was signed and had as object to sell the ship. This agreement was under a condition that the ship would be time-charted back to them; however, on several occasions, the hire payment was made later than agreed. To respond, the claimant sent a message by Telex, which gave notice of withdrawal of the ship from service; this message was sent during normal office hours. The problem arose because the defendant did not read it until the next day and had made the payment.

The issue was whether the notice of withdrawal of service was effective before the defendant's payment of hire. It was held that the withdrawal was effective when Telex message was received and not when the message was read. A corollary of this is that any withdrawal of an offer sent through a form of instantaneous communication, as Telex, would be effective when it could have been read by the other party, not when it was read.

3. The exception to the need for the communication of the acceptance

As it was stressed previously, the main and general rule is that an acceptance, to be valid, shall be communicated to the offeror because it must be brought to

7 [1979] EWCA Civ J0330-3.
8 [1975] QB 929.

the offeror's attention. This general rule, however, has certain exceptions, that is, situations where the law does not require communication of the acceptance. These exceptions are as follows:

- Unilateral offers.
- The postal acceptance rule.

Unilateral offers recall the concept of unilateral contract: the latter is a contract where one party makes an offer to pay another if that other party performs some act or refrains from some act. The other party need make no promise to do the act or refrains from the act. In these cases, acceptance of the offer occurs through performance and there is no need for communicating acceptance in advance of performance.

The case is the just discussed *Carlill v Carbolic Smoke Ball Company*: full performance constitutes the acceptance of the offer; thus, there is no need to communicate the attempt to perform.

As far as postal acceptance rules, it is worth stressing that communication by post gives special practical difficulties that may be explained as follows:

- An offer is posted.
- The offeree receives the offer and posts her acceptance.
- The letter of acceptance will take several days to arrive.

From two problems arise: (1) at what point is the acceptance good? (2) how will the offeree know when the letter was received?

To overcome these obstacles, courts shaped an exception to the general requirement of communication, and this exception is encapsulated in two cases: *Adams v Lindsell*[9] and *Household Fire and Carriage Accident Insurance Co Ltd v Grant.*[10] In these, the "postal acceptance rule" has been theorised: in force of this the acceptance is complete when posted. Again, it constitutes an exception to the general rule that requires communication. The main consequence to this exception is that the risk of both delay and loss is put on the part of the offeror.

In *Adams v Lindsell* the question for the court was when an acceptance was effective: when it arrives at the address or, pressingly later, when the defendant saw it? The court held that the offer had been accepted as soon as the letter had been posted. As far as Adams is concerned, some theories were elaborated, such as:

- This rule prevents an offeree from accepting by post but then nullifying this acceptance by rejecting the offer by a quicker means of communication.
- Without the rule, an offeree would not be able to know for certain whether they had entered a contract or not.

9 [1818] 106 ER 250.
10 [1879] 4 Ex D 216.

- If the offeror, expressly or impliedly, indicates that postal acceptance is sufficient to beat the consequence of postal rule.
- The agreement between the two parties is complete at the moment that acceptance is posted.
- This rule does not apply if (1) the offeree (the party accepting) knew that the postal service was at that time disrupted; (2) where acceptance is made by post in response to an offer made by email, telex or telephone.
- This rule applies when it seems reasonable to use the post as a means of communicating acceptance.

From *Adams v Lindsell* three main consequences arise:

- A posted acceptance prevails over a previously posted withdrawal of the offer which had not yet reached the offeree when the acceptance was posted.
- Acceptance takes effect on posting even where it never reaches the offeror or only does so after delay.
- The contract is taken to have been made at the time of posting to take priority over another contract made after the original acceptance was posted.

In *Household Fire and Carriage Accident Insurance Co Ltd v Grant* the "postal rule" was applied. This rule means that the acceptance is effective when it is mailed if the parties consider the post as an acceptable way of communicating. It was stressed that "postal rule" shaped a "meeting of mind" from which, the first consequence is the creation of a binding contract.

In *Entores v Miles Far East Corp,*[11] the court clarified under which circumstances "postal rules" does not apply, that is, it does not apply for instantaneous communications.[12]

Finally, with the emergence of technology, contracts are formed on internet and cyberspace. Therefore, it seems that the "postal rule" should not apply. However, this may be applicable on the e-mails in the case where it is a time lap between offer and acceptance, but it is more correct to say that "postal rule" will not apply. Therefore, the postal rule:

- Does not apply to *e-contract*.
- Has been changed into "receipt rule".

4. "Postal rule" in IT law

The last paragraph opens the room for further cogitations, the application of "postal rule" to instantaneous communication. It has been suggested that general

11 [1955] 2 QB 327.
12 See also *Brinkibon Ltd v Stahag Stahl* [1982] 2 WLR 264.

acceptance rule should not apply because the there is no actual space between the sending and the acceptance of the offer.[13]

Therefore, the question is if "postal rule" should apply to email correspondence too. To investigate the matter, a comparative approach between US and UK seems to be appropriate.[14]

In the US, laws are active in determining the time and place of dispatch and receipt of electronic messaging. The UNCITRAL Model Law on Electronic Commerce[15] is the main source. The US approach rejects the application of postal acceptance rule for electronic communication because it adheres to the general rule for two main reasons. The first one is that the application of the general rule depends on whether the method of communication is instantaneous or "substantially instantaneous as two-way communication", such as contracting by fax or telephone. Since email cannot be described as a direct and instantaneous communication, this argument is not successful. The second reason is that US laws and more precisely the Uniform Electronic Transactions Act[16] clarifies the moment when a message is considered as having been received by the recipient and when it could be accessible to be received.

More in detail, UETA possesses a section, titled "Time and Place of Sending and Receipt", which stipulates that an electronic record is deemed to be sent when it is properly addressed or directed to another recipient, is in a form capable of being read by other parties' system and when it is out of the control of the sender, but however, it does not establish when the acceptance becomes effective and the contract is formed. Moreover, subsection 15(b) UETA stipulates that "an electronic record is deemed received when it enters an information processing system designated by the recipient for receiving such messages (e.g., home office)", and "it is in a form capable of being processed by that system".

A further act, the Uniform Computer Information Transactions Act 1999,[17] provides with detailed provisions: these indicates the application of the general rule in contracting by electronic means. Moving forward, Article 215 states that electronic messages are to be in effect at the time of receipt, regardless of whether any individual is aware of the receipt. The latter is defined as follows:

> In the case of an electronic notice . . . coming into existence in an information processing system or at an address in that system in a form capable of being processed by or perceived from a system of that type by a recipient, if the recipient uses, or otherwise has designated or holds out, that place or system for receipt of notices of the kind to be given and the sender does not know that the notice cannot be accessed from that place.[18]

13 (Hill 2001).
14 (Al Ibrahim, Ababneh, and Tahat 2007).
15 Henceforth UNCITRAL.
16 Henceforth UETA.
17 Henceforth UCITA.
18 Article 102(A) UCITA.

Additionally, Section 203 UCITA, entitled "Offer and Acceptance in General", states that "if an offer in an electronic message evokes an electronic message accepting the offer, a contract is formed . . . when an electronic acceptance is received".

This is coherent with Restatement (Second) of Contracts: it stipulates that mutual assent is reached after one party has made an offer and the offer is "followed by an acceptance by the other party". The acceptance may be made by any medium used by the offeror or by any other means that is "customary in similar transactions at the time and place the offer is received". Additionally, the Restatement encompasses different rules depending on how an offeree transmits his acceptance:

- The acceptance "completes the manifestation of mutual assent as soon as put out of the offeree's possession, without regard to whether it ever reaches the offeror".
- An acceptance under an option contract is not operative until received by the offeror.
- If an acceptance occurs by telephone, teletype or any means that is "substantially instantaneous two-way communication", the acceptance "is governed by the principles applicable to acceptance where the parties are in the presence of each other". In the just mentioned cases, the acceptance, to be effective, must be received by the offeror.

On the English law side, courts tend to apply the general rule to email communications to avoiding any business uncertainty regarding the timing of email contracts. Indeed, emails are considered as a non-instantaneous method of communication, thus potentially affected by delays.[19] Therefore, contracting by email has been considered as the digital equivalent of the postal system.[20]

Finally, a more recent case should be mentioned: *Reid-Roberts v Mei-Lin*.[21] In an *obiter dictum* it has been suggested that any WhatsApp message will be unavoidable to be signed. The same logic should be extended to email too. The issue – relating to an insolvency context – was whether the bankrupt had made a disposition of his interest in a family home by way of disposition in writing to his former spouse. The latter lived with their children. According to Section 53(1), Law of Property Act, such disposition must be in writing and signed. The Judge held that there was no valid disposition by the reason of the ongoing divorce proceedings. Despite this, the Judge suggested that the formality requirements were met by both email and WhatsApp messages. This statement was not controversial for email, which were conventionally signed off by the bankrupt. Yet the WhatsApp messages were said to be signed by the bankrupt because "his name is in the header of the message for

19 For example, in *Brinkibon Ltd v Stahag Stahl und Stahlwarenhandel GmbH*, ([1982] All ER293) the court held as follows: "No universal rule can cover all such cases; they must be resolved by reference to the intentions of the parties, by sound business practice and in some cases a judgment where the risks should lie".

20 (Gardner 1992).

21 [2024] EWHC 759 (Ch).

the purpose of identifying the Bankrupt as the sender and authenticating the message as originating from him". It is quite controversial such position for different reasons: (1) the header of such message can be altered by the recipients; (2) the integrity of the assertation may be compromised; (3) there is no reference to *SA v Mehta*[22] where it was said that the mere inclusion of a person's email address in the header of the email did not constitute a signature of such document.

5. The method of acceptance

In some cases, an offeror may stipulate that acceptance is to be made using a specific method; in other cases, the required method for communicating acceptance may also be inferred from the making of the offer.[23]

In *Manchester Diocesan Council for Education v Commercial and General Investments*[24] the court held that, in general, it was not a prescribed or mandatory method acceptance of a tender. If the offeror wanted to create a mandatory acceptance method, this would need to be made clear and explicit to the other parties. Further, an equally effective method of acceptance would be enough to form a valid contact.

What about an offeree using another method of acceptance? If another method is used and it results no less advantageous to the offeror, the result consists in the conclusion of the contract. This constitutes the answer, unless the offeror stipulates a certain method of acceptance and further stipulates that only this method of acceptance is good.

It is critical to explain *Manchester Diocesan Council of Education v Commercial and General Investments Ltd.*[25] Manchester Diocesan Council of Education, the claimants, called for a tender relating to property; the defendant, Commercial and General Investments, submitted an offer to buy the property. It was stated that the acceptance of tender would be notified to the person by a posted document and to the address that was to be given by the defendants. They sent their acceptance of the tender; however, they sent the document to the defendant's solicitor and not to the address given on the offer. Later, the complainant sent another acceptance to the defendant's address detailed in the tender. Subsequently, the defendants argued that the time they had received the correct acceptance document, the offer had lapsed.

The court held that there was no prescribed or mandatory method for acceptance of a tender; if the offeror wanted to create a mandatory acceptance method, this would need to be made clearly and explicitly to other parties. Thus, an equal method of acceptance would be enough to form a valid contract.

22 [2006] 1 WLR 1543 (HC).
23 See *Quenerduaine v Cole* [1883] 32 WR 185.
24 [1970] 1 WLR 241.
25 [1969] 3 All ER 1593.

6. The end of an unaccepted offer

It is well-known that an offer does not last indefinitely; it is not open for an indeterminate time. A linked rule is that no legal commitment exists until contract has been concluded by the acceptance of an offer.

Bearing in mind this, either party may change their mind and withdraw from negotiation any time before there is acceptance. In this respect, it is critical to read an old English contract case *Payne v Cave*[26] which stands for the preposition that an auctioneer's request for bid was not an offer rather than an invitation to treat.

Where an offeror has stipulated that the offer will be open for a certain period, he/she can withdraw the offer within this time. This will not be the case, but where the offeror is obliged, by a separate biding collateral contract to keep the offer open for a specified period. In this respect, in *Routledge v Grant*[27]: the court held that the original letter did not bind the defendant to keep the offer for a full six weeks, and as such it had been validly withdrawn by the defendant. This is based on one of the most important principles of contract law: one party cannot be bound whilst the other is not. The underlying issue was whether the defendant was contractually bound by his original letter to keep the offer open for six weeks, and by extension whether he was therefore bound by the claimant's acceptance within that period.

As far as the revocation of an offer is concerned, it is effective only if it be actual communication of this revocation.[28] It is important to clarify that it is not necessary for revocation to be communicated by the offeror: it is sufficient for the latter to do so through a reliable source. In *Dickinson v Dodds*[29] the issue was whether the defendant's promise to keep the offer until Friday morning was a binding contract between the parties. A further question was if he was allowed to revoke this offer and sell to a third party. The decision of the court laid down the following pillars:

- A promise, as the statement made by Mr Dodds, was not a binding contract.
- There was not a "meeting of minds" between the parties.
- A communication made by a friend or other party that an offer had been withdrawn was valid as well as it would be treated as if it came from the persons themselves.

Unilateral contract has a particular problem: as the act stipulated as acceptance of a unilateral offer may take some time to complete. Thus, an offeror may try to revoke the unilateral offer after the offeree has begun, but before he has completed

26 (1789) 3 TR 148.
27 [1828] 172 ER 415.
28 See *Byrne v van Tienhoven* [1880] 5 CPD 344.
29 [1876] 2 Ch D 463.

performance of the stipulated act. It looks like that a unjust revocation was allowed. In *Errington v Errington*,[30] it was held that:

- When the offeree begins performing a unilateral offer, the offer can no longer be revoked even if the offeree is still performing the unilateral offer.
- A unilateral offer is accepted by performing the terms of the offer.

In *Luxor (Eastbourne) Ltd v Cooper*[31] the House of Lords explained that the revocation of a unilateral offer after the offeree has begun performance of the act stipulated would not be possible in most cases because a term would be implied into the contract. Consequently, the offeree would not seek to revoke his offer. As a result of this, the case in which an offeror can revoke after performance has begun will be rare.[32] As far as the method to revoke an offer is concerned, the case comes from the US and it is *Shuey v US*,[33] applicable also in the UK. In this case, the US authorities placed an advertisement in various newspapers displaying a certain amount of money that would be paid as a reward in exchange for information leading to the arrest of several criminals. In a second time, the president of the US made a proclamation that cancelled the reward, and it was publicised also in the newspapers. After this advert had been published, Shuey identified one of the wanted men and claimed the reward. Shuey had seen the original advertisement but not the revocation.

The Supreme Court held that, as an offer had been made through a general advert to the world at large, as opposed to him personally, he ought to have realised the withdrawal in the same way.

An offer terminates where the offer is made subject to a condition which is not fulfilled: the condition, in this case, may be implied.[34]

As far as the death of offeror is concerned, the court decisions are not totally clear.

In *Bradbury v Morgan*[35] it was held that the deceased offeror's estate was liable on the offer of a guarantee after the death of the offeror. By contrast, *obiter dicta* encompassed within *Dickinson v Dodds* stressed that death of either party terminated the offer because there could not be any agreement. Potentially, the best interpretation shall be that a party cannot accept an offer once notified of the death of the offeror. However, in certain circumstances the offer could be accepted in ignorance of death. Further, the death of an offeree, probably, terminates the offer in that the offeree's personal representative could not purport to accept the offer.

30 [1952] 1 KB 290.
31 [1941] AC 108.
32 See *Schweppe v Harper* [2008] EWCA Civ 442.
33 (1875) 92 US 73.
34 See *Financings Ltd v Stimson* [1962] 3 All ER 386.
35 (1862) 158 ER 877 (Ex).

Finally, an offer lapses when the offeror may set a time limit for acceptance; once this time has passed, the offer lapses. In many cases, the offeror can revoke the offer before the time lapses, if offer has not been accepted.[36]

If no period is stipulated for the offer, an offeree cannot make the offeror wait forever; consequently the offeror is entitled to assume that acceptance will be made within a reasonable time or not at all. The concept of "reasonable period of time" depends upon the circumstances. In *Ramsgate Victoria Hotel v Montefiore*,[37] Mr Montefiore wanted to purchase shares in the claimant's hotel. He put in his offer to the claimant and paid a deposit to his bank account to buy them in June for a certain price. He did not hear anything until six months later, after the offer was accepted and he received a letter of acceptance from the complainant.

By this time, the value of shares had dropped, and the defendant was no longer interested. Mr Montefiore had not withdrawn his offer; however, he did not go with the sale. The action for a specific performance acted by Ramsgate Victoria Hotel was unsuccessful, because the offer made in June was no longer valid to form a contract. In this case, six months was considered a reasonable time before an automatic expiration of the offer of shares. Consequently, for other properties, the concept of reasonable period would be decided by the court in the individual case.

7. Offer and acceptance in platform environment

In the platform world, it is arduous to find terms such as "contract conclusion", "offer", or "acceptance" because it is common to read expression such as "order", "reservation" or "booking". Additionally, from a traditional perspective, the conclusion of a contract requires parties' consent, an element that is not required in the platform contracts.

To elucidate, a contract concluded within online platforms consists of consequent steps, named interactions, on a digital interface. An order is made possible by an initial, often public interaction by one of the platform users; this interaction is responded to by the other user. The response may or may not require a new interaction to finalise the order: it depends on both the platform and the user's preliminary choices. The just described interaction should be qualified as offer.

According to this line, an acceptance occurs when either an interaction by the users gives rise to the immediate obligation to platform interface or to enter or confirm details for later payment.

For example, Airbnb has two options: direct reservation or not. In the case of direct reservation, the receiver may directly book his accommodation; in the second one the provider receives a notification about a request of reservation, which should be confirmed or declined.[38]

36 See *Offord v Davies* (1862) 12 CBNS.
37 [1866] LR 1 Ex 109.
38 (Keukeleire 2022).

Furthermore, the communication between platform and users may be either open or close: in the first case, parties are able to send any kind of message to each other. By contrast, in a close communication, the interaction is governed by default message, similar to "your order has been accepted".[39]

The epitome of this sea-change is constituted by *Athena Brands Ltd v Superdrug Stores PLC*:[40] Athena was seeking summary judgment to determine whether a contract was formed between parties through email exchanges. Thus, the claim was based on email communications between parties. The court stated that email communications between parties formed a binding contract for the purchase of products.

A further evolution is if a contract signed through WhatsApp may allow its enforcement, for instance. In *Southwest Terminal Ltd v Achter Land and Cattle Ltd*,[41] the court of King's Bench for Saskatchewan stated that the use of "thumbs-up" emoji over a text message constitutes a valid signature. In other words, "thumbs-up" emoji represents an acceptance of a contract.

As to the narrative of the case, after a telephone conversation, one party sent to the other a text message. In the latter, the attached documents were (1) a picture of a contract (2) and this message: "please confirm flax contract". The counterparty answered with "thumbs-up" emoji.

The court found that this emoji represented a no-traditional means to sign a document. It is even more true where the historical contractual and business relationship is a long-term relationship. In this specific case, after a long telephone conversation on contract terms, the response, again through emoji, should be qualified as an electronic form of acceptance of a contract.

Another example comes from India: under Indian Contract Act of 1872 an electronic agreement signed via WhatsApp is both legal and enforceable.

More recently, in *Jaevee Homes Ltd v Fincham* (t/a Fincham Demolition),[42] it was found that a legally enforceable agreement had been struck once one party said "yes" in confirming whether the job offer was accepted. More precisely, to the question, namely "Are we saying it's my job mate?", a legal controversy arose from an ordinary conversation: after an exchange of email correspondence, parties turned to WhatsApp where a friendly and informal conversation took place. The court held that, if a WhatsApp conversation includes discussion about timing, pricing and payment practices, this constitutes a contract. This, fundamentally, corroborates a growing judicial trend: if the essential elements of a contract (e.g., scope, price, intention) are discernible from informal exchanges, the court could not hesitate to uphold them. Further, the court stressed that, if ancillary terms are surrounded by uncertainty (such as the precise start dates or payment calculations), this does not vitiate contract formation.

39 (Tai 2018).
40 [2019] EWHC 3505.
41 [2023] SKKB 116.
42 [2025] EWHC 942 (TCC).

The decision is perfectly aligned with recent judicial approaches, for example S*outheaster Maritime Ltd v Trafigura Maritime Logistics Pte Ltd*[43] and A*chter Land & Cattle Ltd v Southwest Terminal Ltd.*[44]

In the first one – *Southeaster Maritime Ltd v Trafigura Maritime Logistics Pte Ltd* – a WhatsApp negotiation for charterparty was held to give rise to bidding obligations. The second one – *Achter Land & Cattle Ltd v Southwest Terminal Ltd* – alludes to thumbs-up emoji: it was held that this emoji may be read as a signature under Canadian sale of goods.

References

Al Ibrahim, Marwan, Ala'eldin Ababneh, and Hisham Tahat. 2007. "The Postal Acceptance Rule in the Digital Age." *Journal of International Commercial Law and Technology* 2 (1): 47–53.

Gardner, Simon. 1992. "Trashing with Trollope: A Deconstruction of the Postal Rules in Contract." *Oxford Journal of Legal Studies* 17: 170–90.

Hill, Simone W.B. 2001. "Flogging a Dead Horse: The Postal Acceptance Rule and Email." *Journal of Contract Law* 17: 151–62.

Keukeleire, Artuur. 2022. "Online Platforms and National Contract Law: Unknown Parties, Unknown Rules?" *European Journal of Consumer Law* 3: 369–86.

Tai, Eric Tjong Tjin. 2018. "Platformen als uitdaging voor het privaatrecht." *WPNR: Weekblad voor privaatrecht, notariaat en registratie* 7124 (149): 835–41.

43 [2024] EWHC 255.

44 [2024] SKCA 115.

4 Intention of the parties and certainty of agreement

Chapter Overview

1. Introduction

To understand if and under which conditions parties want to create a legal relationship, called contract, it becomes quintessential to analyse their will, as well as their intention. Furthermore, strategic features of a contract are constituted by the certainty of agreement and the completeness. To elaborate, terms of an agreement should not be vague and do not require further development and/or clarification.

Traditionally, the law distinguishes between domestic and social agreements, on one hand, and commercial agreements, on the other hand. In the first case (social and domestic agreements) there is a presumption that parties do not have any intention to create a legal relation. By contrast, in case of commercial agreements, the law presumes that there is an intention to create a legal relation. In both cases the presumption is rebuttable.

The determination of whether the parties intended to enter legally binding relations is an objective: the courts will not examine the states of mind of the parties to the agreement but will ask whether reasonable parties to such an agreement would possess an intention to create a legal relation.

It was explained in *Edmonds v Lawson*[1]: it constitutes a labour law case regarding the National Minimum Wage Act 1998 and who is or is not included. In this

1 [2000] EWCA Civ 69.

DOI: 10.4324/9781003645948-4

case, the claimant, Rebecca Jane Edmonds was undertaking a criminal law pupillage with Lawson: she won an unfunded pupillage consisting of two sets of six months with different barristers at the chambers. The claimants argued that she was entitled to be paid the national minimum wage during her pupillage; the issues were (1) if a contract between parties did exist and (2) whether this was an employment contract.

It was held that the claimant was entitled to be paid national minimum wage during her pupillage because there was a contract of apprenticeship.

Furthermore, in *President of the Methodist Conference v Preston*,[2] the United Kingdom Supreme Court held that a Methodist Minister, Ms Preston, was not an employee because there was not any contractual intention between parties. More in detail, the Supreme Court stressed that the ministry was a vocation with candidates submitting themselves to the discipline of the church for life. Consequently, duties and rights of Ms Preston arose from her status within the church, not from a contract.

2. Social and domestic agreements

As far as social and domestic agreements are concerned, the leading case is undoubtedly constituted by *Balfour v Balfour*.[3] In this controversy, it was held that there is a rebuttable presumption against an intention to create a legally enforceable agreement when the agreement is domestic in nature. Mr Balfour was a civil engineer and worker for the Government in Ceylon, a British colony that time, now an independent State called Sri Lanka. Mrs Balfour was living with him. They came back to England; however, Mrs Balfour had developed a rheumatoid arthritis. The husband promised to pay his wife £30 per month whilst she remained in England due to illness. Subsequently parties divorced, and an issue arose whether the agreement was enforceable. It was held that the agreement was not enforceable due to the matrimonial relation existing between the parties. More in depth, there was not a contract because parties did not intend that they should be affected by legal consequences of these arrangements. Natural love and affection were not enough features of a contract.[4]

According to this line of reasoning, it was held that

- An agreement between a mother and her adult child did not create a contract.[5]
- An agreement to take a friend to work in exchange for petrol money was an arrangement which lacked contractual intention.[6]

An opposite case is *Merritt v Merritt*.[7] Parties married in 1941 and kept their matrimonial home in joint names. In 1966 Mr Meritt left family home to live

2 [2013] UKSC 29.
3 [1919] 2 KB 571.
4 (Parker 2019).
5 *Jones v Padavatton* [1969] 2 All ER 616.
6 *Coward v MIB* [1963] 1 QB 259.
7 [1970] 2 All ER 760.

with another woman and agreed to pay £40 per month to Mrs Meritt. Under Mrs Meritt's request, he signed an agreement in which it was written that, when she had repaid the balance of the mortgage, he would transfer the matrimonial home into her sole name. Mrs Meritt paid off the mortgage and acquired a declaration that the house belonged to her, but Mr Merritt appealed. The appeal was unsuccessful due to the fact that parties were already in the process of separating; in fact they were already separated: ultimately, the presumption of there being no intention to create legal relations did not apply. The arrangement was sufficiently certain to be enforceable.

An application of this is concerned with prenuptial agreement, or "prenup". In *Radmacher v Granatino*,[8] the United Kingdom Supreme Court stated that the anti-nuptial agreement was valid since the rule in force of which such agreements are contrary to public policy should no longer apply. It was highlighted that an agreement should be upheld if parties entered freely, with all information available and in the absence of pressure.

A particular situation shall be referred to agreements which are entered also by non-family members, although such an agreement relates to a domestic contract.

Ms Simpkins was a paying boarder at Ms Pays house who lived with her granddaughter. Ms Simpkins habitually took part in newspaper competitions. As far as the Sunday newspaper competition is concerned, they agreed that Ms Simpkins would fill in a weekly coupon, with each person making three forecasts, yet submitting them in Ms Pays' name and divide the prize in the event of winning. A forecast made by Ms Pays' granddaughter, in one of the coupons submitted, won a prize of £750 under Ms Pays name. Ms Pays refused to distribute the prize and Ms Simpkins claimed for one-third of the prize under their agreement.[9]

In this case, the court held that, differently from what usually occurs in familial relations, there was mutuality in the arrangements between the parties by which they agreed to the manner of the submission of the forecast in Ms Pays name on a weekly basis. In case of success, all three persons would share the prize money, equally. In this case, the filling out of the coupon was not a voluntary service, rather the outcome of an agreement entitling each party to share the result. Ultimately, it was an intention to create legal relations. To summarise, the mutual arrangements constituted a legally binding agreements to divide shares in thirds.

By contrast, in *Wilson v Burnett*,[10] the defendant won a local prize at the Bingo and, as a result, claimed that they had made an agreement with the defendant before the bingo session. Based on this agreement, the potential win shall be shared equally. The court did not find an intention, nor an agreement, between parties to create a legal relation. Although some piece of evidence provided somehow supported the other side, but this was not deemed crucial.

8 [2010] UKSC 42.
9 *Simpkins v Pays* [1955] 1 WLR 975.
10 [2007] EWCA Civ 1170.

3. Commercial agreements

As far as commercial agreements are concerned, the rule consists of the presumption of an intention to create legal restrictions. A strong inference arises when the commercial context is an ongoing employment relationship. In this respect, in "*Dresdner*",[11] it was held that, where a term is introduced into a pre-existing relationship, there is a very strong presumption that that agreement was intended to be legally binding. However, in the specific controversy, it was held that the onus was on the party asserting that there was no intention to create legal relations to establish the fact. Thus, an employer who had made an oral promise to pay relevant employees a guaranteed performance-based bonus had done so with the intention that the promise would be legally binding.[12]

In *Esso Petroleum Ltd v Commissioners of Customs and Excise*,[13] the House of Lords held that the offer of coins did produce a binding contract with any customer who bought more than four gallons of petrol. Parties intended to create legal relations: customers provided consideration by purchasing the necessary amount of petrol. However, the consideration was a contract to purchase petrol.

A niche application of this rule is within a sale of land agreement: the latter is normally made "subject to contract". This wording displaces, in an express way, any presumption of contractual intention. Moreover, in other situations court have found *ad hoc* expression of the agreement displaced any contractual intention. The reference goes to the following:

- Comfort letter: in absence of an expressly stated information to create legal restriction in relation in respect of payment, the court must determine whether the statement, within its context, was intended as a binding legal promise as to the future. To elaborate, if the words were used merely of comfort and of moral responsibility, they did not have the meaning nor effect to create a legal promise of future conduct with legally binding effect.[14]
- An honour clause: a clause as "honourable pledge" demonstrates that parties did not intend the arrangement as legally binding contract.[15]

4. Smart contracts

From contract law perspective, smart contracts represent a difficult category of contract because not always do smart contracts create a legal contract as an enforceable

11 See *Dresdner Kleinwort Ltd v Atrill* [2013] EWCA Civ 394.

12 (Dautaj and Fox 2023).

13 [1975] UKHL 4: Esso offered a World Cup coin with likeness of the England 1970 squad players given to every motorist buying over four gallons of Petrol. HM Customs & Exercise argued these coins needed to be charged with tax because they were produced in a huge quantity for general sale.

14 *Kleinwort Benson Ltd v Malaysia Mining Corporation Berhad* [1989] 1 WLR 379.

15 See *Rose and Frank Company v JR Crompton and Brothers Ltd* [1925] AC 445.

agreement between two or more parties because the technology guarantees the performance security of promises.[16] For a scholar,[17] smart contracts are contract according to common law rules. The reason for that is fundamentally twofold: (1) smart contracts are contract if some terms are capable of being automatically performed; (2) smart contracts satisfy the requirements for an enforceable contract under English law. Thus, smart contracts should not be treated "as being different in principle from conventional contracts".[18]

Nevertheless, the perspective is quite different from a comparative perspective:

- In Italy, smart contracts are defined as a computer program that works "on technologies based on distributed registers and whose execution automatically constrains two or more parts on the basis of effects predefined by them".[19]
- In France, the smart contract

  is like a self-executing program registered in a blockchain and which is backed by an electronic smart contract in the form, for example, of general conditions of use or sale (CGU and CGV) that the users would be called to accept in advance. . . . Thus, "the term of the contract is a bit overused in that the computer program shares few common characteristics with the legal object of the contract within the meaning of the civil code". The smart contract is therefore an accessory of the real contract.[20]

- In Switzerland

  the term "smart contracts as computer programs. Smart Contract" designates a computer program based on blockchain technology which is executed automatically when certain conditions are met, which has a decentralized structure, and which is secured by means of cryptography. It immediately appears from these doctrinal and legal definitions that the term "Smart Contract" is particularly badly chosen, given that a "Smart Contract" is neither a contract in the sense legal of the term, nor contract in the legal sense of the term, but a computer program used for the conclusion and execution of real Consequently, civil law seems to answer the question.[21]

Therefore, smart contracts are not subject to the same legal framework as contracts as new regulation is required to validate the public trust in such instruments.[22]

16 (Durovic and Willet 2023).
17 (Procopie 2021).
18 The LawTech Delivery Panel, Legal Statement on cryptoassets and smart contracts (2019), para 136.
19 Translation from Italian Gazzetta Ufficiale No. 36, February 12, 2019, p. 13, accessed November 6, 2020, www.gazzettaufficiale.it/.
20 (Bruno 2018).
21 (Müller 2018).
22 (Procopie 2021).

Therefore, a conclusion is that smart contracts should be enforceable under English, Singapore or US law. To elaborate, according to Rome I Regulation and the Rome Convention, the parties can elect English law as a governing law of the contract.[23] The consequence is English courts can enforce such contracts. In addition, such decision of the English courts will be recognised and enforced in other jurisdiction based on international convention on foreign judgments enforcement.[24] It should be highlighted that Rome I convention applies only in the EU. Consequently, after Brexit, Rome I stopped applying to the UK on a reciprocal basis, except as provided for in part three of the UK-EU withdrawal agreement in respect of contracts concluded before the end of the transition period.

Based on this approach, smart contracts should be read as computer programs that can, under specific circumstances, assist in automating the performance of specific contractual obligations. This perspective clarifies also that smart contracts do not provide with commercial certainty simply because smart contracts, as computer programmes, are susceptible to programming errors and vulnerabilities. The latter, vulnerability, alludes to a mistake in the implementation of a system design that results in programs not providing the intended functionality or producing unexpected results. The former, programming errors, is malicious misuse of system implementation to achieve effects contrary to its goal, known as "exploits".

Moreover, smart contracts are affected by a lack of transparency: despite the common opinion that smart contracts are *per se* transparent, the reality is quite different. Hence, inspecting the code may reveal coding errors. It is unclear therefore whether smart contracts will achieve the agreed results or whether they encompass security vulnerabilities.[25] In addition, transparency may be helpful only for experienced and sophisticated coders, not to the average user.[26]

From a descriptive perspective, smart contract means an automatable and enforceable agreement stored in a blockchain that is automatically executed when pre-determined terms and conditions are met. Consequently, smart contracts are based on the following approach: "if/when . . . then". It appears clear that smart contracts are self-executing contracts: it means that they come into force automatically, when and if certain circumstances materialise. The most important element is the lack of human supervision: again, where certain events and/or circumstances occur, the algorithm initiates the transaction automatically. In essence, smart contracts are "self-executing digital transactions using decentralised cryptographic mechanisms for enforcement".[27]

It is vital to stress the relationship between smart contracts and blockchain: smart contracts are executed on blockchain, but smart contracts are not like blockchains. Further, smart contracts are created by human developers and deployed on

23 Ibid.
24 For example, the reference goes to 2005 Hague Convention on Choice of Court Agreements.
25 (Ghaleb and Pattabiraman 2020).
26 (Mik 2025).
27 (Cornell and Werbach 2017).

blockchain: from a technical perspective, smart contracts are not executed directly on blockchain but on virtual machines (Ethereum Virtual Machine).[28]

In other words, smart contracts are executed by the individual nodes which form the blockchain and run the consensus of algorithm that generates individual blocks, yet smart contracts are not validated by such algorithm. The latter or, better, consensus algorithms can only confirm the existence and the correct transfer of natives' assets, such as Bitcoin, which are generated by this algorithm. More in depth, consensus algorithms cannot determine if the contract is correct or not because blockchain technology, *de facto*, executes both good and bad code.

The main characteristics of smart contracts are as follows:

- Self-execution.
- High-speed and fast.
- Unchangeable because they are mapped on a blockchain.
- Decentralisation.
- Cheap.
- Accurate.

On 25th November 2021 the Law Commissions published its advice to government on smart legal contracts where the conclusion was that the current legal framework in England and Wales is able to facilitate and support the use of these contracts. In this moment, the consultation is concluded, and the further stage will be the publication of the report.[29]

Under this publication, smart legal contract is defined as "computer programs which run automatically, in whole or in part, without the need for human intervention". Furthermore, smart legal contract is "a legally binding contract in which some or all of the contractual obligations are defined in and/or performed automatically by a computer program".

In this respect, one main problem is that smart contracts are deployed on blockchain technology, so they become immutable, and their code cannot be modified simply because the code of a smart contract lies on a stone. Additionally, immutability encompasses technical aspects of the code and the substantive rules that should be executed.[30]

In addition, a smart legal contract can unfold in three different forms:

- Natural language contract defined also "external contract" where the code is outside the scope of the parties' legally binding agreement.

28 (Buterin 2015).

29 Law Commissions, Smart legal contracts Advice to Government, November 2021.

30 In Ethereum website it is written that "a smart contract is code that lives on the Ethereum blockchain and runs exactly as programmed. Once smart contracts are deployed on the network you can't change them. . . . This also means you need to design your contracts very carefully and test them thoroughly".

- Hybrid contract, where some obligations are defined under natural language and others under the code of computer program language.
- A wholly smart contract, where all contractual terms are defined and performed automatically by the code of a computer program.

Smart legal contracts are suitable for use in the following contexts:

- Facilitating DeFi or decentralised finance.
- Service level agreement.
- Real estate transactions.
- Aviation refuelling.
- Managing supply chain.

The main question concerns the consideration in smart contract: it was noted that it is difficult to identify consideration for promises defined by code. A solution may be to identify consideration in the operation of the code itself.

A further challenge is linked with the interpretation of the contract. To elaborate, when terms of smart legal contracts are recorded solely or partly in code, the latter, that is, the code, does not have a meaning because it's linked with either performance or output. Potentially, the interpretation may sense where there is a discrepancy between what codes mean to the parties and what is its effect upon execution. Consequently, it becomes quintessential to define the meaning of "code" under a legal sense.

The proposal is to adopt a "reasonable code test": the expert coder will have the role to explain the effect of certain combination of words and coding logic. Moreover, the expert also has a duty to explain what the code instructs the computer to do. The "reasonable code test" may have some positive consequences, such as the following:

- It provides an insight into what parties intend the code to do.
- It applies, *de facto*, the concept of reasonable person with the background knowledge available to the parties at the time the contract was made.
- It will be objective.

In addition, if a conflict between the coded terms and natural terms arise, it is suggested that parties' stipulated terms will take precedence.

Another topic concerns consumer protection. The suggestion is that traders, whilst offering B2C smart legal contracts which encompass coded terms, would need to provide clear and informative pre-contractual literature to the consumer. The goal is to explain terms and how these terms operate. Traders have also another duty: design B2C smart legal contract that gives all instructions and means to consumers relating to the exercise of the right to treat the contract at an end. At the very least, the existing consumer protection rules should be reviewed. B2C contracts have become sophisticated and prevalent. Therefore, the need is the adequacy of the existing consumer protection regulations.

Finally, the jurisdiction problem shall be discussed. More in detail, the reference is to the problem of "digital location", and it constitutes a significant challenge when these rules shall be applied. Therefore, the recommendation is to include both a jurisdiction and the choice of the law in the agreement.

It is worth mentioning that smart contracts may have some benefits in the property sectors also because they have revolutionised the way transactions are conducted. More precisely, by automating tasks – such as transferring funds and registering tiles – smart contracts streamline the process, reducing the need for manual intervention and minimising the risk of human error. This automation means also: speeding up transactions; lower transactions costs and improving parties' experience. Moreover, smart contracts enhance security and help prevent fund in property transactions. Additionally, automation as well as real-time tracking provide greater transparency and accountability in the transaction process, reducing the potential for delays and disputes.[31]

One of the key characteristics of smart contracts is their ability to act proactively. Once parties voluntarily enter a primary smart contract, such contract can autonomously initiate additional agreements with other parties. This second agreement – known as secondary contract – is based on predefined conditions and logic embedded in the code. For example, the primary contract deals with the shipment of goods from a manufacturer and the secondary contract – the smart contract – automatically notifies customs, triggers insurance policies, or initiates payment to the shipping company once the goods are confirmed delivered.

A further example is that the bank and borrower can agree on a framework agreement, whereby if the borrower's bank balance drops below a pre-agreed threshold, the software will automatically accept, provided that certain pre-programmed conditions are met.[32] Therefore, the question is if a software might be seen as a party to a smart contract. In *R (on the application of) v HM Customs & Excise*,[33] the UK court found that an automated system could not be regarded as an agent. The reason was that only a person with a mind could be an agent in law. Consequently, the software is a mere messenger: it does not assume a decision, rather it executes human decisions within the limits of pre-set parameters. Moreover, according to this line of reasoning, parties' actions when programming the software could be characterised as the issue of a conditional offer and acceptance.[34]

Under European Union perspective, the EU Data Act defines a smart contract as a "computer program used for the automated execution of an agreement or part thereof, using a sequence of electronic data records and ensuring their integrity and the accuracy of their chronological ordering".[35] Data Act aims to allow users

31 (Brymer 2024).
32 (Madir 2019).
33 [2007] EWHC 971.
34 (Onyiuke and Anene 2024).
35 Article 2 (39), Regulation of the European Parliament and of the Council on harmonised rules on fair access to and use of data and amending Regulation (EU) 2017/2394 and Directive (EU) 2020/1828 (henceforth Data Act).

to access data they generated when using connected devices and to share such data with third parties to enable a range of data-driven services.[36] It promotes, fundamentally, the use of smart contracts for executing data sharing agreement and prescribes certain requirements for developers who create or integrate such smart contracts.[37]

Furthermore, according to the Data Act approach, the term execution means performance of the agreement in the traditional sense. Additionally, Data Act does not associate smart contracts with blockchain technology and, *de facto*, under the EU Act smart contracts seem to be automatic data sharing agreement.

A partially different definition of smart contracts under the EU law is provided by the EU Blockchain Observatory and Forum: the latter defines smart contracts as "more efficient and enhanced mechanism of agreement, transacting, and transferring value"[38] as well as "an event-driven programme that runs on a decentralized, distributed shared and replicated ledger, which can take custody over and instruct the transfer of assets on that ledger".[39]

Finally, it is possible to affirm that smart contracts are mechanisms that transfers or controls crypto-assets, and every operation appears in the change of the state of a database, the blockchain. Thus, smart contracts are mechanisms relating to transmission and control of various crypto-assets on blockchains.[40] At the same time, smart contracts may be read as acts that manifest parties' intentions that could lead to the formation of a contract. For example, one party can write a smart contract and deploy it on the blockchain, and the other party can accept it. In the described scenario, smart contract represents the parties' intention to contract according to terms embodied in its code. The problem arises because smart contracts are written by a developer and deployed on a blockchain for others to use.[41] This is clear from the terminology: anyone can create smart contracts, and anyone can use smart contracts. Thus, smart contracts are created and used, not performed.[42]

5. Certainty of terms

From a general perspective, it is possible to affirm that a contract consists of several terms; it is essential to distinguish terms from statement of opinion ("mere puff", which has no legal effect) and mere representation (these generate a claim for misrepresentation). If a statement is a contractual term, a mere representation depends on the intention with which the statement was made. Factors that should be considered are the importance of statement and the knowledge of parties.

36 Article 1, Data Act.
37 Article, 36 and Recital 80, Data Act.
38 EU Blockchain Observatory and Forum, Smart Contracts (2022, 29).
39 Ibid., 2.
40 (Cohney, Hoffman, and Sklaroff 2019).
41 (Zhou, Milani Fard, and Makanju 2022).
42 (Mik 2025).

A contract, to be enforceable, shall encompass certainty terms; in other words, an agreement to be contract needs to have clear terms: if an important term is not settled, the agreement is not a contract.

This conclusion is warranted by *Scammell v Ouston*[43]: an agreement was not enforceable because the relevant terms were uncertain and required a further agreement between parties. In other words, a lack of certain terms means that parties did not conclude a real agreement, due to the absence of a *consensus in idem*. The *ratio* is that, if it is not possible to determine terms with certainty, there is no contract because the court does not have the role to create the terms of a contract. The role of the court is, in fact, to try to give legal force to the parties' attempt to make a contract only if it is possible or legal to do this.[44]

Based on such a background, it was clarified that an agreement to operate two aircrafts from an airport for ten years was not void for uncertainty, simply because, allegedly, it did not specify a minimum number of passengers. Thus, the agreement encapsulated clear terms to determine the level of performance.[45]

Although the foregoing conclusions are true, under such circumstances, when the parties have relied upon an agreement, courts will infer or imply a term that is essential for the contract. In *Hillas v Arcos*,[46] where the court stated the contract was not an "agreement to agree" due to the circumstances in force of which the only thing necessary for the agreement to be brought into existence was for the buyers to decide to exercise their option to purchase the wood. Furthermore, the only thing that parties did not negotiate was the price because it changed yearly.

In a similar way, in *RTS Flexible Systems Ltd v Molkerei Alois Muller Gmbh & Co KG*,[47] the United Kingdom Supreme Court affirmed that an objective interpretation of the parties' words and deeds suggested that they intended to enter a binding contract even though certain terms were not yet confirmed.

Furthermore, if parties do not agree on critical terms such as the price and delivery dates, a contract has not been formed.[48]

6. A complete agreement

A complete agreement shall have all the major elements of a contract: in one word the contract shall be complete. By contrast, if an agreement is not complete, a court is unable to state with certainty what agreement has been made between the parties.

43 [1941] AC 251.

44 See also *Scammel v Dicker* [2005] EWCA Civ 405.

45 *Durham Tees Valley Airport v Bmibaby* [2010] EWCA Civ 485.

46 [1932] All ER 494.

47 [2010] UKSC 14. The claimant was a supplier of automated machines and agreed to manufacture an automated system in the defendant's factory. The work began based on a letter of intent with a long form contract to follow; however, the letter of intent expired, while negotiations on the long form contract continued. A dispute arose as to whether the defendant's performance requirements were satisfied by the machines delivered by the claimants.

48 See *British Steel Corp v Cleveland Bridge and Engineering Co Ltd* [1984] 1 All ER 504.

Consequently, if an agreement does not encompass all the essential elements of a bargain, there is no contract.

To understand what constitutes an essential element, it is quintessential to analyse the contract: in other words, what is essential for the contracts depends upon the nature of the contract. Further, a complete bargain may exist which may be supplemented by further implied terms.

An implied term is a term that has not been expressly agreed between the parties because it has been implied into the contract either by common law or by statute.

Wells v Devani[49] constitutes a case where a principle was established that a court can imply terms into a contract. To elaborate, the United Kingdom Supreme Court held that a binding oral agreement was reached between an estate agent and property developer; the result was that agent was entitled to payment of commission. This decision shows the importance of ensuring written terms are agreed and provided prior to proceeding with the marketing of the property of an estate agent.

It is crucial to stress that the position of the Court of Appeal was different: indeed, the Court of Appeal said that parties could not imply a term into a defective contract to make it legally binding. Consequently, no commission was owed.

An agreement to agree shall not be existed. For instance, in *Courtney & Fairburn Ltd v Tolaini Bros (Hotels) Ltd*[50] the issue was if an agreement to agree should be defined as a contract. The court held that in this case the "agreement" in question was incomplete, hence the result depended on the respondent's quantity surveyor agreeing terms with the appellants. More in general, an agreement to enter into an agreement is not binding contract because it is too vague to enforce, as well as impossible to calculate damages. In a nutshell, a contract to negotiate is unenforceable due the nature of negotiation, that is, the fact that parties might never reach an agreement.

In a similar way, a side letter does not constitute a legally binding agreement, because it does not show that parties have the intention to create legal relations. Moreover, also if the side letter is signed by parties and initialled on each page does not change the conclusion. If the letter refers only "terms to be agreed", it constitutes evidence of an agreement to agree.[51]

The underlying *ratio*, potentially, is that the agreement is incomplete; consequently the court does not complete a contract because the duty of the court is to interpret the contract, not to create one.

Finally, it is necessary to focus on the attention on the lockout agreement, an issue linked with the concept of the agreement to agree. The general rule is that an agreement to agree is not binding for the parties, but in commercial property transactions the lockout agreement, a similar form, is quite in use. Its aim is to secure a pre-contractual exclusivity period for a potential buyer to enable the buyer to carry out searches, surveys and investigations before committing himself/herself to the

49 [2019] UKSC 4.
50 [1975] 1 All ER 453.
51 See *Barbudev v Eurocom Cable Management Bulgaria* [2011] EWHC 1560.

purchase. At the same time, it avoids the risk that a landowner accepts another offer in the meantime. They do not bind either party to proceed with the transaction.

In most lockout agreements, the period of exclusivity is of a very short duration; by contrast it is unlikely that the landowner agree to an unnecessary long period of exclusivity, unless there is some valuable consideration paid to incentivise her/him. In other words, a lockout period tends to fall within a range of a few weeks up to six months based on circumstances.

The lockout agreement should define the scope of the buyer preliminary investigations during the agreed lockout period.

If the landowner breaches the obligations, since he/she is accepting a much more attractive offer from a third party, the prospective buyer will be entitled to claim damages.

To summarise, a lockout agreement may be defined as an exclusivity agreement, as well as a negative agreement: seller is required not to negotiate with third partis during a fixed lockout period. A seller can only deal with the buyer during such period.

Further, lockout agreements shall be supported by valuable consideration: frequently, seller seeks a cash sum in the form of a non-refundable deposit.

The leading case is *Pitt v PHH Asset Management Ltd*[52]: the claimant sent the defendant an offer to buy the property, which the defendant accepted. The latter, then, received a higher offer from a third party and withdrew the acceptance he made to the claimant. When the claimant threatened to sue for an injunction and causing trouble with a third party, the defendant appeased the claimant by entering into a lockout agreement. Based on such new contract, the defendant agreed not to consider any further offers if the claimant exchanged contracts within a period of two weeks of receipt of the draft contract. Although the claimant complied with the agreement, the defendant sold the property to a third party at a higher price. Consequently, he was sued for a breach of contract. The Court of Appeal held that the defendant breached a binding contract because the claimant possessed a consideration, because the lockout agreement constituted valuable consideration sufficient to support the agreement.

References

Bruno, Ancel. 2018. "Les smart contracts: Révolution sociétale ou nouvelle boîte de Pandore? Regard comparatiste." *Communication-Commerce Électronique* 15–18.

Brymer, Stewart. 2024. "Smart Contracts." *Property Law Bulletin* 192: 1–3.

Buterin, Vitalik. 2015. "Ethereum White Paper: A Next Generation Smart Contract and Decentralized Application Platform." https://github.com/ethereum/wiki/wiki/White-Paper.

Cohney, Shaanan, David Hoffman, and David Sklaroff. 2019. "Coin-Operated Capitalism." *Columbia Law Review* 119 (3): 591–676.

Cornell, Nicolas, and Kevin Werbach. 2017. "Contracts Ex Machina." *Duke Law Journal* 67: 313.

52 [1994] 1 WLR 327.

Dautaj, Ylli, and William Fox. 2023. *International Commercial Agreements*, 7th ed. Kluwer Law International.

Durovic, Mateja, and Chris Willet. 2023. "A Legal Framework for Using Smart Contracts in Consumer Contracts: Machines as Servants, Not Masters." *Modern Law Review* 86 (6): 1390–421.

Ghaleb, Asem, and Karthik Pattabiraman. 2020. "How Effective ARE Smart Contract Analysis Tools? Evaluating Smart Contracts Static Analysis Tools Using Bug Injuction." In *Proceedings of the 29th ACM SIGSOFT International Symposium on Software Testing and Analysis*. ACM.

Madir, Jelena. 2019. *FinTech: Law and Regulation*. Edward Elgar Publishing.

Mik, Eliza. 2025. "The Sense and Nonsense of Smart Contracts." In *Web3 Governance: Law and Policy*, edited by di Joseph Lee and Jyh-An Lee, 46–67. Routledge.

Müller, Christoph. 2018. "Les smartcontracts en droit des obligations suisse." *Le journée des droits de la consommation et de la distribution* 51–114.

Onyiuke, Tochukwu, and Oge Anene. 2024. "The Transformation of Decentralised Finance: Legal Aspects of the 'Internet of Value'." *Computer and Telecommunications Law Review* 30 (7): 162–67.

Parker, Stephen. 2019. *Family Law Agreements and Consent Orders*. The Law Society.

Procopie, Luminita. 2021. "Are Smart Contracts Actually Contracts? How Smart Contracts Can Work Globally." *Journal of International Banking Law and Regulation* 36 (1): 25–30.

Zhou, Haozhe, Amin Milani Fard, and Adetokunbo Makanju. 2022. "The State of Ethereum Smart Contracts Security: Vulnerabilities, Countermeasures, and Tool Support." *Journal of Cybersecurity and Privacy* 2 (2): 358–78.

5 The regulation of the terms of the contracts

Chapter Overview

1. Introduction

The main and most important characteristic of the law of contract is the fact that, differently from other areas of law, it relies upon the concept of consensual agreement and on its enforcement. From a purely theoretical perspective, parties to a contract are free to choose their own contractual terms, and they are bound by these terms. Although this is true, this theoretical approach shall be interpreted in the light of contemporary law. More recently, many individuals are bound by terms that they have no choice, although they formally agree on them.

The scenario just described represents the "tip of the iceberg" of the standardisation form of contracts.

A standard contract constitutes a contract used by businesses; the main characteristic is that this contract – standard contract – is not the result of a negotiation between two parties. Furthermore, this kind of contract often offered on a "a take it or leave it basis" as a common part of the daily life.

DOI: 10.4324/9781003645948-5

From a historical perspective, and based on what it was just mentioned, at the beginning judges had no means of directly controlling these clauses, since common law allowed courts to exercise, merely, an indirect control.

2. The exclusion or exemption clauses

Exclusion or exemption clauses are stipulated to guarantee that one or both parties to a contract will not be liable in the case of breach of one or more of their obligations. Therefore, the aim of exception clauses is to modify the rule of liability, otherwise applicable, in the case of violation of a term or some terms of a contract.

It is important to clarify that exclusions clauses constitute an inflammatory topic of contract law in each jurisdiction, without any distinction between common law and civil law legal system.

Under ancient Roman law, there were two main principles relating to exemption clauses. The first one was that parties to an agreement were not capable of relieving the obligor when he acted deliberately.[1] In addition to this, the second main principle was about the nature of obligation for the breach for which the contractual provision is banned. Therefore, if this clause refers to an essential obligation, then it was banned.

As far as English common law is concerned, exemption clauses have two different levels of regulation: common law and statute.

Under common law, exemption clauses are defined as clauses, indeed, based on which terms of the contract which excludes or limits the liability of the contractor for a breach. Another definition stresses that limitation clauses exclude or limits liability or appears to exclude or limit liability if a breach of contract or some other obligation.

Exoneration clauses are different from other clauses, such as the following:

- Penal clauses that can benefit both parties.
- Arbitration clauses only provide machinery for determining the rights.

Exclusions clauses may be read, also, under a different and opposite perspective, that is, the defence one. To elaborate, if a contract does not encompass a limitation clause, in case of a breach of contract or obligations of contract, the problem of interpretation may arise. By contrast, under this line of reasoning, an exclusion clause prevents an interpretation because the only objective of these peculiar clauses is to define the scope of contractual duties.[2]

Furthermore, two main problems are relating to exclusions clauses:

- The problem of interpretation.
- The problem of incorporation.

1 D.50.17.23.
2 (Peel 2020).

Under the traditional contractual principles, a clause to be enforceable should be incorporated into the contract. In case a contract is integrated into a document, the signature is sufficient to guarantee the clause incorporation. However, an exclusion clause may be incorporated also by notice: this circumstance may materialise when a clause is encapsulated into a document given to the other party or displayed where the contract is made. The objective of this process is to guarantee that the obliged party has the knowledge of this clause or, alternatively, takes the appropriate steps to attract the attention of the party.[3] All these conditions shall be satisfied before the conclusion of the contract.

Moreover, exclusion clauses are construed *contra proferentem*; however, the English court does not apply the *contra proferentem* rule with the same rigor.[4]

Finally, it is worth noting that, often, exclusions clauses are named as "clauses which appear to exclude liability" or "clauses which purpose is to negotiate terms normally applied in favour to the buyer".

Exemption clauses have their main legal source in the Unfair Contract Terms Act (1977): it invalidates some exemption clauses and other subjects to the test of reasonableness.

The exemption clauses that invalidated are clauses that exclude liability for a negligently caused death or injury to the body, exclusions of liability for a breach of statutory implied duties of the seller or the owner as to the title in sale or hire, purchase, and for a breach of statutory implied duties of the seller or the owner as to the conformity of goods in sale or hire purchase.

The test of reasonableness is constituted by different factors:

- The relative bargaining position of the parties.
- If the customer has received an inducement to agree to the term or had the opportunity to contract on different basis.
- If the customer had known, or ought reasonably to have known, about the exemption clause.

The leading case is *Photo Production Ltd v Securicor Transport Ltd.*[5] In the agreement signed by the party one clause prescribed that Securicor would "under no circumstances be responsible for any injurious act or default by any employee . . . unless such act or default could have been foreseen and avoided by the exercise of due diligence on the part of [Securicor]". Based on this, Securicor argued that they were not liable even if damages were caused by the conduct of its agent. By contrast, Photo Production replied that also the action of Securicor's agent constituted

3 In *Interfoto Picture Library v Stiletto Visual Programmes* [1988] 2 WLR 615 it was said that where a clause is particularly onerous (the fees are exorbitant at ten times the level of other photographic library), the party seeking to rely on the clause must show they have taken reasonable steps to bring the clause to the other party's attention. If a party fails in doing so, as in the specific case, the clause would not be incorporated.

4 (Adams and MacQueen 2010).

5 [1980] AC 827.

a fundamental breach of the contract. As a result of this, the entire contract should be invalidated with the exclusion of the clause. The Court of Appeal stated that Securitor was liable. By contrast, the House of Lords held that Securitor was not liable for the damage. The *ratio essendi* may be explained as follows:

- The case was decided on the doctrine of fundamental breach by the Court of Appeal.
- The House of Lords stressed that the doctrine of fundamental breach was not relevant. The case was a matter of construction of the contract. The exclusion clause did cover the damage in question.

The concept of fundamental breach could be viewed from two different perspectives:

- The breach relates to a particular obligation which is central to the contract.
- A deliberate refusal to perform obligations under the contract.

It was clarified that the doctrine of fundamental breach, in the contemporary, shall not be read as presumption against any exclusion clause being interpreted to cover a fundamental breach of the contract. More precisely, it constitutes a rule of law.[6]

3. The incorporation

An exclusion clause, to have effect, shall become part of the contract, and where the contract has been signed, the party signing will be bound by the clause.

Often, many exclusion clauses are contained in unsigned documents or notices; these may incorporate into the contract based on principle shaped in *Interfoto Picture Library v Stiletto Visual Programmes*, discussed previously.

Incorporation occurs when and if all the following three conditions are satisfied:

- Notice aimed to ensure that all reasonable steps are bringing to capture the attention of the party. It is sufficient that document indicates the existence of the clause and it can be consulted.[7] It does not apply in the consumer contract topic as well as some clauses, in order to be valid, shall be "printed in red ink on the face of the document with a big red hand pointing' at them".[8] Furthermore, other elements should be taken into account, such as the following:

  1. A deck chair ticket is not contractual in nature as a reasonable person would regard it as a mere receipt to show that the claimant had paid for the chair.[9]

6 *Suisse Atlantique Société d'Armament Maritime SA v Rotterdamsche Kolen Centrale NV* [1967].

7 *Thompson v London, Midland and Scottish Railway Co* [1930] 1 KB 41.

8 *J Spurling Ltd v Bradshaw* [1956] 1 WLR 461 and later see *Thornton v Shoe Lane Parking* [1971] 1 QB 163 (Lord Denning).

9 *Chapleton v Barry Urban District Council* [1940] 1 KB 532.

2. The innocent party must either know the clause or the party relying on the clause must have taken reasonable steps to bring it to other's notice before the contract is finalised.[10]

- Timing requires that any term which is to be part of a contract must be brought to the attention of the parties before or at the time of contracting.
- Nature of document: if terms are in a written document, that document must be one which the party would reasonably believe to have contractual force. For instance, a ticket which encompasses a contractual notice does not need to prove that a successful payment has been made.

Furthermore, incorporation may be by signature and by consistent course of dealing between parties.

Incorporation by signature occurs when a person signed a contract and clauses are incorporated into this contract. There are some exceptions to this rule:

- If the clause is "regrettably small" and it is illegible.[11]
- The exemption clause will not be incorporated if the effect of this clause is described inaccurately (misrepresented) and the innocent party has reasonably relied on the inaccuracy description entered the contract.[12]
- The clause is unusual and onerous and is not fairly and reasonably drawn to the attention on the other party.[13]

As far as incorporation by consistent course of dealing between parties, it is important that the dealings must be both consistent and amount to course of dealing, that is enough regular dealings. For example, in *Kendall (Henry) & Sons v Lillico &*

10 *Parker v South Eastern Railway* (1877) 2 CPD 416, CA.

11 By contrast, in *L'Estrange v Graucob Ltd* [1934] 2 KB 934 it was held that the clause was regrettably small but legible, thus the clause was incorporated into the contract because the contract was signed.

12 *Curtis v Chemical Cleaning* [1951] 1 KB 805: the claimant took her wedding dress to the cleaners. She was asked to sign a form, and she asked the assistant what she was signing; the assistant told her that it excluded liability for any damage of the beads. The form encompassed a clause excluding all liability for any damage howsoever caused. The dress was returned badly stained. It was held that the assistant had misrepresented the effect of the clause and therefore could not rely on the clause in the form even though the claimant had signed it.

13 *Blu-Sky Solutions Ltd v Be Caring Ltd* [2021] EWHC 2691 (Comm): a mobile phone supplier was not entitled to enforce a cancellation in its standard terms. It was an unduly onerous term which had not been fairly and reasonably drawn to the purchaser's attention before it had signed an order for 800 mobile phone connections with a monthly rental fee and then cancelled it prior to connection to the network. The court stated that the clauses relied upon by the claimant were not incorporated into the contract as they were unduly onerous and not fairly and reasonable brought to the defendant's attention. If they were not incorporated, they would be considered void penalty clauses. It was emphasised that the clauses were not clearly identified as marking provision for the contractual relationship between the claimant and the defendant.

Sons Ltd[14]: if two businesses had dealt with each other three or four times a month for three years. After each contract was made, a sold note would be sent to the buyer. The note contained exemption clauses. The court decided the clauses were incorporated in the latest contract because of the previous consistent course of dealings. By contrast, in *Hollier v Ramble Motors*[15] it was held that while the claimant had had a car service by the defendant's garage only three or four times over five years, this did not amount to a course of dealings. Further, a course of dealing a clause will not incorporate unless the dealings are consistent. In *McCutcheon v David MacBrayne Ltd*[16] despite the parties had dealt with each other many times, sometimes the document containing the exemption clause had been signed and sometimes it had not. The House of Lords decided that exemption clauses had not been incorporated as the dealing had not been consistent.

A golden rule is that all these principles may be applied less strictly where both parties are commercial entities.[17]

The main idea of this doctrine is that when there is a breach that is so fundamental to the operation of the contract, the waiver contained in the agreement should either be narrowly interpreted or be held entirely unenforceable.

To understand the enforceability of waivers in contracts, a test was shaped. This test is based on three main questions:[18]

- As matter of interpretation, did parties intend that the exclusion clause apply in the circumstances?
- Was the clause unconscionable at the time the contract was made?
- Is there an overriding public policy that would preclude its enforcement?

4. Construction

If a contract encapsulates a particular clause, it becomes quintessential to decide whether this clause covers the breach which has occurred. The main principle, applied by the court, is the *contra proferentem* rule.

As far as this rule is concerned, *contra proferentem* rule:

- Is complex, as far as its application is concerned, even if the underlying principle is simple.
- Shall be related to the interpretation of all contractual provisions.
- Allows new consumers to be protected by dedicated legislative provisions.

14 [1969] 2 AC 31.

15 [1971] 2 QB 71, CA.

16 [1964] 1 WLR 125, HL.

17 *British Crane Hire Corp Ltd v Ipswich Plant Hire Ltd* [1975] QB 303.

18 *Tercon Contractors Ltd. v British Columbia (Minister of Transportation and Highways)*, (2010) 397 N.R. 331 (SCC).

- Takes a more relaxed approach to clauses which merely limit liability, instead of excluding it.

If a contractor has the intention to exclude liability in respect of his own negligence, the interpretation process shall comply with the following principles:[19]

- If the clause contains express language exempting a person from the consequence of the negligence, effect must be given to it.
- If there is not any express reference to negligence, the court must consider whether the words used are wide enough in their ordinary meaning to cover it.
- The court must consider whether liability may be based on some grounds other than negligence.

Negligence, from a general perspective, arises when one party does not exercise reasonable care or skill in fulfilling their contractual responsibilities. More in detail, negligence embodies a party's failure to uphold their end of a contractual bargain in a manner that exercises reasonable care, resulting in detriment to the other party.

Thus, it is vital to distinguish between condition and warranty. If the court decides that a term is a condition, and the contract has not been fully performed, the innocent party will usually have the option to terminate the future performance of the contract as well as obtaining damages for any additional loss suffered. By contrast, if the court decides that term is a warranty, the innocent party cannot terminate the contract but can only sue for damages for loss suffered. This applies even if the innocent party has suffered serious loss or damages. A more recent approach does not distinguish between conditions or warranties but stresses the concept of innominate term: it is neither a condition nor a warranty. The reference is to *Honk Kong Fir Shipping Co Ltd v Kawasaki Kisen Kaisha Ltd*[20]: not all terms should be classified as conditions or warranties. Some terms should classify as intermediate or innominate terms. In this case, it is necessary to wait until the breach of contract has occurred to decide whether the innocent party should be allowed to terminate the future performance of the contract. If the breach deprives the innocent party of substantial or the whole benefit of contract, they can terminate.

Finally, it is quintessential to refer to a recent case law: *Disclosure and Barring Service v Tata Consultancy Service*.[21] The decision provides a summary of the principles of interpretation in the context of a condition precedent. Furthermore, this case stresses the importance of clear language, commerciality and the need to consider the contract holistically. The Court of Appeal affirmed that:

- When a sentence begins with the word "if", it is conditional.
- When a sentence is structured according to "if . . . then" scheme, it represents a paradigm of conditionality.

19 *Canada Steamship Lines Ltd v The King* [1952] AC 192.
20 [1962] 2 QB 26 [1961] EWCA Civ 7.
21 [2025] EWCA Civ 380.

- Although parties did not adopt the words "condition precedent" to exercising delay-related remedies, the construction of the contract confirmed the existence of a condition precedent to exercise this remedy. Hence, the structure and language ("if . . . then" formulation) made clear that compliance was mandatory before the right to claim arose.

Further insightful principles have been clarified:

- Effect shall be given to the words used: the importance of adopting a clear, precise, consistent and well-structured language.
- There is no specific formula necessary to shape conditionality.
- Clauses will be interpreted within their wider context.

In these principles, the Scottish *FES v HFD Construction*[22] echoes: in the latter it was held that no specific language was necessary to give rise to a condition precedent.

5. Consumer contract

A consumer contract is a contract where parties are constituted by a "trader" and a "consumer". The first one is "person acting for purposes relating to that person's trade, business, craft or profession".[23] By contrast, a consumer is "an individual acting for purposes that are wholly or mainly outside the individual's trade, business, craft or profession".

The term individual means that a company cannot be considered as a consumer.

Based on EU Directive 93/2015,[24] a term could not be set aside as unfair where that term was not "individually negotiated".

Based on Section 62(4), Consumer Right Act, an unfair term is a term "contrary to the requirement of good faith . . . causes a significant imbalance in the parties' rights and obligations under the contract, to the detriment of the consumer". As a result of this, an unfair term has two elements:

- A requirement of good faith.
- A significant imbalance between parties' rights and obligations.

Good faith encompasses two aspects:

- Procedural: an unfair term's existence comes as a surprise to the party subject to do it.

22 Court of Session [2024] CSIH 37.

23 Section 2(1), Consumer Protection Act 2015.

24 Council Directive 93/15/EEC of 5 April 1993 on the harmonisation of the provisions relating to the placing on the market and supervision of explosives for civil uses.

- Substantive: it means that there will be some terms that will always be regarded as unfair whatever steps are taken to publicise them.

To ascertain if a term is fair or unfair, Section 62(5) stipulates that the court must take "into account the nature of the subject matter of the contract' and 'all the circumstances existing when the term was agreed and . . . all of the other terms of the contract". The assessment of fairness is made when the contract is concluded; further it does not constitute a retrospective judgment.

Before to Consumer Regulation Act, the precedent Regulations contained a list of terms which will be presumed to be unfair, named grey list. Schedule 2 part 1 of Consumer Regulation Act encompasses a list as indicative and non-exhaustive of terms of consumer contract that may be unfair. For instance, terms of the grey list are as follows:

- Terms which permit the trader to determine the characteristics of the contractual subject matter after the consumer has become bound by contract.
- A term which requires a consumer who does not fulfil his obligations to pay a disproportionately high sum in compensation for services that have not been supplied.

If a term is found to be unfair, the rest of the contract continues so far as practicable to have effect in other respect. However, the unfair term is not binding on the consumer.

In the digital age, consumer rights have become even more complex as well as a crucial topic of maintaining fairness and balance in the marketplace. In the European Union the Consumer Rights Directive provides a comprehensive legal framework for safeguarding consumer rights in the context of online transactions.[25] The US counterpart is the Federal Trade Commission.

The challenges in the digital age for consumers rights includes:

- Data and privacy security: personal data may be collected, stored and processed by businesses, thus ensuring data protection constitutes a paramount.
- Online transactions and fraud: phishing, credit card fraud and deceptive online marketplace, for instance.
- Misleading advertising and information.
- Unfair contractual terms.

To elaborate, e-commerce and platform economy consumers have wider access to a wider range of products and services from different brands and sellers around the world. Consequently, they can easily search information, compare prices, read

25 Directive 2011/83/EU of the European Parliament and of the Council of 25 October 2011 on consumer rights, amending Council Directive 93/13/EEC and Directive 1999/44/EC of the European Parliament and of the Council and repealing Council Directive 85/577/EEC and Directive 97/7/EC of the European Parliament and of the Council Text.

reviews and make purchases without geographical restrictions. Moreover, consumer consumption patterns have changed due to a new lifestyle, the digital one. This means that also companies may change their approach to business to optimise their approach in the virtual world.

In such scenario, regulation plays a critical role: it shall encourage the adoption of responsible and consumer-protection-oriented business practices as well as strengthen data privacy policies. In a nutshell, it is important that governments, regulatory agencies and businesses work together in the formation and enforcement of regulation. The last goal, again, is the protection of the consumer.

From an EU perspective, the most important directives are as follows:

- The Right to Repair Directive (R2R).[26]
- The Regulation on Toy safety to protect children from risks related to use of toys.[27]
- The Regulation on date collection and sharing for short-term accommodation rental services to achieve a sustainable tourism ecosystem.[28]
- The directive to empower consumers for the green transition.[29]
- Regulations about circular economy.[30]
- Crypto assets regulation.[31]
- Digital Services Act (DSA).[32]
- Regulation on general product safety (GPSR).[33]
- Digital Markets Act (DMA).[34]

26 Directive (EU) 2024/1799 of the European Parliament and of the Council of 13 June 2024 on common rules promoting the repair of goods and amending Regulation (EU) 2017/2394 and Directives (EU) 2019/771 and (EU) 2020/1828.

27 Proposal for a Regulation of the European Parliament and of the Council on the safety of toys and repealing Directive 2009/48/EC COM(2023) 462 final 2023/0290 (COD).

28 Proposal for a regulation of the European Parliament and of the Council on data collection and sharing relating to short-term accommodation rental services and amending Regulation (EU) 2018/1724 COM(2022) 571 7.11.2022 2022/0358(COD).

29 Directive (EU) 2024/825 of the European Parliament and of the Council of 28 February 2024 amending Directives 2005/29/EC and 2011/83/EU as regards empowering consumers for the green transition through better protection against unfair practices and through better information.

30 Communication From the Commission to the European Parliament, The Council, The European Economic and Social Committee and the Committee of the Regions A New Circular Economy Action Plan for a Cleaner and More Competitive Europe COM/2020/98 final.

31 Regulation (EU) 2023/1114 of the European Parliament and of the Council of 31 May 2023 on markets in crypto-assets, and amending Regulations (EU) No. 1093/2010 and (EU) No. 1095/2010 and Directives 2013/36/EU and (EU) 2019/1937.

32 Regulation (EU) 2022/2065 of the European Parliament and of the Council of 19 October 2022 on a Single Market for Digital Services and amending Directive 2000/31/EC.

33 Regulation (EU) 2023/988 on general product safety, amending Regulation (EU) No. 1025/2012 and Directive (EU) 2020/1828, and repealing Directive 2001/95/EC and Directive 87/357/EEC.

34 Regulation (EU) 2022/1925 of the European Parliament and of the Council of 14 September 2022 on contestable and fair markets in the digital sector and amending Directives (EU) 2019/1937 and (EU) 2020/1828.

5.1 Consumer protection in platform economy

The contemporary era is endowed by digital platforms as essential infrastructure of electronic commerce, online communication and digital social relationship. Platform signifies an online venue or a technical tool without legal personality: more appropriate, platforms are masking corporations who hide behind them to avoid the legal responsibilities stemming from their status as social institutions.

As a result of this, consumer law becomes complicated to apply, due to the creation of conditions that frustrate the traditional distinction between professionals and consumers. The reason of that is quite simple: on one side any user can provide services and sell or share their personal goods. Yet on the other side, the online transaction permits companies, which used platform, to facilitate peer-to-peer transactions.

Upon the described scenario, to guarantee consumer protection constitutes an arduous work because consumer protection law is shaped according to business-to-consumer (B2C) relationship: information asymmetries make the consumer the weaker party of the contract, by justifying the introduction of special system of protection. Within platform economy, the legal scenario shifts from the traditional scheme because platforms shape a new player: the prosumer. The latter is a hybrid figure which, at the same time, offers goods, services and digital contents to those interested in purchasing them. Thus, an entrepreneurial organisation is not required for this to work: ownership of assets and internet connection are the only two elements necessary and sufficient for the economical organisation.

An additional challenge lies its roots on legal qualification about the notion of professional. More accurate, the legal qualification of parties offering goods, services and digital contents requires that party's purpose be defined, therefore, the demarcation line between personal and professional purposes. From an EU point of observation, consumer is defined in negative terms: a consumer acts for the purposes outside those an economic activity such as trade, craft or business listed in the definition of a professional. Consequently, mixed transactions are controversial.[35]

Finally, it is worth mentioning that the online environment allows the consumer to compare products and traders more easily: only with a click, rather than walking. Yet the online environment can give firms incentives to obfuscate price or other features of their offering to make comparison more difficult.[36] Obfuscation has an impact on consumer protection law. To better explain, the differences between online and offline markets may be explained as follows:[37]

- In an online market consumers do not have a direct physical interaction with trader or the product.

35 (Quarta 2020).
36 (Glenn and Fisher Ellison 2009)
37 (Flecther et al. 2023).

- Whilst in an offline market advertising and marketing shall be clearly flagged and clearly separated from other content; online markets are affected by a lack of transparency in the interest of the platform.
- If in an offline market a consumer can assess the quality of products or services speaking face-to-face with a salesperson, an online consumer is required to develop further and different skills. These, for example, are peer reviews and ratings.
- In an online market, often products are offered based on ongoing subscription-based contracts, and sometimes, subscriptions are in the form of fixed-term contracts often set to auto-renew. Consequently, the service continues unless it is proactively cancelled.
- The online market is based on data money: services are provided for no monetary price since they are monetised by other means, such as advertising or data collection.

5.2 The European Union Regulation

The Single Market for Digital Services Regulation[38] partially replaces E-Commerce Directive setting out a comprehensive new regulatory framework for online platforms and internet/digital services. The aim of this regulation is to provide protection for consumers if the seller – who uses the platform to supply its services – breaches the contract with the consumers.

According to EU position, it is mandatory to distinguish between intermediation together with control and "merely intermediation".[39] The allocation of liability to the platform for trader's breach of contract would result from the fact that it created the impression for the consumer that the contract was concluded with the platform, and it was the platform's responsibility to perform the contract. In essence, this signifies that DSA shall apply only if platforms acting as intermediaries:[40] if the intermediation service provided is part of an overall service whose main element is not remote (transport), the intermediation service is still subject to the rules of DSA.

If the platform exercises the control and/or otherwise gives the consumer the idea that it is the other party of the contract, DSA prescribes tailor-made duties of care depending on the nature and the size of the intermediary undertakings.[41]

Article 6.3, DSA, is the specific legal provision aimed at those platforms acting as online marketplaces: it covers only contracts between businesses and consumers (B2C), thus, contracts between peer (B2B or C2C) are excluded.

Article 6.3., DSA, stipulates that in online marketplace specific pieces of information should be determined objectively on the basis of all relevant circumstances whether the presentation could lead an average consumer to believe that the

38 Henceforth DSA.
39 (Hacker 2018; Bush 2021).
40 Article 2.2., DSA.
41 (Arroyo Amayueias 2023).

information in question was provided by online platform itself or by traders acting under its authority and control.[42] Despite this, consumers do not receive sufficient protection because Article 6.3:

- Does not define the notion of "average consumers".
- The rule is affected by vagueness.

5.3 Transparency in digital venue

The analysis of this topic needs to start from the fact that digital economy changes the conditions of consumers' participation in markets and society[43] since the digital markets are characterised by the centrality of data and algorithmic management. From consumers' perspective, this means that services are more complex to understand than products, due to the underlying demarcation line between goods and services. Furthermore, some items consumed by consumer, traditionally bought in a physical form as product, are only digital and intangible.

Algorithmic and data management exacerbate the opacity because of profiling activity: consumers' data are acquired through sophisticated commercial surveillance techniques. Personalised is carried out through data extracted from users without their input, for example inferred from monitoring their previous uses of the platform and confronting it with data of other consumers.[44]

Consequently, it appears clear that consumers face uncertainty in relation to the type of input, the type of data of the algorithm relies on and the rules that lead to the decision. Thus, a new notion of transparency shall be built due to digital and online market complexity.

From a general perspective, transparency constitutes an attractive instrument as a natural answer to various forms of closure and complexity in markets and society, including the growing opacity and complexity of digital markets.[45]

Moreover, transparency may assume different meanings, not mutually excluded and often build upon each other. Thus, transparency may be defined:[46]

- As access to medium over time.
- As presentation of information that facilitates understanding.
- As formulations that facilitate understanding.
- As non-ambiguity and logical intelligibility.
- As the absence of deception and confusion.
- As completeness and specificity.
- As non-arbitrariness.

42 Recital 24 DSA.
43 (Willson 2017)
44 (Laux, Wachter, and Mittelstadt 2021).
45 (Alloa and Thomä 2018; Bergers 2021).
46 (Jabłonowska and Tagiuri 2023).

Nevertheless, transparency has attracted criticism for three main reasons:

- The limitation of consumers' perception: transparency as a mere informational duty does not work, because behavioural biases prevent consumers from accessing, understanding and acting upon the information they receive.[47]
- The false promise of unmediated access to reality and its susceptibility to abuse: transparency is embedded in power relations as well as it is "enacted by the same author of the information-object, who has, in addition, the power to control the form of disclosure, the information disclosed and, arguably, the way in which that information is received".[48] In order words, transparency may give the incorrect idea that the relevant powers holders can be seen, checked and made accountable.
- The inability to tackle structural asymmetries in digital economy: digital markets are the outcome of the structural inability of consumers to deploy their agency to shape the outcome of economic interactions. This inability derives from platform design.

As a result of this, consumers are affected by vulnerabilities, called digital vulnerability that is both relational and architectural.

5.4 Platform economy: contract law, labour law and competition law

In an American case, *District of Columbia v Doordash, Inc.*,[49] the District alleged violations of D.C.'s Consumer Protection Procedures Act for deceptive trade practices: more precisely, it alleged that Doordash told both consumer and their workers that tips would go to the workers, instead, Doordash used them to pay base wages. The District used Doordash communication to consumers that their tips would go 100 percent to drivers as evidence of the deception because the tips were used to subsidise the workers' base wage. The complaint differentiated between "consumers" of the Doordash service and Doordash delivery workers. According to the complaint, it was very likely precluded from including drivers as consumers due to the D.C. statute's definition of "consumer and consumer goods" as goods and services for "personal, household, or family purposes".[50]

Despite the suit was brought on behalf of deceived customer-consumers, part of the settlement paid the affected workers. Yet this case demonstrates the limits of regulatory effectiveness where statutory definition limits those who can have a cause of action. If the D.C. statute had enjoyed a broader definition of consumers, the suit could have defined both the customers and the workers as consumers.

47 (Ben-Shahar and Schneider 2014).
48 (R. Adams 2021).
49 *District of Columbia v Doordash, Inc.*, No. 2019 CA 007626 B (Sup. Ct. D.C. 2020).
50 D.C. CODE § 28-3901(a)(2)(B) (2022).

Ultimately, a broad definition of consumer allows prosecutors and regulators to seamlessly bring suits against gig-work companies who engage in unfair and deceptive practices towards their workers. Thus, status with the broader definition of unfair and deceptive practices, without excepted industries or classification, offers a viable tool to police the gig economy.

Moreover, such consumer protection law may serve as effective regulatory tools for government agencies interested in regulating the working conditions of gig-economy workers.[51]

To elucidate, in the United States, some consumer protection statutes prohibiting unfair or deceptive acts or practices in scope to "consumer transactions".[52] Whilst rider-share-platform user agreements characterise gig workers as independent contractor, it does not follow that this characterisation predetermines the applicability of consumer protection law. Additionally, even if consumer protection law might characterise a professional driver is beyond the scope of consumer protection law in her contract with a gig platform. According to some consumer law, the touchstone is whether a person enters into the agreement for "personal, family, or household purposes".[53] One potential suitable criteria to understand the difference is put the attention if the employee "invokes the statute not to protect itself as a consumer, but to protect its business relationship".[54] It is possible to affirm that courts have a *penchant* to place a "worker hat" on consumers in employment contract because an array of labour and employment laws are expected to provide a legal framework deterring employer overreach. Similarly, according to consumer law, not every contract formed with the expectation of earning money is treated as a business or employment contract.

Moving forward, to understand if consumer protection law should apply to gig worker contracts, it is quintessential to approach the topic through labour law and antitrust law. Gig economy platforms would place their coercive practices within a soft point just beyond the simultaneous reach of labour and employment law. Thus, it seems that the matter may be under consumer protection law, labour law and antitrust/competition law. According to this line of reasoning, even if the platform treats gig workers as an independent contractor, antitrust and consumer protection law should be applied to constraint coercive rideshare platform practices.[55]

5.5 Data protection and privacy: "pay or consent rule"

Collecting data represents a vital activity for every kind of platform: for example, for an e-commerce platform it is arduous to complete any online transaction

51 (Kaplan 2022).

52 (Pridgen, Alderman, and Cuaresma 2022–2023).

53 For example, see E.g., Truth in Lending Act, 15 U.S.C. § 1602(h); Fair Debt Collection Practices Act, 15 U.S.C. § 1692a(5); Magnuson Moss Warranty Act, 15 U.S.C. § 2301; U.C.C. §§ 2A 103(e), 9-102(a)(22)–(24) (AM. L. INST. & UNIF. L. COMM'N 2022).

54 *Cooperman v R.G. Barry Corp.*, 775 F. Supp. 1211, 1214 (D. Minn. 1991).

55 (Peterson and Steinbaum 2023).

without collecting some form of personal information of the users, such as identity and financial information. Moreover, other platforms, such as Facebook or, better, Meta, the current owner of Facebook, previously worked with the slogan "It is free and always will be". Offering free services is aimed to encourage the enrolment; however, these services are not truly be free since these are funded by an advertising model built on users' personal data. From this, it raises the "pay or consent" rule, introduced in November 2023 by Meta. The concept is quite simple: either a consumer pays a fee up to 251.88 euro, or consent to his/her personal data being processed and used for behavioural advertising. In order words, the "consent or pay" rule signifies that controller offers to data subject a choice between at least two options to get access to an online service provided by controller. This choice is in between paying a fee to gain access to the service without getting their personal data processed or consenting of personal data for a specific purpose.

From a European Union perspective, General Data Protection Regulation (GDPR) and Digital Markets Act (DMA) require explicit consent to the collection and use of personal data whether is it collected inside or outside the platform. To better explain, the DMA states that gatekeepers that provide core platform services, including Meta (owner of both Facebook and Instagram), to request consent adhering to GDPR for collection and use of off-Meta data for personalised advertising.[56] As a result of this, Meta relies on consent to collect on-Meta and off-Meta data and, since 30th October 2023, a paid version is offered to users who do not want to consent the use of their data.

Therefore, according to "pay or consent" rule, users may have three main options:

- Pay for the ad-free version, if they do not want to give consent.
- Use the ad-supported version if they do consent.
- Find a competing provider if they are unwilling to pay or to give consent.

It appears clear that "pay or consent" rule constitutes a grey area: indeed, GDPR requires that users have a genuine choice between accepting or declining consent. It is hinged upon the fact that users have realistic alternative to the ad-supported free version when they want to withhold consent.[57]

In *Meta Platforms Inc and Others v Bundeskartellamt*[58] the Court of Justice of the European Union considered the legal bases relied on by Meta for processing personal data, including for personalised advertising. The reaction of Meta and others explored the use of subscription models as a way to preserve revenue while enabling users to avoid personalised advertising. Moreover, in April 2024, the European Data Protection Board (EDPB) adopted Opinion 08/2024 on "Valid the

56 See Recital 36 and 37 DMA.

57 (Carugati 2023).

58 Judgment of the Court (Grand Chamber) of 4 July 2023. *Meta Platforms Inc and Others v Bundeskartellamt* (C-252/21.

Context of Consent or Consent in Pay Models Implemented by Large Online Platforms" in which data protection requirements for a valid "consent or pay" model has been clarified. This opinion originated after a request of Dutch, Norwegian and Hamburg Supervisory Authorities on the circumstances and conditions under which "pay or consent" model can be implemented in a way that complies with GDPR, particularly in respect of the conditions for valid consent. The conclusion of EDPB was that

> in most cases, it will not be possible for large online platforms to comply with the requirements for valid consent if they confront users only with a binary choice between consenting to processing of personal data for behavioural advertising purposes and paying a fee.

Moreover, the EDPB set out conditions for valid consent under GDPR with a focus on the requirement for consent to be "freely given". It is critical to ensure that data subjects: (1) have freedom of choice; (2) have a real choice; (3) shall not feel compelled to consent or suffering any negative consequences because of not consenting.[59]

A consent is freely given if the following conditions are met:

- A free alternative is available; thus, controllers should consider providing an equivalent alternative to the paid version, which does not require payment of a fee. Therefore, the importance to encourage an equivalent alternative to the paid version which does not require payment of a fee.
- Detriment to the data subject, this alludes to the importance that an individual is able to refuse or withdraw consent without suffering any harm or damages because of doing so. The detriment includes financial harm or inability to use the service. It should be noted that in the contemporary era platforms might impact users' access to important information, including during public emergency, ability to engage in public debate, participation in social life as well as their emotional and psychological well-being. Thus, a potential detriment may influence and impact on users' ability to make a genuine choice.
- Imbalance of power where controllers' position in the market is a critical factor to consider as in the extent of data subjects' reliance on the service. Additionally, the prevalence of social media in day-to-day life could impact whether users have a genuine choice to use this service or not.
- Conditionality notion plays an important role whether users were being asked to consent to unnecessary data processing to access the service. If a controller processes data in a way that is not necessary to provide the service, data subjects will only be given a genuine choice over the processing of their personal data if they can withhold consent without losing access to the service. Thus, an

59 For a comment, see (Erskine-Fox 2024).

equivalent alternative shall be offered, and it shall be "genuinely equivalent". In doing so, the controller shall adopt a case-by-case approach.

From a UK perspective, on 23rd January 2025,[60] the UK Information Commissioner's Office (ICO) published a guidance on the data protection implication of using the "consent or pay" model to fund online services. The "consent or pay" scheme is not prohibited by data protection law; however, it is vital to implement it in a coherent way. The controversial element alludes to a dilemma: how to obtain an individual's consent to data processing in a way that it meets the strict requirements set by the UK GDPR: freely given, specific, informed and capable of being withdrawn without detriment. According to the ICO's guidance, "consent or pay" model shall consider four factors:

- Power imbalance between provider and user: for example, service provider has a dominant position in the market so that users have limited choice whether to use the service. If a power imbalance exists, it will be difficult to demonstrate that users can freely give or withdraw consent without experiencing an unfair penalty. Ways to address the imbalance are, for example, offering a further alternative option to access the service with contextual (rather than personalised) advertising, or offering ways for users to transfer information to a comparable service provider.
- Appropriate fee, if the fees are excessive, individuals may feel they have no real choice other than to consent.
- Equivalence means that the same service shall be offered under each option (pay or consent) according to an objective test shaped on the following elements: product or service features, functionality, content, personalisation and control over personal information.
- Privacy by design requires that the choice is presenting clearly and enabling storage and access technologies for non-essential purposes only after consent is provided.

5.6 ESG and consumer protection

One of the most well-known concepts existing in ESG[61] agenda was developed in a matter relating to consumer protection. Greenwashing was coined in 1980s by Jay Westerveld: it reflects on a holiday resort's policy of asking its costumer to reuse their towel to protect the environment, yet it constituted an issue where there is the convergence of several and sometimes contrasting economic interests.[62]

Consumer sale of goods contracts is subject to an intense regulation, but only recently the attention turns on environmental and social-sustainability issues.[63]

60 For a comment, see (Treacy 2025).
61 As far as ESG in contract law, see Chapter 18.
62 (Schammo 2023).
63 (Micklitz 2019).

Consumers have become worried about the planet; therefore, they are more likely to buy the brand if they perceive that the company is "green". From this, ESG disclosure exacerbates greenwashing concerns because they may be inconsistent between a company's ESG claims and their actual practices. In this respect, greenwashing has been defined as "the act of misleading consumers [and investors] regarding the environmental practices of a company (firm-level greenwashing) or the environmental benefits of a product or service (product-level greenwashing)".[64] Strictly connected with this is "climate washing": it is a species of greenwashing, and it refers to misleading of overstanding claims related to carbon-neutral or net-zero pledges. Moreover, it highlights the gap between state and non-state actors' words and action about climate change.[65]

As a result, litigation trends about ESG may be classified into three main categories: product level greenwashing, firm-level greenwashing,[66] claims of climate-washing. Due to the consumer matter, the attention will be focused on product level and climate washing.

The first one, product level greenwashing, refers to an act of misleading consumers and shareholders about the environment benefits of a product or service by businesses. A claim arises when consumer purchases a product based on misleading environmental claims; consumer believes that this product is eco-friendly, although its choice is misled and harmed by a false advertisement. In this lawsuit it appears clear the importance of laws and regulations: the latter have a duty to identify the terms used by businesses when labelling products.

Climate washing claims are generally related to carbon neutral, climate neutral, net zero and carbon zero. A claim arises when companies make carbon neutral or net zero claims without transparently disclosing their progress towards goals. Consumers feel misled by such claims and reacting through litigation because company, supported by consumer, does not align with its promise.[67]

From an EU perspective, the amendment of the Unfair Commercial Practices Directive[68] prohibits on misleading information concerning the environmental

64 (Delamas and Burbano 2011, 66). Greenwashing is a term misleading a consumer about either firm environmental performances or environmental benefits of a product or service.

65 (Benjamin et al. 2022).

66 This typology of litigation occurs when a company makes false or misleading claims about its overall environmental practices, policies or performance rather than a specific product (Delamas and Burbano 2011).

67 *Dorris v Danone Waters of Am.*, No. 22 Civ. 08717, 2024 WL 112843 (S.D.N.Y. 10 January 2024): the defendant's representation was that the product is carbon neutral was false because it causes carbon dioxide.

68 Directive 2005/29/EC of the European Parliament and of the Council of 11 May 2005 concerning unfair business-to-consumer commercial practices in the internal market and amending Council Directive 84/450/EEC, Directives 97/7/EC, 98/27/EC and 2002/65/EC of the European Parliament and of the Council and Regulation (EC) No. 2006/2004 of the European Parliament and of the Council ("Unfair Commercial Practices Directive").

or social sustainability of a product or service. Thus, greenwashing is banned by businesses.[69]

Despite this, the most developed legal system is the American one and, more precisely, the State of California: California has been the predominant venue for consumer claims. For example, in *Koh v S.C. Johnson & Son, Inc.*[70] In this controversy, a California district court agreed with the plaintiff that the company's use of label that referenced "Greenlist Ingredients" gave consumer the false impression that the product had been reviewed and approved by a third party, when the Greenlist was created by defendants. By contrast, in *Hill v Roll Int'l Corp.*,[71] another Californian court dismissed a class action consumer claim that alleged that a green water droplet on Fiji bottled water represented a "seal of approval" due to its similar appearance to recognised environmental seals of approval. The court stated that a reasonable consumer would not view the water droplet as indicative of an environmental endorsement: the droplet did not bear the name or logo of any third-party group. More recently,[72] in 2020, the Earth Island Institute field consumer claims against several consumer goods companies, alleging that recycling symbol on their plastic packaging and their assertation about recycling are deceptive. More precisely, they damaged marine life and environment.[73]

Further, the US Court of Appeal of the Ninth Circuit clarified the standard required to companies about the disclose of product labels. In *Hodsdon v Mars*[74] – a case linked with a class action against Mars – it was alleged that company failed to disclose on its product packaging that its cacao suppliers employed child labour. Whilst Mars website addressed the company efforts to combat labour abuses, the plaintiff claimed that Mars had a duty to disclose any poor labour practices associated with its supply chain on its product label. The court stated that an omission, to be actionable, "must be contrary to a representation actually made by the defendant, or an omission of a fact the defendant was obliged to disclose".[75] Child labour in the supply chain did not affect the central functionality of the chocolate or its quality, thus Mars had no duty to disclose such information.

Finally, one of the most recent, and perhaps important case is *Swartz v Coca-Cola Co.*[76] The company was sued for making false and misleading statements regarding the sustainability and environmental friendliness of its plastic bottle. The case was dismissed by the Northern District of California, since "[n]o reasonable consumer

69 (Pflücke 2020).

70 010 WL 94265 (N.D. Cal.).

71 128 Cal. Rptr. 3d 109 (Cal. Ct. App. 2011).

72 Further cases are *Gardner v StarKist Co.*, No. 19-02561 (N.D. Cal. May 13, 2019); *Duggan v Tri-Union Seafoods LLC*, No. 19-02562 (N.D. Cal. May 13, 2019); *Duggan v Bumble Bee Foods LLC*, No. 19-02564 (N.D. Cal. May 13, 2019).

73 *Earth Island Inst. v Crystal Geyser Water Co.*, No. 20-1213 (Cal. Super. Ct. 26 February 2020); *Earth Island Inst. v Crystal Geyser Water Co.*, No. 20-02212 (N.D. Cal. 1 April 2020).

74 891 F.3d 857, 859 (9th Cir. 2018).

75 891 F.3d 857, 859 (9th Cir. 2018) at 864–65.

76 No. 21-cv-04643, 2022 WL 17881771, at *1 (N.D. Cal. 18 November 2022).

would understand '100% recyclable' to mean that the entire product will always be recycled or that the product is part of a circular plastics economy in which all bottles are recycled into new bottles to be used again". Moreover, the court stated that, "whether a product is properly labelled 'recyclable' under the Green Guides depends on whether it is comprised of materials that can be recycled by existing recycling programs – not, as plaintiffs say, on whether the product is converted into reusable material". To better explain, "100% recyclable" does not mean that the product will be recycled but that it is capable of being recycled: "recyclable' is an adjective that means capable of being recycled" or "a noun that denominates an object that can be recycled", and it "does not mean a promise that an object will actually be recycled, as plaintiffs would have it". In essence, the plaintiff's interpretation was not aligned with the Green Guides and California rules.[77]

6. Consumer development: the prosumer

The concept of prosumer stays in between consumer notion and IT evolution simply because during the recent years, the attention has been turned into energy and digital economy. It should be noted that prosumer notion dates to 1980 when Alvin Toffler in "The Third Wave"[78] alludes to individuals who blur the line between producers and consumers by engaging in the production of good and services. In doing so, their aim is to use and/or share these goods and services within a community. It appears even more clear that prosumer does not identify the traditional economic roles since this new paradigm integrates consumption with production activities within the purpose to create value for both them and others. This different approach has been emphasised by the technological development and platform economy: these new technologies facilitate this two-fold role enabling peer-to-peer transaction.[79]

As said just before, prosumer deals with energy sector too: the integration of distributed generation technology (wind turbines) has enabled consumer to actively participate in energy production. Thus, not only do prosumers generate energy for their own but also, they supply excess power to the grid enhancing the resilience and sustainability of energy systems.

Consequently, prosumers play a critical role given their impact on societal development and their importance among different fields: in essence they contribute to innovation, value creatin and distributed flexibility, green promotion, sustainable and technological progress.

Furthermore, prosumers possess specific characteristics:

- They tend to be well-educated, financially secure and technologically adept.

77 (Ballan and Czarnezki 2024).
78 (Toffler 1980).
79 (Ertz, Cao, and Barragán Maravilla 2024).

- They participate in an active manner in both consumption and production process.
- They have higher incomes in energy sector and are integrated in digital platform economy.
- The proactive and creative nature process newer houses with individual heating systems.

Thus, a prosumer acts as both a consumer and a producer: this concept has been shaped though different theories. The first one is the prosumption theory (PT)[80] which stresses the role of prosumer: a consumer that takes part in the production process becoming co-producers of products. Prosumers are involved in various processes, such as designing new products and advising in communication helping company to better understand customers and, consequently, adapt their offering to meet individual needs. It appears clear the shifting from passive consumption to active consumption in product development.

The second theory is called co-creation theory:[81] it highlights the prosumers' active participation in creating value. To elaborate, prosumers, at the same time, consume what is offered and participate in creating and enhancing value of those offering. Thus, the underlying theory illustrates the collaborative nature of the value of those offering it: prosumers contribute actively with ideas, feedback, labour resulting in products and services. The latter becomes ever more close to their preferences and needs.

A further theory is prosumer creativity and focus model (PCFM)[82]: it connects prosumers' creativity with company innovation efficiency. Creativity and innovation create additional value thanks to consumers' participation in the production process, that is, marketing strategies.

Moreover, the MOA theory (motivation, opportunity, ability) used to analyse and predict prosumer behaviour. Thus, three are the fundamental pillars:

- Motivation: the inner drivers that propel prosumers to engage in service activities; motivations may be both intrinsic (personal satisfaction) and extrinsic (financial rewards).
- Opportunity encapsulates the external contextual elements that either constraints or facilitates prosumers' ability to provide services.
- Ability alludes to skills and knowledge that prosumers have which enable them to deliver services effectively. Knowledge means understanding customer needs and managing shared properties, for example.

80 (Chandler and Chen 2015).
81 (Lang, Botha, and Kietzmann n.d.).
82 (Seran and Izvercian 2014)

References

Adams, John N., and Hector MacQueen. 2010. *Atiyah's Sale of Goods*. Longman Pub Group.

Adams, Rachel. 2021. *Transparency: New Trajectories in Law*. Routledge.

Alloa, Emmanuel, and Dieter Thomä. 2018. *Transparency, Society and Subjectivity: Critical Perspectives*. Palgrave Macmillan.

Arroyo Amayueias, Esther. 2023. "Consumer Protection in Online Marketplaces." *Revista da Faculdade de Direito da UFMG, Belo Horizonte* 83: 183–95.

Ballan, Barbara, and Jason J. Czarnezki. 2024. "Disclosure, Greenwashing, and the Future of ESG Litigation." *Washington and Lee Law Review* 81 (2): 545–654.

Benjamin, Lisa, Akriti Bhargava, Benjamin Franta, Karla Martínez Toral, Joana Setzer, and Aradhna Tandon. 2022. *Climate-Washing Litigation: Legal Liability for Misleading Climate Communications*. Institute at Brown for Environment and Society.

Ben-Shahar, Omri, and Carl Schneider. 2014. *More Than You Wanted to Know: The Failure of Mandated Disclosure*. Princeton University Press.

Bergers, Stefan. 2021. *Cultures of Transparency: Between Promise and Peril*. Routledge.

Bush, Christoph. 2021. "Rethinking Product Liability Rules for Online Marketplaces: A Comparative Perspective." *Consumer Law Scholars Conference in Boston* 2: 1–43.

Carugati, Christophe. 2023. "The 'Pay-or-Consent' Challenge for Platform Regulators." *Digital Economy and Innovation* 32 (online).

Chandler, Jennifer, and SteEven Chen. 2015. "Prosumer Motivations in Service Experiences." *Journal of Service Theory and Practice* 25 (2): 220–39.

Delamas, Magali A., and Vanessa Burbano. 2011. "The Drivers of Greenwashing." *California Management Review* 54 (1): 64–87.

Erskine-Fox, Emma. 2024. "Pay or OK? 'No Way, Not Today', Says the EDPB (Well, Sort of)." *Privacy & Data Protection* 24 (6): 4–6.

Ertz, Myriam, Xinyuan Cao, and José Maria Barragán Maravilla. 2024. "The Prosumer." *Encyclopedia* 4: 1263–78.

Flecther, Amelia, Gregory S. Crawford, Jacques Crémer, David Dinielli, Paul Heidhues, Michael Luca, Tobias Salz, M. Schnitzer, F.M. Scott Morton, K. Seim, and M. Sinkinson. 2023. "Consumer Protection for Online Markets and Large Digital Platforms." *Yale Journal on Regulation* 40: 875–914.

Glenn, Ellison, and Sara Fisher Ellison. 2009. "Search, Obfuscation, and Price Elasticities on the Internet." *Econometrica* 77 (2): 427–52.

Hacker, Philip. 2018. "UberPop, UberBlack, and the Regulation of Digital Platforms After the Association Professional Elòite Taxi Judgement of the CJEU." *European Review of Contract Law* 14 (1): 80–96.

Jabłonowska, Agnieszka, and Giacomo Tagiuri. 2023. "Rescuing Transparency in the Digital Economy: In Search of a Common Notion in EU Consumer and Data Protection Law." *Yearbook of European Law* 42 (3): 347–87.

Kaplan, David. 2022. "Consumer Rights Are Gig Workers' Rights? Regulating the Gig Economy at the Intersection of Consumer Protection Law and Employment Law." *Seton Hall Law Review* 53: 281–317.

Lang, Bodo, Elsamari Botha, and Jan Kietzmann. n.d. "How to Grow the Sharing Economy? Create Prosumers!" *Australasian Marketing Journal* 28 (3): 58–66.

Laux, Johann, Sandra Wachter, and Brent Mittelstadt. 2021. "Neutralizing Online Behavioural Advertising: Algorithmic Targeting with Market Power as an Unfair Commercial Practice." *Common Market Law Review* 58: 719–20.

Micklitz, Hans-Wolfgang. 2019. "Squaring the Circle? Reconciling Consumer Law and the Circular Economy." *Journal of European Consumer and Market* 8 (6).

Peel, Edwin. 2020. *The Law of Contract*. Sweet and Maxwell.

Peterson, Christopher L., and Marshall Steinbaum. 2023. "Coercive Rideshare Practices: At the Intersection of Antitrust and Consumer Protection Law in the Gig Economy." *The University of Chicago Law Review* 90 (2): 623–57.

Pflücke, Felix. 2020. "Making Influencers Honest: The Role of Social Media Platforms in Regulating Disclosures." In *The Regulation of Social Media Influencers*, edited by di Catalina Goanta and Sofia Ranchordas, 299–322. Edward Elgar.
Pridgen, Dee, Richard D. Alderman, and Jolina C. Cuaresma. 2022–2023. *Consumer Protection and the Law*. Thomson Reuters
Quarta, Alessandra. 2020. "Narratives of the Digital Economy: How Platforms Are Challenging Consumer Lawa nd Hierarchical Organization." *Global Jurist* 2: 1–21.
Schammo, Pierre. 2023. "Greewashing." *Company Lawyer* 44 (4): 105–6.
Seran, Sabina, and Monica Izvercian. 2014. "Prosumer Engagement in Innovation Strategies: The Prosumer Creativity and Focus Model." *Management Decision* 52 (10): 1968–80.
Toffler, Alvin. 1980. *The Third Wave*. New York: Morrow.
Treacy, Bridget. 2025. "'Consent or Pay': Examining the ICO's Guidance." *Privacy & Data Protection* 25 (4): 8–10.
Willson, Michele. 2017. "Algorithms (and the) Everyday." *Information, Communication & Society* 20: 137.

6 Consideration and estoppel

Chapter Overview

1. Introduction

For a contract to be enforceable, it shall be supported by consideration. The word "consideration" means something which is of some value in the eye of the law or "something in return" for a promise, for example the price for which the promise of the other is bought.

In *Currie v Misa*[1] consideration was defined (Lush LJ) as "some right, interest, profit or benefit accruing to one party, or some forceable, detriment, loss or responsibility given or undertaken by the other".

Another definition is encompassed into *Dunlop Pneumatic Tyre Co Ltd v Selfridge & Co Ltd*[2]: consideration is "an act for forbearance of one party, or to promise thereof, is the price for which the promise of other is bought, and the promise thus given for value is enforceable".

A simpler approach to consideration is "the price paid for the promise" or the *quid pro quo* element of the contract. Further, the consideration in a contract constitutes into a promise of performance rather than performance itself. Thus, a contract has a legal effect from the moment it is agreed: it can be enforced even if the party is not yet due to pay or perform.

1 (1874) LR 10 Ex 153.
2 [1915] AC 847.

DOI: 10.4324/9781003645948-6

In a purchase agreement, consideration:

- For A is goods or promise of goods.
- For B is the money or the promise of money.

Finally, also from a general perspective, consideration is required to be present in all contracts except those made by deed. The latter, deed, is a written document which complies with certain formalities: the document must make it clear that it is intended to be a deed; it must be signed and witnessed.

It is worth stressing that Scots legal system, still within the UK, does not recognise consideration as a necessary requirement of the contract. Similarly, Louisiana refuses to accept consideration requirement as well as it is focused on the agreement of the bargaining.[3]

2. Consideration in legal theory

The underlying idea of consideration is the reciprocity as an essence of law of obligations. In addition, legal system shall not recognise legally binding and binding all promises for different reasons:

- Courts will be paralysed by litigation.
- Some problems of evidence may arise.
- May lead to unjust outcomes.

Moreover, consideration relates to the idea of reciprocity, summarised with the Latin expression "*quid pro quo*", defined also as the requirement of mutuality. Consideration, therefore, constitutes a requirement that "something of value" should be given for a promise to make it enforceable.

Consideration achieves three main functions:

- Evidentiary function: consideration provides a proof of existence of a valid contract.
- Cautionary function: consideration refrains parties from undertaking reckless legal actions.
- Challenging function: consideration represents a simple test of enforceability of a contract as it gives to the contract a "badge of enforceability".

Moreover, it was also highlighted that consideration achieves also the objective to realise the "justice of the case".[4] In this respect, considerations play, also, a crucial role:

3 Article 1906, Civil Code of Louisiana, stipulates as follows: "A contract is an agreement by two or more parties whereby obligations are created, modified, or extinguished". Further, Article 1966 stipulates as follows: "An obligation cannot exist without a lawful clause".

4 (Atiyah 1986).

- If interpretation of terms of contracts is difficult.
- The implied condition in a contract recognised to purchase the right to receive adequate value for money.
- If consideration is grossly inadequate this may give rise to strong suspicion of fraud or undue influence.

From a comparative perspective, the scenario shall be summarised as follows:

- European legal systems are focused on the enforceability that promisor really intended to be bound by his promise.
- Civil law system adopts the concept of "causa" and distinguishes the latter from the concept of the motive for which parties contracting. "Causa" constitutes the reason for contracting and implies a certain level of court's enquiry. By contrast, consideration is aimed to help to establish parties' intention.

In English contract law consideration, although different, is distinct from the concept of privity,[5] that is, with the general rule that only a party to contract can enforce it. The rule of consideration moves from the promise, although it is not necessarily true that it moves to the promisor. There is no need for a direct benefit to the promisor, so even entering by a promise into a contract with a third party can be seen as a valid consideration.

Based on *The Contracts (Rights of Third Parties) Act 1999*, third parties are allowed to enforce a contract which was concluded by them. Furthermore, it is possible to affirm that third parties may enforce terms of the contract under two circumstances:

- If third party is especially mentioned in the contract as someone authorised to do so.
- If the contract "purports to confer a benefit" on him.

As far as consideration is concerned, it is possible to affirm that consideration serves more as an additional formality concerned with gratuitous contracts than a serious material requirement of validity. More in general, the performance of an existing legal duty cannot constitute a valid consideration.

In *Stilk v Myrik*[6] the principle shall be explained as follows: a valid contract requires an offer and acceptance. Although this is true, the underlying principle is

5 It is worth mentioning that "privity" in smart contracts has a different meaning hence it signifies the property that knowledge about the contract should only be spread to the participants with a contractual need to know (Köpke 2020).

6 [1809] EWHC KB J58: the return voyage between London and Baltics was in peril when two of the crew abandoned the ship. The seamen were due to receive wages for £5 per month during voyage. The captain offered the remaining crew an equally divided share of the deserted seamen's salary if they could return sail the ship to London with reduced crew. Although the ship was to return to London by the remaining seamen, the additional payment was not made.

that offer and acceptance require consideration too: the lack of consideration leads to the no-existence of a contract. Therefore, each party must be given something in return for the bargain they receive under the contract and without which the contract will not be valid. In a nutshell, it was stated that agreements cannot be altered without the provisions of fresh consideration to underpin the promise and contractually binding the parties.

To simplify, this case was relating to the problem of enforcing a benefit promised after the formation of a contract and resolves this by making enforcement conditional upon the supply of fresh consideration to support the promise. It encapsulates a strong approach to consideration based on which an employer is at liberty to resile from an unsupported promise formally and freely given as well as seriously intended. As a result of this, *Stilk v Myrik* encapsulates the "orthodox doctrine" of consideration.

Since its origin, the doctrine of consideration has undergone many changes, and its rules have been subject to many modifications. It is also linked with the new economic reality.

For instance, the consequences of *Stilk v Myrik* have been softened or even limited. *In Williams v Roffey Bros & Nicholls (Contractors) Ltd*,[7] the court held that the doctrine of *Stilk v Myrik* needed to be redefined. More precisely, it was stated that a promise to make bonus payments to complete work on time was enforceable if the promisor obtained a practical effect and the promise was not given under duress or by fraud. The main statements were that the court should take "a pragmatic approach to the true relationship between the parties".

It is important to clarify that the aim of "William" is not to overrule the requirement required *in Stilk v Myrick*. To elaborate, the *dictum Williams v Roffey Bros* does have the following elements:

- It refers to the commercial *rationale* for preserving relationships.
- It has a focus on the following conclusion: the cost of engaging in a new contract is higher than to keep the existing contract functioning.

Finally, a modern approach to consideration doctrine requires to read consideration as a need for not being the object of the promisor's desire for which he offers his promise in exchange. By contrast, the correct approach seems to be to read consideration as an element required if an action shall be enforceable as a result or natural consequence of a promise.

7 [1991] 1 QB 1: the appellants were builders who were contracted to refurbish 27 flats belonging to a house corporation. The contract had a penalty clause for late completion. The appellants sub-contracted some work to William, a carpenter. He fell behind with his work, the appellants offered him bonus payment to finish on time; Williams carried on working until the payments stopped. As a result of this, he sued the appellants for breach of contract.

3. When "consideration" is missing: a comparative approach

It is important to emphasise that consideration represents a peculiarly English concept. In other jurisdiction, a "*nudum pactum*" (i.e., a bare promise) with a clear intention to be bound can be sufficient for formation of a binding contract.

A pragmatical example is the mixed legal system and the Scottish one. The latter was under the influence of the medieval canon law: it is possible that the emphasis was upon performance as the moral right and duty flowing from promises and agreements. Based on such background, Lord President Stair wrote "Institutions of the Law of Scotland": it constitutes a basic scheme of the law of obligations. Despite the influence of common law systems, some areas were not affected by this shift: for example, consideration and privity.

Partially different was the development in South Africa where the Roman-Dutch law flirted for a long time with consideration requirement. The latter had been rejected in 1919.[8] The "issue" arose because Roman-Dutch law had used the concept of "*causa*" as a tool of distinguishing enforceable from unenforceable agreements. For some lawyers, "*causa*" was, fundamentally, consideration but called in a different way.

In Scotland,[9] the approach was different due to the influence of Spanish and Grotius approach; thus, the rejection of the fact that promises without equivalent onerous cause do not produce obligation or action.[10] According to this line of reasoning every *pactum* produces action, in essence *pacta sunt servanda.*

From this a new problematic topic arises: whether a promise or an agreement will create legal obligations; thus, how to investigate if an agreement is legally binding or not. In other words, if parties do not have the intention to create an enforceable agreement, the consequence is that the agreement cannot be legally enforced. This question is, theoretically, a question of fact despite the difficulty to assess the subjective intentions of individuals whenever a dispute arises about an enforceable promise or contract.

Therefore, the law presumes that in certain circumstances the promisor, or the parties to an agreement, intended to enter legal obligations and in different circumstances the law presumes that they did not intend the promise or agreement to be legally binding. For example, where a promise or agreement is made in a commercial context, there is a presumption that the parties intend to enter legal relations. A different conclusion is when the promise or agreement is made in an entirely social context (an invitation to dinner). In this case, the presumption is that the arrangement is not intended to be legally binding. Further, if an agreement or promise is made between members of a family or cohabitants, it is presumed too to not be legally enforceable.

In both cases, presumption may be rebutted where the promisor or the parties have expressly stipulated that the promise or agreement is intended to be legally

8 See *Conradie v Roussow* [1919] AD 279.
9 See (MacQueen 2013).
10 (Sellar 2000).

binding, or such intention can be inferred from the particular facts of the case. Moreover, if the contract should be encompassed into the two mentioned categories, the court has the power/duty to determine whether the agreement was intended to be legally binding.[11]

4. Requirements for consideration

To be valid, a consideration shall comply with the following criteria. These are as follows:

- Consideration shall not be past.
- Consideration shall move from promise/claimant.
- Consideration shall be legal: consideration cannot be something or some act which is illegal, immoral or contrary to the public morals.
- Consideration shall have an economic value.[12]
- Considerations shall be express or implied request by promisor to promisee for consideration.
- Shall be sufficient because shall provide some benefits to promisor or some detriment to promisee. Furthermore, consideration shall have, also, some economic value even if negligible. In this respect, consideration cannot consist, solely, of sentimental or otherwise emotional value, for instance following someone's wishes or promising.

It is crucial to clarify that consideration needs to be assessed alongside whether there was an intention to create legal relations.

In this respect, it is worth mentioning *White v Bluett*[13]: Mr Bluett had lent his son some money; when he died, his executor – Mr White – sued the son to pay back the money. The son argued that his father said that the son need not repay if the son stops complaining about how Mr Bluett would distribute his property in his will among the children. The court said that the son had not provided consideration for the father's promise. It was emphasised that consideration was on one side, so it was a *nudum pactum*. Consequently, the most important points are as follows:

- There was no consideration given by the son which would absolve him of having to repay the debt to his father's estate.
- The son had no right to complain as the father was free to distribute his property as he wished.

11 (MacQueen 2020).

12 See *Thomas v Thomas* (1842) 2 QB 851 where it was involved the rental of a property for the cost of £1. This amount of money was not a valid consideration because the actual value of the property rental exceeds the £1 of value. Therefore, the court ruled that this was irrelevant for the fact that the existence of consideration made it valid. The expression "some consideration" refers to anything that has an economic value.

13 (1853) 23 LJ Ex 36.

By contrast, an American case law – which may not be followed in England – is *Hamer v Sidway*[14]: it establishes that forbearance of legal rights, voluntary abstaining from one's legal rights, on promises of future benefit made by other parties can constitute valid consideration. Further, unilateral contracts were valid under New York law. This decision is influenced by the "benefit-detrimental theory": the consideration exists if one party benefits from a contract while the other party suffers a detriment.

Moreover, in some circumstances consideration was defined as insufficient to form a binding contract. Along these circumstances there are also some exceptions.

As far as the limitations are concerned, these are three:

- Performance of an existing duty.
- Past consideration.
- Part-payment of a debt.

Performance of an existing duty encompasses different exceptions:

- Performance of legal obligations which are independent of any contract: the general rule is that performance of an existing obligation does not constitute a valid consideration.[15]
- Performance of a duty already promised in a different contract.
- Performance of a duty owed to a third party: to better explain, the performance of an existing duty owed to a third party may be valid consideration if it allows the party to enforce a direct obligation against the other.[16]

However, in *Williams v Roffey*[17] some circumstances may constitute a valid consideration even if performance of a duty was already promised in a different contract. These are as follows:

- If A has entered a contract with B to do work or to supply goods or services to B in return for payment by B.
- At some stage before A has completely performed his obligations under the contract B has reason to doubt whether A will not, or will be able to, complete his side of the bargaining.

14 124 N.Y. 538, 27 N.E. 256 (N.Y. 1891). William Story promised his nephew that if he would stop drinking alcohol, smoking, swearing and gambling until he was 21 years old, William would pay him $5,000. His nephew agreed, and he fully performed the agreement. However, the nephew occasionally drank alcohol and smoked.

15 See *Glasbrook Bros v Glamorgan County Council* [1925] AC 270: an individual requested police protection in the form of a constant presence on his property. The police did not have the resources to do so but did in exchange for a financial contribution. It was held that one of the legal obligations of police is to protect members of society; however, the consideration was valid as it required the police to go above and beyond their ordinary duties.

16 See *New Zealand Shipping Co Ltd v AM Satterthwaite & Co Ltd (The Eurymedon)* [1975] AC 154.

17 [1991] 1 QB 1.

- B promises A an additional payment in return for A's promise to perform his contractual obligations on time.
- B obtains a benefit or obviates a disbenefit because of giving his promise.
- B's promise is not given because of economic duress or fraud on the part of A.

Past consideration is insufficient to form a legally enforceable agreement due to the fact that only consideration which is given at the time or after the promise for which it is given is enforceable. The leading case is *Re McArdle*[18]: a sum of money was promised for some building work. However, this promise was made after the building work being completed. In this respect, building work was "past consideration".

By contrast, a past consideration may valid if the following are present:

- The consideration that is past would have operated as valid consideration if the act was done at promisor's request.
- There was an understanding there would be the conferment of some kind of reward payment or benefit for the act. In *Re Casey's Patents*,[19] the court stressed that due commercial relationship of the parties, it was presumed payment would eventually be promised despite it not being so at the time of performance of the contractual requirements. Thus, a mutual understanding should be identifiable.
- The consideration would have been valid had it been promised in advance of the contract.

It should be noted that a contracting party can stipulate for what consideration he chooses. In *Chappell & Co Ltd v Nestle*[20] the question was if the contracting party can stipulate for what consideration he chooses. In this case, the defendant, Nestle, launched a marketing promotion where they offered a discount music record for their customers in exchange for three wrappers of their chocolate bars; wrappers are no monetary value as they are eventually thrown away by Nestle. Thus, the question was if the wrappers bars were part of the consideration. The House of Lord held that the wrappers were part of the consideration since it conferred a benefit upon Nestle by inducing people to try their chocolate and the offer was addressed to everyone; it means that it may be accepted by a person who was induced to try it. Therefore, wrappers were not just a condition because conditions limit the offer to persons qualified, such as members of a club. By contrast, in this specific case, the qualification confers a benefit only sufficient for a sale and must be re-acquired before another. Consequently, repeated acquisitions of qualifications are parts of the consideration.

Finally, as far as part-payment of debt is concerned, the general rule is that part-payment of a debt is never good consideration to discharge that debt. To

18 [1951] Ch 669.
19 [1892] 1 Ch 104.
20 [1960] AC 87.

elaborate, part-payment of a debt represents simply the performance of an existing duty.[21] For example, the payment by cheque made no difference to the principle that late payment of a less amount did not equal satisfaction of the total amount owing. In the specific case, builders had been under duress to accept a reduced amount due to their financial position, which not only was the other party aware but also took advantage of. Consequently, an acceptance arising from a threat does not amount to a settlement.[22]

An exception of this is constituted by part-payment of a debt. It is valid if something else is exchanged along with/instead of money. The underlying reason is that court may presume that mobile phone has some value which goes beyond the debt, even if it does not.

A further exception was represented by the case in which payment was made in a different form or at a different location. For example, if A is required to pay via bank transfer, but is later asked to pay in person, the part-payment of a debt can be sufficient consideration. The reason is both the effort and expense of travelling helps to amount sufficient consideration.

Finally, it is possible to stress the differences between *Stilk v Myrick* and *Foakes v Beer*.

In the first one – *Stilk v Myrick* – the rule is that if there is a contract between A and B, and A agrees to pay B more money if B will complete B's obligations the consequences is that the performance of an existing contract duty owed to the other party is not sufficient consideration for a promise to pay more.

In the second – *Foakes v Beer* – if there is a contract between A and B and A has fully performed A's obligations and agrees to accept a reduced payment from B, the consequence is that partial payment of a debt is not sufficient consideration for a promise by a creditor to forgo the balance.

5. Promissory estoppel

"Estoppel" does not constitute a term with an English origin due its Latin origin, *stupa*, that means hemp or tort. This element, considered alone, is useful to understand the goal of promissory estoppel: to reduce shortcomings of the doctrine of consideration. It is also true that it is also one of the roles played by equity: to reduce the rigidity of common law rules.

The concept of promissory estoppel is important to recall some elements of the *culpa in contrahendo* notion in the continental jurisdictions. The latter assumes that it would be dishonest to withdraw from one's promise, if the other party had previously relied on it. However, promissory estoppel, different from *culpa in contrahendo*, cannot be used as a basis of action.

21 *Foakes v Beer* (1883) LR 9 App Cas 605.
22 See *D & C Builders v Rees* [1966] 2 QB 617.

Promissory estoppel shall be applied only if it complies with certain requirements, that is:

- A clear or unequivocal promise or representation: it means that a promise should be aimed at promisor's legal rights and intended to amend the legal relationship between the parties. This test is led with the standard of reasonable person's understanding.
- The promise must have relied on the promise of his behaviour; in some cases, also the "detriment" in reliance on the promise is required.
- It shall be inequitable for the promisor to go back on his promise: promissory estoppel constitutes an equitable doctrine: thus, the court will apply it with a discretion.

To summarise, the general rule of the effect of promissory estoppel is that it suspends their enforcement; by contrast it does not extinguish legal rights. As a result of this, for more years, the promissory estoppel was read to diminishing the concept of the doctrine of consideration. More precisely, the evolution of promissory estoppel provided successful defence in cases relating to claims based on part payment. Furthermore, promissory estoppel, as part of equity, is aimed not to mitigate common law rules rather than to create a counter-rule to reduce the inconvenience of consideration requirement.

The leading case is *Central London Property Trust Ltd v High Trees House Ltd*[23] where the High Court reaffirmed the doctrine of promissory estoppel in contract law in England and Wales. The important part is the *obiter dictum* where Denning J stated that estoppel shall be applicable if

> a promise was made which was intended to create legal relations and which, to the knowledge of the person making the promise, was going to be acted on by the person to whom it was made and which was in fact so acted on.

More precisely, it was held that:

- CLPT could not go back on its promise to accept reduced rent for the period when flats were not fully occupied.
- CLPT made a promissory representation base on which other parties rely on; consequently, they were stopped from reneging.
- Once conditions went back to normal, the original agreement could be enforced and the claim for full rent for the last quarters of 1945 was successful.

23 [1947] KB 130. In 1937 Central London Property Trust Ltd (CLPT) leased a block of flats in London, the High Trees House Ltd. As a result of the World War II there was a drastic under-occupancy of the flats; thus, CLPT agreed to reduce the rent. This rent was paid until the end of 1945; after, flats were again fully occupied. CLPT claimed for the full rent for the last two quarters of 1945.

Based on this case, the principle of promissory estoppel means that, once a promise is made and relied upon, it cannot be reneged on without an agreement if

- (also) not supported by consideration.
- This would be inequitable.

Moreover, the effect of promissory estoppel is only suspensive. In other words, it only temporarily varied the rent payable; therefore it does not permanently extinguish rights.

The doctrine of promissory estoppel has its origin in equitable waiver: the judge is not obliged to apply this principle in automatic way because there is a residual discretion. The latter appears when the judge can decide that an enforced promise should not qualify as "fair". Thus, inequitable concept covers situation in which the promise has extracted the promise by taking advantage by the promisor.

Between promissory estoppel and waiver lies a difference. The second, waiver, refers to the situation in which party waiving their rights is only waiving the right to claim damages for breach of contract or to terminate for breach where applicable. By contrast, in promissory estoppel payment could not be claimed.

To summarise, as far as promissory estoppel is concerned, it is possible to say that:

- Rules are developed in equity.
- The doctrine only applies where one party relied on the promise of another.
- Rights are only suspended, not extinguished.
- It represents a shield, not a sword.

Promissory estoppel is applicable only if the follows conditions are met:

- The existence of a contractual relationship.
- It is a promise as well as a reliance.
- It appears inequitable to enforce strict legal rights.
- It shall be inequitable for the promisor to go back on the promise.
- The promise or representation shall have influenced the conduct of the promise in some way.
- Can be only used as a defence since its equitable nature.[24]
- It is available only at the discretion of the court.
- Future rights do not destroy.
- New rights should not be created.

24 The general rule is that "equity is a shield, not a sword".

References

Atiyah, P.S. 1986. *Essay on Contract*. Oxford: Oxford University Press.

Köpke, Julius. 2020. "Towards Modeling Privity and Enforceability Requirements for BPM Based Smart Contracts." *Modellierung (Companion)* 53–55.

MacQueen, Hector L. 2013. "Scots and English Law: The Case of Contract." Research Paper Series 2013/41. University of Edinburgh.

MacQueen, Hector L. 2020. *MacQueen and Thomson on Contract Law in Scotland*. Bloomsbury Professional.

Sellar, David. 2000. "Formation of Contract." In *A History of Private Law in Scotland*, edited by Kenneth G.C. Reid and Reinhard Zimmermann, 155–58. Oxford University Press.

7 Capacity in contract

Chapter Overview

1. Introduction

Contractual capacity may be defined as the ability to understand the consequence of a contract. More in detail, contractual capacity constitutes the ability of an individual or an entity to enter a contract which may legally bind such a party. In doing so, parties commit themselves, or the entities they are acting for, to both obligations and consequences that flow from the contract.

Moreover, contractual capacity represents a key element of a contract, as well as offer, acceptance and consideration.

Based on this, capacity is a complex area of breach of contract. A party, to avoid the consequences of a contract, must prove, at the same time, that he/she was not mentally sound when signing the contract and that the other party was aware of the fact. According to this line of reasoning, disputes may arise if the party was deemed not able to act for himself or herself. In this respect, we can refer to minors. These

DOI: 10.4324/9781003645948-7

are individuals under the age which is required for an individual to be a party to a contract, that is, 18 years old.

More in general, also in other circumstances contracts may be considered voidable if signed by, or with, parties who lack capacity. These parties are as follows:

- Mentally incapacitated is a person that lacks the ability to understand the consequences of his/her contracts. All contracts signed by a person who is mentally incapacitated are void.
- The intoxicated is a person who is using, legal or illegal, drugs. The main question is if this individual can understand the consequences of his/her contract. Further, it is quintessential to stress that, typically, intoxication is of a voluntary nature.

Capacity represents a crucial element in contract law, and this happens for different reasons:

- To protect vulnerable parties, because it is critical to ensure that individuals who lack the ability to fully comprehend the terms and consequences of a contract do not take advantage of it.
- To ensure that consent is given voluntarily: in this respect, capacity plays an important role to guarantee that parties entering a contract do so willingly, with their own consent. This is aimed to maintain the integrity of contractual agreements.
- To uphold legality since contracts signed by parties without the required capacity may be void or voidable. In other words, these contracts may not be enforceable before a court of law.

Contractual capacity has also an impact on commercial law or, better, on business organisations under different aspects, for instance:

- Risk mitigation, because if company has engaged someone who lacks the capacity to contract, the business enterprise may be in a legally precarious situation.
- Legal compliance, because ignoring the capacity in issue may lead to non-compliance with the law.
- Financial stability, because to sign a contract with an individual who lacks contractual obligations can disrupt cash flow and lead to financial issues.
- Reputation management, because to enter contracts with parties lacking capacity can lead to disputes, legal actions and, finally, also to negative publicity.
- Legal costs.

Finally, it is central to stress that the general rule in English law is that any person is competent to bind himself to any contract he/she chooses to make, if this it is not illegal or void for reasons of public policy. Common law recognises, also, exceptions to this rule: corporation, minors, mentally incompetent and intoxicated persons.

Between 1870 and 1949 married women were categorised as competent: however, since 1949 this further exception has been abolished. Consequently, a married woman has full contractual capacity.

2. Corporations

A corporation created by Royal Charter has always the same contractual capacity as an ordinary person; however, a company incorporated under the Companies Act 2006 can make a contract if it is under the umbrella of the scope and objects defined in its memorandum of association. If it is beyond, it is *ultra vires*, therefore void.[1]

The leading case is *Ashbury Railway Carriage and Iron Co. Ltd v Riche*.[2] Its importance has been diminished because of Companies Act 2006 and, more precisely, by Section 31. The *ultra vires* doctrine was shaped in this. As a result of this, every act carried out by company shall be entered into the border of the Memorandum of Association.

The Ashbury Railway Carriage and Iron Company Ltd.'s memorandum, clause 3, prescribed that its objects were

> to make and sell, or lend on hire, railway carriages and waggons, and all kinds of railway plant, fittings, machinery and rolling stock; to carry on the business of mechanical engineers and general contractors; to purchase, lease, work and sell mines, minerals, land and buildings; to purchase and sell as merchants, timber, coal, metals, or other materials, and to buy any such materials on commission or as agents.

Clause 4 stated that activities beyond this should obtain a special resolution.

Despite this, the company agreed to give Riche and his brother a loan to build a railway from Antwerp to Tournai, in Belgium. In a second moment, the company repudiated the agreement: Riche sued, and the company pleaded that the actions was *ultra vires*.

The House of Lords held that, if a company pursued objects beyond the scope of the memorandum of association, the company's action was *ultra vires*. More in detail, and in the specific case it was highlighted that the contract was not ratified by the unanimous assent of the whole corporation.

Important changes came from Section 108, Companies Act 1989, that substituted the initial prescription. As a result of this, the "ancient" Section 31 stipulates as follows: "The validity of an act done by a company shall not be called into question on the ground of lack of capacity by reason of anything in the company's memorandum".

As a result of this, if Section 35 had applied to *Ashbury Railway Carriage and Iron Co. Ltd v Riche,* the conclusion would be different. More in depth, the directors

1 (Fimmanò, de Gioia Carabellese, and Della Giustina 2024)
2 (1875) L.R. 7 H.L. 653.

committed a breach of duty by signing a contract. However the contract was made, its validity could not be questioned, provided that the making of the contract was "an act done by the company". A potential objection shall be referred to any act that was made, due to the lack of powers of directors to sign the contract.[3] It is also true that an *ultra vires* act by the directors may be ratified but only by special resolution, which does not affect any liability incurred by the directors or any other person.

In a nutshell, this case shows that, because of changes, the decision of the court should be different.

3. Minors

Minor is a young person under the age of 18 years old: the law does not consider that a minor has the same capacities as an adult with full mental capabilities. One of these capacities is the ability to enter a legally binding contract.

It is crucial to stress that a minor constitutes a different concept of infancy. As far as the infant is concerned, the law prescribes that an infant is not bound by the contracts which he/she enters. The only exception is the purchase of necessaries and for useful contract of service.

Given the general rule, therefore, a minor is not bound by a contract which he/she entered into during his/her minority. The aim is to protect minors against their own inexperience and improvidence by relieving them of ability on contracts made by them, but in some cases, the rights of the other party must in fairness be allowed to prevail over this policy of protection.

Law recognises the ability of minors to sign a contract to necessaries: the latter is defined by Section 3(3), Sale of Goods Act 1979. Based on this definition, necessaries are "goods suitable to the condition in life of the minor . . . and to his actual requirements at the time of the sale and delivery". Necessaries means goods which are suitable to the minor's condition in life. Furthermore, this condition refers, also, to a minor's status in life: in *Peters v Fleming*,[4] it was held that rings, pins and watch-chains were under the umbrella of "necessary goods". The underlying reason was that the minor, in this specific case, was a child of a Member of the British Parliament. Furthermore, in *Hands v Slaney*[5] servant's uniform was necessary goods when purchased by a gentleman.

Nash v Inman[6] constitutes an important English case relating to the concept of "necessaries". The plaintiff was a Savile Row tailor, the defendant was a minor doing undergraduate studies at Trinity College, University of Cambridge. The plaintiff sent his agent to the university to see if he can find people who might be interested in buying high-class clothing. The plaintiff sued the minor for the

3 See Section 35A(1): "In favour of a person dealing with a company in good faith, the power of the board of directors to bind the company, or authorise others to do so, shall be deemed to be free of any limitation under the company's constitution".

4 [1840] 6 M & W 42.

5 (1800) 8 Term Rep 578.

6 [1908] 2 KB 1.

payment of the price of clothing: the student claimed that the contract was not enforceable against him as he was a minor.[7] The court could not uphold the claim made by the plaintiff against the defendant for the price of clothing: according to the judgment, the plaintiff could not establish that the goods supplied to the minor were "necessaries". Further, the court noted that there was enough evidence that the minor's father was an architect; therefore he was in a good position with a town and country house. As a result of this, the clothes supplied were suited to the minor's conditions in life and standard cost of living. Nevertheless, the father showed that the defendant had adequate clothes of such type at the time when the plaintiff had delivered clothing.

Consequently, the Court of Appeal held that, although the goods supplied were suitable to the young man's condition in life, they could still not be regarded as "necessary". It was because of the evidence provided by the father: the defendant possessed a sufficient wardrobe of clothes.

Although this reasoning is correct as a matter of principle, an element to be stressed is that a minor may be liable for breach of an executory contract. In *Roberts v Gray*[8] the court ruled that the contract signed between Roberts and Gray was for the benefit of Gray, the minor, and did not encompass harsh terms. As a result of this, the contract was binding on the minor, and he was liable for breach of contract.

By contrast, a minor is generally bound by a contract of employment if this contract is beneficial for him. The reference goes to contracts of apprenticeship, training or employment and professional engagement.

In *Doyle v White City Stadium*[9] the court stated that the rules of the fight were meant to protect the infant boxer – this was for his benefit. Consequently, the terms of the contract were considered binding on him.

By contrast, in *De Francesco v Barnum*[10] it was held that the contract between the plaintiff and the minor was largely to the benefit of the plaintiff, not to the one of the defendant, the minor. The contract was one-sided and unreasonable; it could not be considered as a valid contract. Since the contract was void, the plaintiff could not sue the defendant for breaching a non-existent contract.

7 It is important to stress that during the time zone of this case law, people were considered minor until 21 years of age.

8 [1913] 1 KB 520. Robert was a professional billiard player who agreed to take Gray on a world tour playing billiards to teach Gray how to play billiards. It was agreed that Roberts will pay all the expenses associated with the tour and be reimbursed out of the money made on the tour. Whilst the contract was still executory, a disagreement ensued between them, and Gray refused to embark on the trip. Despite this, Robert had already incurred some costs planning the trip.

9 [1935] 1 KB 110. An infant boxer entered a contract to fight for £3,000; the contractual terms stated that he will not be entitled to the prize money of £3,000 if he was disqualified for breaching the rules of the fight. The infant boxer breached the rules and got disqualified. He claimed the prize money.

10 [1880] 43 Ch D 165. A minor signed a contract with the plaintiff to learn stage dancing: the minor was to serve the plaintiff for seven years and will only be paid if employed by the plaintiff. However, the plaintiff was not under obligation to employ her. Further, the plaintiff could terminate unilaterally the contract but the minor could not; nevertheless, the minor left plaintiff and went to defendant. Thus, the plaintiff argued that the defendant induced the minor to breach his contract.

More in general, the minor may rid himself of his obligations if he repudiates the contract before attaining the age of 18 or within a reasonable time after this moment. In other words, the contract is voidable at the minor's option. To elaborate, a voidable contract constitutes an existing contract, but the law recognised to one party the right to set aside or render void.

Finally, at common law, all contracts, different from all these contracts signed for necessaries, did not used to be binding on the minor, unless he ratified them after reaching majority age. By contrast, these contracts could be enforceable by the minor if this was his/her choice.

The Minors' Contracts Act 1987 introduced a new remedy of restitution in favour of other contracting parties; however, it constitutes a discretionary remedy.

In *Stocks v Wilson*[11] it was held that, if a minor obtains goods through fraudulent means, he can be compelled to return the goods if they are still in his custody or make refunds if the goods are no longer with him.

Furthermore, in *Leslie v Sheill*[12] it was stressed that enforcing void contract would be equivalent to making a minor liable for any restitution for damages. Since the minor's use of the money cannot be tracked, restitution should not be sought in this situation. Furthermore, if the products may be tracked back to the third party, equity will only permit the plaintiff to establish a right of action against the third party for tort of conversion.

As far as the narrative is concerned, to acquire a loan from the plaintiff, the defendant falsely represented age at the time of transaction. The child spent the entire sum and made no repayments. As a result of this, he was sued by the defendant to recover the money. The issue was the infant's fraud responsibility. Indeed, Sheill, the defendant, was a minor who fraudulently claimed to be an adult to acquire two financial loans from the plaintiff, Leslie Ltd.

The court ruled that Sheill was not responsible for making reparations; restitution constitutes a type of equitable relief, according to the court, and infants are typically exempt from equitable remedies. Therefore, the court distinguished between:

- Debt payment.
- Money restitution.

The latter, money restitution, is permitted if the advantage gained by the minor under the agreement includes property, provided that the property can be in accordance with the equitable doctrine of restitution.[13]

11 [1913] 2 KB 235.

12 [1914] 3 KB 607.

13 By contrast, in *Stock v Wilson*, the court ordered that infant refund the sum he had made from the sale of the furniture to the original seller.

4. Agency

Agency may be defined as the relationship which arises when the agent acts on behalf of another, the principal, and has the power to affect the principal's legal position as regarding a third party. For example, agents are travel agents, insurance brokers, ticket agents, shop assistants and auctioneers. To create a binding contract between a principal and a third party, an agent must have authority, which may be either actual or apparent.

Actual authority occurs when the principal has given to the agent the required authority to contract on his behalf. This means that agency, normally, arises by an express appointment through which the principal will expressly appoint someone to act as their agent to do some specific things.

Apparent authority means that the agent does not have authority from the principal, although the agent could still be able to form a binding contract because he has a different form of authority. The appearance of authority should be created by the principal, and this representation must have been intended to be, and was acted upon, the other party. The following conditions should be satisfied:

- The principal must have been represented, by words or conducts, that the agent had the authority.
- The third party must rely on this representation, believing that the agent has authority.
- The third party must alter their position by entering the contract, for example.

As far as the effects of agency are concerned, it should be distinguished between authorised and unauthorised agent.

The first one has no rights or obligations under the resulting contract: the agent is authorised to enter the contract on behalf of someone else, the principal, and the resulting contract is between the principal and other party.

The unauthorised agent is an agent who is acting on behalf of another with a lack of authority. The consequences are as follows:

- The principal cannot sue the third party or be sued by a third party: the agent did not have authority to bind the principal.
- The agent cannot be sued on the contract.
- The third party may sue the agent in deceit where the agent knew they had no authority or for breach of implied warranty or authority.

To summarise, an agent, indeed, is appointed by his principal to enter into negotiations and conclude contractual agreements with third parties. Then, the agent shall be dropped out of the usual legal equation (party of the contract v. third party), simply because in this case principal and third party are locked into the same contract.

Second, the creation of the agency is made by:

- Actual authority where a principal and agent have created an agreement.
- Apparent authority: the principal makes a representation to the third party that the agent has the authority to contract when the agent has no such

authority. Consequently, the principal is stopped from going back to the third party.[14]

- Usual authority: the agent has the authority that someone in the position of the agent usually has. If the principal does not disclose it, he is liable.[15]
- Ratification: it means that the principal, in a retrospective way, agrees to the contract that the agent has formed on his behalf, even if the agent did not have the authority to make the contract.[16]
- Necessity: under certain circumstances, and where it is necessary, the law imposes an agency arrange.

5. Remedies

As far as voidable contracts are concerned, examples of these are buying shares in a company, entering a partnership and buying or leasing property. All these contracts tend to be of a continuous or permanent nature. Furthermore, they are considered valid unless the minor repudiates them either during minority or within a reasonable time of attaining majority.

In *Edwards v Carter*,[17] the House of Lords held that the settlement was voidable, not void, for the husband. He was required to repudiate it within a reasonable time after coming of age, and he was presumed to know the contents of the deed regardless of his actual knowledge. Further, if he did not repudiate the settlement within a reasonable time, he was bound by its terms. In a nutshell, for the House of Lords the repudiation was too late.

A contract is enforceable against a minor until its repudiation by the minor. Accordingly, liability attaches to a minor for rent until the lease is forfeited.[18] In a similar way, a minor is liable for calls on shares until they are repudiated. In *Steinberg v Scala (Leeds) Ltd*,[19] a minor applied for shares in a company and paid the amounts due on application and at the first call. She received no dividends and attended no meetings. Eighteen months later, while she was still a minor, she repudiated the contract and asked for her money back. It was held that:

- She could repudiate the contract.
- The money paid was irrecoverable as the allotment of shares was a benefit as shares at one period had value.

14 *Spiro v Lintern* [1973] 3 AER 319.

15 *Watteau v Fenwick* [1893] 1 QB 346. An undisclosed principal can be held liable for the actions of an agent who is acting with an authority that is reasonable for a person in the agent's position regardless of whether the agent has the actual authority to do so.

16 Kelner v Baxter (1866) LR 2 CP 174.

17 [1893] AC 360. The husband's father, through a marriage settlement, agreed to pay an annuity to trustees for the benefit of his future daughter-in-law and any children or grandchildren from the marriage. The husband, who was minor at the time, agreed to vest any property inherited from his father in the trustees. A month after signing the settlement, the husband came of age, his father passed away four years later. Over a year after his father's death, the husband repudiated the settlement.

18 *See Blake v Concarmon* IR 4 CL 323 (1870).

19 [1923] 2 Ch 452.

Finally, Section 1(6), Law of Property Act 1925, prevents a minor from holding a legal estate in land.

If a contract with a minor is not non-binding or repudiated, there are some remedies to enforce a contract. In this respect, remedies are as follows:

- Recovery of money paid by minors: a minor cannot recover money paid or property transferred by the minor under a contract unless the minor can demonstrate that there was a total failure of consideration.
- Remedies against a minor are (1) liability in restitution and (2) restitutionary liability under the Minor's Contracts Act 1987.

As far as liability in restitution is concerned, a minor who is not obliged to execute a contract may still be liable to make restitution to an adult about any enrichment resulting from the adult's performance of the contract. To elaborate, it is possible to affirm that the general approach to the law is aimed to safeguard minors as the weakness part.[20]

Consequently, the law seeks to avoid the indirect imposition of liability on an immature contracting party, such as if a minor is ordered to repay a loan or to pay a reasonable price for non-necessary goods and services.[21]

Section 3(1), Minor's Contracts Act 1987, provides a statutory method of ordering children to make restitution where the contract is not enforceable. Thus, the court may order the minor to transfer to any other party:

- Any property acquired by the child under contract.
- Any property representing it.

Therefore, the minor is under an obligation to offer up any goods acquired in exchange for non-necessary goods if ordered to do so by the court. In other cases, the minor cannot be sued for the price.

6. Other cases of incapacity

As just mentioned at the beginning, an adult person can also lack capacity: it occurs in the case of mentally incapacitated persons and intoxication.

In the first case, mentally incapacitated persons, Section 2, Mental Capacity Act 2005 stipulates that a person lacks capacity if he/she is "unable to make a decision for himself in relation to the matter because of an impairment of, or a disturbance in the functioning of, the mind or brain" at the time in which the contract is made. This occurs if impairment is permanent or temporary.

20 See *R Leslie Ltd. v Sheill* [1914] 3 KB 607.

21 In *Lempriere v Lange* (1879) 12 Ch D 675 minor obtained a lease by falsely representing himself to be full age.

Impairment in respect of the inability consists of the inability to do the following:

- Understand the information relevant to the decision.
- Retain that information.
- Communicate his decision, whether by talking, using sign language or any other means.

The relevant information is relating to reasonably foreseeable consequences of deciding one way or another or failing to make a decision. A mentally incapacitated person is liable to pay a reasonable price for necessary goods and services.

Under common law, a contract signed by a person who, for these reasons, is not able to understand what he/she is doing is valid unless he/she can prove the following:

- He/she does not understand the nature of the contract.
- The other party is aware of his impairment.

In *Hart v Connor*[22] the court held that an agreement to sell land was affirmed even if the claimant was shown to be mentally incapacitated. The underlying reason was that mental incapacity was not apparent to the buyer.

The same *ratio* shall be applicable to intoxication made by alcohol or intoxicating substances. Consequently, a contract signed by a person who, by reason of intoxication, is incapable of understanding what he/she is doing is valid unless the individual demonstrates the following:

- He/she does not understand the nature of the contract.
- The other party was aware of his impairment.

Therefore, a contract is voidable if one party knew the level of intoxication of the other party. Moreover, the mentally incapacitated party is liable to pay a reasonable price for necessary goods and services.

For example, in *Matthews v Baxter*[23] the court held that the contract made by an intoxicated person was not void but merely voidable: in this case the drunken party, upon coming to his senses, ratified the contract. Therefore, he was bound by it.

7. New subjects of law: robot and non-human entities

7.1 An overview

In the contemporary era "new" kinds of rights seem to emerge on the horizon: animal rights as well as the right of synthetic beings. The latter seems to be shaped

22 [1985] 2 All ER 880.
23 (1873) LR8 Exch 132.

according to the concept of electronic person. This notion shall be suitable to refer to robotic entity to recognise him/her the legal personality[24]: this notion, electronic personhood,[25] is opposite of human personality. The need to assign a personality and establish liability for robots is necessary in establishing who would be liable for ensuring damage.[26]

Not only does the recognition of robots' rights arise from the recognition of animals' rights, but also, it is the expression "future generation".

This notion has been developed in international law debate as linked with the climate change issue. The latter, indeed, represents the key to open the door to the debate about the importance of future generation rights. Future generation is the human of tomorrow, which populates the world in the next years, the contemporary "young". Therefore, the dilemma is: "who is the human of the future world?" Is this person again a human being or a robotic entity? The assumption was, and is, that future generation is represented by the young which are entitled to reclaim a better world, without emergency and uncertainty, where they will live.[27]

Bearing this in mind, it is not totally futuristic a world where the workplace becomes as a space where human and synthetic beings work together in Industry 5.0. The fundamental idea is that AI could also be a person, or better, a digital person.[28] A concrete example is shown by SmokeBot[29]: this is a robot created to perform dangerous tasks in an emergency, such as a house fire or indoor gas leak. It is controlled remotely by rescue workers. It can assist the fire service department in its rescue operations. In other words, the crew is both human and robotic.

7.2 The British Company law perspective

It is worthy to mention that, under English common law, the debate about differences between human person[30] and artificial one is not unknown, nor is it merely

24 For example, in 2017 Saudi Arabia granted "citizenship" to a humanoid robot, named Sophia. She is a chatbot with a face. Further, in Tokyo, an online system with the persona of a 7-year-old boy was granted "residency" in Tokyo. From a regulatory perspective, a resolution of European Parliament achieved the objective to take into the consideration the possibility to shape an ad hoc legal status for robots (European Parliament Resolution with Recommendations to the Commission on Civil Law Rules on Robotics (2015/2103(INL)) (European Parliament, February 16, 2017) para 59(f)). See (Chesterman 2020).

25 It was stressed that if a synthetic entity would confer legal personality this has some benefits: "(a) registration/incorporation of the robot, (b) a head of responsibility, with specific rules and an entity to be considered in terms of liability and insurance, and (c) the ability to enter into contracts with each other and with humans with specific responsibilities arising out of the breach of such contracts". (Lucchetti 2017).

26 (Janal 2020).

27 From a recent perspective, see (Roger, Fernández-Planells, and Pérez-Altable 2024).

28 European Parliament resolution of February 16, 2017 with recommendations to the Commission on Civil Law Rules on Robotics (2015/2103(INL)).

29 (Fan, Hernandez Bennetts, and Schaffer 2019).

30 The word "person" in legal jargon may be defined as generic term. To elaborate, a human being, albeit always a person in a real and ordinary world, may or may not be qualified as "person" in contemplation of law. Similarly, a corporation, albeit always both artificial and fictitious entity, may be or not to be a legal person. (Griffin 1950).

contemporaneous. To elaborate, reference shall be made to scholars who have extensively opined on the concept of legal personality of a firm or, better, have referred to contractual activity that a company shall carry out.

In this scenario, there are, at least, two main golden rules. The first one is the authority to sign a contract with third parties. The latter has power to sell and to buy assets in name of company as well as to sign contracts. In this respect, the concept of "delegated managers" shall be recalled: the latter have the power to bind a company in a contract, as members of the board of directors. A rule linked to this is the *ultra vires* doctrine.

A second principle alludes to a procedural mechanism whereby both a firm and its counterparties shall observe in cases where proceedings were issued again.

To summarise, thanks to the "entity shielding doctrine", there is a common expectation, among creditors and other counterparties, relating to the effects that an enforceable contract binds these parties and guarantee creditors' rights.

Bearing in mind these "rules", separate legal personality means that an entity complies with these rules, therefore, separate legal personality is a way to summarise this kind of compliance.

It is worth emphasising that a company is a person, therefore the logical/legal consequence is its capacity to enter contracts, owning its own property, delegating authority to agents, suing and being sued in its own name.[31] In order to understand the concept of separate legal personality, it becomes mandatory to recall *Salomon v Salomon*.[32] The latter constitutes the British landmark case in this macro-area of law.[33] In this *decisum*, the House of Lords affirmed the principle in force of

31 (Armour, Hansmann, and Kraakman 2009).

32 [1897] AC 22. Mr Salomon transferred his business of boot making. In the beginning, it was run as a sole ownership but, at a further stage, this business became a company, the Salomon Ltd. The members were Mr Salomon and members of his family, particularly his children. The price to Mr Salomon for the transfer to the newly established company to, was paid by shares and debentures having a floating charge on the assets of a company. After a while, Salomon Ltd started struggling, and the business went into liquidation: therefore, Salomon's right of recovery stood before the claims of unsecured creditors. This happened because Salomon's rights were secured through floating charge. The liquidator, on the part of unsecured creditors, argued that this company was, *de facto*, an agent of Salomon; because of this, Mr Salomon was the principal and personally liable for its debt. The theory behind this approach was a separation between the personality of Salomon Ltd from its member, Mr Salomon, as the other members of the family, although it is Mr Salomon who is the nearly absolute owner of the shares. The latter should be personally liable for company's debt only if he continued the business individually. As far as the ruling is concerned, it shall be divided between the Court Appeal position from the House of Lords. The first one, Court of Appeal, stressed that Mr Salomon should be responsible for the debt, because he is an agent of Salomon Ltd: the company was created in contrast with the true and real intent of Companies Act 1862. By contrast, the House of Lords held that because of incorporation, the company was an independent person with its rights and liabilities. There is a legal fiction relating to "corporate veil" between the company and its owner/controllers that, in this case, was Mr Salomon.

33 *Salomon v Salomon & Co* [1897] AC 22.

which a company is generally considered to be a new legal entity, separate from its shareholders.[34]

Moreover, a company is perceived both a "human product" and artificial product; at the same time, a company is perceived as an "alien" for the natural law. Thus, the company as an artificial person is created and shaped by human minds to achieve a goal. To elucidate, the company represents a means of achieving some objectives and has a specific purpose or, better, purposes.[35]

From a metaphorical perspective, a company is a "human structure", populated by humans and where the latter channel their ambitions, activities and aspirations. It is obvious that company is not *per se* either a good thing or bad one; it simply epitomises a connection, a tie, between an end achieved by humans, with the latter controlling the company.

Although companies are artificial (or not-being persons), they live in the economic and juristic legal world. Evidence of this is that companies are entitled to have a "name" as human persons. More precisely, a company shall have both a name and a logo that is an image that, *mutatis mutandis*, is the body of a person.

Thanks to the logo everyone can create an image in its own mind relating to the major activities to be carried on by a company. With a logo, everyone will associate it with the company's name; ultimately, this shows the degree of success of a company to live in people's minds.

The metaphor shall be the following one: as God created humans, humans have the power to create artificial person, the company. In this respect, it is critical to emphasise the difference between humans and non-human persons.[36] The latter, which encapsulates also company, shall be a means, a device, a way to achieve objectives decided by humans, the operators of the company. Nevertheless, it is also possible to affirm that human person and artificial person share some characteristics, such as name; "shell", that for the company is logo and, by contrast, for the human being body; vitality – hence both artificial person and human person are "living".

34 Although *Salomon v Salomon* represents the leading case, the modern approach is encompassed in *Adams v Cape Industries* [1991] 1 All E.R. 929. In the latter, the Court of Appeal refused to lift the corporate veil. See (Moore 2006).

35 From a comparative perspective, Section 19(5) of the Singaporean piece of statute addressed to companies qualifies and recognises the incorporated company as a "body corporate". By contrast, from an America common law perspective, "The plain and evident meaning of the section is, that persons to whom the equal protection of the law is secured are persons born or naturalized or endowed with life and liberty, and consequently natural and not artificial. This construction of the section is strengthened by the history of the submission by congress, and the adoption by the states of the 14th amendment, so fresh in all minds as to need no rehearsal". *Insurance Co. v New Orleans* (C.C.La. 1971) 13 F. Cas. 67, 68. Toward the same direction, the Supreme Court held that corporations were not "citizens" within other provisions of the Constitution, see *Bank of U.S. v Deveaux*, 9 U.S. 61 (1809).

36 For example, the Non-human Rights Project (NhRP) represents the opportunity and possibility to extend and, consequently, grant human rights to non-human persons. In a nutshell, based on such project, certain non-human beings should enjoy some rights, freedom and protections. Traditionally, the latter are ensured only to humans under the law. See (Thurzo 2021).

7.3 The doctrine of personality

Upon the described scenario, it is necessary to approach the underlying theories of corporate personhood. In this respect, the relevant theories are three: (1) artificial and dependent person theory; (2) an aggregate person theory; (3) a real and independent theory.

The first one – artificial and dependent person theory – stresses that a physical existence of a corporation there due to an abstract idea constructed by law. Consequently, a corporation is just a legal construct, an artificial creation of law and humans. Thus, personhood is a legal fiction conferred by law solely for the facilitation of trade and commerce.[37] In addition, the name of a corporation is basically an abbreviation used in law and commerce to confer specific rights on, and perform duties by, individuals contractually or otherwise related to or affected by entity.[38]

The second theory – aggregate person theory – does not recognise a corporation as a separate and distinct person. According to this theory, a corporation is not an artificial entity nor merely a creation of law; rather it is an organisation or association of a group of people. Without the "human" side corporation does not have any identity of its own or any ability to function toward its goals. In a similar way, a corporation is virtually a manifestation of natural persons because it is created, owned, managed and administered by those who thus become the ultimate actors of the body corporate. For example, in *Santa Clara County v Southern Pacific Railroad Company*[39] the court held that company's properties are those of the individuals behind it. In essence, the emphasis is on the fact that rights and duties of a corporation are factually those of corporators rather than those of an imaginary person. Moreover, a corporation is not fiction but does not exist as an aggregate of individual, not as a separate person independent of its corporators.

The latter – real and independent person theory – argues that corporate personality is both real and natural, as opposed to fictitious. A body corporate or a corporate organism has been created by a group of human beings. A body corporate or a corporate organism is founded, per se, which is recognised by law to facilitate trade and commerce. The existence of a corporation is an objective fact, and entities have a real presence in society: corporate life comes into existence independently of law, and States only officially recognise the pre-existing fact.[40]

7.4 Artificial person: from company to robot

It is also important to note that, because of IT development, the concept of "artificial person" should not be confined only to companies, nor persons. The reference goes to human robots if we accept that they are human "constructure" and not

37 (Ripken 2010).
38 (Wolff 1938).
39 (1886) 118 U S 394.
40 (Solaiman 2017).

living in the natural world.[41] Furthermore, the idea that the company is an entity that lives like it's human is also reminiscent of the concept of human remote operator that is a hot topic in the era of unmanned vehicles and that comes from the area of maritime law.

In other words, if a synthetic being is under an "incorporation process" – in a similar way to which an entity is incorporated under company law – this means that (1) the synthetic being possesses a "registration number";[42] (2) the natural person is the owner, or has the ownership, of this robot.[43]

The dichotomy is, therefore, human being, on one hand, and synthetic beings, on the other hand. The latter are better known as "robots". To elaborate, it was stressed that to understand if a robot[44] is entitled to claim the existence of its right,[45] a way out is to observe how the legal system treats animals.[46] A different approach is to read the controversial issue under a historical perspective. In this case, the underlying allusion is to slavery: for instance, the ancient Roman law did not recognise legal personality to slave. The latter was considered as mere agent for his master.[47]

To summarise something about personality concept, it is critical to highlight that legal personhood is not necessarily synonymous with or confined to human beings.[48] To elaborate, the term "personality" when it comes to legal concepts, conferring this status, personality indeed, on an entity depends upon a given jurisdiction having an independent legal system. This is the reason why there is no uniformity across legal systems in recognising an entity as a legal person.[49] Moreover, the recognition of legal personality is a means of mutually respecting persons' rights and enforcing legal control against any breaches. It signifies mutual duties, mutual rights vital in establishing a legal relation between two persons.

The idea of personhood arose in canon law and continues to dominate the administration of justice to date. Later, it was read in recognition of chimpanzees'

41 The differences between corporation and robot are emphasised. More in detail, it was affirmed that the "crucial difference between a corporation and a robot is that corporations always act through humans", and the latter, the human being, makes the final decision (Eidenmueller 2017).
42 *Mutatis mutandis*, the registration number may be the national insurance number for the robot.
43 (Chester Cheong 2021).
44 (Fosch-Villaronga 2019).
45 It is important to clarify one point. From a merely legal theory perspective, the question about the rights of the robot requires a further question: do robots want such rights? If the answer is affirmative, the consequent problem is linked with the recognition of these rights.
46 (Kurki and Pietrzykowski 2017).
47 (Katz 2008; Ashrafian 2015).
48 See *Byrn v New York City Health & Hosp Corp* 1972: "the Constitution does not confer or require legal personality . . .; the Legislature may, or it may do something less . . . and provide some protection far short of conferring legal personality" (at 203).
49 (Gray 1909).

rights.[50] According to this line of reasoning, the requirements or attributes of legal personhood are as follows:

- A person shall be capable of being subject to law.
- Being a legal subject entails the ability to exercise rights and perform duties.
- To be able to exercise awareness and choice.

Moving forward a robot as a possessor of artificial intelligence has five characteristics: (1) the ability to communicate with others; (2) internal knowledge; (3) external or outside world knowledge; (4) some degree of intentionality; (5) some degree of creativity. Yet they are recognised as "quasi-persons".[51] This means that robots enjoy only some rights, or partial rights and duties.

Others[52] discuss about the "borderline status" regarding robots because the underlying process that produce robots' behaviour is relatively like the process of a human mind.

7.5 From robot to other non-human entities

Not only does the question about legal personality refer to "robot", but also to other legal entities, different from humans, animals, environment, etc. A practical example is the "idol": a statute created and worshipped by humans as a god or goddess most popular in Hindu religion. Idol, according to Hindu religion, has been held to have peculiar desires and a will of its own which shall be respected.[53] Furthermore, idols have been judicially recognised in some jurisdiction as a legal person founded upon religious customs.

To elucidate, Hindu idols:[54]

- Are like a legal entity to which such dedication might be made.
- Might be borrowed from human beings who are lawfully entitled to manage them with all the powers as with a guardian or manager of an infant and his/her assets.
- Are legal persons as good as human beings and body corporates.

50 Matter of Nonhuman Rights Project, Inc v Stanley [2015] NY Slip Op 31419(U) 1156 Stanley (2015).

51 (Asaro 2007).

52 (Solum 1992).

53 See *Pramatha Nath Mullick v Pradyumna Kumar Mullick* (1925) 27 BOMLR 1064. It was said as follows: "A Hindu idol is, according to long established authority, founded upon the religious customs of the Hindus, and the recognition thereof by courts of law, a 'juristic entity'. It has a juridical status with the power of suing and being sued. Its interests are attended to by the person who has the deity in his charge and who is in law its manager with all the powers which would, in such circumstances, on analogy, be given to the manager of the estate of an infant heir, It is unnecessary to quote the authorities; for this doctrine, thus simply stated, is firmly established".

54 (Duff 1927).

- Have capacity which does refer to that of managers of respective idol: the idol guardian or manager has the duty to pronounce the will of idol.

Another example is based on the "Earth-centred law"[55] promoting nature's integrity, intrinsic values and ecological limitations in legal formulation, interpretation and application. Nature is viewed as a subject of rights deserving protection. Consequently, the need to grant legal personhood to natural entities (e.g., rivers, forests, ecosystem).[56] One of the main problems is that environmental law, from a traditional perspective, is based on the nature/human dichotomy. However, in 1972 in *Sierra Club v Morton*,[57] Justice Dougles said that

> is the living symbol of all the life it sustains or nourishes – fish, aquatic insects, water ouzels, otter, fisher, deer, elk, bear, and all other animals, including man, who are dependent on it or who enjoy it for its sight, its sound, or its life. The river as plaintiff speaks for the ecological unit of life that is part of it.

A similar approach has been developed in 2017 and, more precisely, in *Mohd. Salim v State of Uttarakhand & others*:[58] Rivers Ganga and Yamyna are read as "breathing, living". Additionally, the Colombian Constitutional Court recognises Río Atrato as a subject of rights.[59] Consequently, environmental law is going to recognise a growing number of these rivers as legal persons and/or living entities.[60]

References

Armour, John, Henry Hansmann, and Reinier Kraakman. 2009. "The Essential Elements of Corporate Law: What Is Corporate Law?" Harvard Law School Working Paper 134. http://ssrn.com/abstract=1436551.

Asaro, Peter M. 2007. "Robots and Responsibility from a Legal Perspective." *Proceedings of the IEEE* 14 (4): 20–24.

Ashrafian, Hutan. 2015. "Artificial Intelligence and Robot Responsibilities: Innovating Beyond Rights." *Science and Engineering Ethics* 21: 317–26.

Chester Cheong, Ben. 2021. "Granting Legal Personhood to Artificial Intelligence Systems and Traditional Veil-Piercing Concepts to Impose Liability." *SN Social Sciences* 9 (1): 231–49.

Chesterman, Simon. 2020. "Artificial Intelligence and the Limits of Legal Personality." *International & Comparative Law Quarterly* 69 (4): 819–44.

55 Henceforth ECL.

56 (Lopez Porras 2024).

57 *Sierra Club v Morton*, 405 U.S. 727, 743 (1972).

58 *Mohd. Salim v State of Uttarakhand & others WPPIL* 126/2014 (High Court of Uttarakhand) 2017 (India).

59 Centro de Estudios para la Justicia Social 'Tierra Digna' and Others v the President of the Republic and Others [2016] Corte Constitucionál Sala Sexta de Revision (Colombia) No. T-622 of 2016 (November 10, 2016).

60 (O'Donnell 2020).

Duff, Patrick W. 1927. "The Personality of an Idol." *The Cambridge Law Journal* 3 (1): 42–48.

Eidenmueller, Horst. 2017. "The Rise of Robots and the Law of Humans." *Oxford Legal Studies Research Paper* 27. https://ssrn.com/abstract=2941001.

Fan, Han, Victor Hernandez Bennetts, and Erik Schaffer. 2019. "Towards Gas Discrimination and Mapping in Emergency Response Scenarios Using a Mobile Robot with an Electronic Nose." *Sensors* 19 (3): 658–713.

Fimmanò, Francesco, Pierre de Gioia Carabellese, and Camilla Della Giustina. 2024. *Company Law in the UK and EU: ESG and Digitalisation.* Universitas Mercatorum Press.

Fosch-Villaronga, Eduard. 2019. *Robots, Healthcare, and the Law: Regulating Automation in Personal Care.* Routledge.

Gray, John Chiman. 1909. *The Nature and Sources of the Law.* York: Columbia University Press.

Griffin, Robert P. 1950. "Constitutional Law-Corporations-Artificial 'Persons' and the Fourteenth Amendment." *Michigan Law Review* 48 (7): 983–93.

Janal, Ruth. 2020. "Extra-Contractual Liability for Wrongs Committed by Autonomous Systems." In *Algorithms and Law*, edited by Martin Ebers and Susanna Navas, 174–206. Cambridge University Press.

Katz, Andrew. 2008. "Intelligent Agents and Internet Commerce in Ancient Rome." *Society for Computers and Law* 20: 35–38.

Kurki, Visa A.J., and Tomasz Pietrzykowski. 2017. *Legal Personhood: Animals, Artificial Intelligence and the Unborn.* Springer.

Lopez Porras, Gabriel. 2024. "Earth-Centred Law: Challenges and Necessity." *Environmental Law Review* 26 (3): 181–84.

Lucchetti, Stefania. 2017. "Why Artificial Intelligence Will Need a Legal Personality." *LawCrossBorder* (online). https://lawcrossborder.com/2017/05/22/why-robots-need-a-legal-personality/.

Moore, Marc. 2006. "'A Temple Built on Faulty Foundation': Piercing the Corporate Veil and the Legacy of Salomon v Salomon." *Journal of Business Law* 180–203.

O'Donnell, Erin. 2020. "Rivers as Living Beings: Rights in Law, but No Rights to Water?" *Griffith Law Review* 29 (4): 643–68.

Ripken, Susanna K. 2010. "Corporations Are People too: A Multi-Dimensional Approach to the Corporate Personhood Puzzle." *Fordham Journal of Corporate & Financial Law* 15: 97 117.

Roger, Soler-i-Martí, Ariadna Fernández-Planells, and Laura Pérez-Altable. 2024. "Bringing the Future into the Present: The Notion of Emergency in the Youth Climate Movement." *Social Movement Studies* 23 (4): 517–36.

Solaiman, Sheikh M. 2017. "Legal Personality of Robots, Corporations, Idols and Chimpanzees: A Quest for Legitimacy." *Artificial Intelligence and Law* 25: 155–79.

Solum, Lawrence B. 1992. "Legal Personhood for Artificial Intelligence." *North Carolina Law* 70 (4): 1231–87.

Thurzo, Vladimír. 2021. "The Influence of Existentialism and Subjectivism on the Concept of Human Person." In *Spiritual and Social Experience in the Context of Modernism and Postmodernism (Interdisciplinary Reading of the Phenomenon)*, edited by Patrik Maturkanič and Čergeťová Tomanová, 7–34. Verba Theologica.

Wolff, Martin. 1938. "On the Nature of Legal Persons." *Law Quarterly Review* 54 (4): 494–1128.

8 Misrepresentation

Chapter Overview

1. Introduction

An agreement constitutes a universal phenomenon among the humans. More precisely, an agreement represents the result of a business negotiation. To be valid, parties are expected to be *ad idem* while agreeing on the terms of the contract; in the opposite scenario, the contract shall be void. Further, it is quintessential that contract fits into all its main elements: to elaborate, offer, acceptance, consideration, intention to enter legal relations and capacity.[1]

In this respect, consent may be rendered without mistake, misrepresentation, duress and undue influence.[2] Therefore, vitiating elements of a contract may be introduced from the outset: a valid contract requires that parties have agreed to the terms freely, without some form of compulsion or some other defect which may make the apparently valid contract defective. By opposite, if there is an element which may spoil or make such contract defective, this element is called vitiating factor.

1 (Klass 2025).
2 (Atiyah and Treitel 1967).

DOI: 10.4324/9781003645948-8

Vitiating factor of a contract is the technical term to define things which make a contract void or voidable. In other words, vitiating elements are factors able to invalidate a contract. In this respect, vitiating elements of a contract are as follows:

- Mistake.
- Misrepresentation.
- Duress.
- Undue influence.
- Incapacity and illegality.

As far as illegality is concerned, the legal pillars of contract law prescribe that the court will not enforce a contract which is illegal or contrary to public policy. Illegal contracts are contracts prohibited either by statute or common law. In most cases, the illegality affecting the contract sparks off some sanctions. In other cases, the only consequences are represented by a declaration to ascertain the fact that the contract is void and unenforceable.

Illegal contracts constitute a category which encompass the following:

- To commit a crime, a tort or a fraud on a third party.
- That are sexually immoral.
- Which are prejudicial to public safety.
- Liable to corrupt public life.
- To defraud public revenue.

When a contract is adjudicated illegal, it will not be enforced, and such contract will be absolutely void.

2. Misrepresentation: an overview

Misrepresentation may be defined as a false statement of fact made by one party to the other which induces that other party to enter the contract. It is critical to highlight that misrepresentation occupies a border line in the contractual agreement: actually, misrepresentation represents something that induced the contract. As a result of this, misrepresentation falls more naturally in tort law, rather than contract law.[3]

Consequently, it becomes quintessential to distinguish between:

- Fraudulent misrepresentation: when a person makes a false statement which he knows is not true and has no belief in its truth, or which he makes recklessly, not carrying what is true or not.[4]

3 (Farnsworth 1969).

4 *Derry v Peck* [1889] 14 AC 337. The defendant had issued a prospectus containing untrue statement and the plaintiff applied for 50 shares and was allowed the same. Subsequently, he sued the defendant

- Negligent misrepresentation: when a person makes a false statement which he may honestly believe to be true but without reasonable ground for believing it to be true.

Although misrepresentation shares most elements within the area of tort law,[5] its effects are more important also in contract law because misrepresentation induces the contracts even if the party is not part of it.

The consequence of this is that contract law provides that a contract signed because of misrepresentation is voidable for misrepresentation. However, misrepresentation goes beyond the border of contract law: therefore, the remedies are damages and rescission.

Finally, misrepresentation shall be analysed also under a historical perspective: the turning point is represented by 1960s year and, more in detail, by the case "Hedley Byrne".[6] In this case, the House of Lords held that a negligent misstatement may give rise to an action for damages for economic loss. When a party seeking information or advice from another party, who possesses special skills, and trust him to exercise due care, a duty of care will be implied. Therefore, a damage for pure economic loss could arise in situation where these conditions are met:

- The existence of a fiduciary relationship of trusts and confidence between the parties.
- The party preparing the advice/information has voluntarily assumed the risk.
- One party has reliance of the advice/information by the other party.
- This reliance is reasonable in the specific circumstances.

In a nutshell, the court stated that a duty of care would arise when negligent advice was given which resulted in economic loss. There are three requirements for this:

- Reasonable reliance.
- Assumption of responsibility.
- Special relationship of trust and confidence between parties.

---

in damages for fraudulent misrepresentation. It was held that the defendant was liable as they were aware of the falsity of the statements. More in depth, the House of Lords stressed that the statement was untrue, but the directors were not liable for deceit as they honestly believed that the statement was true.

5 (Mitchell 2020).

6 *Hedley Byrne & Co Ltd v Heller & Partners Ltd* (1964) AC 465 (HL). Byrne were advertising that agents were placing contracts on behalf of a client on credit terms; he would be personally liable if a client would default. To protect themselves, Byrne asked its bank to obtain a credit reference from Heller & Partners. The references, given both orally and in writing, were given in gratis, free and were favourable. These references encompassed an exclusion clause to the effect that information was given, that is, "without responsibility on the part of this Bank or its officials". Byrne suffered financial loss when client went into liquidation.

This is named "Hedley Byrne test" that was redefined in *Caparo Industries Plc v Dickman.*[7] In this case a firm of accountants appealed before the House of Lords against a decision of the Court of Appeal in which it was decided that the accountants owed a duty of care to appellant shareholder when producing an audit report required by statute. The claim was for negligent misstatement. Caparo had bought shares in the company of which the report was about as a part of takeover. The appellant had relied upon the results of the report. Later, it was found that the results of the report had misrepresented the profits of the firm; it caused a loss for Caparo.

The House of Lords stated that there was not a duty of care in relation to existing or potential shareholders. The only duty of care the auditors owed was to the governance of a firm. As a result of this, three factors shall exist for duty of care:

- Proximity.
- Knowledge.
- Fair, just and reasonableness.

Until the 1960s there were two main categories of misrepresentation:

- Fraudulent misrepresentation.
- Innocent misrepresentation.

After 1964, misrepresentation encompasses the following:

- Fraudulent misrepresentation.
- Innocent misrepresentation.
- Negligent misrepresentation.

3. Misrepresentation: a definition

Misrepresentation[8] is a statement of fact which induces the other party to sign the contract and operate in the borderlands of contract and tort, allowing contract to be rescinded and, if there has been fault, giving rise to damages under tort and statute.

Basic pillars are as follows:

- False statement: normally, non-disclosure does not amount as misrepresentation. The exceptions are contracts in *uberrima fidei* (insurance contract) or where a party is under a duty to inform the other party to a change in circumstances or where a statement is misleading in light of the information withheld.
- A statement of fact, not a mere opinion.

7 [1990] UKHL 2.
8 (Handley 2015).

- Inducement of an innocent part to enter the contract and misrepresentation need to be the sole clause of the other party to enter the contract, but it shall be a cause.

It is crucial to stress that silence, generally, is not regarded as a misrepresentation of fact. In this respect, the leading case is *Fletcher v Krell*,[9] which encompasses the rule in force of which, normally, misrepresentation arises because of an express statement. Therefore, the failure to disclose a material fact does not amount to misrepresentation. In this case, an applicant for a job as governess failed to disclose the fact that she had previously been married and remained silent on the point. It was held that there was no misrepresentation; the situation was not under the exceptions of the main rule. These exceptions are as follows:

- Change of circumstances.
- The statement is only a half-truth.
- Confidential/fiduciary relationship.

4. Typologies of misrepresentation

Misrepresentation shall be fraudulent, negligent or innocent.

The first one, fraudulent misrepresentation, is known, also, as the tort of deceit. It is possible to affirm that fraudulent misrepresentation occurs when a party makes a false statement and, at the time, does not believe it to be true.

The leading case is the just discussed *Derry v Peck*: in this Lord Herschell defined fraudulent misrepresentation as a statement which is made:

- Knowing it to be false.
- Without belief in its truth.
- Recklessly, careless as to whether it be true or false.

Another case is *Sear v Kingfisher Builders*,[10] which is quintessential in order to ascertain the quantum of claims. In June 2008, Mr Sear and Kingfisher Builders entered a contract for the renovation and extension of Mr Sear's house. By December 2008, Kingfisher said that the other party, Mr Sear, had underpaid. The first one, Kingfisher, left the site prior to completing the works and started a claim for outstanding sums due. The court:

- Dismissed Kingfisher's claim.
- Found that Ms Whale, the partner of Kingfisher, had made a fraudulent misrepresentation to Mr Sear. Consequently, Mr Sear made two claims: one for overpayment and one against Ms Whale for damages of fraudulent misrepresentation.

9 (1872) 42 LJQB 55.
10 (No. 3) [2013] EWHC 21 (TCC).

- Mr Sear was entitled to damages as would put him back into the financial position before the contract was made.

The underlying rationale was that, if Ms Whale did not commit the fraudulent misrepresentation, Mr Sear would not have entered the contract with Kingfisher.

Finally, it is important to emphasise that damages in fraud are unlimited; by contrast damages for breach of a contract are limited.

Negligent misrepresentation is aimed to extend the common law tort of negligence to cover negligent misstatement that are in loss. In this respect, it is worth mentioning *Hedley Byrne & Co Ltd v Heller & Partners Ltd.* In this case, the House of Lords established that in limited circumstances, if a duty of care arose in the making of statements, pure economic loss in tort could be recoverable in English law. To elaborate, a negligent misstatement may give rise to an action for damages for economic loss: when a party seeking information or advice from another possessing special skills, and trusts him to exercise due care. Furthermore, when that party knew or ought to have known that the claimant was relying on his skills and judgement, a duty of care will be implied.

A specific misrepresentation is the statutory misrepresentation. Pursuant to the Misrepresentation Act 1977, the "fiction of fraud" has been shaped. The legal source is Section 2(1), Misrepresentation Act 1977:

> Where a person has entered into a contract after a misrepresentation has been made to him by another party thereto and as a result thereof he has suffered loss, then, if the person making the misrepresentation would be liable to damages in respect thereof had the misrepresentation been made fraudulently, that person shall be so liable notwithstanding that the misrepresentation was not made fraudulently, unless he proves that he had reasonable ground to believe and did believe up to the time the contract was made the facts represented were true.

Fiction of fraud means that, if a claimant can prove that there was a misrepresentation, bringing a claim under the act, the burden of proof is shifted to the representor to show that they had reasonable grounds to believe and did believe that the statement was true.

The leading case is *Howard Marine and Dredging Co Ltd v A Odgen and Sons (Excavations) Ltd.*[11] It was explained the test of "reasonable grounds for belief" under the Misrepresentation Act 1967, particularly Section 2(1). This section stipulates that where a person enters a contract after a misrepresentation was by another party and he suffers loss, the person making the misrepresentation will be liable even if the misrepresentation was not made fraudulently. The exception is where the person making misrepresentation proves that he had reasonable ground to believe and did believe up to the time the contract was made that the facts represented were

11 [1978] QB 574.

true. To summarise, the court held that where a representor had made a statement on the honest but mistaken belief that it was true, based on the term "accident", this was a misrepresentation not made fraudulently but negligently. The fictions consist in the fact that the remedy provided is the same as if the statement was made fraudulently.

Innocent misrepresentation occurs when the element of misrepresentation can be proved but the misrepresentor genuinely believed it was true and did not act negligently. It is crucial to highlight that, before 1964, an innocent misrepresentation that referred to any non-fraudulent misrepresentation was not relevant, because there was no liability to pay damages in respect of anything other than a fraudulent misrepresentation. However, more recently, liability for negligent misrepresentation existing under both common law (*Hedley Byrne & Co Ltd v Heller & Partners Ltd*) and statute (Misrepresentation Act Section 2(1) may engender liability. Thus, "wholly innocent" misrepresentation is used to describe both a non-fraudulent and a non-negligent misrepresentation.

A niche nuance of misrepresentation is pre-contractual misrepresentation linked with the topic of supervening falsification, discussed in *With v O'Flanagan.*[12] Supervening falsification involves a change in the facts between representation and reliance; thus the importance to distinguish this situation from a different scenario in which the representor learns of falsifying facts that are innocently unknown to him at the time when the representation was initially made. In this respect, a pre-contractual misrepresentation occurs when a representation, though perfectly true when made, and unknown to representee throughout, has become substantially false by the time it induces the representee to enter into the contract in question. Pre-contractual misrepresentation and supervening representation are linked by each other because the latter arises whenever there is an appreciable interval of time between the moment when a representation is made and the time when the party to whom it was made, reasonably, altered his position on the faith of it.[13]

Furthermore, the notion of continuing misrepresentation shall be introduced. In *Smith v Kay*,[14] Lord Cranworth stated as follows:

> It is a continuing representation. The representation does not end for ever when the representation is once made; it continues. The pleader who drew the bill, or the young man himself, in stating his case, would say, Before I execute the bond I had been led to believe, and I therefore continued to believe, that it was executed pursuant to the arrangement.

In a more recent decision (*Cramaso LLP v Ogilvie-Grant*),[15] the UK Supreme Court held that a negligent misrepresentation is capable of having a continuing

12 [1936] 1 Ch. 575.
13 (Bigwood 2005).
14 (1859) 7 H.L.C. 750; 11 E.R. 299.
15 [2014] UKSC 9.

effect until the time when the contract is concluded. This applies if the person to whom the misrepresentation is addressed becomes the agent of the person by whom the contract is concluded. In a nutshell, this means that a contract entity would be entitled to sue for rescission and damages even though the negligent misrepresentation was not actually made to it.

5. Remedies

Remedies for misrepresentation are rescission of the contract and damages: the first one is available for all types of misrepresentation; damages are available for fraudulent or negligent misrepresentation under the tort of deceit and Section 2(1) Misrepresentation Act.

As far as the rescission is concerned, it constitutes the principal common law remedy: it is available whether the representation was innocent, negligent or fraudulent. In this scenario, rescission means that the contract is set aside, and the parties are put into the position they would have been in, had the contract never been made. Any goods or money which have been exchanged must be returned. The equitable remedy of rescission must be sought by the claimant, because it does not occur automatically. The consequences of this are as follows:

- Until rescission, the contract will continue to exist.
- Misrepresentation renders a contract voidable rather than void.
- The right of rescission will be exercised by giving notice to the other party; however, there is one authority which holds that rescission can be effected, by giving notice to the relevant third parties.[16]

In some circumstances the right to rescind the contract will be lost; these are called "bars" to rescission and are the following:

- Where a party to the contract, aware of the other party's misrepresentation, continues with the contract: in this case, the representee must be aware of both the circumstance that gives rise to the right to rescind and to the fact that right has arisen.
- Where there is a significant lapse of time between the making of the contract and the discovery of the misrepresentation, for instance a gap of five years.
- If the restitution is impossible.
- If the rescission would affect the rights of a third party, for example where goods have been sold to the "misrepresentor" who has sold them on to an innocent third party before the contract has been avoid.

16 *Car & Universal Finance Co v Caldwell* [1965] 1 QB 525: the seller of a car wished to rescind a contract when the purchaser's cheque bounced. It was held that notifying the police and the Automobile Association was sufficient.

Right for damages was later recognised for non-fraudulent misrepresentation. At the beginning, there was merely a recognition of only an indemnity for necessary expenditures incurred, as a party to the contract rescinded, and this happened by way of monetary compensation. By contrast, if misrepresentation was fraudulent, damages were recoverable under the tortious action for deceit. Once it was established that the statement was fraudulent, all losses which were directly attributable to the deceit are recoverable. Thus, the normal rule of "remoteness" does not apply.

As far as negligent misrepresentation is concerned, more recently, we need to refer to Section 2(1), Misrepresentation Act 1967. In this respect, the crucial pillars are as follows:

- The burden of proof: claimant is under a duty to prove that a misrepresentation was made and that it induced the contract. By contrast, the defendant will be liable for damages unless he/she can prove that there were reasonable grounds for his/her belief that the statement was true.
- The measures of damages: in *Royscot Trust Ltd v Rogerson*,[17] the Court of Appeal held that damages under Section 2(1) should be calculated as the same way as if the statement had been made fraudulently. The consequence is that all losses are recoverable.

6. The exclusion of liability for misrepresentation

The exclusion of liability for misrepresentation in contracts between a trade and consumer will be subject to a test of fairness rule, shaped by Section 2 and Schedule 4, Consumer Right Act 2005. The other cases dealt with Section 3, Misrepresentation Act 1967: it states that any clause which attempts to limit liability for misrepresentation shall satisfy the requirement of reasonableness.

Nevertheless, the right of a party to exclude damages caused by an innocent or negligent misrepresentation did not extend to a fraudulent misrepresentation. If a fraudulent misrepresentation occurs, the party deceived retained the right to rescind the contract and sue for damages.[18]

Another issue is the case in which an entire agreement clause encapsulates a statement in force of which one party places no reliance on representation of the other can prevent liability for misrepresentation. Although such clause could be effective to restrict liability for statements made by an agent of the party concerned, the line adopted by the court is that such clause does not fall within the scope of Section 3.[19]

17 [1991] 2 QB 297.

18 See *HIH Casualty & General Insurance Ltd v Chase Manhattan Bank* [2003] 1 CLC 358.

19 See *Cremdean Properties v Nash* [1977] 1 EGLR 58; *Inntrepreneur Estates (CPC) Ltd v Worth* [1996] 1 ELGR 84; *Thomas Witter Ltd v TBP Industries Ltd* [1996] 2 All ER 573; *Inntrepreneur Pub Co (GL) v East Crown Ltd* [2000] 2 Lloyd's Rep 611.

7. Misrepresentation in IT era: between misrepresentation and mistranscription

Contracts may face malfunctions in the digital world too; however, the problem is that blockchain governance would uphold the unexpected result due to the so-called law code: parties agreed to the code, and the code represents the only solution. To better explain, blockchain technology is based on community's political aversion to any kind of intervention (judicial or otherwise) on code-legal executions that could strip the code of its certainty. From a contract law perspective, this means an excessive interpretation of the freedom to contract principle: one golden rule of contract law is that individuals are free to make and enter into agreements. Moreover, it is required that there be consensus ad idem for the contract to be enforceable – the so-called meeting of minds. From a smart contract perspective, the burning issue is if parties' consensus covers code law too. Thus, how to manage mistranscription and misrepresentation in smart contracts: following blockchain's rule, the approach is to adhere to code and not investigate what is really written in the contract.

To commence, mistranscription occurs when parties negotiated the terms of an agreement outside the code and one party was charged with creating a smart contract based on what they discussed. In a traditional contract, mistranscription is read as a mechanical error that occurs after the contract has been made as the "only contract the parties have made is the oral contract".[20]

Partially different is the scenario in smart contract: if parties agree to their terms before inscribing them in the code, the coded version of the contract should act as a transcription of their original agreement. Moreover, if parties have a natural-language explanation of terms to accompany the smart contract or emails or other business documents demonstrating the original intent, the burden on the party claiming harm becomes easy. From an empirical perspective in a platform like Ethereum, contract reformation does not constitute an impossible task, despite blockchain's rigid formalities. For example, parties may have some opportunities:[21]

- They may ask to a court to change contract.
- They can mutually decide to "undo" a contract through self-destruct, delegate call or call code functions.
- They can create a new correct contract.

It should be noted that mistranscription is available even if one party has intentionally mis-transcribed a party's contract. In other words, the blockchain governance system cannot stop a code-writer from committing a fraud *in factum*.

A different scenario occurs if negotiation was done in code, and the code, that is, the IT system based on blockchain, executes an action or result that neither party intended.

20 (Eisenberg 2018).
21 (Bill and Juels 2016).

Finally, misrepresentation in smart contract too may materialise. For example, the distributor made some claims about the product that they knew were not true but critical to the re-seller's decision whether to contract or not. Provided re-seller relied on the claims and suffered harm because of the untruth: a fraudulent misrepresentation is met, but the problem is blockchain governance. The latter, alone, has no system for dealing with such situations; therefore, judicial intervention is required.[22]

A practical legal example is *Quoine Pte Ltd v B2C2 Ltd*[23]: it involves the decision of a Singaporean court about transactions involving the exchange of Ether for Bitcoin on a platform (Quoine, indeed). Quoine installed a software that aimed to ensure that transactions were concluded according to instructions given by algorithms. An additional software was installed with the purpose to ensure that transactions were concluded by identifying applicable market prices from external cryptocurrencies exchanges.[24] A company, B2C2, user of such platform, following instruction given by Quoine installed a "fail-safe deep-price" in the system equivalent to 10 Bitcoins in exchange for 1 Ether. Yet due to an error on the side of the platform, the exchange rates were not updated, and some transactions were executed at an exchange rate approximately 250 times higher in favour of B2C2 with the disadvantage of two other companies with which it had concluded smart contracts for the exchange of cryptocurrencies. In this scenario, on its side, Quoine cancelled all transactions concluded by B2C2 with the other companies. On its side, B2C2 considered this cancellation as a violation of the legal relationship.

The Singaporean court held the following[25]:

- Transactions were not voidable because Quoine had breached the terms of the contracts between user and platform: the action is irreversible once the fulfilment of the order has been communicated.
- The contract had been concluded without intermediation between the users, even though they were also contractually obliged to Quoine because of the conditions of the use of the Platform (the Agreement) and in particular of the aforementioned irreversible action clauses.
- The invalidity of the contract between B2C2 and the two companies for mistake should have concerned an essential element also due to the knowledge of the mistake by the contracting parties at the time of the conclusion of the contract.
- Quoine had no reason to cancel the transactions because B2C2 could not have known about the alleged mistake of the two companies with which it had traded cryptocurrencies.

22 (Sillanpaa 2020).
23 *Quoine Pte Ltd v B2C2 Ltd SGHC(I)* 03[2019] e SGCA(I), 02 [2020].
24 (Nathaniel and Tey 2022).
25 (Matthew 2021).

References

Atiyah, Patrick S., and Guenter H. Treitel. 1967. "Misrepresentation Act 1967." *The Modern Law Review* 30 (4): 369–88.

Bigwood, Rick. 2005. "Pre-Contractual Misrepresentation and the Limits of the Principle in with V. O'Flanagan." *The Cambridge Law Journal* 64 (1): 94–125.

Bill, Marino, and Ari Juels. 2016. "Setting Standards for Altering and Undoing Smart Contracts." In *Rule Technologies. Research, Tools, and Applications: 10th International Symposium, RuleML 2016, July 6–9, 2016*, 151–66. Stony Brook, NY: Springer International.

Eisenberg, Melvin A. 2018. *Foundational Principles of Contract Law*. Oxford University Press.

Farnsworth, E. Allan. 1969. "The Past of Promise: An Historical Introduction to Contract." *Columbia Law Review* 69 (4): 576–607.

Handley, Ken R. 2015. "Causation in Misrepresentation." *Law Quarterly Review* 13 (2): 275–90.

Klass, Gregory. 2025. "Misrepresentation and Contract." In *Research Handbook on the Philosophy of Contract Law*, edited by di Chen-Wishart Mindy, 2471. Edward Elgar.

Matthew, Oliver. 2021. "Contracting by Artificial Intelligence: Open Offers, Unilateral Mistakes, and Why Algorithms Are Not Agents." *ANU Journal of Law and Technology* 2 (1): 45–87.

Mitchell, Paul. 2020. "Implied Terms as to Description and Misrepresentation." In *Sale of Goods*, edited by di Paul Mitchell, 317–37. Informa Law from Routledge.

Nathaniel, Kevin, and Samuel Tey. 2022. "Can Smart Contracts Outsmart the Law: The Law of Contract in Light of Smart Contracting." *Singapore Comparately Law Review* 93–113.

Sillanpaa, Tiffany M. 2020. "Freedom to (Smart) Contract: The Myth of Code and Blockchain Governance Law." *Indonesian State Law Review* 7 (2): 38–51.

9 Mistake

Chapter Overview

1. Introduction

Through a mistake, a contract is analysed and scrutinised in the tents and dealings running to the conclusion of such an agreement. More specifically, 'dealing' represents the outward manifestation of the agreement to be judged by objective standard.[1]

Therefore, mistake constitutes a vitiating factor of the contract: it alludes to a situation where both parties have entered a contract under the same fundamental mistake, which will render the contract void. It is crucial to emphasise that the main consequence of a void contract, because of mistake, is that parties do not have any other choice but for the law to automatically state that the contract is void.

The circumstance just described is helpful to define the demarcation line between the position of a contract affected by mistake, which is void, and the one prejudiced by misrepresentation, which is voidable.

From a legal theory perspective, sometimes, mistake has the effect of preventing the formation of a contract. In order words, if the main rule is that law gives effect to the will of the parties of an agreement, if the promise is made under the influence of a mistake, such promise should not be enforceable.

If the will of the party has a legal effect, recognised by law, the consequence should encourage to adopt a rule in any cases in which the enforcement of the

1 (Tylor 1948).

DOI: 10.4324/9781003645948-9

promise of a party to the contract would not accord with his will in the situation. The reason is quite simple: party made the promise under the influence of a mistake; thus, the promise should not be enforced.[2]

From a historical perspective, mistake represents a remedy which originates from both common law and equity. Nevertheless, it has been limited to common law since the *Great Peace Shipping Ltd v Tsavliris Salvage International Ltd* decision.[3]

To elaborate, this decision constitutes an important milestone in mistake, because it is the first one where the concept of mistake is analysed under common law. More in detail, it is possible to affirm as follows:

- If the "mistake" refers to the quality of performance of the contract (e.g., the distance between two different places, for example), it does not make the contract impossible to perform.
- A common mistake requires the vitiating element to make the contract performance impossible. Therefore, the consequence is that the contract is void.

Moreover, this case is also crucial, because it ruled the "equitable mistake" doctrine encapsulated in *Solle v Butcher*.[4]

Before explaining this doctrine, it is quintessential to distinguish between mistake in common law and in equity.

As far as mistake under common law is concerned, mistake renders a contract void in limited cases, such as the inexistence of goods (good perished before sale, for example) or the lack of title of the goods (good belonged to the buyer). Other forms of mistake do not render a contract void.

From another perspective, that is, equity, there are two different categories of mistake:

- Unilateral mistake relating to terms or identity: the consequence of this is that contract is voidable, not void.
- Common mistake, relating to quality, renders a contract voidable.

More in depth, in *Bell v Lever Bros*,[5] it was held that common mistake that renders a contract void should be:

2 (McClintock 1944).

3 [2003] QB 679. The main issue was if the location of the stricken vessel could constitute a mistake and, consequently, if the contract was void. To elaborate, the distance was 35 miles as per parties' agreement; however, it became 410 miles in the reality.

4 [1950] 1 KB 671.

5 [1932] AC 161. More in detail, it was stressed that "Mistake as to the quality of the thing . . . will not affect assent unless it is a mistake of both parties and is as to the existence of some quality which makes the thing without the quality essentially different from the thing that it was believed to be" (Lord Atkin).

- Relating to existence of the contract. The principle is that the subject matter of the contract shall exist at the time of making the contract; otherwise, there is no contract.[6]
- Relating to the title. For instance, the buyer is already the owner of what the seller is selling. Therefore, the principle is that the mistake relating to the title will be a mistake for which the contract can be voided.[7]
- Relating to quality. In this specific case, a mistake will not affect the validity. The exception is when the mistake affects both parties and it is of essence, as far as the quality or a specific quality of the goods are concerned. This quality makes the object of the contract, if devoid of that quality, essentially different from the thing as it was believed to be.

Bearing this in mind, equitable mistake doctrine means the following one:

> A contract is also liable in equity to be set aside if the parties were under a common misapprehension either as to facts or as to their relative and respective rights, provided that the misapprehension was fundamental and that the party seeking to set it aside was not himself at fault.[8]

2. Differences between mistake and misrepresentation

Both mistake[9] and misrepresentation are based on incorrect information; consequently, it is crucial to highlight the difference between these two vitiating factors.

Mistake alludes to a situation where one or both parties are involved in a contract or agreement and an error relating to their understanding of the terms occurs.

By contrast, misrepresentation refer to a situation where one party intentionally or unintentionally provides false information to the other party. As a result of this, the other party misunderstands the terms of agreement.

Misrepresentation and mistake are based on incorrect information as well as defined as vitiating factors relating to consensus. However, it is worth clarifying as follows:

- In mistake, incorrect information arises from an unintentional error.

6 See *Couturier v Hastie* [1856] UKHL J3. The principle is that if there is a contract for the sale of specific goods, and the goods without the knowledge of the seller have perished at the time when the contract is made, the contract is void. Now it is encompassed into Section 6 Sale of Good Act.

7 See *Cooper v Phibbs* (1867) LR 2 HL 149. In this controversy, an uncle told his nephew, being in error, that the uncle was entitled to a fishery. A nephew leased a fishery from his uncle. His uncle died. When the lease came up for renewal the nephew renewed the lease from his aunt. It later transpired that the uncle had given the nephew a life tenancy in his will. The lease was held to be voidable for mistake as the nephew already had a beneficial ownership right in the fishery. It was held that (1) the lease was voidable rather than void; (2) the claim was based on equity; (3) it is related to beneficial ownership as opposed to legal ownership.

8 Denning LJ.

9 (McTurnan 1963).

- In misrepresentation, incorrect information constitutes a deliberate or negligent falsehood.

To summarise, as far as the mistake is concerned:

- It is hearer oriented.
- It prevents the creation of rights and obligations.
- It does not involve the making of a false statement.
- It does not constitute a deliberate effort to hide the true facts in the making of a mistake.
- It is not actionable, but for some exceptions. If established, it renders the contract void *ab initio*.

Misrepresentation, by contrast, may be summarised as follows:

- It is speaker oriented.
- If it is present, rights and obligations are created.
- It involves the making of a false statement.
- It constitutes a deliberate effort to hide or withhold the true facts. It
- It is actionable, even if innocent.
- If established, it renders the contract voidable.

3. Mistake: an overview and unilateral mistake

It is possible to affirm that mistake shall be as follows:

- Common. It refers to (1) quality of bargain; (2) to the subject matter (*res estincta*); (3) to title (*res sua*).
- Mutual. In this case parties misunderstand each other's intentions and so are at cross-purposes. The result is that both parties have not reached consensus, therefore, the contract does not exist. In this case, mistake shall be referred to terms of contract and/or the subject matter of the contract.
- Unilateral means that only one party is mistaken, the other one is aware of his mistake. Unilateral mistake shall refer to contractual terms as identity.
- *Non est factum*.

To understand what "*non est factum*" means, it is important to explain *Saunders v Anglia Building Society*.[10]

Mrs Gallie signed a document which stated it was the sale of her interest in her home to Mr Lee; the latter used this document to obtain a mortgage from Anglia Building Society. He failed to keep up repayments on the mortgage, thus the building society sought possession of the property. Mr Lee was a friend of

10 [1970] AC 1004.

Mr Parkin, who was Mrs Gallies' nephew. Mrs Gallie knew the wishes of the two friends and told them that she would assign her house to the nephew as a gift on condition that he allowed her to remain there rent-free for life. She told the two men that:

- The document she signed had the effect to that agreement.
- She signed the document in both their presence, but she could not read it – she did not find her glasses.
- In the action against the building society, Mrs Gallie raised the plea of *non est factum*.

The House of Lords stated that the document was not radically different from that which Mrs Gallie believed it to be. Moreover, the plea of *non est factum* should not be applied. In other words, this plea shall be applicable if the individual is unable to read the document (blind) or he is illiterate or incapacitated through age.

Unilateral mistake occurs when one party takes advantage of the other when he/she knows that the other has made a mistake. It shall be referred either to contractual terms or to identity.

As far as contractual terms are concerned, the principle is that a contract is void where there is a mistaken statement of intent made by one party and the other knows it is mistaken. For example, a contract for the sale of 30,000 hare skins: the latter are traditional (trade practice) sell by skin. However, sellers mistakenly contracted to sell them by weight. The court held that the mistake would have been known to the buyers. Consequently, the contract was void as there was a material mistake made as to the terms of the contract.[11]

To understand how unilateral mistake works, it is worth mentioning that a test has been shaped in force, of which the mistake will be operative under these conditions:

- The innocent party is mistaken over a material term of the contract without fault.[12]
- The other party should have known about the mistake.[13]

11 See *Hartog and Colin v Shields* [1939] 3 All ER 566. In another case the court affirmed that a contract will be void where the innocent party is mistaken over a material term of the contract without fault; see *Sybron Corp v Rochem Ltd* [1983] 2 All ER 706.

12 *Sybron Corp v Rochem.*

13 *Wood v Scarth* (1858) 1 F&F 293. The defendant offered in writing to let a pub to the plaintiff. After a conversation, the plaintiff accepted by letter believing that £63 rental was the only payment under the contract. The defendant had intended not only to charge £63 per year, but to demand a further payment of £500 and the clerk was told about this. The defendant refused to complete it, and the plaintiff brought an action for specific performance. It was held that contract was not void because it was not sufficiently ambiguous despite the mutual mistake.

Another typology of unilateral mistake refers to identity: the "innocent party" is under a duty to demonstrate that he/she intended to deal with someone else. The applicable principle differs whether the contract is made:

- Written correspondence: the principle is that it must be shown that there was an intention to deal with some other person than the one with whom he appears to have made the contract. Further, the mistaken party must prove that the other party was aware of the intention. In this respect, the correct identity of the party is crucial when trade is made at a distance.
- Face-to-face: the presumption is that the defrauded party intended to deal with the person in front of them. Therefore, the only mistake would be of the person's creditworthiness. The latter constitutes a quality of the person, not his identity.[14]
- At distance.

To conclude the unilateral mistake, two cases law shall be read together: *Cundy v Lindsay*[15] and *Shogun Finance v Hudson*.[16]

In *Cundy v Lindsay*, Lindsay sued Cundy to reclaim handkerchiefs after being defrauded by a rogue who had sold the goods to Cundy. Lindsay received some correspondence from a man named Blenkarn who falsely represented himself as Blenkiron & Co. Since Lindsay mistakenly believed that the correspondence came from the business Blenkiron & Co., she then delivered a large order of handkerchiefs to Blenkarn. The rogue sold the goods to Cundy, who was an innocent party. The House of Lords held that:

- Lindsay had intended to deal only with Blenkiron & Co.
- There was no agreement or contract between Lindsay and the rogue.
- The contract was void, not voidable: there was only one side to the contract, but a contract, to be valid, requires two sides.

By contrast, in *Shogun Finance v Hudson* a car dealer sold a car to a fraudster who produced stolen licenses as his own. The dealer signed the hire-purchase contract in the same name written on the license. The fraudster took physical possession of the car. The defendant purchased the car from the fraudster in good faith. Upon discovery of the false payment by the fraudster and the failure to make payments, Sought Finance brought an action against Hudson for conversion. Hudson counterclaimed stressing that he had obtained the right title to the vehicles.

First and foremost, it should be clarified that, under the Hire Purchase Act 1964, good title passes to an innocent buyer if an agreement exists. The House of Lord held that:

- The contract was void for mistake.

14 *Philips v Brooks* [1919] 2 KB 243.
15 (1878) 3 App Cas 459.
16 [2003] 3 WLR 1371.

- The contract signed between the finance company and the rogue was made *inter absentes*, that is, at a distance. Thus, the identity of the person was crucial to the contract.
- The dissenting judges argued that it should be a distinction between contract made inter absenter and contracts *inter praesentes*.

To summarise, an individual, to successfully claim unilateral mistake, has a duty to prove the following:

- An intention to deal with some other person.
- The other party knew his intention.
- The identity played a fundamental role.
- He had taken the reasonable steps to verify the identity.

4. The doctrine of common or mutual mistake

The underlying doctrine of common or mutual mistake lies on the principle that sometimes parties misunderstand each other's intentions. Common mistake shall encompass two different situations:

- Each party makes a different mistake, and this mistake refers to either terms of contract or the subject matter.
- Both parties have not reached consensus, therefore a contract does not exist.

If the mistake falls into a term of contract, the main principle is that the role of the court is to give an objective interpretation of the contract, if possible. Therefore, the court will ask what an imaginary reasonable third party would understand by the contract in line with one or both parties' arguments. In cases where it is not objectively possible to decide to which terms of contracts parties referred to, the contract would not exist.

Moreover, it is important to distinguish between mistake on a term from mistake on a quality.

In the first case, that is, mistake on a term of a contract, a party knows that the other party agrees to a different term. Therefore, it is not possible to enforce the contract on the grounds that there is only a unilateral mistake relating to terms of a contract.

In the second scenario, that is, mistake on quality, there is not a mistake over the terms of a contract. Consequently, the party is obliged to buy despite the unilateral mistake.

To understand this, the reference is to *Smith v Huges*[17]: it was held that only a mistake on the terms of a contract, if known to the farmer, would prevent an agreement arising between the farmer and the racehorse trainer. In this specific case, the

17 *Smith v Hughes* (1871) LR 6 QB 597.

racehorse trainer thought that he was buying old oats. By contrast, the farmer said that any reference to the quality of oats was made.

It is critical to stress that the doctrine of common mistake is dependent on the construction of the terms of the contract. To elaborate, it is not possible to decide whether there is an operative common mistake without looking at all the circumstances of the contract and whether its terms properly construed put the risk of mistake on one or other of the parties.

An example of this comes from the High Court of Australia. In *McRae v Commonwealth Disposal Commission*[18] it was held that on the facts of this case the true construction of the contract meant that there was an implied promise from the sellers that the tanker existed. The latter did not exist, so the sellers were in breach of the contract and had to pay damages to the buyer.

Another distinction shall be between the following:

- Common mistake means that both parties made the same mistake.
- Cross-purpose mistake[19] is the mistake made by one or all the parties, but the mistake is different.

To summarise all, the scenario seems to be the following one:

- Common mistake is where both parties make the same mistake.
- Mutual mistake is where both parties think the other is in agreement, but in reality, they are at cross-purposes.
- Unilateral mistake is where one party takes advantage of the other, when he/she knows that the other has made a mistake.

Finally, mistake differs also from frustration.[20] The latter, frustration, can be seen as primarily about risk allocation. Although both common mistake and frustration deal with the same issue, that is, the risk allocation, frustration refers to this topic but in relation to events occurred after contracting. In other words, frustration is concerned with the impact of subsequent events on initially valid contracts which have already been agreed.

18 (1951) 84 CLR 377. Two parties agreed to buy and sell a tanker but both parties operated under a mistake: the tanker did not exist.

19 *Raffles v Wickelhaus* [1864] EWHC Exch J19. Parties entered a contract for the sale of some cotton shipped by the *Peerless* from Bombay; the *Peerless* had a sailing from Bombay in October and December. The defendant thought it was the October sailing, and the claimant believed it was December sailing which had been agreed. An objective test has been applied: it was held that a reasonable person would not have been able to state with certainty which sailing had been agreed. Thus, the contract is void because there was no *consensus ad idem*. In essence, term is objectively ambiguous.

20 Frustration will be discussed and analysed in depth in Chapter 12.

While there is no question if the contract is void from the beginning, by contrast, through the lens of frustration, the question is whether the events which have occurred should terminate the contract.

5. Mistake in smart contract

In the contemporary era it becomes vital to understand how traditional contract law categories face the IT challenges, therefore the topic of mistake in smart contract.

A mistake in smart contract means error brought about by a fault in a smart contract's coding causing it to operate beyond its programmed instructions. It is a mistake, hence it was no way intended or comprehended because the human parties to the contract assumed it could not operate in that way, and it was conceived *ex ante*. In this respect, it appears clear that mistake doctrine will not serve to vitiate a smart contract because a successful claim of mistake is contingent upon the existence of a fundamental error in the underlying assumption of that contract. More in detail, as will be discussed, a party has made a legal mistake when a smart contract makes a decision that is unfavourable yet feasibly within the parameters of the contract's coding, vesting smart contracts with the capacity and responsibility to assume decisions at the margin of their coded instructions.[21]

The existing literature in this niche IT area tries to apply mistake doctrine to situation of errant smart contracts that tend to focus on two different scenarios. The first one occurs when parties did not understand what the coding of their smart contracts meant or how it would translate to outputs by the smart contracts.[22] The second one alludes to a situation where a party became implicated in a transaction that was neither foreshadowed nor desired due to the action of a third party, for example a hacker or a person that "legitimately" exploited gaps in the smart contract code to bring about unintended consequences.[23]

Moreover, it should be noted that in smart contracts, not every decision shall be predicted by parties: whether parties look to the smart contract's coding itself or to plain-language summaries of the same, the parties' understanding of the perimeter of the contract's authority will be case-specific. In other words, in agreeing to have the smart contract decide for them, parties are likely to be considered "consciously ignorant" of future risks associated with this agreement.

Consequently, a vital legal activity is to include terms allocating liability in the event the smart contract makes an incorrect decision. In this way, from a first stage, smart contract's errant decision would be expressly attributed to one or both the parties. In addition, programmers – as intermediaries – would distance themselves from any liability for the AI-driven smart contract's subsequent behaviour through disclaimer contained in a separate agreement for the development of the smart

21 (Giancaspro 2022).
22 (Ryan 2017).
23 (Chilaeva and Dutton 2018).

contract.[24] In addition, if terms stipulated required that parties live by the decision of the smart contracts and bear responsibility for the same, the mistake doctrine would not operate.[25] Also through the lens of mistake doctrine, the latter should not apply to a mistake as to one's belief regarding future risks or event and would instead need to be tested according to the more rigid and stringent criteria for relief according to frustration's doctrine.[26]

To elaborate, when and if an AI-driven smart contract assumes a decision that is untendered, irrational and undesirable, a party might be tempted to affirm that its purpose has been frustrated. Yet this doctrine should not apply if this particular risk had been allocated by express term simply because the risk would have been foreseen and accounted for. Frustration doctrine should not work for an additional reason: it is based upon the occurrence of some events which, on the one hand, have a fundamental impact upon parties' bargain, on the other hand, render it something different to what was agreed. More appropriately, the decision may be inconvenient.[27]

From a more practical perspective, the case law is *B2C2 Ltd v Quoine Pte Ltd*[28] managed by Singapore International Commercial Court: it analysed the doctrine of mistake in the context of an algorithmic trading contract on a cryptocurrency exchange. Before approaching the decision of Singapore International Commercial Court, it is worth highlighting that under Singaporean law, the common law doctrine of unilateral mistake requires that a party can demonstrate that it both acted and cooperated under a mistake of fundamental terms of the contract. Moreover, the other party, the non-mistaken party, had actual knowledge of the mistaken party's error.[29] According to the doctrine of unilateral mistake in equity, the constructive knowledge shall substitute the actual knowledge, on the part of the non-mistaken party; also it requires the mistaken party to show that the non-mistaken party engaged in unconscionable conduct in relation to the mistake in order to establish that the contract is voidable.[30]

The decision of Singapore International Commercial Court is constructed on the following main pillars:

- The price was a fundamental term of the agreement determined by parties' respective algorithms. Therefore, the fundamental term, the price, was not mistaken.

24 (Levy and Bell 1989).

25 This is corroborated by the approach in force of which a party "bears the risk of a mistake when (a) the risk is allocated to him by agreement of the parties". See *Campbell v Edwards* [1976] 1 WLR 403, 407 (Eng.); *Wamo Pty. Ltd. v Jewel Food Store Pty. Ltd.* (1983) 2 BPR 9611, 9615 (Austl.).

26 (Corbin 1952).

27 (Giancaspro 2022).

28 Just discussed in the previous Chapter 8.

29 B2C2 Ltd [2019] SGHC(I) 03 at 77.

30 (Harsimar 2021; Cassar 2023).

- Determining the intention or knowledge underlying the machine's mode of operation requires to define the conduct of the operator or controller of the machine. The purpose is to assess if the operator or controller has actual knowledge of the trading operation, that is, the possibility of trades at that price being executed.
- There was a breach of contract and a breach of trust on the part of Quoine: Quoine's unilateral action (reserving the dispute trade orders) constituted a breach of the Terms and Conditions and, more precisely, of the Irreversible Action Clause.

References

Cassar, Damian P. 2023. "The Notion of Mistake in Blockchain-Based Smart Contracts: An Analysis of B2C2 Ltd v Quoine Pte Ltd from a Comparative Perspective." *European Journal of Comparative* 10 (2): 253–82.

Chilaeva, Maya, and Pia Dutton. 2018. "Smart Contracts: Can They Be Aligned with Traditional Principles or are Bespoke Norms Necessary?" *Journal of International Banking and Financial Law* 8: 479–88.

Corbin, Arthur L. 1952. *Corbin on Contracts: One Volume Edition*. West Group.

Giancaspro, Mark. 2022. "'I, Contract': Evaluating the Mistake Doctrine's Application Where Autonomous Smart Contracts Make 'Bad' Decisions." *Campbell Law Review* 45 (1): 53–86.

Harsimar, Dhanoa. 2021. "Making Mistake with Machines." *Santa Clara Hight Technology Law Journal* 37 (1): 99–118.

Levy, Lawrence B., and Suzanne Y. Bell. 1989. "Software Product Liability: Understanding and Minizing the Risks." *High Technology Law Journal* 5 (1): 1–28.

McClintock, Henry L. 1944. "Mistake and the Contractual Interests." *Minnesota Law Review* 28: 460–82.

McTurnan, Lee B. 1963. "An Approach to Common Mistake in English Law." *The Canadian Bar Review* XLI (1): 1–53.

Ryan, Philippa. 2017. "Smart Contract Relations in e-Commerce: Legal Implications of Exchanges Conducted on the Blockchain." *Technology Innovation Management Review* 7 (10): 10–17.

Tylor, Theodore Henry. 1948. "General Theory of Mistake in the Formation of Contract." *Modern Lae Review* 11 (3): 257–68.

10 Duress and undue influence

Chapter Overview

1. Introduction

The doctrine of duress and undue influence constitute, for an individual, a means of avoiding an already concluded contract: these two doctrines operate when an individual has been forced, or even coerced, into a contract by threats, unfair pressures or unreasonable influences. The underlying *ratio* of this doctrine preventing that one party taking unfair advantage of another. The consequence, or the effect, of this is that the contract shall be voidable at the request of the aggrieved party.

Furthermore, there is also a difference between duress and undue influence. The first one, duress, involves the application of illegitimate pressure so that the relevant contract or contractual modification is unsafe and should be set aside. Normally, the pressure will take the form of a threatened legal wrong (crime, breach of contract etc). In exceptional circumstances, it might be the threat of a lawful act, such as reporting a person to police or some other authority.

As far as undue influence is concerned, it constitutes an equitable doctrine; more in detail, undue influence is broader than coercion even if it can take the form of coercion. Once undue influence is shown, there is no need to show that the transaction is objectively unfair and unbalanced. The common situation where this legal concept is evoked is the abuse of relationship by someone occupying a superior or dominant position. These relationships may be found in some circumstances, such as solicitor/client; teacher/pupil; spiritual advisor/follower; trustee/beneficiary. In just mentioned cases it is presumed undue influence.

DOI: 10.4324/9781003645948-10

In a nutshell, it is possible to affirm that:

- Undue influence constitutes an equity remedy that deals with cases where one person has acquired influence over another.
- Duress is a common law doctrine under which a contract may be avoided where the complainant was induced to enter it by illegitimate pressure, such as threat of physical violence, a threat to seize or damage property or economic pressure.

Moreover, the common law doctrine of duress refers to the procedure, or the mechanism, by which a contract was agreed, by contrast the equitable doctrine of undue influence is focussed upon the relationship between the parties.

Finally, it is critical to highlight that both undue influence and duress constitute a response to the use of illegitimate pressure.

2. Duress

If a person uses an illegitimate power to force a party to contract, this contract may be voidable for duress. The doctrine of duress was developed in common law in a slow way: at the first time, only duress to the person, that is, a threat to the personal security of an individual, was recognised as duress. With time, the law expanded to encompass duress to goods and economic duress.

Duress may be defined as a common law doctrine allowing a contract to be set aside because it was entered into because of illegitimate pressure or threats such that the other party had no realistic choice other than to agree.

More in general, it is possible to say that under English common law there are some examples of the forms of duress:

- Duress by threat of violence.[1]
- Duress by threat of imprisonment.[2]
- Duress by creating a threatening environment.[3]
- Duress to threat to damage property.[4]
- Duress by economic pressure.

The duress has the effect to render the contract voidable, rather than void. The apparent consent of the victimised party is treated as revocable: they can affirm or not to affirm the contract. In case they choose not to affirm the contract, it is void.

To amount to duress, the threat made must be sufficient in its nature: usually, the indicator the courts have used is whether the threat is illegal. If the threat is illegal, there is a presumption that this will amount to a sufficient threat. The illegal act

1 *Barton v Armstrong* [1976] 1 AC 104.

2 *Williams v Bayley* (1886) LR 1 HL 200: it involves a case relating to forgery and invalid contract obligations based on undue pressure. It was argued that an agreement with a bank was not free and voluntary when it was based on a forged signature.

3 *Antonia v Antonia* [2010] EWHC 1199.

4 *Dimskal Shipping Co SA v International Transport Workers' Federation, The Evia Luck* [1991] 4 All ER 871.

shall be a criminal act: in *Barton v Armstrong*[5] physical duress can be established when a threat is held to be a cause of the threatened party to enter a contract. It only requires that the threat shall be the potential cause that contributed to the signing of the contract. It is true even if there is a possibility that the threatened party would have entered the contract anyway. In a nutshell, a person who agrees to a contract under physical duress may avoid the contract.

In *Universe Tankships of Monrovia v International Transport Workers Federation (The Universe Sentinel)*[6] it was held that duress rendered the contract void. C's ship, named the *Universe Sentinel*, had been blacklisted by ITF, a trade union. Tugmen on the direction of ITF refused to operate their tugs, therefore *Universe Sentinel* was unable to sail. To lift the blacklisting, Cs agreed to pay into ITF's seamen's welfare fund. C sued ITF for economic duress. As a result of this, it was held that C was entitled to have back the money paid to the fund.

To ascertain the existence of duress, it is important to distinguish between the case where the threat results in a claimant voluntarily entering the contract and the claimant involuntarily entering the contract. In the first case, the claimant has an alternative to enter the contract, therefore, the conduct was not held sufficient to amount to duress. In this respect, *Northern Ireland v Lynch*[7] explains this concept. To elaborate, the judges accepted that even in extreme circumstances there is always an option, but this option may be realistically available. More in detail, the defence of duress is available to a person accused of murder as a principal in second degree. The plea of duress is available when the will of the accused has been overborne by threats of death or serious personal injury. The commission of the alleged offence was no longer the voluntary act of the accused. By contrast, in non-homicide cases, the degree of criminality or blameworthiness can and should be reflected in the punishment meted out, a course which the mandatory life for murder prohibits.

The effect of finding that duress renders a contract voidable has some consequences, for example:

- The party subject to the duress must act promptly to set aside the contract.[8]
- A third party can acquire good title to goods even though his vendor has acquired those goods pursuant to a contract which was brought about by duress.

It is quintessential to refer to *Halpern v Halpern*:[9] the Court of Appeal considered an application for summary judgment to enforce an alleged compromise of a Beth Din

5 Alex Barton was the managing director of a company, Landmark Corporation Ltd, whose main business was property development. Its project passing through "Paradise Waters"; Barton executed a deed whereby the company would pay a certain amount of money to Armstrong, an NSW state politician, as well as buy his shares for $80,000. Armstrong was the chairman of the board.

6 [1983] 1 AC 366.

7 [1975] AC 653. Lynch was convicted of murder and sentenced to life imprisonment. He appealed to the Court of Criminal Appeal in Northern Ireland, arguing that he had acted under duress. The Court of Criminal Appeal allowed the appeal and ordered a new trial. The Director of Public Prosecutions for Northern Ireland appealed to the House of Lords.

8 *North Ocean Shipping v Hyundai Construction* [1979] QB 705.

9 [2007] EWCA Civ 909.

arbitration. The application raised two interesting issues: the extent to which parties are able, under the provisions of the Rome Convention, to apply Halakha, Jewish law, which is not the law of any "country". Furthermore, there was also the issue relating to the extent to which rescission of a contract for duress at common law. This requires that the claimant makes a counter-restitution. The Court of Appeal held that choice of Jewish law would not be effective under Rome Convention. It declined to determine the issue relating to counter-restitution, holding that these questions should not be addressed until the court had heard all the pieces of evidence.

In this case, the Court of Appeal took the opportunity to clarify two aspects:

- The rescission for duress should not be any different in the principle than rescission for other vitiating factors, such as misrepresentation.
- The practical effect of rescission would always depend upon the circumstance of a particular case.

3. Duress through the lens of Roman law and legal theory

According to Roman law rule, a well-known concept was *laesio enormis*: it allowed relief for inadequacy of price. Under common law, there was a refusal to review the "adequacy" of consideration during the 19th and 18th centuries: according to economic individualism theory, a judicial interference with processes of price determination began to be described as both impracticable and dangerous. The official doctrine of common law of contract reaffirmed, through 19th century, all enquiry about "adequacy". In the described scenario, equity plays a central role, particularly in the broader field of usury. From statute it is possible to infer the rule based on which a transaction may invalidate for excessive interest as well as the standard of equivalence that define a reasonable rate.

Equity developed a special rule for "confidential" and "fiduciary" relationship: for these specific cases, it was clear that ordinary process of bargaining was considered inappropriate due to unusual reliance on personal honesty and good faith that exist for performance of fiduciary functions. In these cases, the person securing an advantage from a confidential or fiduciary relationship is required to prove his own full disclosure of all the relevant facts and the fairness of the transactions.

In essence the attention was on the adequacy of a price and when the latter was perceived as inadequate the expression used were "shock the conscience" or "fraud". These expression received legal effect through the legal instrument of cancellation: for example, a specific performance was refused where the inadequacy of the price was "such as shocks the conscience, and amounts in itself to conclusive and decisive evidence of fraud".[10] Moreover, some cases shaped a truly "shock-the-conscience" tests based on some specific elements, such as oppression, personal inequality, misleading conduct, short of positive misrepresentation.[11]

10 Lord Eldon in *Coles v Trecothick*, 9 Ves. 234 (1804).

11 *Lester v Mahan*, 25 Ala. 445 (1854); *Shaffer v Security Trust and Sav. Bank*, 4 Cal. App. (2d) 707, 41 P. (2d) 948 (1935); *Hardy v Dyas*, 203 Ill. 211, 67 N.E. 852 (1903); *Marshall v Billingsley*, 7

The essence of this approach is to investigate an extreme disproportion in values in a bargaining transaction, that is, the importance to obtain an explanation. The latter, often, has been found in misplaced reliance on the opposite party's good faith, some misleading partial disclosure, some extreme inequality of the parties in knowledge, experience or economic resources. Therefore, judicial remedies should not be read as a danger for economic foundations of an individualistic society but as a policing function.

From a methodological perspective, duress or, more specifically, economic duress, shall be approached as a situation in which inequality in the values exchanged has inspired judicial attack on unfair bargains. Further, the problem of inequality shall be approached in a case-by-case method, that is, according to specific conditions which affect the bargaining power and the motivations of individuals in particular transactions.

According to this line of reasoning, duress was describing the pressure as inherently improper, since process intended for the vindication of public interests are misapplied when used to enforce civil liability. Thus, doctrine of duress is based on a fundamental question: whether and if it is rightful using types of pressure for the purpose of extracting an excessive or disproportionate return.[12]

4. The form of duress

Duress can appear in three different forms:

- Duress to the person.
- Duress to goods.
- Economic duress.

The first form, duress to the person, represents the first form of duress recognised by the common law. More in detail, duress to the person materialises when one party to a contract forces another to contract with him through threats of violence. The law finds an apparent contract voidable where duress constitutes a reason for the contract, but the duress does not have to be the reason for the contract. In case a party enters a contract for several reasons, of which the duress is only one reason, this contract is still voidable. In *Barton v Armstrong* the court held that where there is duress to the person, there was no obligation to show that he would not have entered the agreement but for the threat, it simply being sufficient that the death threats were a cause.

As far as duress to goods is concerned, this kind of duress may occur where one person takes or destroys or threatens to destroy or takes the goods for another unless a contract is entered into. This type of duress is the threat of damage to the

Ind. 250 (1855); *Matthis v O'Brien*, 137 Ky. 651, 126 S.W. 156 (1910); *Barker v Wiseman*, 51 Okla. 645, 151 P. 1047 (1915); *Birdsong v Birdsong*, 39 Tenn. 289 (1859); *Kuel kamp v Ridding*, 31 Wis. 503 (1872).

12 (Dawson 1947).

victim's goods rather than to his person. In *Astley v Reynolds*[13] the court, King's Bench, found that money paid to release goods which had been unlawfully detained could be recovered. In this case, a pawnbroker refused to release the pawned goods until Astley paid back for more than the legal rate of interest: it was held that the contract be voidable.

By contrast, *Skeate v Beale*[14] stated that the unlawful detention of another's good does not constitute duress. The reason is that duress to goods does not render an agreement voidable. Although it is true, in *Dimskal Shipping Company SA v International Transport Workers Federation (The Evia Luck),* it was said that it was wrong the thesis where the only duress to the person renders voidable a contract. Therefore, also duress to good can form the basis of a claim and can render the contract voidable.

Economic duress occurs when one party uses its superior economic power to force the weaker party into an agreement. The main challenge in this area consists in drawing a demarcation line between unacceptable commerce pressure and acceptable commercial pressures.[15] As far as the structure is concerned, economic duress has two elements:

- An illegitimate threat.
- A compulsion of victim.

The latter, compulsion, is established by considering a list of factors including (1) the presence or absence of protest; (2) any alternative courses of action available to the victim; (3) whether the victim had independent advice.

The concept of economic duress appears for the first time in *Occidental Worldwide Investment Corp v Skibs A/S Avanti (The Siboen and The Sibotre)*[16] where it was stressed that to amount to economic duress there had to be a coercion of the will so as the vitiate consent. In this respect, commercial pressures were not sufficient. The development of this doctrine arrives only in *Pao On v Lau Yiu Long*[17]: it was said that under the general doctrine of economic duress, it shall be demonstrated that the victims' consent to the contract did not constitute a voluntary act on his part. It is required that there is a level of coercion of the will.

13 (1731) 2 Str 915.

14 [1840] 11 Ad & El 983.

15 In *Alec Lobb Ltd v Total Oil* [1983] 1 All ER 944, acceptable commercial pressures were not considered as duress. More in detail, the defendant had extracted hard terms in a contract with the claimant. The defendant had done this, because it was reluctant to contract with the claimant. Further, the commercial pressures upon the claimant originated with parties other than the defendant.

16 [1976] 1 Lloyd's Rep 293.

17 [1979] UKPC 17. The claimant had threatened not to complete the main contract unless subsidiary agreements were met, including a guarantee and indemnity. The claimant then sought to enforce the guarantee, but the defendant sought to have the agreement set aside for economic duress. The defendant did not protest at the time: he enforced the contract of sale through specific performance; therefore, he had another avenue of redress available to him. He had taken legal advice and took no steps to avoid the agreement, before the claimant sought to enforce the guarantee.

A successful claim to economic duress shall encompass the following:

- Pressure, which is illegitimate,[18] that means the lack of commercial or other justifications.
- The pressure shall be significant, that is, the victim or, the innocent party, is induced to enter the contract but for the duress would not have entered the contract.
- The practical effect of the pressure is that there is compulsion on, or a lack of practical choice or realistic alternative for the innocent party.

As far as illegitimate pressure is concerned, there is not an absolute test to distinguish illegitimate pressure from the normal pressure of normal commercial bargaining. To determine whether there is an illegitimate pressure, courts usually consider different elements, such as the following:

- The breach of contract.
- The party exerting the pressure has acted in good faith or bad faith.
- The innocent party has any realistic alternative.
- The innocent party protested at the time.
- The innocent party affirmed and sought to rely on the contract.

These factors[19] do not constitute exhaustive elements, rather than a support to define what is legitimate and illegitimate.

5. Undue influence

Undue influence represents a remedy that comes from equity: it operates when there exists a relationship between the parties which has been exploited by one party to gain an unfair advantage. Influence is acceptable because only when it becomes undue is it not acceptable from the law. Undue influence means that there is an imbalance of power between the parties and has been used illegitimately by the influencer. The level of influence is at such a level that the influenced party has lost autonomy in deciding whether to enter a contract.[20]

In *Royal Bank of Scotland Plc v Etridge (No. 2)*,[21] Lord Nicholls described undue influence as "one of the grounds of relief developed by the courts of equity as a

18 See *Attorney General for England and Wales* (2003): the "wrong duress" possessed two elements: (1) pressure; (2) illegitimacy of the pressure.

19 In *Progress Bulk Carriers Ltd v Tube City IMS LLC (The Cenk Kaptanoglu)* [2012] EWHC 273, the court held that what constitutes an economic duress was to be considered on a fact-specific basis; there was no requirement than an unlawful act had been committed although would be unusual to have economic duress in a commercial context without an unlawful act having been committed.

20 (Du Plessis and Zimmermann 2003).

21 [2002] UKHL 44. Wife provided security home for loan by bank to her husband's business. Home was being repossessed and wife alleged she had not understood the legal advice.

court of conscience. The objective is to ensure that the influence of one person over another is not abused".

Undue influence shall be the following:

- Actual undue influence.
- Presumed undue influence.

These two categories were shaped in *Allcard v Skinner*.[22]

The first one, actual undue influence, materialises when a person is subject to direct pressure or coercion by another. This might include threats, harassment or manipulation. To prove actual undue influence, the party shall demonstrate that someone has actively coerced the testator[23] into writing their will a certain way. More in detail, the person shall prove that influence was excessive, improper or unconscionable, but there is not any presumption of actual undue influence.

By contrast, presumed undue influence refers to a situation where a relationship of trust and confidence exists between parties and the person in dominant position takes advantage of the other's vulnerability or dependence. The law presumes that person in the dominant position may have taken advantage of the other person's vulnerability or dependence. The person that claims to be influenced is not under a duty to prove undue influence: it is sufficient that the existence of the relationship based on trust and confidence is demonstrated. The person in the dominant position to disprove the presumption of undue influence shall show that the other person acted freely and independently.

Relationships where "trust and confidence" arise include the following:[24]

- Parent and child.
- Doctor and patient.
- Solicitor and client.

Finally, there are other cases, named 2B relationship,[25] where undue influence is presumed. To elaborate, in this case, claimant can establish the existence of a

22 (1887) 36 Ch D 145. A had inherited her family's wealth; she became a member of the "protestant sisters of the poor", and this involved giving up her property. She gifted her property to sisterhood. She left the order, but it was six years before she sought to reclaim her property. The Court of Appeal held that although she had been unduly influenced, she could not recover due to delay and acquiescence since leaving sisterhood.

23 (Herrmann et al. 2022).

24 For example, in *Barclays Bank Plc v O'Brien*, [1994] 1 AC 180 it was held that undue influence encompasses: (1) actual undue influence; (2) presumed undue influence; (3) presumed undue influence from readily ascertainable facts raising suspicion of undue influence.

25 See also *Goodchild v Bradbury* [2006] EWCA Civ 1868 where LJ Chadwik said that "A gift which is made without informed consideration by a person vulnerable to influence, and which he could not have been expected to make if he had been acting in accordance with the ordinary motives which lead men's actions, needs to be justified on the basis that the donor knew and understood what he was doing. In this case, that requirement was not met".

relationship of trust and confidence on the facts. This raises a presumption that influence has been exercised and that presumption will be undue where there is something in nature of the transaction which calls for an explanation. For example, the case is *Lloyds Bank Ltd v Bundy*:[26] Mr Bundy placed trust and confidence in the bank manager with regards to his financial affairs. He was persuaded to change his home as security for the debts of his son's company. The Court of Appeal set this aside for the undue influence by the bank. The principle established by the court was that undue influence was presumed: a relationship of trust and confidence arose on the facts.

Undue influence by a third party on a claimant give rises to a claim for undue influence where the third party is exercising undue influence on the claimant. The situation may be described as follows:

- Party A, a bank, are contracting with party B to guarantee the loan for the third party, party C.
- Party C has used undue influence to force party B to guarantee their debt.
- This contract may be voidable so long as party A is aware of this undue influence.

Barclays Bank v O'Brien confirmed the "doctrine of notice":

- The first category is actual notice: party A has actual knowledge of the undue influence.
- The other category is constructive notice.

The remedy to contrast undue influence is rescissions: the contract is voidable; therefore, the parties are to be restored to their original positions. In *Dunbar Bank plc v Nadeem*[27] the Court of Appeal reasoned that there was not any duty to make restitution as a condition for the setting aside of the legal charge to restore the other party. The underlying reason was that no evidence of actual undue influence was seen.

References

Dawson, John P. 1947. "Economic Duress – An Essay in Perspective." *Michigan Law Review* 45 (3): 253–90.

Du Plessis, Jacques, and Reinhard Zimmermann. 2003. "The Relevance of Reverence; Undue Influence Civilian Style." *Maastricht Journal of European and Comparative Law* 10 (4): 345–79.

Herrmann, Nathan, Kimberly A. Whaley, Deidre J. Herbert, and Kenneth I. Shulman. 2022. "Susceptibility to Undue Influence: The Role of the Medical Expert in Estate Litigation." *The Canadian Journal of Psychiatry* 67 (1): 5–12.

26 [1974] EWCA Civ 8.
27 [1998] EWCA Civ J0618-12.

11 Discharge of a contract

Chapter Overview

1. Introduction

From a general perspective, it is possible to affirm that a contract may end in one of the five ways detailed here, more specifically:

- Through performance.
- By agreement of the parties.
- By breach.
- Operation of the law.
- By frustration or, better, impossibility deriving from frustration.

The two most frequent and normal ways to end a contract are performance and breach of a contract. These two phenomena are the two sides of the same coin, since breach may be read as a defective performance of a contract.

In dealing with discharge of a contract,[1] the following ones are the main subareas usually associated and/or linked:

- Force majeure clauses.

1 (English 2025).

DOI: 10.4324/9781003645948-11

- The liquidation of damages.
- Mitigation.
- The penalty clause.
- Repudiation by the innocent party.

Bearing this in mind, the two main topics are the performance of the contract, on one hand, and the breach of a contract, on the other hand. As it was just highlighted, these two elements constitute two opposite sides of the same coin.

2. The discharge of a contract through performance

The "natural way" to end a contract is the performance of the promised obligation which is the subject matter of the contract. Although this seems a tautological expression, a contract requires performance of the promised obligation. Some contracts may be defined as "entire obligation" contracts: in these contracts the mere performance will satisfy the obligation. A party cannot recover payment for the partial performance of an "entire obligation". Until the entire obligation is performed, the party performing the obligation cannot recover any payment for it.

An example of this may be seen in the case *Cutter v Powell*.[2] In this controversy, Cutter contracted with Powell to be the second mate on a ship bound from Jamaica to England. Cutter was to be paid 10 days after the ship would arrive in Liverpool. A term of the contract stated that "he [Cutter] proceeds, continues and does his duty as second mate in the said ship from hence to the port of Liverpool". However, for unfortunate circumstances, Cutter died shortly before the ship reached Liverpool and, as a result, his window sued to recover payment for the period where Cutter had acted as a second mate. This payment was denied, based on the explanation that the contract was not fully performed. There was no pay until the performance to make the payment and, on the other hand, there would not be any partial payment for partial performance.[3]

As far as this legal technique is concerned, the ability to stipulate that payment will not be made until performance is complete may be the only effective way householders can ensure the prompt and proper performance of small building works. While this is true, the Court of Appeal noted that it was "relatively unusual" in commercial construction contract and contracts for professional services for the payment obligation to be entire.[4]

2 (1795) 6 TR 320.

3 In a similar way see *Bolton v Mahadeva* [1972] EWCA CIV. 5. The claimant agreed to install a heating and hot water system into the defendant's house; however, the latter discovered some defects on the installation, and the plaintiff refused to fix it. As a result of this, the defendant refused to pay the initial cost. In this case, the court held that it was more serious breach: the plaintiff was not entitled to receive any amount of money, while the defendant would be discharged of any obligation.

4 In *Smales v Lea* [2011] EWCA Civ 1325, it was held that a lump sum contract does not mean that the entire performance was a condition precedent to payment. The claimant's cause of action for payment of fees, a cause of action in contract, accrued when the obligation to negotiate with insurers

To mitigate the general rule just explained, courts have been shaping a lot of remedies, thanks to which a party may allow to receive some recompense for a partial performance. These are the three remedies:

- Interpreting the contract as series of obligation: a court may interpret the contract not as being an entire contract but as a contract which is made up of a series of entire obligations. In other words, the contract is divided into a series of stages of performance: when a stage has been completed, the performing party can recover payment for this stage.
- The substantial performance of obligations: the party, albeit theoretically in breach, has substantially performed his obligations. If the performance has been substantially performed, the breach constitutes a minimal consequence, for instance a breach of a warranty. The case to recall is *Hoenig v Isaacs*,[5] where the court held that, where a party has substantially performed his obligations under contract, he is entitled to claim for payment in an action for the agreed sum, subject to the deduction of any cost of repairs for defects in his performance.
- The existence of a statutory exception (Sale of Goods Act 1979) when the buyer does not contract as a consumer. In this circumstance the buyer is required to collect the goods despite a delivery shortfall, or a delivery excess, in circumstances where such a shortfall is so slight that it would not to be "reasonable" to do so. By contrast, the innocent party may be liable to compensate the performer for a partial performance where the innocent party accepts the partial performance. The difficulty is that the other party may have no choice but to accept the partial performance even if the parties signed a contract for a complete performance. The relevant case is *Sumpter v Hedges*:[6] the main question in this controversy was whether, if a contract is only partially performed, the party in breach cannot claim for the partial performance, unless a new contract may be inferred. The court focused on whether the innocent party had the option not to accept the partial performance when inferring whether a new contract had been performed. In this scenario, the claimant cannot claim *quatum meruit* either, unless there is a fresh contract permitting this. Further, the court stressed that the defendant had no choice but to accept partial performance as he was left with half completed house on his land.

---

concerning claimant's fees became impossible to fulfill. Furthermore, the Court of Appeal held that the claimant was entitled to sue for his fees before his negotiation with insurers had either concluded or broken down.

5 [1952] 2 All ER 176. A contract was concluded for the decoration of a one-room flat for a lump sum: upon completion. There remained an outstanding a balance of money for the contractor's work and labour. There were certain defects in the bookcase and wardrobe. The employer refused payment of the outstanding balance, claiming a repudiatory breach of the contractor due to a failure to perform the contract.

6 [1898] 1 QB 673.

3. The concept of actual breach

Ascertaining if a breach of contract has occurred is quite a difficult and arduous exercise. On one hand, if a party refuses to continue performing or commits an act which prevents further performance, a breach of contract has occurred. This constitutes a repudiatory breach.

On the other hand, where there is a partial performance or an inadequate performance, it is difficult to determine whether such repudiatory breach has occurred. A repudiatory breach means a breach which entitles the innocent party to terminate the contract: a party who alleges that a repudiatory breach has occurred is under duty to prove that it has occurred. Therefore, a repudiatory breach is a breach which entitles the innocent party to terminate the contract, but a party who alleges that a repudiatory breach has occurred has to prove that it has occurred.

The definition of repudiatory breach[7] of contract is linked with the terms of the contract; in this respect, there are two main areas:

- The standard of performance.
- The type of term breached, sometimes it is called as actual breach of the contract: it means that the time for contractual performance has arrived, and the promisor has failed to deliver that performance.

As far as standard of performance is concerned, different terms impose different standards; these can be divided between the following:

- A standard for strict liability: the general rule stipulates that contracts for the supply of goods impose a strict standard of liability of performance about the quality and quantity of the goods to be supplied. The fault of the party who supplies the goods is immaterial: the party in breach may exercise all reasonable care to ensure that the goods conformed to the standard required.
- A standard of reasonable care that imposes a duty on the party to use reasonable care and skill in the performance of their contractual obligations. In this case, the fault of the party in breach is relevant. The general rule relating to contracts for supply of services require that the party exercise reasonable care and skills in the performance of their contractual obligations.

4. Anticipatory breach

An anticipatory breach occurs when, before a performance is due, a party either renounces the contract or disables himself from performing it.

A renunciation shall be a clear and absolute refusal to perform and can be expressed or indicated by the conduct of the party involved. The inability to perform shall involve the breach of a contractual obligation but does not have to be the fault of the party in breach.

7 (Carter, Courtney, and Tolhurs 2018).

An anticipatory breach gives rise to an immediate right of action: the injured party does not have to wait until the time due for performance to terminate the contract. This means that an anticipatory breach gives rise to a right to terminate if its prospective effects are such as to satisfy the requirement of substantial failure in the performance.

One element shall be duly highlighted: an anticipatory breach does not entitle an individual to give rise to an immediate right of action. More appropriate, the damages are determined and can be claimed at once, before the time is fixed for performance.

Hochster v De la Tour[8] represents a landmark case in English contract law, relating to anticipatory breach of contract. The main rule is that, if a contract is repudiated before the date of performance, damages may be claimed immediately. More precisely, the court established the following principles:

- When a contract provides for a promise for future conduct, a party refusinf to perform the agreement, thus renouncing the contract, becomes liable for breach of contract.
- A contract for a future contract constitutes an implied promise: in the meantime, neither party will prejudice the performance of that promise.
- The renunciation of a contract of future conduct by one party dissolves immediately the obligation of the other party to perform the contract.
- A breach of a contract by renouncing the duty to perform the future obligation immediately renders the party liable to suit of action for damages by the injured party.

In *Universal Cargo Carriers Corp v Citati*,[9] the court stressed two principles. The first one is that a party cannot be exempt from liability for negligence unless it is explicitly stated in the agreement. Furthermore, the court emphasised that the defendant had the control over the ship and its servants: the defendant had a duty to ensure that the ship was not damaged.

In case of renunciation, a party shall prove that the party in breach has "acted in such a way as to lead a reasonable man to conclude that he did not intend to fulfil his part of the contract". The consequent question concerns the nature of the refusal; it is vital to determine whether the injured party was reasonable in their position, that is, the refusal was sufficiently clear and absolute to give them the right to terminate.

One of the effects of an anticipatory breach of contract is that the innocent party may elect to affirm the contract and continue with a performance that is not wanted

8 [1853] EWHC J72 (QB).

9 [1957] 2 QB 401. Universal Cargo Carriers Corporation charted a ship to Citati: the ship was to be used for a voyage from the US to Italy. The charter party agreement included a clause that stated that the ship was to be returned in the same condition as it was received; the only exception was ordinary wear and tear. During the voyage, the ship was damaged due to the negligence of Citati's servants.

by the other party.[10] The innocent party's ability to affirm the contract and continue with the performance is qualified in two different ways:

- The innocent party cannot carry on with performance where he/she needs the cooperation of the party in breach.[11]
- If the innocent party did not have a legitimate interest in performing the contract other than claiming damages, he/she ought not to saddle the other party with an additional burden. The innocent party would be found to have an insufficient legitimate interest in performing the contract, when such performance would be "wholly unreasonable" or "perverse".

A further effect of an anticipatory breach is if the innocent party elects to affirm the contract, he/she runs the risk that the contract may later be discharged by frustration. In this case, the innocent party will not be able to claim for the earlier breach. In a similar way, if the innocent party affirms the contract and subsequently breaches it himself, he will not be able to rely upon the other party's earlier breach of contract.

5. The consequences of a breach

It is quintessential to clarify that a breach of a contract does not automatically end a contract. In *Decro-Wall SA v International Practitioners in Marketing*,[12] it was stated (Buckley LJ) that "the breach must be such as to deprive the injured party of a substantial part of the benefit to which he is entitled under the contract". It would be unfair to hold the injured party to the contract and leave them to their remedy in damages. The fundamental principle is that the contract may only be terminated by the plaintiff where the breached term is a significant one, a repudiatory breach.

However, a breach of condition or a sufficiently serious intermediate/innominate term gives the innocent party the option to terminate the contract. The terms used to describe this option to terminate is different from an election to the right to rescind: in cases where the right is described as one of rescission, this sparks off consequences which are very different from a rescission which operates in relation

10 *White and Carter (Councils) Ltd v McGregor* [1961] UKHL 5: this constitutes an English contract law case relating to the right to terminate a contract and the duty to mitigate. The innocent party can affirm a repudiated contract if (1) it can perform without the cooperation of the defaulting party; (2) it has a legitimate interest in doing so; (3) the right of innocent party is not an absolute right. In this case, facts involved an anticipatory breach, which is a repudiatory breach where one party tells the other that it will not perform ahead of the date where the obligation to perform kicks. It was also highlighted that the innocent party can sue for damages immediately without waiting till the date when performance by the defaulting party is due.

11 *Hounslow LBC v Twickenham Garden Developments Ltd* [1971] Ch 233.

12 [1971] 1 W.L.R. 361.

to a vitiating element, such as misrepresentation. The latter, however, may take different forms, because:

- A rescission for breach ends only future obligations.
- A rescission for misrepresentation ends all obligations.

Upon a breach of contract, other consequences occur upon, such as the following:

- The innocent party, regardless of whether he decides to terminate the contract, will have the right to sue for damages.
- The party in breach may also be unable to sue upon the contract.

The innocent party has a duty to communicate to the party in breach that he/she has elected to terminate the contract.[13] A court has to consider any steps taken by the party in breach to remedy accrued breaches of a contract. For example, an important factor is that the injured party purports to exercise the right to termination.

In *Ampurius Nu Homes Holdings Ltd v Telford Homes (Creekside) Ltd*,[14] the Court of Appeal considered what constitutes a repudiatory breach. In this case, the Court of Appeal stressed the importance of determining the core benefit to be derived under the contract before commencing an analysis relating to consequences of a breach. More in detail, the Court of Appeal held that:

- Whether anticipatory or actual, a breach of contract is capable of being remedied.
- The court should give due consideration to whether the breach has been remedied at the time that an injured party seeks to exercise its right to terminate the contract.
- An injured party wishing to terminate the contract shall be careful not to "jump the gun" and strike too soon when seeking to exercise its right to terminate a contract for repudiatory breach.
- The correct time to assess the effect of the breach should be the date at which the injured party seeks to exercise its rights and not when it reserves its position.

The nature of a breach of contract is prospective because if the innocent party elects to terminate the contract:

- Future obligations are no longer binding and are discharged.
- Past obligations remain.

13 *Vitol SA v Norelf Ltd* [1996] A.C. 800; [1996] 3 W.L.R. 105; [1996] 3 All E.R. 19.
14 [2013] EWCA Civ 577.

To summarise, a contract has no future, although it does have a past: this means that those rights which have been unconditionally acquired are still binding.[15] *Johnson v Agnew* is important also because it encapsulated major principles relating to termination, these principles are:

- Termination for a breach of a contract is "prospective": repudiatory breach of contract discharges both parties from future performance of their contractual obligations.
- A claimant for a specific performance does not forfeit his rights to terminate the contract by accepting a defendants' repudiatory breach.
- When a specific performance decree is made, the only role of the court is to determine whether the obligation can be discharged.
- Common law damages are assessed at the date of the breach of the contract.

More in general, damages could only recover where the performance was not necessary. More in detail, there are two main pillars:

- Cooperation of the other party is not required.
- The injured party does not have a legitimate interest in performing the contract other than to claim damages.[16]

Another case is *Geys v Societe Generale*[17]: it is a labour case concerning wrongful dismissal. However, the Supreme Court's decision is also important for the contractual repudiation. To elaborate, a repudiatory breach of contract does not terminate a contract: a contract is only terminated when the innocent party chooses to accept the repudiation. Therefore, the acceptance must consist of a conscious intention to bring the contract to an end or doing something inconsistent with the contract continuing. From a labour law perspective, the repudiatory dismissal does not terminate the employment contract because the claimant affirmed the contract. As a result of this, the defendant was not entitled to rely on the termination right in the handbook without providing the claimant clear and unequivocal notice that it was making a payment in lieu of notice in reliance of that clause. Ultimately, in the employment context, notice shall be clear and unequivocal to have effect.

15 See: (1) *Heyman v Darwins Ltd* (1942) 72 Ll.L.Rep. 65; (2) *Johnson v Agnew* [1980] AC 367. The first one is relating to an arbitration clause: the House of Lords said that although parties' contract was terminated by an accepted repudiation, the arbitration clause survived, which meant the parties had to resolve their dispute by arbitration. In *Johnson v Agnew* it was emphasised that the word "rescission" was often used interchangeably with termination at the time the case was heard, generating confusion as to the effect of termination.

16 See *Clea Shipping Corpn v Bulk Oil International Ltd* [1984] 1 All E.R. where the main question was the following one: "whether, and if so in what circumstances, an innocent party may during the performance of a contract decline to accept a repudiation by the other party to the contract".

17 [2012] UKSC 63.

6. Breach of conditions

Partially different from a breach of contract is the breach of a condition. The latter refers to conditions, warranties and innominate terms. Moreover, a demarcation line shall be painted between the following:

- Breach of condition, where the contract is discharged and party may claim damages.
- Breach of warranty, where the contract continues and it is also possible to claim damages.

The effects relating to a breach of conditions are two. The first one consists of the acceptance of the breach as discharging the contract: the innocent party can claim damages. The second one is strictly linked with affirmation or waiver. More in detail, the law of affirmation or waiver can be either expressed or implied. In this scenario, the innocent party will have full knowledge of the facts, and rather than terminating the contract, he elects to continue with it.

In *Pilbrow v Pearless de Rougemont & Co*[18] the court stressed the importance of full disclosure by legal service providers to clients regarding the qualification of the individuals providing services. Failure to disclose such information may result in discharge of a contract for legal services and relieve the client from payment obligations.

7. Discharge by agreement

The golden rule is that as the contract arises from an agreement, an agreement can also extinguish a contract. The discharge may be either bilateral or unilateral.

A bilateral discharge refers to a situation in which both parties have yet to carry out their obligations under the contract, wholly or partially, and their respective promises to discharge the contract shall be supported by consideration.

Traditionally, the expression to describe this is "accord and satisfaction": it means the need for new consideration to support the discharge agreement. A better explanation is encompassed in *British Russian Gazette Ltd v Associated Newspaper Ltd*,[19] where Scrutton Lj said as follows:

> Accord and satisfaction is the purchase of a release from an obligation, whether arising under a contract or tort by means of any valuable consideration not

18 [1999] 2 Costs LR 109. Mr Pilbrow contacted a solicitors' firm, seeking legal advice on a family matter. He was referred to Ms Haswell, who was not a solicitor, although he held a position within the firm. The firm sued Mr Pilbrow for payment for their services. Consequently, Mr Pilbrow claimed that there was an implied representation that the fee earner was a solicitor; this would entitle him to the rescission of the contract. The Court of Appeal held that the contract for legal services was discharged by the firm's breach of failing to disclose that the fee earner was not a solicitor. In other words, the firm's failure to disclose that the fee earner was not a solicitor amounted to non-performance of the contract for legal services.

19 [1933] 2 KB 616.

being the actual performance of the obligation itself. The accord is the agreement by which the obligation is discharged. The satisfaction is the consideration which makes the agreement operative.

To discharge a contract the law does not require formalities, the only exception being where a contract to be discharged is a new one put in place.

There are two forms of discharge:

- Warries – it occurs when one party requests an alteration of the terms of the contract and the other party agrees not to insist on strict compliance with the terms of the contract.[20]
- Express provisions for discharge – where parties express or imply in their contract that it will become discharged, should certain circumstances arise. For example, parties have agreed that the operation of some subsequent conditions will have the effect of discharging contract.

Different from bilateral discharge is unilateral discharge: the latter arises where one party has fully performed their obligations under the contract, and the other party has yet to do so.

Finally, the classification of terms of a contract is important in relation to a breach of a contract because not all breaches give rise to a right to terminate the contract. More in detail, only the breach of a condition, or a sufficiently important intermediate/innominate term, gives rise to a right to terminate the contract.

In this respect, a recent court decision clarified the distinction between (pre-contractual) representations and contractual warranties. To better explain, the former – representations – are pre-contractual statements of fact which allowed the other party to rescind the contract and/or claim damages. The latter may be claimed in the form of reliance interest if the statement was false and induced the other party to sign and enter the contract.

The second one – warranties – is contractual promises: consequently, if breached, the innocent party may claim remedies that are normally available for breach of contract; damages for the performance interest are included too.

In the mentioned court decision, *Veranova v Johnson Matthey*,[21] contractual documents encompassed statement of the facts; in this respect, these documents could be qualified as representations if they are general. Specifically, the Commercial Court dismissed an application of summary determination of whether actionable representation could be found in a draft disclosure letter sent in course of negotiation (M&A transaction). The defendant said that warranties drafts constitute merely contractual promises, thus they are not actionable representations. The position of

20 *Charles Rickards Ltd v Oppenheim* [1950] 1 ALL ER 420.

21 *Veranova BidCo LP v Johnson Matthey PLC and others* [2025] EWHC 707 (Comm), Sean O' Sullivan KC, at para 72.

the defendant was that this principle should be extended to a draft of disclosure letter: its purpose is to provide content to the warranties, not representations.

The claimant, on its side, emphasised that there is no legal principle which would justify a summary dismissal of a misrepresentation claim since the draft disclosure letter could not give rise to actionable representation.

The court held that a draft disclosure letter could also impart information and could form the basis of actionable representations. More precisely,

> it seems to me that there is no "rule" about what can or cannot amount to a representation when parties exchange what are to become contractual documents, save only that agreeing to provide a warranty will not, without more, amount to making a representation of fact . . . In my judgment, there is nothing inherently absurd or implausible about saying that a disclosure letter provides factual information upon which the recipient might reasonably rely, just because its primary contractual function will be to qualify the content of the warranties. If the question is "why are these words here?", it does not seem to me that the only possible answer is "in order to qualify the warranty". I cannot see why, depending on the detailed facts, a disclosure letter cannot have a dual purpose, or a secondary effect.[22]

References

Carter, J.W., Wayne Courtney, and Gregory Tolhurs. 2018. "Two Models for Discharge of a Contract by Repudiation." *The Cambridge Law Journal* 77 (1): 97–123.

English, Jordan. 2025. *Discharge of Contractual Obligations*. Oxford University Press.

22 [2025] EWHC 707 (Comm).

12 Frustration

Chapter Overview

1. Introduction

In the real world of contract law, business organisations often enter into agreements with the expectation that all parties involved will fulfil their respective obligations. However, sometimes, because of unforeseen circumstances, the performance of the contract becomes either impossible or radically different from what was initially envisioned.

In such a scenario, the doctrine of frustration comes into play, because it provides a potential remedy for the parties. Frustration in contract law refers to a situation where an unforeseen event occurs after the formation of a contract.[1] This event renders the contract performance impossible, illegal or fundamentally different from what parties originally agreed. It is critical to stress that frustration applies only in exceptional circumstances: therefore, it does not represent a substitute for breach of contract.

A successful demonstration of frustration requires that the following elements shall exist:

- Supervening event: this event shall occur after the formation of the contract. Furthermore, it is required that it shall be beyond of the control of the parties at that time the contract was made.

1 (Mitchell and Mitchell 2008).

DOI: 10.4324/9781003645948-12

- Beyond control: again, the event or, more precisely, the supervening event shall not be under the control of parties.
- The obligations' nature becomes totally different: this is a consequence of the supervening event.
- The event does not constitute the result of fault or negligence of the parties.

To summarise, under the doctrine of frustration, performance of contractual obligations becomes impossible or radically different.

2. The concept of frustration

In the area of contract law, the general rule is that where a breach of contract materialises, the injured party needs to elect whether to treat the contract as discharge by breach or not. The just described discretion does not arise in the case of discharge by frustration since it terminates automatically all obligations under the contract.

Frustration may be the following:

> Frustration occurs whenever the law recognises that without default of either party a contractual obligation has become incapable of being performed because the circumstances in which performance is called would render it a thing radically different from that which was undertaken by the contract . . . It is not this I promised I would do.[2]

Therefore, the doctrine of frustration may be defined as a remedy in case of change of circumstances. Although this seems to be contradictory with the basic principle which the law of contract and the contractual freedom are informed to, there is a rationale behind this. To understand this, it is vital to explain the legal mechanism underpinning the frustration doctrine.

From a historical perspective, the doctrine of frustration was born in Roman contract law and further implemented for extinguishing obligations of innocent parties where the thing has been destroyed without an act or a default of the debtor.[3] For example, this doctrine was applied if a slave dies before delivery date, a horse dies before it is delivered or a painter or the author of a book dies before the competition of the work.

2 Lord Radcliffe in *Davis Contractors Ltd v Fareham UDC* [1956] AC 696. To summarise, a change in circumstance makes a contract more difficult or more impossible to perform but does not frustrate it. As far as the facts are concerned, a building contractor agreed to build houses for local authority for a fixed fee in eight months. Due to the storage of labour and materials, the costs exceeded the fee, and the project was only completed in 22 months. The building contractor claimed that at some point the contract was frustrated due to the delay and it was entitled to restitution of quantum meruit from that point onwards. The claim was rejected because the contract was not frustrated even with the existence of delays.

3 (Kiley 1960).

From a British perspective, the leading case is *Paradine v Jane*;[4] the rule was that under irrelevant of changes of circumstances parties could never be freed from their contractual obligations. Paradine brought an action against Jane for the rent arrears for the lands that Paradine had leased to Jane; Jane acknowledged that he owed the money for the rent. However, the reason why she did not pay it was because the land was invaded by the enemy of the King: his castle was driven away, and she was expelled from the land. Thus, she, effectively, could not enjoy it.

The final decision of the court, which was against the lessee, was based on three pillars:

- If a party creates a duty or charge upon himself by virtue of a contract, he/she is bound to perform the duty or pay the charge, notwithstanding any accident.
- In the lack of an express covenant, the lessee is equally liable as the rent constitutes an obligation created upon the reservation.
- In the specific case, the lessee was bound to pay rent, even though the house may have been expelled from the land or the land may have been inundated.

The doctrine of frustration was shaped in *Taylor v Caldwell*[5]: the claimant hired out a music hall in Surrey for the purpose of holding four grand concerts. The claimant went through great expenses and made many efforts to organise the concert. A week before the first concert took place, the music hall was destroyed by an accidental fire. The claimant sought to bring an action for breach of contract for failing to refund damages for the expenses incurred.

Under the existing doctrine, that is, the doctrine of absolute obligations, the defendants would be liable to the claimant: under the signed agreement, though, parties would no longer be able to perform their obligations which had been contracted for, that is, the use of music hall for four days. In this specific controversy, the harshness of these contractual obligations did not go unnoticed by the court: consequently, it was held that the defendant was released from their obligations under the doctrine of frustration. The reason was quite simple: the fire destroyed the music hall, and the contract was not doable under the terms agreed by parties. Furthermore, the court highlighted that there was an implied term in the contract, such as the existence of the concert hall at the time of the contract.

To understand the ratio under frustration, *Davis Contractors Ltd v Fareham Urban District Council* shall be recalled.[6] In this specific case the contact was not frustrated since the obligations have become more difficult but not radically different or impossible. Moreover, it is also possible to affirm that this case was decided under the construction approach. The latter imposes an assessment of the changes in light of the context of the contract to assess whether the performance is impossible or radically different.

4 [1647] EWHC KB J5.
5 (1863) 3 B & S 826.
6 It was just described previously.

Finally, a quintessential case is *Maritime National Fish Ltd v Ocean Trawlers Ltd*[7]: it established that foreseeable or self-induced frustration will not render a contract frustrated. Parties contracted for a charter of a fishing ship; then, during the currency of the contract because of a new law passed in Canada, it became unlawful for a ship to use otter trawl, the only equipment available to the ship, without a license. Further, the number of licenses, for the respondent, Ocean Trawlers, were restricted to three, whereas their fleet included four ships. In the election of the three ships, out of four, which needed to be fitted with a licence, Ocean Trawlers did not include the ship which was the subject matter of the charterparty. As a result of this, the owner of the ship claimed that they were no longer bound by the charterparty as it was frustrated by the refusal of the Minister to grant a licence in respect of the steam trawler in question.

It was held that there was no frustration of the charterparty as the absence of a licence since the appellants' choice of vessels, which were to be granted licences. Therefore, the contract remained valid and enforceable.

3. The test of frustration

To understand if a frustration applies to a contract, it is required to ascertain whether the following elements are presented:

- The allocation of the risk of the event.
- The existence of a radical change in obligations.
- The radical change constitutes the consequence of the fault of one party.

As far as the allocation of the risk is concerned, frustration operates only where parties have not themselves allocated the risk of loss between themselves in the contract.

Furthermore, obligations under contract law may change in different ways, for example: non-occurrence of an event, increased expense, destruction of subject matter, illegality, alteration of manner of performance or impossibility by one party, outbreak of war, delay or interruption.

Finally, the third element refers to the fault of one of the parties: if one party is at fault for the frustrating event, it is difficult that the contract is frustrated.

In *The Super Servant Two*[8] it was explained that a frustrating event should be both uncontrollable and an extraneous change of situation: in a nutshell, the frustrating event should be beyond the control of parties. Moreover, if one party is at fault of the frustrating event, although that party may not make a claim for frustration, the innocent party can do so and can be able to claim damages for any loss that resulted from the contract. In this respect an important case is *The*

7 [1935] AC 524.

8 [1990] 1 Lloyd's Rep 1.

Eugenia, Ocean Tramp Tankers Corporation v V/O Sovfracht[9]: the vessel *Eugenia* was lent to a charter for a trip to India via the Black Sea; the *Eugenia* was delivered in Genoa. Based on the agreement signed between parties, the vessel was not to be brought within any zone which is dangerous as a result of any actual or threatened act of war, war hostilities or war-like operations, unless the consent of the owner was obtained.[10] After the negotiation, the agents of two parties realised that Suez Canal might be closed; the problem was that under contract there was not any terms to meet this eventuality. The vessel was delivered in Genoa on 20th September 1956 and sailed off from Odesa to India on 25th October 1956, the customary route being via the Suez Canal. The vessel arrived in a moment when the Egyptian anti-aircraft guns were in action and the zone was regarded as "dangerous" under Clause 21. The vessel entered Suez Canal on 31st October, and the Canal was blocked by the Egyptian government. Thus, the vessel was trapped. The passage was declared northwards at the beginning of 1957, the vessel arrived in Alexandria on 12th January 1957. The charter argued that the charterparty contract was frustrated because of the blocking of the canal.

The decision made by the court may be summarised as follows:

- The essence of the charterparty was that the vessel was placed at the disposal of the charterers, consequently it was under the charterers' orders. The charterer was in breach of the Clause, no. 27, when they ordered the vessel to enter the Suez Canal knowing that there was a war.
- The charterers were in breach of contract.
- The blocking of Suez Canal did not bring a fundamentally different situation to justify a frustration of the contract.

4. The nature of a "frustrating event"

It is not possible to provide a comprehensive list of events that can lead to the frustration of a contract, because it is the effect of the event to frustrate the contract, not the event. The main consequence of this is that the court, in deciding whether a contract has been frustrated, applies a "multifactorial approach".[11]

9 [1964] 2 QB 226.

10 (MacMillan 2014).

11 In this respect the reference goes to *Edwinton v Tsavliris (The Sea Angel)* [2007] EWCA Civ 547. The *Sea Angel* was a vessel used by Tsvaliris to assist in the salvage operations concerning the Tasman Spirit, a tanker loaded with light crude oil, which on 27 July 2003 grounded in or near the approaches of the port of Karachi. On 13 August the Tasman Spirit broke into two, which resulted in a major pollution incident. Tsavaliris entered a contract with the owners of the Tasman Spirit to salvage the causality. The salvage contract encompassed a compensation, protection and indemnity clause. However, it was impossible to return the *Sea Angel* because the authorities in Karachi had refused to issue it with the certificate showing that it did not own any port fees for months. In the end, the *Sea Angel* was returned on 1 January 2004. Tsvaliris did not pay any hire fees for the *Sea Angel* after 18 September 2003. The claimant took legal action to recover the hire fees. The Court of Appeal stated that (1) the purpose of the charter had been performed, and there was no radical or

In this respect, factors that courts should consider are as follows:

- The terms of the contract itself, its matrix or context.
- The parties' knowledge, expectations, assumptions and contemplations.
- The nature of the supervening events.
- Parties' reasonable and objectively ascertainable calculations as to the possibility of the future performance in the new circumstances.

In any case, the quintessential element is that the event has made the contract impossible, illegal or radically different. By contrast, it is not enough that the contract has simply become more difficult or expensive for one party. There are two clear circumstances where a contract shall be frustrated:

- The destruction of subject-matter, that means that something central to the performance of contract no longer exists. Consequently, the court will find that the parties' obligations should come to an end.
- Personal incapacity where parties have agreed that the contract is to be carried out by a particular individual and the latter passes away or is too ill to perform the contract. It is required that the contract shall be done by the individual who is unavailable.[12]

Furthermore, several cases are related to the cancelled coronation of King Edward in 1903. For example, in *Krell v Henry*[13] a room overlooking the route of coronation procession had been hired for the purpose of watching it. When the procession was cancelled, the contract for the hire of the room was held to be frustrated. In *Krell v Henry* it is possible to affirm that the doctrine of frustration of a contract was implied.[14] The doctrine of the frustration was boosted in *North Shore Ventures v Anstead Holdings*.[15]

---

fundamental change in the circumstances to establish frustration; (2) the supervening event came at the very end of the charter, therefore, the effect of the detention on the performance of the charter was purely a question of financial consequences of the delay; (3) the risk of detention was purely on the defendants from Tsavaliris. Moreover, the risk of detention was foreseeable by the salvage industry and provided for in the compensation, protection and indemnity clause.

12 See *Condor v Barron Knights* [1966] 1 WLR 87. A 16-year-old individual agreed by contract to play the drums for the defendant band for seven nights per week for five years. The claimant suffered a mental breakdown and was told by his doctor that he should not perform more than four nights per week. The band dismissed him; thus, he brought a claim for wrongful dismissal. It was held that claimant's action was unsuccessful as his medical conditions made it possible for him to perform his contractual obligation. The conclusion was that the contract was frustrated.

13 [1903] 2 KB 740.

14 See also *Chandler v Webste* [1904], 1 KB 493. Webmaster agreed to rent a room to Chandler so he could witness the king's coronation. Chandler paid for his room based on agreement, but the coronation never took place. Chandler's claim for a refund was rejected by the court.

15 [2010] EWHC 1485 (Ch).

Also relating to coronation celebrations, another case is *Herne Bay Steam Boat Co v Hutton*.[16] In this second case, by contrast, the court held that the contract was not frustrated. More in detail, a boat had been hired to tour the fleet and watch the King's review of it. However, King's illness imposed to cancel the event. The court emphasised that the contract was not frustrated since the tour was still possible; this tour represented a significant element in the contract. Thus, the hirer remained obliged to pay for the use of the boat.

Other events that may lead to the frustration of the contract are the following:

- The war, because in time of war a government may make trading with companies based in enemy territory illegal.[17] For example, the requisitioning of property which had been allocated to a contract may lead to the frustration of that contract.[18] It is important to stress that the frustration need not result direct government action: for example in *Finelvet AG v Vinava Shipping Co Ltd*,[19] the continuing war between Iran and Iraq trapped certain ships in the Gulf for a lengthy period, consequently contracts relating to the charter of these ships were held to be frustrated.
- Reasons of health and safety,[20] as well as listing of building house as architectural and historical interest build may frustrate the contract.[21] Further events that may frustrate a contract are industrial action[22] and accidental running aground of a ship.[23]

16 [1903] 2 KB 683. It constitutes a case that may be encompassed into the main category of "coronation cases".

17 *Fibrosa Spolka Akcyjna v Fairbairn Lawson Combe Barbour Ltd* [1942] UKHL 4, where the main issue was if, under common law and specifically contract law, a restitution was available for benefits conferred prior to termination of the contract by frustration where there was a total failure of consideration. In this respect, it was held that a total failure of consideration is required for restitution.

18 See *Metropolitan Water Board v Dick Kerr* [1918] AC 119. The House of Lords held that the contract was frustrated because the delay clause was intended to cover temporary difficulties and not fundamental changes in the contract's nature.

19 [1983] 1 WLR 1469. In a nutshell, this case involved the court balancing judgment between the length of detention of a vessel, on one hand, and the length of time of the charter as provided in the contract, on the other hand. Because the court did not predict the future, the approach adopted was a "wait-and-see" approach.

20 *Gamerco SA v ICM/Fair Warning Agency* Ltd [1995] 1 WLR 1226. The court stated that the contract was frustrated because it became incapable of performance due to the cancellation of the permit by authority. Although it was an implied term to take all reasonable step to attain the permit, this does not mean that it was an obligation to ensure it remained in force.

21 *Amalgamated Investment and Property Co Ltd v John Walker & Sons Ltd* [1977] 1 WLR. In a nutshell, the court stated that the listed building did not make the contact something radically different from the one contemplated by the parties.

22 See *Pioneer Shipping Ltd v BTP Tioxide Ltd (The Nema)* [1982] AC 724.

23 *Jackson v Union Marine Insurance Co Ltd* (1874) LR 10 CP 125. To summarise, the court held as follows: (1) a breach of contract did not materialise on the part of the charterer because it was excused by the non-availability of the ship, which made the shipment impossible; (2) the delay was not too long for the charterer to make the shipment; (3) there was an implied "condition precedent" that the ship should have arrived in time to pick up the nails.

All these examples constitute evidence that the categories of frustrating events are not close-end. In this respect a special mention shall go to Covid-19 virus and health emergency pandemic. This global event should have frustrated some contracts. In this respect, two are the sectors hinted by these exceptional events: airline industry and commercial property.

As far as airline industry is concerned, there are two main cases:

- *Salam Air SAOC v Latam Airlines Groups SA*[24]: the claimant sought an injunction to restrain the defendant from making demands in relation to underlying leases of three aircraft. The claimant argued that the contract was frustrated due to regulation issued by the Public Authority of Civil Aviation from Oman, which led to a substantial decrease in demand for flying. The court stated that there was not a sufficient basis for frustration; therefore, parties were not exempt from performing their contractual obligations.
- *Wimington Trust SP Services (Dublin) Ltd v Spicejet Ltd*[25]: in this case parties entered into three lease agreements for the provision of aircraft. This lease was a "dry lease": it means that the defendant had assumed the entire risk of the commercial operation for the aircraft for ten years. The defendant failed to make payments as it was significantly curtailed by the Covid-19 pandemic. Thus, two aircrafts were grounded by Indian government. The court held that the lease was not frustrated because the risk of the entire commercial operation was on the part of the defendant.

The case relating to the topic of commercial property is *Bank of New York Mellon (International) Ltd v Cine-UK Ltd.*[26] The tenants argued that their lease of the commercial premises had been "temporarily" frustrated since they were forced to close due to the government's legislation arising from Covid-19 pandemic. This argument was not successful: an 18-month forced closure in the context of 15-year lease does not make contract impossible to perform or radically different from what was originally planned. In a nutshell, it was not recognised as a temporary frustration.

5. The effect of frustration

As far as the consequences of frustration are concerned, there are two rules: one comes from the common law and the other one is encapsulated into Law Reform (Frustrated Contracts) Act 1943. First and foremost, it should be noted that common law rules are applicable even when the act is applicable too.[27]

24 [2020] EWHC 2414.

25 [2021] EWHC 1117.

26 Ibid., 1013.

27 See *Hirji Mulji v Cheong Yeong Steamship Co Ltd* [1926] AC 497 and *The Super Servant Two* [1990]1 Llyod's Rep 1. In *Hirji Mulji v Cheong Yeong Steamship Co Ltd*, it was stressed that: (1) the legal effect of the frustration of a contract does not depend on the intention, opinions or knowledge

The principle under common law is that any loss arising from frustration lies where "it fell": the starting point is that all future obligations are discharged. However, obligations incurred prior to the frustrating events are expected to survive. Further, where the loss depends entirely on what the contract said in advance, then the payment shall be made, or work shall be done according to the terms of the contract.

The Law Reform (Frustrated Contracts) Act 1943, a piece of legislation passed because of the uncertainty of this area, encompasses two elements: the main rule; the relevant exceptions.

The first one, the main rule, is encapsulated into Section 1(2) and Section 1(3). Section 1(2) stipulates as follows:

> All sums paid or payable to any party in pursuance of the contract before the time when the parties were so discharged (in this Act referred to as "the time of discharge") shall, in the case of sums so paid, be recoverable from him as money received by him for the use of the party by whom the sums were paid, and, in the case of sums so payable, cease to be payable.

To better explain, it is possible to affirm that:

- Monies paid are recoverable, despite total failure of consideration.
- Court can award discretionary expenses, based on a just and equitable sum.

Section 1(3) says that:

> Where any party to the contract has . . . obtained a valuable benefit . . . before the time of discharge, there shall be recoverable from him by the said other party such sum (if any), not exceeding the value of the said benefit to the party obtaining it, as the court considers just, having regard to all the circumstances of the case and in particular – the amount of any expenses incurred before the time of discharge by the benefited party in, or for the purposes of, the performance of the contract. . . . and the effect, in relation to the said benefit, of the circumstances giving rise to the frustration of the contract.

Section 1(3) covers a situation where a party has received a benefit, not money, before the frustration; the other party should receive a sum for that thing done. In this case, the court should: (1) identify the valuable benefit; (2) give the benefit a financial value.

of the parties; (2) the frustration of the charterparty brought an end to the whole contract. In *The Super Servant Two*, the court made some important clarifications: (1) a contract was not frustrated when the frustrating event was self-induced by the party; (2) termination of contract by frustration is automatic.

As far as the exceptions are concerned, Law Reform (Frustrated Contracts) Act does not apply to the following contracts:

- Contracts for the carriage of goods by sea.
- Contracts for insurance.
- Contracts for perishable goods.

6. The limitation of the frustration doctrine

The essence of the doctrine of frustration is that the occurred event constitutes a surprise: this justifies the conclusion in force of which the risk of the event occurring has not been allocated by the parties.[28] Thus, the court should intervene.

Bearing this in mind, the principal limitations on the doctrine of frustration are as follows:

- The frustrating event has been foreseen and provided for in the contract, that is, the express provision in the contract.[29]
- The "self-induced" frustration: the principle is that self-induced frustration does not constitute frustration.[30] Self-induced frustration may occur when one party has control over an event which they claim prevents their contractual performance. In this scenario, any non-performance will represent a breach of contract.
- The existence of an alternative performance: if an alternative is possible, then it will not frustrate a contract. It is true even if the alternative is more expensive.
- The performance has become more expensive.[31]

7. Contract law and Covid-19 pandemic

Covid-19, a global pandemic[32] which realised disruption to individual contracts: it is well-known that diseases have the capacity to realise profound change upon law.[33]

28 (Treitel 2014).

29 *Pacific Phosphate Co Ltd v Empire Transport Co Ltd* (1920) 36 T.L.R. 750 (KBD). In this case, a clause giving the parties the option to suspend a 4-year long contract of carriage in the event of a war engaging Great Britain and providing for the adding of any suspended time to the contract upon the termination of the war was found not to preclude the frustration of the contract altogether by the Great War. Despite this, the court stated that the contract was frustrated upon the outbreak of the First World War, because the parties had not contemplated a war on such a long duration and with such dislocating effects.

30 See the just discussed *Maritime National Fish Ltd v Ocean Trawlers Ltd.*

31 See the just discussed *Davis Contractors Ltd v Fareham Urban District Council.*

32 As regards the Covid-19 pandemic, see also Chapter 14, paragraph 8, entitled "Good faith during Covid-19 pandemic".

33 (Palmer 2001).

Based on "frustration test", it is quintessential to consider three main elements to consider whether Covid-19 has frustrated a contract:

- The event must arise without the fault or election of either party.[34]
- There must be such a change in the significance of the obligation undertaken.[35]
- The question is if the foreseen event can be a frustrating event.[36]

During the Covid-19 pandemic, parties affected by the restrictions can perform some contracts and not others; therefore, where a party actively makes such a choice, those contracts not performed are unlikely to be discharged by frustration.

However, in some cases during the Covid-19 pandemic, some contracts have become illegal to perform due to coronavirus legislation. In other words, during lockdown, an enormous number of contracts stand to be discharged through frustration arising from a supervening illegality.[37] Moreover, during the pandemic some contracts were illegal due to a contrast with government guidance, rather than legislation: the former, the guidance, in some cases exceeded the legislative prohibition and could be reinforced in some instances by police action.

A different challenge was when a performance of a contract was not illegal but impracticable, undesirable or purposeless. For instance, in March 2020 businesses selling food for consumption on the premises were required to close. A food distribution company with a contract to sell food to restaurants did not find itself with a contract rendered illegal, but the linked illegality made the performance impracticable.

Under English contract law frustration of purpose was relating to *Krell v Henry* as well as within the problem to identify the fundamental purpose of the contract for determining whether this purpose has become impossible.[38]

It is worth mentioning that English common law does not recognise a defence of force majeure or allow for adjustment or termination of the contract on the grounds of changed circumstances. To elaborate, either the contract encapsulates force majeure clause or, if the circumstance is unforeseen, the legal instrument is frustration notion.

A force majeure clause in a contract stipulates that, if something sufficiently bad happens, and it is not under a party's control, it would be enough to suspend performance. According to Black's Law Dictionary, force majeure is "an event or effect that can be neither anticipated nor controlled; esp., an unexpected event that prevents someone from doing or completing something that he or she had agreed or officially planned to do". From a practical perspective, force majeure provision encompasses a list of events or circumstances that constitutes examples of what

34 *Super Servant Two*.
35 *Davis Contractors v Fareham*.
36 *The Sea Angel*.
37 (Ewing 2020).
38 (MacMillan 2021).

might constitute a force majeure event. In this respect, in *Kel Kim Corp. v Cent. Markets, Inc.*[39] it was said that a party is excused in discharge of its performance only if the force majeure clause specifically includes the event.

A force majeure clause may encapsulate different events, such as the following ones: acts of Good; strikes; lockouts or other industrial disturbances; acts of the public enemy; acts of terror; sabotage, wars; blockades; military actions; insurrections; riots; epidemics; storms or storm warnings; lightening; earthquakes.

To better explain, it is a common understanding that the Covid-19 pandemic had an impact among different sectors: health; business; education, etc. Consequently, the area of contract law was not immune from the pandemic's effects because parties were obliged to renegotiate or litigate their contracts.

Moreover, a contracting party will be able to rely on a force majeure clause to be executed from its obligations where it can establish the following:

- The contract contains a force majeure clause that refers to the relevant event.
- The relevant event has occurred, and it is the sole effective cause of the party's inability to perform its obligations.
- The relevant event was neither foreseeable nor preventable.
- The affected party took reasonable steps to mitigate the effects of the relevant events.
- The affected party notified the other contracting party of the relevant event in accordance with any specific notification requirements.

Finally, if a force majeure clause is inserted into a contract, this signifies that the doctrine of frustration is less likely to apply. This occurs when contracting parties have made express provision for an event that occurs, for example, pandemic and/or act of government. Yet it is also possible that if a contract encompasses a force majeure clause, courts may construct the clause as not covering a specific event. To elaborate, where the force majeure clause is drafted narrowly it is possible to argue that it has not made full and comprehensive provision for what has occurred, and therefore, the doctrine of frustration may become relevant.[40]

The novelty of contract law during pandemic was that public policies were implemented by contractual agreements: the pandemic required parties to change their transaction because of public and health policies recommendations. A further consequence was that also courts were able to redefine their own role. An example of this is *Fu v Note Photography*: a couple planned a wedding and hired a photographer who required a deposit, paid by the couple. However, before the date of the planned wedding, the government restricted the size of the gathering due to Covid-19 spread. The photographer demanded that photographs should be made outside and refused to take photo indoor, as the original agreement prescribed. Thus, the couple sued to return deposit. Based on photographer defence, the court

39 *Kel Kim Corp. v Cent. Markets, Inc.*, 70 N.Y.2d 900, 902–3 (1987).

40 *Bank Line Ltd v Arthur Capel & Co* [1919] AC 435.

had to decide whether government's health and safety guidelines fell in protecting health and safety. In other words, the photographer wanted the court to impose its own public health policy and rewrite the contract.

In the UK, in the aftermath of Covid-19 spread,[41] there was a direct State action that, temporarily, managed the operation of private ordering in the commercial sphere. For example, a landlord's rights to forfeit a business tenancy for non-payment of rent was suspended by statute.

Moreover, a code of practice was passed to ensure negotiations between commercial landlords and tenants were informed to ethical principles going beyond the terms of the agreements of this kind. The focus was on rent payments and arrears: it required parties to act "reasonably, swiftly, transparently and in good faith". The purpose of this was to identify mutual solutions. In a nutshell, parties were under a moral obligation to "do everything reasonable to enable otherwise viable businesses to continue operating through the period of recovery". This represented, in other words, an expectation of honest communication between parties as well as information disclosure.

On 7th May 2020 Government passed "Guidance on Responsible Contractual Behaviour" where it was encouraged a "responsible and fair performance and enforcement of contracts during [the] public health emergency". In this respect, the suggestion was to act

> reasonable and proportionate in responding to performance issues and enforcing contracts (including dealing with any disputes) acting in a spirit of co-operation and aiming to achieve practical, just and equitable contractual outcomes having regard to the impact on the other party . . . the availability of financial resources, the protection of public health and the national interest.

One of the characteristics of the UK approach during Covid-19 pandemic was a proliferation of pandemic codes and guidance on reasonable conduct. The underlying reasons were multifarious:

- The impossibility of comprehending the agreement outside of social and economic context.
- The importance of cooperation.
- The expectation of readjustment and renegotiation of contractual agreement.

One critical topic consists in the qualification of Covid-19 under contract law "language". The question is if Covid-19 was related to "force majeure clause" or to Act of God. It is worthy to stress that the word "pandemic" does not present under the concept of "force majeure": more in detail, it encompasses the term "epidemic".

41 Keith Markham, *COVID-19, Force Majeure and Frustration of Contracts. The Essential Guide* (Law Brief Publishing, 2020).

Accordingly, Covid-19 shall be qualified as force majeure clause if a link with government laws shall be found. Therefore, if a State orders people to stay at home and businesses cease operations, these events constitute force majeure for the entire length of the order.

Relating to force majeure clause, there are two court decisions. The first one is *Football Association Premier League Limited v PPLive Sports International Limited.* In this decision, it was stated that although there were significant changes to scheduled matches, these did not constitute "fundamental change" to the format of the competition. Thus, even with the existence of Covid-19 pandemic, the application of force majeure clause followed the usual principles relating to contractual interpretation.

By contrast, in *European Professional Club Rugby v RDA Television LLP*, the court recognised that Covid-19 constituted a force majeure event. In this specific case, indeed, the contract signed between parties stipulated that a force majeure event was "any circumstances beyond the reasonable control of a party affecting the performance by that party of its obligations under this Agreement including . . . Epidemic".

As far as Act of God is concerned, the question is if Covid-19 pandemic shall be viewed as a natural disaster, such as hurricanes. The most problematic aspect is that Act of God has been considered only on few occasions by the English courts. According to these limited applications, it is possible to affirm that Act of God includes storms, flooding and lightning and heavy snowfall. Moreover, Act of God should possess the following characteristics:

- Exclusively the consequences of natural causes.[42]
- Extraordinary or overwhelming.
- Cannot be anticipated or provided against.

Where Covid-19 pandemic is concerned, two additional elements should be considered. The first one is termination clauses and the second one is good faith.

Commencing with the first, if a contract encompasses a termination clause which may allow either party to terminate subject to a period of notice. This signifies that during Covid-19, if a party considers that the contract should not continue, the first option is to adopt this clause. In doing so, not only are frustration and force majeure clauses avoided, but also it represents a non-contentious solution.

As far as good faith is concerned, despite being established that English contract law does not recognise an implied duty of good faith in all contracts, such duty could be implied in certain contracts, such as necessary for business efficacy and relational contracts.[43]

42 *Nugent v Smith* [1876] 1 C.P.D. 423.

43 *Yam Seng PTE Ltd v International Trade Corporation Ltd* [2013] EWHC 111 (QB) (1st February 2013).

References

Ewing, Keith D. 2020. "Covid-19: Government by Decree." *King's Law Journal* 31 (1): 1–24.
Kiley, Roger. 1960. "The Doctrine of 'Frustration'." *American Bar Association Journal* 46 (12): 1292–94.
MacMillan, Catharine. 2014. "English Contract Law and the Great War: The Development of a Doctrine of Frustration." *Comparative Legal History* 2 (2): 278–302.
MacMillan, Catharine. 2021. "Covid-19 and the Problem of Frustrated Contracts." *King's Law Journal* 32 (1): 60–70.
Mitchell, Charles, and Paul Mitchell. 2008. *Landmark Cases in the Law of Contract*. Hart.
Palmer, Robert. 2001. *English Law in the Age of the Black Death 1348–1381*. University of North Carolina Press.
Treitel, Guenter. 2014. *Frustration and Force Majeure*. Sweet & Maxwell.

13 Illegality in contract law

Chapter Overview

1. Introduction

A contract shall be affected by illegality, in connection with different circumstances: if it is concluded to commit a legal wrong; to promote immoral values and/or goals; if it is performed illegality and where it does not comply with the procedure prescribed by statute. To elaborate, making a contract is prohibited under the following circumstances:

- If an express statutory prohibition exists.
- If there is an implied statutory prohibition.
- If the goal of the agreement is to commit a crime.
- If the agreement is contrary to the public policy.

Furthermore, a contract may be statutory illegal or common law illegal. Moreover, another distinction occurs between contracts that are illegal at the time they are formed, on one hand, and contracts that are illegal at the time of their performance, on the other hand. The latter, the contract illegal as performed, is a legal contract, but the performance does not comply with legal rules.

DOI: 10.4324/9781003645948-13

The general rule should be that courts will not enforce a contract which involves an illegality. Despite this, in some cases, a policy-based approach to each case has been proposed, for example:[1]

- To deter parties from such conduct.
- To prevent parties from benefiting from their own wrong.
- To punish wrongdoers.
- To preserve the dignity of the court and integrity of legal system.
- For reasons of public policy.

In more recent *dicta*, British courts have taken the opportunity to review this area of law. As a result of the latest decisions, two main and distinct approaches have emerged.[2]

The first one is focused on the importance to adopt a policy-driven scheme to each individual case.

By contrast, courts have emphasised the importance of adopting a "clear cut test" of enforceability.

2. *Petel v Mirza* and its development

In the area of illegality, the leading case is *Patel v Mirza*[3]: Petel paid £620,000 to Mirza to gamble on the movement of shares in a bank based on inside information. This agreement amounted to a conspiracy to commit the offence of insider dealing in contrast with Section 53, Criminal Justice Act 1993. Patel tried to reclaim his money from Mirza.

Mirza sought to argue that the monies should not be returned to Patel on resulting trust, because Patel would have to rely on his own unlawful conduct to establish his interest in monies. Patel argued that the illegal act had not become effective, and there was no justification to allow Mirza' unjust enrichment to persist. Further, he argued that it would be unjust to allow one co-conspirator to keep all monies.[4] Allowing Mirza to keep the monies would positively encourage the commission of such offences, since he had profited from encouraging the commission of such offences, so deterrence as a policy argument in this context is problematic. All judges agreed that Patel was entitled to see his money duly returned: the majority of the judges affirmed this, on the basis that the enforcement of Patel's claim would

1 In this respect, see *ParkingEye Ltd v Somerfield Stores Ltd* [2012] EWCA Civ 1338. The court found that the application of illegality principle was "unduly sanctimonious" or not proportionate.

2 (Gloag 1929).

3 [2016] 3 WLR 399.

4 In this respect, the reference goes to *Tinsley v Milligan* [1994] 1 AC 340. This is a leading case in English contract law relating to the presumption of advancement and illegality. Scholars criticised this decision due to its creating results. More in detail, the House of Lords rejected the application of a public policy test for illegality defence in the context of resulting trusts and stuck with the old "reliance test". Despite this, the public policy test was adopted by the Supreme Courts in different cases.

not undermine the integrity of the legal system, whereas a minority of the court suggested the "narrower rule-based approach".

The UK Supreme Court dismissed Mr Mirza' s appeal: it recognised that Mr Patel could recover the money he had paid to Mr Mirza.

For the sake of completeness of analysis, it is worth noting that the formal test shaped in *Tinsley v Milligan* should not represent the actual law. To elaborate, the court stressed that the "*Tinsley* test" is not consistent with the concept of coherence and integrity of the legal system. Thus, different factors should be considered to establish if the public interest is harmed by the enforcement of the illegal agreement. These elements are as follows:

- The purpose of the prohibition which has been transgressed and whether the purpose would be enhanced by the denial of the claim.
- Any relevant public policy on which the denial of the claim may have an impact.
- Whether the denial of the claim would be a proportionate response to the illegality bearing in mind that punishment is a matter of the criminal courts.

The rule shaped in *Patel v Mirza* was applied in *Stoffel & Co. v Grondona*[5]: In the latter, the court found that a negligent solicitor could not invoke the illegality defence, even if the negligent advice arose whilst assisting a client in a fraudulent transaction by client.[6]

To better explain, while in *Patel v Mirza* the Supreme Court established new rules around illegality in tort law, in *Stoffel & Co. v Grondona,* these rules were restarted, confirmed and applied. More in depth, this new approach in "*Stoffel*" can be explained as follows.

From the court perspective, denial of the claim – the civil remedy against the solicitor for their negligence in failing to register the transfer – would not guarantee the protection afforded by the law in mortgages. Further consideration dealt with standards of diligence which solicitors are required to comply with.

Finally, it was said that it was not necessary to consider the proportionality[7]: tit is only to be considered if the defence is still in issue after analysing the first two limbs.

Finally, "*Stoffel*" can be summarised according to three main pillars:

- The main justification is avoiding inconsistencies damaging to the law.
- The prevention of profiting from one's own wrongdoing is merely a peripheral consideration.
- Professional standards are persuasive arguments but are secondary to the core ground of legal incoherence.

5 [2020] UKSC 42.
6 (Green and Bogg 2018).
7 (Tan 2020).

3. Statutory illegality

In cases where a contract is illegal, it is void *ab initio*, since the beginning. This harsh position is due to the consideration that the illegality has been present since the outset of the contract. For instance, a statute may expressly prohibit certain contracts. As a result, where the contract is void, the issue is whether a party, who is innocent because he/she is not responsible for any wrongdoing, can recover a benefit conferred by the contract. This constitutes a controversial issue.[8]

In *Re Mahmoud & Ispahani*,[9] the court held that the contract should be enforced, due to the statutory provisions. To elaborate, this is a statutory implied prohibition. In this specific case, the statute prohibited unlicenced dealing in linseed oil. To determine if an implied provision is operable, the court shall ascertain the objective achieved by legislation.

There are two rules:

- The contract is not illegal itself, where the sole object of the statute is to increase national revenue. This rule refers to statutes which require individuals to have a license to trade in a particular area or with goods. An example is constituted by fishing licence or license to sell tobacco.[10]
- An analysis relating to the aim of the statute is required. This concept may be explained through a question, more specifically: "Does the statute contemplate that the prohibited act will be done in the performance of a contract?"

The second case is *Mohamed v Alaga & Co (A Firm)*[11]: the Court of Appeal held that, although the legislation prohibited any contract aimed to introduce refugees, it was possible to recover a *quantum meruit* basis for the translation services provided in relation to the refugees. These services, translation services, were not covered by the legislation, nor in force of public policy rules, because they would not be offended by allowing such recovery.

From a different perspective, a contract may be illegal in its performance. The reference goes to *St John Shipping Corporation v Joseph Rank Ltd.*[12] The defendant argued that, as it was legally performed, the plaintiffs could not enforce rights that resulted from their own crime. Further, the contract could not be sued upon. It was

8 (Zimmermann 1996).

9 [1921] 2 KB 716. In this case, the purchaser of the oil claimed that he had a license to purchase the oil, but in fact he did not it. When the seller delivered the oil, the purchased refused delivery. He explained that he did not actually have a license. The contract could not be enforced due to a statutory provision, even if the seller of the oil was completely innocent.

10 See *Smith v Mawhood* (1845) 14 M & W 452.

11 [1999] EWCA Civ J0630-9.

12 [1957] 1 QB 267. St John Shipping Corporation owned a ship that was expected to sail from a port in the US to the UK. Mr Rank held a bill of lading in respect of some of the ship's cargo. Whilst the ship was in the US, the charterers took on additional cargo, which overloaded the ship. On arrival in the UK, the master was prosecuted and fined.

held that performing an illegal contract did not render the contract illegal unless the statute meant to prohibit that contract.

In addition, in *Parkingeye Ltd v Somerfield Stores Ltd*,[13] it was held that, where a claimant's contractual performance could have been carried out lawfully, illegality would not have constituted a defence against the claim.

Finally, in some cases, the Parliament declared that a certain type of contract is void. It may also provide that no action can be brought to recover a benefit derived from such void contract. For example, Section 4(1), Marine Insurance Act 1906, stipulates as follows: "Every contract of marine insurance by way of gaming or wagering is void". Statutes may also provide that the performance, or certain mode of performance, is illegal.

4. Common law illegality

In some circumstances, the illegality arises from a common law prohibition. Under common laws, it is possible to see two different situations:

- The commission of a legal wrong.
- Contracts contrary to public policy.

The second category may be problematic because public policy represents a concept with a changing nature.

Indeed, public policy encompasses the following:

- Morality.
- Illegality.
- Public morals customs.
- Contracts out of the jurisdiction of the court.
- The restriction of a trade.[14]

Public policy has the effect to rend contract void and not illegal: an illegal term in agreement taints the whole contract and including, also, collateral transaction. By contrast, a void term does not have this effect.

5. The effect of illegality

To ascertain whether illegality has occurred is a difficult and complex activity. The underlying reason is that there is not a single form of illegality. Additionally,

13 [2012] EWCA Civ 1338.

14 This is considered in two contexts: (1) employment law; (2) where a business is sold and the purchaser seeks an undertaking from the vendor not to compete with him. In the two cases there are two opposite different interests: (1) the interest of employer and the businessman, on one side; (2) the public policy, on the other side. Further, in this specific matter there are statutory controls upon anti-competitive agreements, as well as the control delivered by regulatory authorities.

illegality seems to have a strange – and not usual – effect upon contracts,[15] because the contract is not without any effect. As a result of this, the better way to explain the effect of illegality is to affirm that an illegal contract is unenforceable rather than void for illegality.

Coherently to this is the fact that property may pass under an illegal contract. By contrast, if a contract is void due to a mistake of identity, ownership does not pass to the buyer, even by delivery.

For example, in *Singh v Ali*,[16] the principle established was that, if two persons are involved with an illegal transaction, one of them can enforce his rights under such transaction if he/she is able to show that he/she was unaware of illegality. To elaborate, a party can escape liability by the proof that he/she is not in *pari delicto* with the other party.

In this respect, Lord Denning emphasised as follows:

> Although the transaction between the plaintiff and the defendant was illegal, nevertheless it was fully executed and carried out: and on that account it was effective to pass the property in the lorry to the plaintiff . . . The reason is because the transferor, having fully achieved his unworthy end, cannot be allowed to turn round and repudiate the means by which he did it – he cannot throw over the transfer, and the transferee, having obtained the property, can assert his title to it against all the world, not because he has any merit of his own, but because there is no one who can assert a better title to it.

The court did not confiscate the property because of the illegality as it had no power to do so; therefore, in the words of Lord Eldon: "Let the estate lie where it falls".

Although an illegal contract is not enforceable, a claimant may have also the interest to bring a different claim to obtain redress from a defendant. In this respect, it is also well-known that, if the contract is void for illegality, the claimant should not be able to succeed simply by pleading the same facts as the basis for an estop pel or a tort. Nevertheless, the winner strategy may be represented by a claim in unjust enrichment.

Nevertheless, the complexity of illegality leads to the conclusion in force of which restitutionary claim constitutes a safety net. In this respect, there are, at least, two opposite sides of the coin.

The first one is *Parkinson v College of Ambulance Ltd*.[17] The claimant said that he was entitled to reclaim money he had paid as he had been induced by fraud to enter the contract. It was stated that this was not possible, because the agreement was not a contract but a donation. The latter was only a gift which was irrecoverable, once it was made. Further, the agreement signed between parties was improper and illegal because it achieved the purchase of an honorary public title.

15 (Burrows 2016).
16 [1960] 1 MLJ 52.
17 [1925] 2 KB 1.

The second case is *Patel v Mirza*. This case placed a great emphasis on the availability of restitution and restoring the parties to *status quo ante*.

To summarise, the best approach seems to be more appropriate to deter illegal activities. From a general perspective, restitution should be available through a claim of unjust enrichment.[18] Illegality itself may justify the practical response of the courts to put parties back on their original position before the illegal transaction. This approach shall resolve that the initial difficulties relating to property transferred under an illegal contract can be recovered.[19]

Also, in property law, if a party seeks to withdraw from an illegal transaction within the "locus poenitentiae" or time to repentance, that party can rely upon evidence of the illegal scheme to recover property transferred pursuant to that scheme.

6. Illegality in Scots law

Due to English influence, modern Scots law describes the main effect of illegality of a contract as unenforceable.[20]

The leading case in Scots law is *Cuthbertson v Lowes* ("*Cuthbertson*").[21] The legislation at that time declared contracts for the sale of produce where the price was determined with reference to Scots acre (opposed to the Imperial acre) to be null and void. The pursuer had sold and delivered potatoes to the defender with reference to the Scots acre. The defender refused to pay, arguing the illegal nature of the contract. The court stated that the contract could not be enforceable, yet the pursuer was entitled to recover the market value of the potatoes. Illegal contract was not basis for awarding the market value of the potatoes to the pursuer. In this respect, two main elements are worth mentioning: (1) the lack of turpitude or immorality involved in the selling potatoes; (2) it would be equitable for the defender to retain potatoes without accounting for their value.

A further important case is *Jamieson v Watt's Trustees* ("*Jamieson*"):[22] the wartime legislation required that licences be obtained to perform certain building works. The pursuer worked as a joiner and had a licence to perform work to the value of £40. Nevertheless, in violation of the legislation, he performed work for the defender to the value of £114. Once the defender refused to pay the balance of the unauthorised work, the pursuer sought to claim the money by relying on

18 If a claimant has paid money over to the defendant and received nothing in return, or provided services for nothing in return, then the claimant sues the defendant for restitution of the money paid or services rendered. This constitutes unjust enrichment.

19 For example, in *Bowmakers Ltd v Barnet Instruments Ltd* [1945] KB 65, it was held that the claimant did not plead the illegal agreement in making their claim. By contrast, the claim was based on their ownership of the machine. As a result of this, they did not need to rely on their illegality to succeed in the claim.

20 *Malik v Ali* 2004 SLT 1280.

21 (1870) 8 M 1073.

22 1950 SC 265.

"*Cuthbertson*". The court dismissed the claim by holding that "*Cuthbertson*" constituted a unique case confined to its circumstances. To elaborate, in "*Cuthbertson*" the effect of the statute was to render the contract void; by contrast, in Jamie it rendered the contract illegal. Furthermore, "Cuthbertson" fell under the case in which the law will not allow to operate, but "Jamieson" fell under the umbrella of the case in which contracts are contrary to law. To elucidate, the degree of illegality is different in the two cases: in "Cuthbertson" there was little to no turpitude in the transaction; in "Jamieson" there was a serious contravention of the law.[23]

The last important case is *Dowling & Rutter v Abacus Frozen Foods Ltd* ("*Dowling*"):[24] it was about a contract in terms of which the pursuers supplied workers to be employed at the defenders' fish processing factory. These workers were foreigners who did not have the necessary work permits required by immigration law. The defenders refused to pay for the labour on the basis that the pursuers performed their side of the contract unlawfully by supplying the unauthorised labourers. Therefore, as per Lord Johnston's words,

> [T]he issue is essentially one of equitable remedy in the sense that a person who is seeking to rely knowingly on his own illegal act cannot gain by it but equally should not lose by it if the illegal act is committed by somebody else completely out with his own knowledge, actual or constructive.[25]

It was held that it would have been inequitable to deny pursuers the right to sue upon an otherwise perfectly legal bargain. The critical element was that the pursuers were unaware of the illegality, and the contract was not prohibited, but it was performed in an illegal manner.

To conclude, while *Patel v Mirza* is not a Scottish case, it is very influential in any future Scottish case involving illegality.[26] The reason for that is simple: in the past Scottish courts have often taken English case law into account when deciding disputes pertaining to illegal contracts.[27]

References

Burrows, Andrew. 2016. *Restatement of the English Law of Contract*. Oxford University Press.

Gloag, William M. 1929. *The Law of Contract: A Treatise on the Principles of Contract in the Law of Scotland*. W Green & Son Ltd.

Green, Sarah, and Alan Bogg. 2018. *Illegality After Patel v Mirza*. Hart Publishing.

23 (Macgregor 2000).
24 2002 SLT 491.
25 2002 SLT 491 para 20.
26 *Ezike & Macleod* (2018) ERPL 281. Among Authorities, see *D Geddes (Contractors) Ltd v Neil Johnson Health & Safety Services Ltd* [2017] CSOH 42.
27 The reference goes to *Jamieson v Watt's Trustees* 1950 SC 265 271. Among Scholars, see (MacQueen and Thomson 2020).

Macgregor, Laura J. 2000. "Pacta Illicita." In *A History of Private Law in Scotland*, edited by Kenneth G.C. Reid and Reinhard Zimmermann, 129–56. Oxford University Press.
MacQueen, H.L., and J. Thomson. 2020. *Contract Law in Scotland*. Edinburgh: Bloomsbury Professional.
Tan, Zhong Xing. 2020. "The Proportionality Puzzle in Contract Law: A Challenge for Private Law Theory?" *Canadian Journal of Law & Jurisprudence* 33 (1): 215–44.
Zimmermann, Reid. 1996. *The Law of Obligations: Roman Foundations of the Civilian Tradition*. Oxford University Press.

14 Good faith

Chapter Overview

1. Introduction

The golden rule relating to good faith is that, traditionally, English law has always been very cautious to adopt an overriding principle of good faith.[1] Despite this, English legal system has shaped and developed alternative solutions to respond to problems of unfairness.

These solutions include different topics, such as the following:

- Vitiating factors.
- Equitable doctrine, for example promissory estoppel, repudiation and rules against penalty.

The English hostility to good faith may originate from different circumstances and scenarios:[2]

1 (de Gioia Carabellese 2023).

2 *Yam Senge Pte Ltd v International Trade Corporation Ltd* [2013] EWHC 111 (QB).

DOI: 10.4324/9781003645948-14

- The traditional legal approach in England and Wales is based on a case-by-case approach: English common law prefers to develop a "bottom-up" methodology, rather than a "top-down" one. The latter tends to apply an abstract principle to a particular case.
- English law prefers to find solutions where there is a demonstrated problem of unfairness.[3]
- The ethos English law is endowed with a principle of individualism: parties are free to achieve their own interests in both negotiating contract and performing them.
- A principle of good faith may engender too much uncertainty, since the content of obligations may become too vague and subjective.

Through the lens of legal theory, good faith represents a notion linked with public law/constitutional law: freedom of contract is built upon private autonomy. To illustrate, freedom of contract signifies that a person is free to decide whether and with whom and under which conditions he/she enters a contract. More in detail, freedom of contract relates to personal liberty and the right of self-determination.[4]

From a comparative law perspective, this seems to be peculiar. For example, Roman law required parties to act in good conscience in fulfilling their obligations. This was under the expression "*obligatio ex fide bona*", such as obligations to act in good faith. To elaborate, the state of the art, beyond the UK and English common law, may be summarised as follows:

- Civil law jurisdictions highlight the importance that parties act in good faith. In this respect, both Italian and Germany civil codes are adamant that this obligation constitute general principle of law.[5]
- The US Restatement (Second) of Contracts stipulates as follows: "Every contract imposes upon each party a duty of good faith and fair dealing in its performance and enforcement".
- From a European perspective, Articles 1:201 Principles of European Contract Law stipulates as follows: "Each party must act in accordance with good faith and fair dealing, and this duty cannot be excluded".

2. Good faith: a definition

One of the reasons why there is an English scepticism towards the concept of good faith is because such notion is deemed a vague and abstract concept. It is not a coincidence that to provide a definition of this legal notion is an arduous activity because of the degree of nebulosity surrounding this expression. There is no doubt

3 *R (European Rome Rights Center and others) v Immigration Officer at Prague Airport* [2004] UKHL 55, [2005] 2 AC 1 [59].

4 (Bebchuk 1989).

5 See Article 1137 Italian Civil Code as well as Para 242 German Civil Code.

that good faith was coined with the intention "not only to condemn deception and lack of candour at the time of bargain is concluded but also to require a forthcoming attitude, to condemn chickaree and sharp practise in the carrying out of contractual obligations".[6] Yet in the last years, although good faith does not have citizenship in common law, it has gained its reputation in the area of commercial law.

As per Bingham J's words, good faith

> does not mean that they should not deceive each other, a principle which any legal system must recognise; its effect is perhaps most aptly conveyed by such metaphorical colloquialism as "playing fair", "coming clear" or "putting one's cards face upwards on the table". It is in essence a principle of fair and open dealing.[7]

Nevertheless, good faith may take different meanings, such as the following:

- A party shall not act dishonestly.
- A party has a duty to act in a commercially acceptable way and not in an unconscionable one.
- A party shall consider relevant consideration whilst taking a decision.
- Each party is under a duty to communicate the relevant facts.
- A party does not act dishonestly.
- A party shall act or not act in a particular way depending on the context in which the duty arises.

Furthermore, a good faith test has been shaped and aimed to ascertain whether, contexts, the conduct would be regarded as commercially unacceptable by a reasonable and honest person. This test should be objective; however, good faith remains a difficult idea to understand because the relevant standard, which includes the fair dealing,

> should be understood as comprising a spectrum of norms. At its narrowest end, good faith merely requires honestly in fact . . . At the other hand of the spectrum of good faith, it edges close to fiduciary duties by requiring performance of the contract that takes the interest of the other party into account.[8]

To summarise, good faith shall be understood and interpreted "in context", therefore as a normal aspect of contractual interpretation. According to this line of reasoning, good faith may be accepted as a term of a contract signed by parties. Good faith may be moulded by the parties to an agreement to ensure that it does enjoy an autonomous meaning. However, in cases where there is a lack of

6 (Burrow 1968).
7 *Interfoto Picture Library Ltd v Stiletto Visual Programmes Ltd* [1989] QB 439.
8 (Hugh 2014).

agreement, because parties are still negotiating, good faith does not constitute a helpful, as well as certain and clear, yardstick.

3. The "perimeter" of good faith

Good faith in English common law constitutes a shadow concept which implies specific contexts where parties act. Consequently, it is quintessential to draw the relevant perimeter which otherwise would be evanescent. Based on the latest case law, it is possible to define the specific area where the principle of good faith operates. In this respect, there are two expressions to adopt: implied duties; expressed duties of good faith.

As far as the first one is concerned, a general understanding is that duties of good faith are implied in every relational contract.

As regards the duties, these may be identified by reference to nine indicators. These indicators are not exhaustive and are the following:[9]

- There shall not be a specific express term in the contract that prevents a duty of good faith being implied into the contract.
- The contract will be a long-term one, with the mutual intention of the parties being that there will be a long-term relationship.
- Parties need to intend that their respective roles be performed with integrity and with fidelity to their bargain.
- Parties will be committed to collaborating with one another in the performance of the contract.
- The spirit and objectives of the parties' venture may not be capable of being expressed exhaustively in a written contract.
- The parties will each repose trust and confidence in one another, but of a different kind to that involved in fiduciary relationships.
- The contract in question will involve a high degree of communication, cooperation and predictable performance based on mutual trust and confidence as well as expectation of loyalty.
- There may be a degree of significant investment by one party, or both, in the venture.
- The relationship shall be exclusive.

9 These indicators were shaped in *Bates v Post Office Ltd* [2019] EWHC 606 (QB). There were various claims against the Post Office and claimants which amounted to around 550. Before 2011, sub-postmasters (henceforth SPMs) contracted with Post Office a new contract, based on which the Network Transformation Contract (NTC), the one signed between Post Office and a major service provider, based in Japan, was introduced. Post Office introduced a computerised electronic point of sale and accounting system, named Horizon. Based on the new agreements in place with Post Office, each SPM would become responsible for losses caused by negligence on the part of the SPM or his or her personnel, including those of the new system, Horizon. It became immediately clear that the latter system was affected by shortfalls and discrepancies in the accounting of different branches of the Post Office. Some claimants paid these shortfalls; other claimants were convicted before criminal courts for false accounting fraud and other offences. The court stated that SPMC and NTC were relational contracts; thus, a duty of good faith could be implied in these contracts.

In a nutshell, a good faith obligation is implied not only in the relational contracts but in restricted circumstances.[10]

By contrast, English courts adopt a precautionary *modus operandi* aimed to recognise an express duty of good faith. An example of this is *Faulkner v Vollin Holdings Ltd*[11]: the Court of Appeal was sceptical about interpreting the express duties of good faith. Furthermore, the court stressed the importance of being aware of rules based on formulas: the best "tactic" is to analyse in detail the specific situation and context where good faith clause, initially, was negotiated. To elaborate, "formulaic principles", or principles based on formulas, such as "acting honestly", "fair and open dealing", "fidelity of parties", might refrain courts from examining the context where a specific good faith clause has been introduced. In other words, it is not a duty of the court to enforce an absolute duty of honesty and/or find dishonesty conclusive. By contrast, an in-depth analysis of the original purpose of the contact and the surrounding circumstances shall suffice.

Finally, it is also worth describing *Phones 4U Ltd (In Administration) v EE Ltd and others*.[12] The court held that an agreement was not a relational contract; therefore, EE was not under a general duty to act in good faith. Indeed, EE had informed P4U that they would not be extending their trading agreement. Consequently, P4U claimed that EE intended to force P4U into administration by terminating the agreement a year before it was due to end, avoiding further payments. P4U argued that:

- The agreement was relational in nature.
- EE was under an implied general duty to act in good faith in relation to the performance of its obligation under the contract.

The court held that this agreement was not a relational contract, therefore there was not a general duty to act in good faith. Further, the court emphasised that the agreement was a professionally drafted as well as a very full contract between sophisticated parties. Consequently, if parties intended to impose a general obligation of good faith, they would have done it in an express way.

Finally, this agreement did not constitute a relational contract: although this contract was a long-term contract and involved collaboration, it has also some

10 This was confirmed also in *Candey Ltd v Bosheh* [2022] EWCA Civ 1103. This case is related to proceedings brought by a firm of solicitors for breach of retainer against its former clients for procuring breach of the retainer and/or unlawful conspiracy. The Court of Appeal analysed the following issues: (1) whether a client was in breach of an implied duty of good faith by settling underlying litigation on terms which meant the solicitor had no entitlement to their costs under a Conditional Free Agreement; (2) whether the solicitors could rely on privileged documents in support of their claims; (3) whether the solicitors could rely on confidential documents which had been provided to them by a third party after the underlying proceedings have settled.

11 [2022] EWCA Civ 1371.

12 [2023] EWHC 2826 (Ch).

differences from the standard of relational contracts. EE, indeed, was not only enabling P4U to supply connections to its network but was in competition with the retailer to supply the connections to customers directly. Therefore, for EE it was natural to reduce its reliance on indirect retailers and instead expand its direct retailing business.

4. The concept of relational contract

Previously, we have just discussed the concept of good faith in the relational contract; therefore, the need to provide a brief definition of these kinds of contracts.

It is possible to say that the adjective "relational" as an opposite expression of "discrete contract". The latter means contracts where one-off transactions shall be made between parties who are not known to one another. By contrast, more contracts are signed between parties who have been known to each other; consequently, their relationship has a value to them and their mutual obligations. One of the main consequences of relational contracts is that it is arduous to define the exact moment when the contract was formed. Further, it is also possible that multiple contracts were signed.

An example of relational contracts is business relationship characterised by an overlap of contract and economic areas. These contracts better explain why parties often do not respect contractual terms because the most important "value" is to maintain good relations.

Bearing this in mind, relational contracts are based on some features:

- They are based on a relationship of trust.
- They establish a partnership mentality and set mutual goals.
- They are ideally for long-term business relationships.

Relational contracts constitute a concept established also in English common law as well as in these contracts a duty of good faith is implied. The latter, that is, the implied duty of good faith, encompasses further elements, such as the following:

- Transparency.
- Trust and confidence.
- Cooperation.

Furthermore, the duty of good faith goes beyond an obligation to act honestly since it requires that parties act as honest people in commercial contracts.

If a contract is relational, the contract depends upon the factual circumstances; nevertheless, courts provided a list of non-exhaustive characteristics that may be relevant. These characteristics are as follows:

- A mutual intention for the long-term relationship.
- An intention for the parties' roles to be performed under integrity, fidelity, confidence and trust.

- A commitment of collaboration.
- The exclusivity of relationships.
- A high level of communication, co-operation.
- Performance is based on mutual expectations of loyalty.

Moreover, other elements are not relevant, for example: the balance power of parties; the presence of onerous terms; bad behaviour by a party, if the contract is a business-to-business contract (B2B).

5. From good faith to duty of rationality

A further angle of perspective of good faith is the duty of rationality: it represents an implied obligation, in the absence of clear language to the contrary, to exercise a contractual discretion in good faith and not arbitrarily or capriciously. Generally, this means that the discretion must be exercised consistently with its contractual purpose.

After the case *Braganza v BP Shipping Ltd*,[13] the duty of rationality is also named "Braganza duty". It constitutes an exception to the general rule of English law that rights are enforceable regardless of whether they are exercised in a reasonable or unreasonable way.

The burning issues in *Braganza v BP Shipping Ltd* were two: (1) which principles governed the exercise of the contractual power; (2) what is the general approach that court ought to adopt when this principle should be applied.

Braganza v BP Shipping Ltd constitutes a landmark case in English common law for different reasons:

- The interconnection between administrative law review and contractual law review: in "*Braganza*" was adopted the scrutiny test based on reasonableness and proportionality principles.
- Both in administrative and contractual law existed implied terms: in the first case the term is implied into law; in the second case the term is implied into agreement signed between parties.
- The review of a contract (whether in-depth or ordinary) is linked with the contract signed between parties: for example, in case of a contract of employment, the review shall be more intensive and in-depth, given the implication of fundamental rights of vulnerable parties, such as employees.

13 [2015] UKSC 17. Mr Braganza and his employer, BP Shipping Ltd signed a contract. Mr Braganza was an engineer of one of BP's vessels; one evening, when the vessel was in the North Atlantic, Mr Braganza disappeared, and it was presumed drowned. According to the contract, Mr Braganza's widow would be entitled to a death benefit, except that it would not be payable. The exception would be relating to the fact that the death resulted from Braganza's own wilful act. As a result of investigation, the conclusion was that the cause of death was suicide, therefore death benefits were not payable. The court held that the conclusion in force of which suicide was the cause of death was not supported on evidence.

- The role of a reviewing court shall be an examination role of the decision-making process than substance.[14]
- The discussion of the "big beast factor": it refers to the power, the resources and legal assistance that big companies, such as multinational ones, can support where the counterparty is a small business. Therefore, the question is if the approach to review of an implied should be different.

It is crucial to clarify that the duty to act rationally is not synonymous with the general duty to act reasonably: reasonableness imposes an external objective standard applied to the outcome of a person's thoughts or intentions.

A test of rationality is objective, although it applies a minimum standard to the relevant person's mental processes. Further, it introduces a requirement of good faith since it requires a logical connection between the evidence, as well as apparent reasons for decisions.

"Braganza duty" arises in limited situations and, typically, when one party acts as decision-maker and makes a subjective decision on a matter relating to parties from which a potential conflict of interest shall arise.

The duty of rationality is necessary to protect against the abuse of power of one party, that is, the party that plays a role as decision-maker. Nevertheless, it is also critical to stress that this does not constitute an absolute contractual right.

To summarise, in "*Braganza*", the test adopted by the court is based on a two-limb test for determining a breach of duty:

- An assessment relating to the exercise of discretion under the contract.
- An assessment relating to the extension of the discretion power, that is, if this was outrageous.

The final decision was that a decision-maker is under duty to act honestly, good faith and genuineness; consequently, the court recognised the existence of an implied term of a contract which requires that the relevant party exercises its discretionary power in a way that is not arbitrary, irrational or capricious.

From a comparative perspective, it is worth noting that several judgments of Irish courts do not recognise the existence of an implied duty to act reasonably.[15] However, in a recent Supreme Court decision, *O'Sullivan v The Health Service Executive*,[16] Braganza test was considered. More in detail, this case involved an appeal to a Court of Appeal decisions where the contract under scrutiny had elements of private and administrative law. The Supreme Court recognised the existence of a discretion and the importance that discretion should be exercised in good faith.

14 This approach echoes administrative judicial review: courts are better placed to scrutinise the process by which decisions are made as opposed to the substance of decisions which implicate qualitative judgments.

15 See *Irish Bank Resolution Corporation Ltd (In Special Liquidation) v Morrissey* [2013] IEHC 208; *Ryan v Danske Bank* [2014] IEHC 236; *Re Flynn Construction Co* [2014] IEHC 458.

16 [2023] IESC 11.

Furthermore, it was also held that it is possible to impugn a contract if there was evidence that:

- No reasonable decision-maker could have reached that decision.
- The decision-making process had failed to exclude extraneous considerations or to take account all obviously relevant ones.

6. Good faith as an implied term

Although good faith represents a complex and contradictory concept, its flexibility permits to achieve flexibility in specific contracts, such as constructions contracts. The latter may have a rigid structure, because they are constructed to carry out their parties' obligations. Furthermore, these contracts are special in their own nature.[17]

According to a Canadian recent case law *Bhasin v Hrynew*,[18] the Supreme Court introduced a new duty, tha tis, the duty "to act honestly in the performance of contractual obligations". Consequently, good faith was perceived as a principle of general organisation of contractual fitness.

Moreover, in an international case law *Yam Seng Pte Ltd. v International Trade Corp Ltd*,[19] governed by English law, it was held that the one-off contract encompassed a "good faith" as an implied term because one element was a promissory "duty of honesty". Although Legatt Judge was sceptical about the role played by good faith in English contract law, he emphasised that in a specific contract, such as relational contracts (long-term contracts), a "mutual trust and confidence" constitutes an implicit element for "parties' understanding and necessary to give business efficacy to the arrangements". Thus, an expectation of honesty as a "paradigm example of a general norm which underlies almost all contractual relationships" exists.[20] From *Yam Seng Pte Ltd. v International Trade Corp Ltd* a new test has been shaped: good faith is breached "whether in the particular context the conduct would be regarded as commercially unacceptable by reasonable and honest people".[21] From this a perspective there is an analogy between the duty of good faith and fair dealing, thus, the prohibition to abuse of right.[22]

7. Good faith in civil law countries

In most civil law countries, based on a written constitution, the good faith principle is perceived as a pre-condition to protect constitutional values in contractual relationships. To elucidate, through good faith, constitutional values enter contractual

17 (Nurhidayah et al. 2022).
18 *Bhasin v Hrynew* [2014] SCC 71.
19 *Yam Seng Pte Ltd. v International Trade Corp Ltd.* [2013] EWHC 111 (QB); [2013] 1 Lloyd's Rep. 526.
20 For a comment, see (Carter and Courtney 2016).
21 *Yam Seng Pte Ltd. v International Trade Corp Ltd.* (2013) 1 CLC 699.
22 (Halberda 2020).

relationship, such as the following ones: freedom, justice, reasonableness, etc. Therefore, thanks to good faith, moral value assumes the level of constitutional values.[23]

From a historical perspective, civil law systems have adopted the principle of good faith as a general principle of the law of contracts since their origin, as general tribute to their Roman roots. Consequently, the concept may be deemed as a keystone on which the entire legal architecture of such legal systems is hinged upon. Not only does the principle reverberate on the phases preceding the conclusion of the contract, the same is also a stronghold aimed to protect each party during the same validity of the contract.

Remarkably, under Roman law "*bona fides*" seems to be associated to the civil proceeding discipline, where distinction is made among "*actiones stricti uris*", "*actions bonae fidei*" and "*actiones arbitrariae*". In short, the second ones are "*actiones civiles in personam*", where the "*iudicium*" confers to the judge an ample degree of autonomy, namely the power to decide according to its discretion everything the defendant is to be bound on doing or on performing according to the good faith principle.

After the Roman empire and at the dawn of the formation of the modern systems, the principle of good faith has been enunciated with specific characteristics. At times, contracts are divided between *contractus bonae fidei* and *contractus stricti iuris*; however, more frequently, it is averred that all contracts are pervaded by the principle of good faith.

Italian law sets forth the fundamental rules according to which "[t]he contract shall be interpreted according to good faith"; in addition, "[t]he contract shall be performed according to good faith", the "objective".[24]

In essence, good faith, emphatically enunciated as governing the performance of the contract, although jurisprudence initially denied that the principle had any degree of autonomy. More recently Italian courts affirm that this concept represents an actual duty of law, consisting of a general duty of solidarity which is imposed on each party insomuch as to preserve the interests of the other parties, irrespective of both specific contractual obligations and of the extra-contractual duty of the *neminem ledere*.[25]

8. Good faith during Covid-19 pandemic

Good faith shall also be interpreted through the lens of the UK Government during Covid-19:[26] the UK Cabinet Office published a non-legally binding guidance in May 2020 titled "Responsible contract behaviour".[27] It was addressed to all

23 (Kull 2022).
24 (de Gioia Carabellese 2023).
25 Italian Supreme Court No. 3250 of 1977.
26 The impact of Covid-19 in contract law will be scrutinised further.
27 Cabinet Office, *Guidance on Responsible Contractual Behaviour in the Performance and Enforcement of Contracts Impacted by the Covid-19 Emergency*, May 7, 2020.

commercial players, and it encouraged that contractual parties acted "responsibly and fairly in the national interest in performing and enforcing their contract".

The main pillars of these Guidelines were as follows:

- An extraordinary response was required from individuals, businesses and public authorities in their contractual arrangements.
- Contractual arrangements played a critical role in the economy.
- During Covid-19 some contracts may become difficult or impossible to perform.

A responsible and fair behaviour was strongly encouraged in specific circumstances defined by the same government in paragraph 15 of the guidelines. This paragraph stipulated that responsible and fair behaviour was aimed to achieve the following goals:

- If possible, to maintain contractual performance.
- To ensure cashflow in those contracts is maintained.
- If it was not possible to continue contractual performance, the preservation of supply chains and market during the emergency should be safeguarded.
- To guarantee that contractual and economic activities could be preserved in the best interests of the growth of the UK productivity.

9. The new role of good faith in smart contracts

The digitalisation of human relation requires to face further challenges, one of this is how to read the notion of good faith in smart contracts. In the latter, human factor does not play a quintessential role simply because smart contracts can be concluded, performed and terminated without the participation of a person.

To understand these contracts, often, US courts adopt a "reasonable communicativeness test". Based on the latter, the focus is on transparency and clear conditions published on Internet website. Thus, good faith becomes transparency in contractual negotiations.[28] In the IT era, the problem is how to mirror good faith principles and reasonable expectations of parties into a code. Therefore, the question is if smart contracts' design is suitable to encompass good faith or if good faith should no longer exist in smart contracts.

References

Bebchuk, Lucian Arye. 1989. "The Debate on Contractual Freedom in Corporate Law." *Columbia Law Review* 89 (63): 1395–415.

Burrow, Josef B. 1968. "Contractual Co-Operation and the Implied Term." *The Modern Law Review* 31 (4): 390–407.

Carter, John, and Wayne Courtney. 2016. "Good Faith in Contracts: Is There an Implied Promise to Act Honestly?" *Cambridge Law Journal* 75 (3): 608–19.

28 (Filatova 2017).

de Gioia Carabellese, Pierre. 2023. *From utmost Good Faith to Algorithmic Faith in Marine Insurance*. Studium.

Filatova, N. Yu. 2017. "The Regulation of Peculiarities of Electronic Contracting: Comparative Analysis." *Problems of Legality* 139: 63–77.

Halberda, Jan. 2020. "The Principle of Good Faith and Fair Dealing in English Contract Law." *Pravovedenie* 64 (3): 312–25.

Hugh, Collins. 2014. "Implied Terms: The Foundation in Good Faith and Fair Dealing." *Current Legal Problems* 67 (1): 297–331.

Kull, Irene. 2022. "Principle of Good Faith and Constitutional Values in Contract Law." *Juridica International* 7: 142–49.

Nurhidayah, Abdullah, Ong Tze Chin, Nur Atiqah Nasir, and Faizal Kurniawan. 2022. "Good Faith in Construction Contract: A Common Law Perspective." *International Journal of Sustainable Construction Engineering and Technology* 14 (2): 88–95.

15 Interpretation of a contract

Chapter Overview

1. Introduction

Any written contract requires to ascertain the real will of the parties. To achieve this objective, it is quintessential to read and peruse the words used in that written document, named contract. Therefore, interpretation may be defined as an activity strictly connected with the construction of a contract, including its terms.

To determine the legal effect of a contract, two factors shall be examined:

- The application of external legal rules, for example the intervention of the statute or some public policy rules.
- The interpretation of the words that parties have not written in the documents originally signed, therefore signed at the time of the conclusion of the contract.

Under common law, the goal of the interpretive activity is to discover the intention of the contracting parties. In *Pioneer Shipping Ltd v BTP Tioxide Ltd (The Nema)*,[1] it was stressed by Lord Diplock as follows: "The object should be achieved in constructing any contract is to ascertain what the mutual intentions of the parties

1 [1982] AC 724.

DOI: 10.4324/9781003645948-15

were as to the legal obligations each assumed by the contractual words in which they sought to express them".

From this proposition, it is possible to infer four main rules:

- Parties cannot give evidence to the court as what their intention really was.
- It is vital to realise that, sometimes, clauses are written at the end of the word document and in small letters.
- Words used by parties do not express their real and true will, in a perfect way.
- The role of the court is to ascertain the hypothetical intention of the parties, not their actual intention. In this respect, it was stressed by Lord Wilberforce as follows: "When one speaks of the intention of the parties to the contract one speaks objectively – the parties cannot themselves give direct evidence of what their intention was – and what must be ascertained is what is to be taken as the intention which reasonable people would have had if placed in the situation of the parties".[2]

As a result of this, the interpretation constitutes "not an exercise in the arcane", rather it is "a logical process in which the interpreter seeks to ascertain the intention of the draftsman as embodied in the instrument".[3]

2. The intention of the parties

To understand the intention of the parties, the first approach is the language used in the agreement. Furthermore, language should be read under the surrounding circumstances, as well as the objective of the contract.

In doing this, it is necessary to adopt an objective approach to the interpretation of the contract, to promote certainty. To elaborate, Lord Goff of Chieveley affirmed that

> the objective of interpretation is of a paramount importance in commercial affairs; commercial men have frequently to take important decisions with some speed, and it is great importance that they all know that they can rely on courts and arbitrators, if any dispute should later arise, to adopt the same objective approach as they themselves have to adopt in the daily administration of their contracts.[4]

In this respect, words have an objective meaning, and often, that meaning does not constitute a mirror of the intention of parties. Thus, the aim of the objective approach is not based on the potential or actual reliance of the promise. Also, conduct after agreement may be relevant: more in detail, the reference goes to the "time of contracting". This latter expression refers to the subsequent conduct in

2 *Readorn-Smith Line Ltd v Hansen-Tangen* [1967] 1 W.L.R.
3 Kriegler J. in *Bekker No. v Total South Africa (Pty) Ltd* [1990] 3 S.A. 159.
4 *President of India v Jebsens (U.K.) Ltd* [1991] 1 Llyod's Rep. 1-9.

cases where contract will be changed, or varied, or an obligation has been varied from the initial scheme.

A problem may arise if words used by parties result as ambiguous or not totally clear. In this scenario, it is necessary to turn the attention to the initial purpose, as well as the aim of the agreement. Further, the interpreter should choose the meaning which seems to be more coherent in the context of the contract considering the factual circumstances.[5]

In *Ireland v Livingston*,[6] it was stressed that, if the intent of the agent's actual authority is ambiguous and the agent placed a reasonable interpretation on their instructions, then the principal would be bound by their actions pursuant to them. If on one hand there is the objective interpretation, on the other hand there is the subjective one. The latter is aimed to look at parties' state of mind in finding both the existence of a contract and the interpretation of the written document. An example is the "snapping up" case, inferable from *Hartog v Collin Shield*:[7] the agreement encapsulated both an objective and subjective element. It was held that there was no contract between parties, because there was a duty to correct mistake that was known to be not the real intention of the person making it.[8]

As far as the meaning of the words is concerned, the "golden rule"[9] is an expression that shall be construed in their grammatical and ordinary sense. Further, if the focus is the meaning of the words, the following rules shall be applicable:

- The ordinary meaning of a word is its meaning in its plain, ordinary and popular sense.
- If a word has both an ordinary and specialised meaning, the first one shall be preferred if parties do not admit the specialised meaning.
- In the case in which words appear imprecise or describe a quality of continuous variation, the court has a duty to decide as a question of fact whether a given set of circumstances is within or outside the contractual stipulation.
- Where a word has a single primary meaning, the choice between meanings is determined by the context in which the word is used.
- If a word is defined by statute, it is inadmissible to contradict the statutory definition.

5 *Vitol B.V. v Compagnie Europeene des Petroles* [1988] 1 Llyod's Rep.

6 (1872) LR 5 HL 395.

7 [1939] 3 All ER 566. Colin and Shields were merchants based in London. Hartog was a furrier from Belgium. The first entered an oral agreement with the second, one to sell him 30,000 Argentinian hare skins. In the agreement there was a mistake: parties wrote that the price was 10d per pound, instead of per skin. This means that the price difference was one third cheaper for the complainant.

8 This complies with the rule shaped by Lord Hoffman in *Investors Compensation Scheme Ltd v West Bromwich Building Society* 4 [1998] 1 WLR 896: "Interpretation is the ascertainment of the meaning which the document would convey to a reasonable person having all the background knowledge which would reasonably have been available to the parties in the situation in which they were at the time of the contract".

9 *Caledonian Railway Co v Noth British Railway Co.* (1881) 6 App. Cas.

3. The "parol evidence" rule

"Parol evidence" rule means that, where parties have signed an agreement, it is not generally permissible to adduce extrinsic evidence:

- To demonstrate what the parties' intention was in entering that agreement.[10]
- To contradict, change, or add something to the terms of the written agreement.[11]

This rule constitutes a presumption against allowing parties to adduce external evidence to contradict the written contract. Although it constitutes the main rule, it is also important to clarify that:

- Parties may enter a collateral written contract, even if this further contract adds or contradicts the main contract.
- Parties may prove that the contract is a written contract whose terms are spread across multiple documents.

It is worth clarifying that, if parties form an oral contract, this constitutes a collateral contract only if it is independent from the main contract and it does not contradict, add or vary the terms of the main contract.

Furthermore, there are important exceptions to the "parol evidence" rule, such as the following:

- When the validity of the contract is in question to establish the existence of consideration, some invalidity clause, etc.
- Where terms or words have a specific meaning by custom[12] or they are technical expression.
- Where an agreement fails to record the agreement/understanding between parties in an accurate way.
- When the aim is to explain words which are ambiguous or, under a merely literal perspective do not have any sense.

Consequently, "parol evidence" rule does not constitute a rigid rule, rather a principle applicable where an objective interpretation shall be adopted. The aim of this rule is to enforce the intentions of parties as they have objectively manifested. It is also important to highlight that this rule does not promote a public policy, nor a need for commercial certainty. More precisely, "parol evidence" rule arises from

10 *Prenn v Simmonds* [1971] 1 WLR 1381. The general rule is that any pre-contractual discussions, made during the negotiation of the contract, is not admissible evidence to assist in determining the construction of the contract. An exception is whether the question of construction arises in a claim for rectification. In this specific case, the reference is to the correction of a document where parties are in complete agreement on the terms, but these terms were written in a wrong way.

11 *Jacobs v Batavia & General Plantations Trust Ltd* [1924] 2 Ch 329 (Ch).

12 *Hutton v Warren*, (1836) 150 ER 517. It was said that where a contract is silent, extrinsic evidence of customary practice and usage is admissible. The latter may be incorporated into the agreement. As a result of this, there is an implied term.

the same agreement as a form of an implied term of the agreement. Therefore, "parol evidence" rule represents a specific application of the more general rule of law, because it is suitable to deliver an objective test for agreement.

4. The new approach

To understand the state of the art of the interpretation of a contract, it is critical to discuss and analyse *Arnold v Britton*[13]: the starting point of this controversy was that, when court interprets a written contract, it adopts an objective approach. The aim is to identify "what a reasonable person having all the background knowledge which would have been available to the parties would have understood them to be using the language in the contract to mean".[14] Therefore, judges are focused on the meaning of the relevant words in their commercial, documentary and factual context. Furthermore, this assessment shall also be carried out considering:

- The natural and ordinary meaning of the clause.
- Other relevant provisions of the document.
- The purposes of clause and document.
- The facts and circumstances known or assumed by parties.
- Commercial common sense.
- Subjective evidence of party's intention.

Arnold v Britton is important due to its focus on the concept of "commercial common sense". More in detail, commercial common sense should not be invoked to undervalue the importance of the language of provisions and should not be invoked retrospectively. In clarifying the meaning of unclear relevant words, the court shall move from their natural meaning. The consequence is that commercial agreements should be interpreted according to the natural meaning of words. The principles to apply, when interpreting commercial contract clauses, are the following:

- The court is under a duty to ascertain objectively the aim of parties.
- The court shall put itself in the position of a reasonable person who possesses all background information reasonably available to parties at the time the contract was entered into.
- If contract encompasses an unambiguous term, the court should give the normal effect to that language.
- If the contract encompasses two possible interpretations, the court shall prefer the interpretation that made the most commercial sense.
- Surrounding circumstances should be ignored by court.

13 [2015] UKSC 36. As far as the factual background is concerned, the owners of land granted several 99-years leases to plots so that holiday chalets could be built. Each lease stated that "it was granted on terms similar in all respects". However, one clause was different in two groups of leases. It was argued that the clause should be interpreted so that the payable rates were not out of proportion with the costs of repairs.

14 Lord Neuberger.

- Commercial common sense, as well as surrounding circumstances, should not be used to reduce the importance of the words used.

Commercial common sense may be defined as an element, part of the agreement, which operates as safety clause or criterion against the absurdity. Nevertheless, textual fidelity should be guaranteed and maintained. In other words, commercial common sense should not be used to re-write the agreement text or to better reconstruct the contract.

Before *Arnold v Britton*, a crucial leading case was *Rainy Sky SA v Kookmin Bank.*[15] As far as the meaning of this case is concerned, the court held that, if there are two possible constructions, the court is entitled to prefer the construction which is consistent with business common sense.

After the analysis of these two cases, it is possible to draw some important inferences:

- *Rainy Sky SA v Kookmin Bank* may lead courts to deliver a non-correct exercise of interpretation. Commercial common sense, in some cases, was used to override the natural meaning of the words.
- *Arnold v Britton* better clarifies the correct approach that a court shall follow when considering commercial implications of a contract, or a clause, as a part of the interpretation process.

Finally, it is vital to recall *Wood v Capita Insurance Services Limited.*[16] This controversy involves the construction of an indemnity clause in an agreement for the sale and purchase of the entire share capital of a company. It was stressed that every contractual interpretation activity should be focused on one main question: "What did the parties mean by the words which they have chosen to express their agreement?". Moreover, in *Wood v Capita Insurance Services Limited* it was also said that both textualism and contextualism should be used to ascertain the objective meaning of a language.

5. The concept of interpretation and construction of a contract

Interpretation and construction represent two pillars to understand the expressions used by parties into an agreement. The question, thus, is concerned with the exact definition of the concept of interpretation and construction of a contract.

Interpretation is aimed to identity the meaning of the words or actions. Therefore, it refers to linguistic and social abilities not related to the area of law. Furthermore,

15 [2011] UKSC 50. Kookmin Bank gave a guarantee in connection with a shipbuilding contract. The guarantee covered the repayment of certain advance instalments of the price by the counterparty to the shipbuilder if ship was not delivered by the shipbuilder. The ship was not delivered; the shipbuilder refused to return the instalments paid. A dispute arose on the terms of the guarantee covered by the instalments that were paid. The court stated that guarantee covered the paid instalments: a different or contrary interpretation did not comply with commercial common sense.

16 [2017] UKSC 24.

interpretation requires that interpreters apply its linguistic ability and social knowledge to understand the meaning of parties' words and actions.

From the opposite pole, construction involves the legal effects of an agreement: to better explain, rules of construction translate the output of interpretation into legal effects. The reason is that it is impossible to understand the meaning of what parties have said if these words would not translate into "action".

Prima facie differences between interpretation and construction seem to be clear; however, in the reality, these two activities are involved where the interpret shall define the exact meaning of an expression used by parties into an agreement. The main reason is that legal interpretation is strictly connected with the rule of construction and, the latter, often, affects the meaning of what parties have written in the document.

In addition, legal interpretation serves construction because the first one (legal interpretation) is based on construction. In a specular way, acts of construction produces legal formalities, therefore, it includes the application of interpretative altering rules. In *Chandris v Isbrandtsen-Moller Co Inc.*,[17] Devlin J. explained:

> A rule of construction cannot be more than a guide to enable the court to arrive at the true meaning of the parties. The ejusdem generis rule means that there is implied into the language where the parties have used words of restriction which are not there. It cannot be right to approach a document with the presumption that there should be such an implication. To apply the rule automatically in that way would be to be make it the master and not the servant of the purpose for which it was designed – namely to ascertain the intention of the parties from the words they have used.

To clarify this point, scholars highlight as follows:

> Just as construction must begin with interpretation, we shall find that our interpretation will vary with the construction that must follow. Finding that one interpretation of the words will be followed by the enforcement of certain legal effects, we may back hastily away from that interpretation and substitute another that will lead to a more desirable result.[18]

6. Interpretation of statutory

A different object of interpretation is statutory. Although statutes may be very lengthy and detailed, they will always require further interpretation as they are applied to new situations by judges deciding cases. In this respect, judges and lawyers have created a set of "rules" by which statutes can be interpreted to apply in

17 [1951] 1 K.B. 240.
18 (Corbin 1950, 11).

different situations. Although Parliament is the source of the statute, courts play a vital role in applying the statutes. Therefore, these rules are not mandatory rules, rather they are tools to aid the judges. The latter have discretion as to whether to use and how to use them.

These rules include the following:

- Literal rule: words should be given their plain, ordinary and natural meaning or their technical legal meaning, where they have one. If the words of the statute are clear, they must be applied as they appear on their face, even if the results are overly harsh or undesirable.
- Golden rule: this rule holds that the plain ordinary meaning of the words should be followed as far as possible but, if this produces an inconsistency, or an absurdity or inconvenience.
- Mischief rule: courts may interpret legislation considering the law that existed before that legislation and the "mischief" (or problem) that the legislation was meant to address because of the decision of the Parliament.
- Purposive approach: the legislation should be interpreted to give effect to its purpose. This has become the preferred approach of the courts, particularly in respect of European legislation.

7. The interpretation of smart contracts

The legal interpretation of smart contracts represents a crucial activity because they are, fundamentally, programmes, and often it is unclear what legal effects the actions of such program may have. The most controversial issue is if smart contracts are interpretable. In this respect, some scholars believe that code possesses only an effect, therefore, there is no room for interpretation simply because "code is law".[19]

By contrast, the Law Commission stated that smart contracts, as contracts, must be interpretable:

> If we say that the code only means what it does when it is executed, the meaning of the code would change in every instance depending on how the code responded to the system upgrade. However, we do not think it makes sense to say that the meaning of the code has changed in each case, because the code itself has not changed; instead, it must be the outcome that has changed. If we accept this, it then follows that there can be a divergence between what the code 'means', and what it does when it is executed, which entails a distinction between meaning and effect.[20]

19 (Cannarsa 2018).

20 Law Commission, Smart Legal Contracts, Advice to Government (Law Com No. 401, 2021), para 4.11.

Furthermore, Law Commission states that standard contractual principles can be applied to interpret smart contracts due to their definition of meaning.[21]

The word "meaning" – from the Law Commission perspective – fits into the entrenched principles of contract relating to the objective interpretation of "traditional" contracts. Additionally, the Law Commission asks to adapt the traditional test, the reasonable person test:[22] therefore, priority should be given to the "natural" meaning of the language. Thus, the reasonable person test becomes the "reasonable coder test"; the latter possesses the benefit of providing an insight into what the parties intended the code to do, regardless of the computer's ultimate performance.

Moreover, the Law Commission has established that an expert may assist the court by translating the code in the same way as any other contract written in a language unfamiliar to the court. Nevertheless, the main problem is that programming languages appear as a suitable tool for reducing linguistic ambiguity; however, programming languages are formal and constructed systems. This means that the relevant community can redefine the programme language in a way that radically alters the meaning of programme written in it. Smart contracts, as contracts based on blockchain, are particularly vulnerable to this; in other words, blockchain smart contracts do not have continual linguistic drift, hence they have occasional "earthquakes".[23]

References

Cannarsa, Michel. 2018. "Interpretation of Contracts and Smart Contracts: Smart Interpretation or Interpretation of Smart Contracts?" *European Review of Private Law* 26 (6): 773–85.

Corbin, Arthur Linton. 1950. *Corbin on Contracts: A Comprehensive Treatise on the Rules of Contract Law*. West Publishing Company.

Green, Sarah. 2018. "Smart Contracts, Interpretation and Rectification." *Lloyd's Maritime and Commercial Law Quarterly* 2: 234–51.

Grimmelmann, James. 2019. "All of Smart Contracts Are Ambiguous." *Journal of Law & Innovation* 2 (1): 1–22.

21 (Green 2018).

22 *Arnold v Britton* [2015] UKSC 36.

23 (Grimmelmann 2019).

16 The doctrine of the privity of a contract

Chapter Overview

1. Introduction

In contemporary era, commercial transactions are no longer confined to individuals, nor to simple sale and purchase deals. With the increase in the number of the parties to contracts, commercial agreements, as well as financial transactions, have become even more complex.

Therefore, the main research – and teaching question – is to ascertain who is entitled to enforce a contract. The subsequent and logical answer may be found under the doctrine of privity of contract. Based on this doctrine, it is possible to affirm that the general rule in English law consists of a straightforward answer: no party can act upon a contract unless he/she is party to this contract.[1]

While this constitutes the general rule, there are also some notable exceptions. Among these, reference can be made to the following:

- Collateral contracts.
- The court procedure to stay proceedings.

1 (Tolhurst 2025).

DOI: 10.4324/9781003645948-16

- Statutory exceptions.
- Damages on behalf of another.
- Agency.
- Statutory exceptions.
- Negotiable instruments.

In a nutshell, the doctrine of privity of contract originates from a question: who can enforce the contract.

Based on such a premise, two consequences can be postulated:

- Only contracting parties are bound by it.
- Only parties to a contract can derive rights and benefits from their contract, therefore from the contract they signed.

2. The doctrine of privity

As highlighted previously, the general rule in common law demands that a contract creates rights and obligations only between parties to this agreement. As a result of this, a third party does not have any right or liability under such agreement. Again, this constitutes the main concept encapsulated into the doctrine of privity of a contract. Thus, this doctrine is applicable to every contractual relationship.

From a historical perspective,[2] the doctrine of privity has its legal roots in Roman law: in the latter legal system, the principal rule was that a contract in favour of a third party, or person, did not have effect, even for the contracting parties. Only within the *Justinian' Institutiones* does it become possible to stipulate in favour of a third party.

The contemporary doctrine of privity of contract means that, even though a contract, or its performance, can affect a third party, this doctrine dictates that the general rule in contract law cannot confer or recognise rights and/or obligations arising under it or any person except the parties to this agreement. Therefore, the consequences of this doctrine are, at least, three:

- A person cannot enforce rights under contract if this person is not a party to that contract.
- A person, who is not party to a contract, cannot have contractual liabilities imposed on him.
- Contractual remedies are not aimed to compensate third parties.

2 (Baker 2013).

It is worth emphasising that, before *Donoghue v Stevenson*,[3] the privity doctrine was read and interpreted in so strict a way that it used to precludes actions in tort by third parties arising from the negligence of a party to a contract.

Before *Donoghue*, the rule was encompassed in *Winterbottom v Wright*[4] where the question was if the duty of care went beyond the contracting parties. It was held that the duty of care did not extend by any means. Although it was recognised in the same *dictum* that this decision was a "hard case", it was also stressed that a changing of standard could, and perhaps should, have created an unreasonable extension of liability.

An important case is *Dunlop Pneumatic Tyre Co Ltd v Selfridge Ltd*[5] where the court emphasised that the fundamental principle in English law was that only a person who was party to a contract could sue on this contract. Furthermore, the court highlighted that there was a lack of consideration; consequently the contract was not enforceable.

Based on such background, the doctrine of a privity of a contract was criticised and in 1967 with *Beswick v Beswick*,[6] it was held, with the approval of the Law Revision Committee's proposal, that when a contract by its express terms purports to confer a benefit directly on a third party, it shall be enforceable by this third party on its name. In other words, a specific performance may be ordered in lieu of nominal damages to produce a just result for a third party. Incidentally, this principle enunciated in this case is now encompassed with a statute, the Contracts (Rights of Third Parties) Act 1999.

Consequently, the approach of the court to this concept has changed: for example, in *Swain v Law Society*,[7] Lord Diplock stressed that non-recognition of a third rights constitutes "an anachronistic shortcoming that has for many years been regarded as a reproach to English private law". Moreover, it was suggested, according to a different and more progressive line of reasoning, that the rule passed under *Beswick v Beswick* should be reviewed.[8]

3 [1932] AC 562. It constitutes a landmark case in Scottish law in tort/delict; more in detail, it represents the foundation of the modern doctrine of modern law of negligence in common law jurisdiction. To summarise, *Donoghue v Stevenson* constitutes a milestone because (1) it establishes the liability of manufactures to consumer with whom they did not have a direct contractual relationship; (2) it established the principle that forms the basis of negligence; (3) it shaped the "neighbour test" or "neighbour principle".

4 (1842) 10 M&W 109. Winterbottom was a coachman who drove a horse pulled mail coach. His employers entered a contract with Wright to maintain the coach in good working order. However, he failed to do this, and Winterbottom injured himself. Consequently, Winterbottom sued Wright: although they were not parties of a contract, the second one, Wright, may have a duty.

5 [1915] AC 847. Dew agreed with Dunlop to buy tyres at a discount; however, Dew did not promise to resell the tyres at less than the list price. Dew sold tyres to Selfridge who also agreed not to sell at below list price, but they did sell tyres at a discount to private buyers. After this, Dunlop sued for damages and made an injunction to prevent Selfridge to continuing his activity.

6 [1967] UKHL 2, [1968] AC 58. PB was in poor health and agreed with the defendant, his nephew, that he would transfer the trade and good will of his coal business to him on the basis that the nephew employed him as a consultant for the rest of his life and paid for it. The nephew agreed to pay BP wife also after BP died for the rest of her life. After the death of PB, the nephew paid PB's wife once but not so longer. Therefore, BP widow brought an action as administrator of BP' estate to claim specific performance.

7 [1982] UKHL J0701, 598, 611.

8 See *Woodar Investment Development Ltd. v Wimpey Construction (U.K.) Ltd.* [1980] 1 W.L.R.

3. The relationship between privity and consideration

In the complex matter of privity of contract, two main questions lie in contract law shall be resolved:

- Which promises are legally enforceable.
- Who can enforce this promise.

The first question is linked with the doctrine of consideration, whereas the second one relates to the doctrine of privity.

Although privity and consideration involve different and separate issues of policy, as soon as the Law Commission started reading the doctrine of privity, the relationship between privity and consideration was also discussed. Thus, the question was if these two concepts are different or not.[9]

The historical law background supported the idea that privity and consideration are two different concepts.

The reference goes to *Dunlop Pneumatic Tyre Co. Ltd. v Selfridge & Co. Ltd.*, where Viscount Haldane L.C. stated as follows:

> My Lords, in the law of England certain principles are fundamental. One is that only a person who is a party to a contract can sue on it. A second principle is that if a person with whom a contract not under seal has been made is to be able to enforce it consideration must have been given by him to the promisor or to some other person at the promisor's request.[10]

This was the approach adopted by the Law Revision Committee, but it was not welcomed with enthusiasm among scholars. More in detail, it was stressed that a contract does not constitute, merely, promise, rather a promise supported by consideration. The critics highlighted that the promise is only the one that a party, who supplies consideration, originates from the party to a contract. Therefore, a third party, C, cannot be treated as a party to a contract if he/she does not supply any consideration.

An example of the uncertainty surrounding the topic of the privity of the contract in English law is the Indian Contract Act 1872. This piece of legislation is since consideration must move from the promise. Despite this, it is also true that most scholars in India have long supported the traditional English approach, specifically the one preceding the 1999 reform. The uncertainty surrounding the topic at stake, at least before the 1999 reform, is confirmed by a further common law jurisdiction: Malaysia. In a judicial case, *Keuons ProsDectins Ltd. v Schmidt*,[11] it was held that a third party could have enforced a contract under a Malaysian ordinance since consideration did not need to move from the promisee.

9 (Furmston and Tolhurst 2015).
10 [1915] A.C. 853.
11 [1968] A.C. 810.

4. The Contracts (Rights Parties) Act 1999

The Contracts (Rights Parties) Act 1999[12] constitutes a significant change in the common law doctrine of privity, because it confers a benefit for a third party. The Contracts Act, more in detail, implemented the recommendations of the Law Commission: it reformed the doctrine of privity, without dismantling it. The reason for that is simple: the doctrine of privity recognises, and gives effect, the intention of the contracting parties.

Considering this reform, third party possesses two benefits:

- A positive benefit: a third party can enforce a term of a contract in his own right in two circumstances: (1) where the contract expressly provides that he/she may; (2) where the terms of a contract purport to confer a benefit upon him and nothing else in the contract denies the purported benefit.[13]
- A negative benefit: Section 1(6) stipulates as follows: "Where a term of a contract excludes or limits liability in relation to any matter references in this Act to the third party enforcing the term shall be construed as references to his availing himself of the exclusion or limitation".

Section 1(3) stipulates as follows: "The third party must be expressly identified in the contract by name, as a member of a class or as answering a particular description but need not be in existence when the contract is entered into".

In *Avraamides v Colwill*[14] the court of appeal clarified that it was not sufficient to rely on an inference as the use of the term "express". Section 1(3) requires that the contract shall refer in an express way to the name of the party.

The right of the third party is additional to any right whereby the promise might have to enforce any term of the contract.[15]

Among the different cases already "blossomed" after the 1999 Act was passed, it is important to analyse *Fortress Value Recovery Fund I LLC & Ors v Blue Skye Special Opportunities Fund LP &. Ors.*[16] In this case, the difference between Section 8(1) and 8(2) was explained. Thus, it was said that:

- Under Section 8(1), the third party is entitled to receive a substantive benefit under the contract, subject to a procedural condition that the third party may enforce it only through a particular process, such as the arbitration.

12 Henceforth the Contracts Act.

13 See Section 1(1)(a)(b).

14 [2006] EWCA Civ 1533.

15 It was said in Section 1(4) as follows: "This section does not confer a right on a third party to enforce a term of a contract otherwise than subject to and in accordance with any other relevant terms of the contract".

16 [2013] EWCA Civ 367. The claimants, in the first instance, brought an action against the defendant even if they were no parties to the partnership. However, it was held that they were entitled to enjoy the benefit of various indemnities and exclusion clause.

- Section 8(2) recognises that a term of a contract confers a unilateral right to the third party to require that a dispute should be submitted to arbitration.

In other words, in "*Fortress*" the court recognised the difference between a right of action and a contractual defence.

Finally, it is critical to highlight that the 1999 Act under discussion provides an enforceable right to third parties which is given in addition to any right or remedy available at common law: this is said by Section 7(1). To elaborate, the various devices developed by the common law to evade the consequence of privity exists.[17] These remedies are as follows:

- To enforce a promise: the estate of a promise was able to enforce the promise.
- If a person booked a holiday on behalf of himself and family member was able to recover damages on behalf of the family members where the contract was breached.[18]
- When the seller and carrier contract in contemplation of a second contract with the buyer, the seller can recover substantial damages on behalf of the buyer where the goods are lost or damaged.[19]

5. Exceptions to the doctrine of privity of contract

The main rule, that is, the rule in force in which a third person has no right to enforce a contract which they are not party to, does not constitute an absolute rule. Therefore, there are several exceptions in both common law and statutes.

As far as statutes are concerned, the most important is the one just discussed.

A second exception refers to statutory exceptions. More in detail, the reference goes to the following:

- Section 56(1), Law of Property Act 1925.
- Section 11, Married Women's Property Act 1882.
- Section 14(2), Marine Insurance Act 1906.
- Section 148(7), Road Traffic Act 1988.

Under common law, exceptions are as follows:

- Collateral contracts: it materialises when a third party makes a promise which induces an innocent party to enter a contract with another. A leading case is *Shanklin Pier Ltd v Detel Products Ltd*[20]: the High Court of Justice King's Bench

17 (Merkin 2000).

18 *Jackson v Horizon Holidays Ltd* [1975] 1 WLR 1468.

19 *The Albazero* [1977] AC 774.

20 [1951] 2 KB 854. The owner of the pier employed contractors to paint the pier, under the contract he has the right to specify what paint to be used. The seller of paint represented to the pier's owner that its paint was suitable for painting the pier and that two coats would last for seven years. As a result of

Division created an exception to the rule of privity of contract where a contract may be given consideration via the stipulation of another contract. In this case, consideration for a collateral contract originates from the stipulation of the main one.

- Damages: in some circumstances it is possible for a person, who is not party to a contract, to recover damages, or have them recovered on their behalf. Although it is true, it becomes mandatory to clarify some elements: (1) third party cannot enforce contract as they have not given consideration: (2) a contracting party can only recover damages for their own loss; (3) a third party could get a contracting party to sue on their behalf, however only nominal damages will be awarded as the contracting party has suffered no damages.
- Trust: in *Dunlop Pneumatic Tyre Company Ltd v Selfridge and Company Ltd*[21] it was held that, although the existence of privity of a contract doctrine does not allow third person action, such right may be conferred by way of property. The reference goes to trust. Furthermore, in *Les Affreteurs Reunis v Walford*,[22] it was recognised that the charterers had the benefit of the contract "on trust" for the respondent. This case constitutes an example relating to the use of the "trust of a promise" concept in their area of privity of a contract. More in detail, the rule shaped by the court applies if the third party "effectively nominated" another to enter the contract for his benefit. Where there is a trust for promise, the party to the contract can sue as a trustee for the third party's benefit.[23]
- Assignment through which a party can assign his rights under the contract to a third persons. There is a limit: a mere right to litigate or sue for damages cannot be assigned, unless the third person has a commercial interest in assuming a litigation right.[24]
- Agency: the reference goes to *Dunlop Pneumatic Tyre Company Ltd.* The court established that an agreement for resale price maintenance was unenforceable as a matter of privity of contract. It is noteworthy that under the new Competition

this, the pier's owner instructed the contractor to purchase this specific paint. After the paint peeled in three months, the pier's owner sued the seller of the paint for compensation. The court stated that the seller was liable for compensation pier's owner for breach of a contract.

21 [1915] AC 847.

22 [1919] AC 801.

23 It is worthy to stress that this should not be confused with a simple contract executed for a benefit of a third party/person. Indeed, not in every contract that involves third person beneficiary there is a trust of contractual right created. In *Re Schebsman* [1944] Ch 83, the court held that there is not any principle in equity which allows the trustee to claim funds which the debtor could not obtain without breach of contract. In this respect, see also *Green v Russel* [1959] 2 QB 226.

24 *Trendtex Trading Corporation v Credit Suisse* [1982] AC 679. Trendtex claimed in England against the Central Bank of Nigeria (CBN) for damages. CBN sought the assistance of Credit Suisse for the recovery the debt, which Credit Suisse was also going to use to help it to recover its own debt from Trendtex. The question was if the assignment of a debt complied with common law rules. The court stressed the importance to understand the context or, more precisely, the transaction in the context. The court held that Credit Suisse had a genuine commercial interest in the success of CNB claim for debt.

Act 1988, an agreement like this should be regulated as anticompetitive agreement. Furthermore, Dunlop was not listed as an agent within the contract; consequently, he could not include as a third-party who had rights to claim on the contract.

- Action in tort.[25]
- Restrictive covenants: for example, in sale and purchase of land, any terms of conveyance will generally be confined to the seller and the buyer, not extending to subsequent buyers and owners. A restrictive, or negative, covenant, such as bar on use of the land for commercial purposes may be carried forward with the land and enforced by the seller against subsequent owner. However, it was upheld in *Tulk v Moxhay*[26]: if an agreement has been a contract instead of a covenant, it would have been enforceable. Ultimately, the covenant was enforceable at equity. In a nutshell, it was said that under certain circumstances a restrictive covenant can "run with the land".

References

Baker, John. 2013. "Privity of Contract in the Common Law before 1680." In *Collected Papers on English Legal History*, 1222–47. Cambridge University Press.

Furmston, Michael, and Gregory Tolhurst. 2015. *Privity of Contract*. Oxford: Oxford University Press.

Merkin, Robert. 2000. *Privity of Contract: The Impact of the Contracts (Right of Third Parties) Act 1999 (Lloyd's Commercial Law Library)*. Informa Law from Routledge.

Tolhurst, Greg J. 2025. *Furmston and Tolhurst on Privity of Contract*. Oxford University Press.

25 It was just discussed previously. Furthermore, in *Junior Books Ltd v Veitchi Co Ltd* [1983] 1 AC 520, the court allowed a claim against a defective construction against the sub-contractors. It was possible because the contract singed was already under the "umbrella" of the main, broader contract.

26 [1848] 41 ER 1143.

17 Damages

Chapter Overview

1. Introduction

Damages constitute a topic relating to remedies and, more in general, to a concept of breach of contract. A breach of a contract occurs when a contracting party fails fulfilling their obligations as agreed under the contract signed with the other party. Subsequently, when a breach of a contract materialises, the innocent party, defined also "non-breached party", is entitled to activate different types of remedy. The latter depends both on matter and the severity of the breach.

If a contract is breached, the remedies available are as follows:

- Termination of a contract
- Damages.
- Equitable remedies which include rescission, rectification, specific performance and injunctions.

Moreover, remedies may also be distinguished between legal remedies and equitable remedies. The first ones, legal remedies, encompass agreed sum/price and damages. Equitable remedies, by contrast, refer to specific performance and injunction accounts of profits.

Furthermore, parties may also agree to reduce, expand or change the remedies available for breach of contract. The legal instruments are as follows:

- Conditions subsequent.
- Limitation and exclusion clauses.

DOI: 10.4324/9781003645948-17

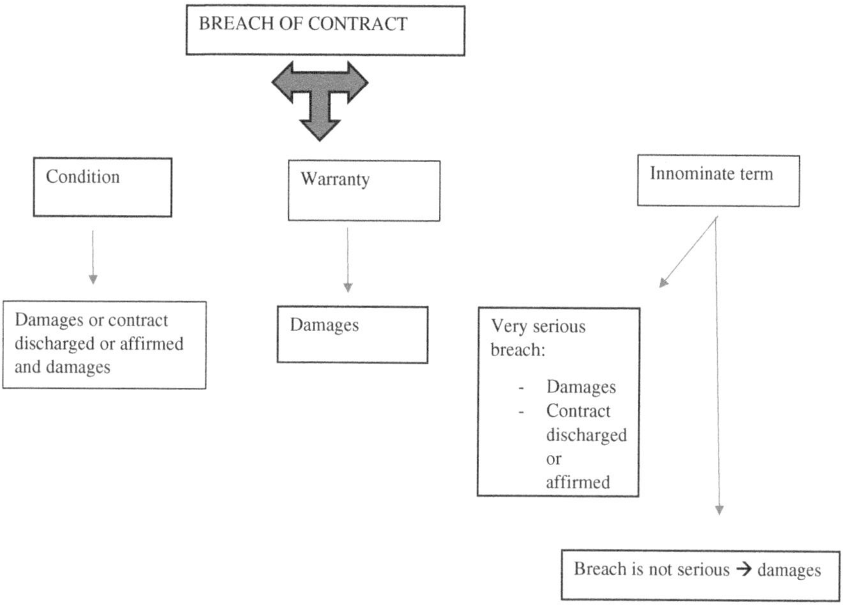

Figure 17.1 Consequences of breach of contract

- Indemnities.
- Set-offs.
- Excluding misrepresentation.
- Liquidated damages.
- Retention to title clauses.
- Time limitations on claims.

Finally, it is crucial to stress that, under English common law, the main rule is that damages are available as of a right for breach of a contract. Thus, every breach of a contract entitles the innocent party to recover damages, even if such damages are only nominal. The latter reflects the fact that claimant's rights have been infringed.

By contrast, punitive damages, named also exemplary damages, are available for all torts. Furthermore, it is possible to affirm that punitive damages shall be recognised for the tort of inducing a breach of a contract. It is worth affirming that punitive damages shall represent an extraordinary remedy of last resort; however, the most appropriate are compensatory, or restitution remedies, as they are usually considered appropriate and/or sufficient to sanction a wrong conduct.[1]

Consequences of a breach of contract may summarise as follows.

1 *Rookes v Barnard* [1964] UKHL 1. Lord Devlin stressed the following concept: "There are certain categories of cases in which an award of exemplary damages can serve a useful purpose in vindicating the strength of the law and thus affording a practical justification for admitting into the civil law a principle which ought logically to belong to the criminal. I propose to state what these two categories

2. Damages

Damages in common law may be compensatory or non-compensatory damages. The first ones, compensatory damages, are an award of a sum of money which aims to compensate the claimant of his loss under the contract.

Non-compensatory damages, by contrast, consists of an award of a sum of money not only to compensate the claimant for his contractual losses. Further, they aim to compensate the claimant in relation to any bad conduct of the other party.[2]

In this respect, the attention will be turned to compensatory damages. First and foremost, it becomes quintessential to define the concept of damage. In *Farley v Skinner*,[3] Lord Scott affirmed as follows:

> The basic principle of damages for breach of contract is that the injured party is entitled, so far as money can do it, to be put in the position he would have been if the contractual obligation had been performed. He is entitled to the benefit of his bargain.

Furthermore, the most important element is to ascertain the loss the claimant has suffered under the contract. The general rule is that the claimant may recover only his own loss.[4] To elaborate, the claimant does not identify an exact amount of loss, because it is sufficient that a loss has occurred. Therefore, the question concerns the quantification of the loss. For example, in *Chaplin v Hicks*,[5] the damage was a lost opportunity: a lost opportunity may become a damage where it is the result of the action of a third party. In *Chaplin v Hicks*, the third party was the panel of judges who would decide the winner of the competition.

To assess the amount of the loss, the court shall focus on the date of the breach.[6] However, the aim of damages is to put the non-breaching party in the position that they would have been had the contract been performed.[7] In order to achieve this result, there are two different approaches:

- Expectation measures.
- Reliance measures.

As far as expectation measures are concerned, the main principle is encapsulated into *Robinson v Harman*[8] where Parke B stated as follows:

---

are; and I propose also to state three general considerations which in my opinion should always be borne in mind when awards of exemplary damages are being made".

2 (Kramer 2017).

3 [2001] UKHL 49, 76.

4 *Alfred McAlpine Construction Ltd v Panatown Ltd* [2001] 1 AC 518.

5 [1911] 2 KB 786.

6 See *Johnson v Agnew* [1980] AC 367.

7 The reference goes to *Robinson v Harman* (1848) 1 Ex 850.

8 (1848) 1 Ex 850.

> The rule of the common law is, that where a party sustains loss for reason of breach of contract, he is, so far as money can do it, to be placed in the same situation, with respect to damages, as if the contract had been performed.

A loss of expectation includes the following:

- The cost of cure or the difference value, that is the amount of money required to pay a third party to perform what was stipulated in the contract.
- Loss of a chance.

It is crucial to stress that in certain circumstances the cost of cure shall not be adopted. These circumstances are summarised as follows:

- If the claimant does not intend to rectify the issues with damages.[9]
- If the cost of the cure becomes not proportionate.[10]

Reliance loss refers to a situation where the claimant cannot prove that a financial benefit would accrue to it had the contract been performed. Its aim is to put the claimant back in the position he/she was before the contract was made.[11]

Another important topic is loss categorisation, that is, whether a loss suffered is actionable. In this respect, the loss may be as follows:

- Financial: it means that the claimant is in a worsened financial position because of the contract.
- The consumer surplus: it is the amount by which a particular consumer values the performance of a contract. It is not a financial loss but a more heterogeneous loss, for example the relaxation on holiday.[12] More in general, it falls within the concept of peace and is considered quite important for the claimant.
- Distress: it is actionable where a contract is signed for a specific purpose relating to enjoyment or entertainment. In this case, damages may be awarded for the disappointment, distress, upset and frustration caused by a breach of contract.[13] Although distress constitutes a different concept from the consumer surplus, *de facto* it materialises an overlap between these two notions.

A successful action for claim damages shall identify three main elements:

- Factual causation.

9 *Tito v Waddell (No. 2)* [1977] Ch 106.

10 *Ruxley Electronics & Constructions Ltd v Forsyth* [1995] UKHL 8.

11 (Yin et al. 2020).

12 *Jackson v Horizon Holidays Ltd* [1975] 1 WLR 1468. In this case, it was recognised that a contract for holiday achieves the objective of providing relaxation. The latter, indeed, falls into the damages actionable by a claimant.

13 *Jarvis v Swan Tours Ltd* [1973] EWCA Civ 8.

- Legal causation.
- The action of the claimant.

Between defendant's wrong and claimant's loss there is to be a connection, a link that shall be legal and factual. Factual causation means that claimant has a duty to recover only losses which have been caused by the breach. It means that the breach of a contract must be "but for" a cause of loss.[14] Legal causation means that the breach of a contract be the direct cause of the loss. Further, it is also required the absence of a subsequent action which breaches the "chain of causation".

The approach is based on the so-called "but-for test". It is a test used in tort law and criminal law which aim is to determine actual causation. This test is based on the question: "but for the existence of X would Y have occurred?".

This test has two problematic aspects:

- Tenuous relations between actions: most things can be construed as but-cause, and therefore, the problem is that a liability may be justified under a remote approach.
- Over causation or merged causes: in the real world, it is difficult to define what has caused the event.

As a result of this, in contract law, a loss will be recoverable only if (1) it arises naturally from the breach itself; (2) was "in the contemplation of the parties", it means that it was foreseeable at the time of contracting as a probable result of the breach.

Finally, it is quintessential that the claimant has taken all reasonable steps to mitigate the loss. In this respect, there are three rules. The first one stipulates that claimant could not claim damages in respect of any loss that he could have reasonably avoided.[15] Furthermore, the claimant has a duty to recover all expenses incurred whilst taking reasonable effort to mitigate loss. Finally, in the case in which claimant avoids further potential losses, these cannot recover for the loss they avoided. The effect of the failure to mitigate is the reduction of damages that might otherwise have been paid.

Another topic is relating to the hypothesis in force of which claimant has contributed to the loss. In this case, the court has the power to reduce the amount of damages the claimant can claim. This reduction shall be proportionate according to the fault of the claimant.[16] The contributory negligence shall arise from the following:

- Contractual provision which does not rely on the negligence of the defendant.

14 *South Australia Asset Management Corporation v York Montague Ltd* [1996] UKHL 10.

15 *British Westinghouse Electric Co Ltd v Underground Electric Railways Co of London Ltd* [1912] AC 673.

16 Section 1(1), Law Reform (Contributory Negligence) Act 1945, stipulates as follows: "Where any person suffers damage as the result partly of his own fault and partly of the fault of any other person or persons, a claim in respect of that damage shall not be defeated by reason of the fault of the person

- Contractual obligation which is expressed in terms of "taking care".
- Tort of negligence and the liability of two parties is the same, and it is independent of any existence of a contract.

3. Equitable remedies

Equitable remedies for breach of a contract[17] are not generally available because it is required that the following elements will exist:

- Damages may be defined as an adequate remedy.
- The performance of the contract requires a constant supervision.
- The contract is signed for a personal service, or it would be the cause of undue hardship for the defendant.[18]

Moreover, equitable remedies are the following ones: specific performance, injunction, restitution, rescission and rectification.

Specific performance constitutes a specific judicial order addressed to the promisor. The latter has the duty to undertake the performance which he obliged himself into a contract. It does not constitute a remedy generally available, because it is not suitable if damages represent an adequate remedy. Further, a specific performance:

- May be activated if there is a breach of a contract to sell a unique item.
- Shall never be used to force a person to perform a service against his will, for example an involuntary servitude.

The secondary remedy is the injunction: it is available both in contract law and tort law. From a perspective of definition, the injunction is a court order directing to a person to stop doing that which this person should not do.[19] If a person violates an injunction, this individual may be held in contempt of court. More in detail, injunction may be as follows:

- Prohibitor, when prevents a person to do something.
- Mandatory, when it obliges a person to do something.

The aim of restitution is to restore to one party of what he/she gave to the other. It constitutes a remedy applicable to several different cases, such as incapacity or misrepresentation. The underlying ratio is that a person who breaches a contract

---

suffering the damage, but the damages recoverable in respect thereof shall be reduced to such extent as the court thinks just and equitable having regard to the claimant's share in the responsibility for the damage".

17 (Barnett 2022).

18 In *Hope v Walter* (1990) 1 Ch 257 the court refused specific performance because it was not appropriate to force someone into a position where they would be the landlord of a brothel.

19 (Halson and Campbell 2019).

should not suffer a punishment as well as the non-breaching party should not be unjustly enriched.

As far as unjust enrichment is concerned, it arises when a party confers a benefit to another party receiving the proper restitution required by law. More in depth, unjust enrichment is focused on what the defendant has been enriched at the claimant's expense; it constitutes a common cause of action. Unjust enrichment is based on three elements:

- The defendant has been enriched or has received a benefit.
- The enrichment of the defendant was unjust.
- The enrichment of the defendant was at the expense of the claimant.

More recently, the Supreme Court stated that an enrichment should not be unjust if it represents the outcome which had been provided for by an agreement between parties.[20]

The rescission is a remedy applicable where and if a party has induced another party to sign a contract. More in detail, this remedy refers to a situation where the innocent party was induced to sign a contract and this contract is abrogated. Rescission allows a party to stop performing its duties under a contract and aims to replace parties in a *status quo*. The traditional reasons for rescission are as follows:

- Misrepresentation of material fact.
- Fraud.
- Duress.
- Unilateral or mutual mistake.
- A lack of consideration.

Finally, rectification constitutes an equitable and discretionary remedy suitable where the contract signed by parties does not reflect their obligations. In other words, rectification refers to a situation where there is a clear mistake in drafting the contract: rectification constitutes an equitable remedy to correct parties' contractual intention.

In *Hamblin & Ors v Moorwand & Ors*[21] the controversy was about an exclusion clause in a contract for payment services. This case alluded to a fraud which induced the claimant to transfer £400,000 via 15 different payments. These payments were executed from their account to an account held with Santander on behalf of PGW Consultants Limited. The claimant sought the bank on the basis of the "Quincecare" duty. This duty was supposed to originate from *Barclays Bank plc v Quincecare Ltd*[22]: a bank has a duty to not execute a payment instruction given by an agent of the customer without making further enquiries. The refusal

20 *Barton and others v Morris and another in place of Gwyn-Jones* [2023] UKSC 3.
21 [2025] EWHC 817 (Ch).
22 [1992] 4 All ER 363.

of the payment by the bank must be based on the reasonable grounds for believing that the agent is attempting to defraud the customer. The essence of the *Quincecare* duty has been clarified in *Philipp v Barclays Bank*[23]: the Supreme Court held that the *Quincecare* duty does not apply to invalidate a payment or give rise to a claim against bank if the customer has unequivocally authorised and instructed the bank to make the payment. In other words, such duty is a simple application of the general duty of care owed by a bank to interpret, ascertain and act in accordance with customer's instructions.

Ultimately, in "*Hamblin*" two individuals were victims of an authorised push payment fraud who brought a claim based on *Quincecare* duty against the Electronic Money Institution (EMI). The decision of the High Court was that, if there were "circumstances of dishonesty apparent to the bank which would cause a reasonable banker before executing the instruction to make inquiries", the bank should execute those enquiries prior to authorising the payment. If the bank did not execute these enquiries, they would be in breach of duty. Therefore, in the case under analysis, court had wrongly equated the company with its agent; the EMI had actual awareness of the need for further enquiries and there were contradictions between the company's stated business and the nature of the transaction carried out.[24] Thus, EMI was expected to have made an enquiry about whether the transactions were not authorised by the company. Consequently, it was ordered to EMI to restore the missing funds to the company's account.[25]

4. Agreed remedies

One of the power of parties of a contract is to insert a clause into their agreement which stipulates what remedy should be applied upon a breach of a contract. If parties choose to insert an agreed damages clause, this should be respected by the court.

In cases where an agreed damages clause operates to punish a breach of a contract, this clause is named "penalty clause" and it is not enforceable. If the clause does aim to punish parties in case of a breach, it is named liquidated damages clause and it is enforceable.

23 [2023] UKSC 25.

24 It should be noted that under Regulation 55 of the Payment Service Regulation 2009 (*SI 2009/209*) (PSRs 2009), a payment transaction is authorised if the payer has consented to the payment order either before, or if agreed, after the execution of the transaction. The form and procedure of the consent must be agreed between the payer and the payment service provider (PSP). The latter – according to Regulation 61(1) – is liable for an unauthorised payment transaction and is obliged to refund the full amount to the customer, and where applicable, put the customer back in the position he would have been in if the payment had not taken place, including refunding any charges or interest paid by and/or owed to the customer.

25 Finally, in a different previous case (*Hayim v Citibank NA* [1987] AC 730 (PC)) the High Court permitted a derivative action on behalf of a company that was used as a vehicle for fraud on the basis that the company held money transferred to it as a trustee. So principle has it that a beneficiary may bring a derivative claim where a trustee commits a breach of trust or in other exceptional circumstances.

Liquidated damages[26] may be defined as a predetermined damage, generally set as a fixed daily sum or a weekly one. It is quintessential to clarify that liquidated damages are not penalties, because they shall be the exact result of mathematic operation when a breach of a contract occurs. Liquidated damages encompass loss of rent, loss of income, storage costs, rental costs, financing costs, etcetera.

By contrast, a penalty clause[27] states that if a person breaks any parts of the agreement, he/she must pay a significantly high amount of money to the no-breaching party. It is even more clear that the penalty clause achieves the objective to deter a party from breaking the contract. In *Dunlop Pneumatic Tyre Company v New Garage & Motor co*,[28] the leading case in English contract law, the court established the principle in force of which a clause is a penalty clause if its aim is to punish the breaching party. Moreover, in this case, the court clarified that the question if a sum is penalty or liquidated damages is a question of construction of a contract that shall be decided under the terms and specific circumstances of each specific contract.[29]

To establish if a clause is a penalty clause or a liquidated damages clause, some principles should be applied. For instance, there is a presumption in force of which a penalty occurs when a "a single lump sum is made payable by way of compensation, on the occurrence of one or more or all of several events, some of which may occasion serious and others but trifling damage".[30]

Moreover, a penalty clause occurs when a sum appears both extravagant and unconscionable in amount: there is a penalty clause if the clause refers to many liquidated damages.[31]

Finally, in penalty clause, damages are not genuinely pre-estimated.

To conclude, it is critical to state as follows:

- Penalty clause does not aim to accelerate an existing liability.
- Parties can stipulate that a certain amount of money shall be paid on an event which is not a breach of a contract.
- Often the word "penalty" plays a purely descriptive role: parties use "penalty" to refer to a liquidated damages clause. Thus, interpretation becomes quintessential to distinguish a liquidated damages clause from a penalty, the latter being an invalid contractual provision.

A recent case is *Pharos Offshore Group Limited v Keynvor Morlift Limited.*[32] The legal dispute was about a marine contracting project. The main issue was if Pharos was contractually obliged to a specific mobilisation for equipment and whether

26 (Halson 2018).
27 (Morgan 2016).
28 [1915] AC 79.
29 *Public Works Commissioner v Hills* [1906] AC 368.
30 *Lord Elphinstone v Monklands Iron and Coal Co Ltd.* (1886) 13 R. (H.) 98, Lord Watson.
31 See *Kemble v Farren* [1829] 130 Eng. Rep. 1234.
32 [2025] EWHC 1764.

delays were attributable to unforeseen circumstances. More in detail, the dispute was on the commencement date, delays caused by customs clearance, whether, technical difficulties as well as seabed conditions, and, finally, the contractual interpretation of payment terms and risk allocation. The court confirmed that delays caused by factors outside a contractor's control, weather and customs clearance, may not constitute breach if the contractor acts with reasonable skills and care within a reasonable time.

5. Guarantees and indemnity

A contract of guarantee is a contract under which a person, the guarantor, guarantees that if another person, the debtor, does not pay back money owed, the guarantor will pay the money instead. In other words, a contract of guarantee is fundamentally a contract in which the guarantor agrees not to discharge the debt in any event but only to do so if the debtor defaults. Consequently, a contract of guarantee constitutes a secondary obligation to pay if and only if the debtor does not pay the money owed.

Furthermore, contracts of guarantee must be evidenced in writing; this means that:

- This contract need not be a written contract.
- There must be evidence of the transaction.
- The evidence must exist before the creditor seeks to enforce the contract and must be signed by the guarantor.

By contrast, indemnity creates a primary obligation: it is effectively where one party promises to reimburse pound-for-pound the other party in respect of a particular loss arising under the contract. It is not required that indemnity be evidenced in writing form.

References

Barnett, Katy. 2022. *Damages for Breach of Contract*. Sweet & Maxwell Ltd.

Halson, Roger. 2018. *Liquidated Damages and Penalty Clauses*. Oxford University Press.

Halson, Roger, and David Campbell. 2019. *Research Handbook on Remedies in Private Law*. Edward Elgar.

Kramer, Adam. 2017. *The Law of Contract Damages*. Hart Publishing.

Morgan, Jonathan. 2016. "The Penalty Clause Doctrine: Unlovable but Untouchable." *The Cambridge Law Journal* 75 (1): 11–14.

Yin, Kenneth, Simon Kozlina, Kelly Green, Luca Siliquini-Cinelli, Emmanuel Larye, and Lisa Spagnolo. 2020. *Contract Law: Cases and Materials*. Cambridge University Press.

18 Sustainability in contract law

Chapter Overview

1. Introduction

Contemporary era is based on one mantra, that is the concept of sustainability often known as ESG principles too. This topic, albeit vital, is discussed only in this chapter for one reason, fundamentally. ESG principles are often part of commercial agreements or financial agreements rather than a merely contracts signed by private parties. This permits to, at the same time, introduce both sustainability and the second part of this research textbook, such as international trade law.

The next paragraphs will be focused on the analysis of ESG criteria and their application to contracts. It should be noted that ESG parameters are in between contract law and company law: if the corporation is a "nexus of contracts",[1] following the contractarian view of the firm, the corporation should be able to contractually agree on ESG provisions. It is possible because these contracts advance their mutual interests.[2]

Before commencing, it should be emphasised the vital role played by contract law in sustainable development. Contract law is essential for two main reasons. The first one is that contract law provides standardisation, certification and conduct codes. The second one is that, in social science area, certification has been analysed as non-state market-driven governance system. Further, in the business literature,

1 (Jensen and Meckling 1967).

2 (Kostritsky, Fox, and Spiller 2023).

DOI: 10.4324/9781003645948-18

certifications are important in the supply chain management or governance, including the global supply chains.[3]

2. The concept of ESG

Sustainable development constitutes a recent notion: it was defined by the Brundtland Commission in 1987 as a "development that meets the needs of the present generation without compromising the ability of future generations to meet their own needs".[4] From this, a heterogeneous regulatory framework has been established at the crossroads of international environmental law, human rights law and international economic law. Furthermore, this approach turns around five main pillars, at the beginning, that are as follows: environmental development, economic development, social development, inter-generational equity (promoting the account of interest of future generations), and intra-generational equity (promoting reduction of poverty and inequalities between different countries and between communities within one State).[5]

Moreover, the 1992 Rio Declaration on Environment and Development defined sustainable development in two Principles, more precisely Principles 3 and 4. The first one, Principle 3, stipulates as follows: "The right to development must be fulfilled so as to equitably meet developmental and environmental needs of present and future generations". The second, Principle 4, states that "[i]n order to achieve sustainable development, environmental protection shall constitute an integral part of the development process and cannot be considered in isolation from it".[6]

It appears clear that the aim of sustainable development is to strike a balance among environmental, economic and social interests, as well as consider the impact on the future generations. Because of this, the clash between rights and interests is something courts deal with daily, and judges can give concrete strength to sustainable development by reasoning around its elements.

ESG factors mean environment, social and governance: in other words, ESG factors are based on three main pillars, again, environment, social and governance. As far as the first one is concerned, environment encompasses the following:[7]

- Pollution.
- Waste.
- Water.
- Natural resources management.
- Supply change management.
- Emissions.

3 (Eberlein, Abbott, and Black 2014).

4 Gro Harlem Brundtland, *World Commission on Environment Development, Our Common Future* (Oxford University Press, 1987), 43.

5 (Folkesson 2013).

6 UNCED Report (1992), Annex 1.

7 (Fimmanò 2024).

- Land use and deforestation.
- Energy.
- Climate impact and asset resilience.
- Renewables.

It is worth nothing that environmental protection has received a lot of attention since the 1972 UN Conference on the Human Environment in Stockholm. The first case law was *López Ostra v Spain*:[8] the court in Strassburg made clear that environmental obligations under the ECHR do not only cover State activities but also activities carried out by private parties. The court held also that environmental degradation directly obscured the applicant's rights to private and family life, encompassed into Article 8, ECHR. Even if there were no grave health risks, severe environmental pollution could affect well-being of individuals and their rights to effectively enjoy their home. Therefore, the conclusion was that the right of private has been violated: Spain had not struck a fair balance between the general interest in having a waste treatment plant nearby and the individual rights.

In *Guerra and Others*[9] the court stressed that environmental responsibilities under Article 8 include an obligation of State authorities to provide affected people with information about the environmental situation that might interfere with their private and family life.

Moreover, in *Giacomelli v Italy*,[10] the court recognised a violation of Article 8 due to environmental destruction.

A further case is *Médecines du Monde International v France*.[11] It deals with the safe, or unsafe, heating, damp, mould and poor energy efficiency in Roma housing of poor quality. The claimants alleged the violation of their right to health because of poor ventilation conditions, "general state of dampness" and danger heating conditions. As the complainants better explained, public authorities failed "to install electricity that conforms to the existing standards": a consequence of this was the occurrence of numerous domestic accidents (e.g., burns, gas poisoning and fires).[12]

It is particularly clear that this case was focused on basic services infrastructure,[13] rather than on the health conditions of applicants. Thus, the court did not find a

8 European Court of Human Rights Application No. 16798/90, Judgment of 9 December 1994.

9 European Court: *Guerra and Others v. Italy*, Application No. 14967/89, Judgment of 19 February 1998.

10 European Court: *Giacomelli v. Italy*, Application No. 59909/00, Judgment of 2 November 2006.

11 *Médecines du Monde International v France* No. 67/2011.

12 See (Della Giustina and de Gioia Carabellese 2025).

13 The right to an adequate standard of living as well as to the continuous improvement of living conditions, including the right of an adequate housing and electricity, is encompassed with two main international treaties: (1) the Convention on the Elimination of All Forms of Discrimination against Women (CEDAW); (2) The International Covenant on Economic, Social and Cultural Rights (ICESCR). In addition, the UN Human Rights Council stresses that the realisation of "the right to housing in the context of climate change requires States to step up efforts to improve the energy efficiency of households. . . . Energy inefficiency, combined with rising energy prices and demands, are creating financial stress for low-income households and contributing to energy poverty. Similarly, energy efficiency standards and retrofits can also negatively affect housing affordability, especially

connection between Article 11(3) and safe heating and electricity access. Ultimately, the right to health requires that member states adopt "appropriate measures to prevent, as far as possible, epidemic, endemic and other diseases as well as accidents".[14]

Social, on the other hand, is a word under which the following topics are encapsulated:

- Health and safety.
- Human rights.
- Modern slavery.
- Stakeholder and community engagement.
- Employee and customer relations.
- Conflict zones/conflicts relations and minerals.
- Relocation and displacement.

The social side dates to 1992 Rio Declaration, Principle 1 stipulates that "Human beings are at the centre of concerns for sustainable development. They are entitled to a healthy and productive life in harmony with nature".[15]

The last pillar is governance, which means, on its turn:

- Anti-bribery and corruption.
- Anti-money laundering.
- Executive pay.
- Financial and corporate reporting.
- Gender pay-gap.
- Diversity and inclusion.
- Data protection and cybersecurity.
- Risk management and oversight.
- Directors' and officers' duties and liabilities.

3. UK and EU Regulation

In the aftermath of the Covid-19 pandemic, the Procurement Policy Note (also, PPN) 06/20 requires key environmental, social and governance (ESG) to be evaluated and assessed in all UK central government procurements from 1st

---

of rentals. These risks need to be explicitly acknowledged, and programmes must be designed to include protections for renters and not undermine affordability and security of occupancy, and to proactively address energy poverty. Rent control is essential to combat green gentrification. Higher costs resulting from building retrofits or green building requirements can also be prevented through tenant protection regulations, requiring the construction of affordable housing in mixed-use developments and by tying retrofit loans to future energy savings". See UN Human Rights Council, 'Report of the Special Rapporteur on the Right to Adequate Housing: Towards a Just Transformation: Climate Crisis and the Right to Housing' (23 December 2022) UN Doc. a/hrc/52/28, 42.

14 *Médecines du Monde International v France* No. 67/2011, 158–63.

15 (Sands, Peel, and MacKenzie 2018, 293).

January 2021. This constituted a first response to Covid-19 pandemic. Therefore, the PNN 06/20 adopted a "social value model": the latter includes the following:

- Covid-19 recovery.
- Tackling economic inequality.
- Fighting climate change.
- Equal opportunity.
- Well-being.
- Improved community integration.

It is worthy to emphasise that the HM Treasury had launched, on March 2023, a public consultation "[f]uture regulatory regime for Environmental, Social, and Governance (ESG) ratings providers". The purpose of this consultation is brought into regulation the direct provision of an assessment of environmental, social or governance factors to a user in the UK.

From a European Union perspective, the regulatory framework may be summarised as follows:

- Corporate Sustainability Reporting Directive (CSRD),[16] whose purpose is to expand sustainability reporting requirements for a wider range of companies, particularly large ones. It covers environmental, social and governance aspects, including climate change impacts, human rights, labour standards and corporate governance.
- Corporate Sustainability Due Diligence Directive (CSDDD),[17] this directive applies to companies exceeding a certain financial threshold and to non-EU companies with significant operations within the EU. The main elements stressed are corporate accountability, requiring companies to identify, mitigate, and address human rights and environmental risks throughout their value chains. The goal is to guarantee that companies are responsible for the environmental and social impacts of their operations and supply chains.
- EU Taxonomy Regulation[18] defines which economic activities can be considered environmentally sustainable. It provides a classification system for sustainable activities, helping to identify and promote investments in environmentally responsible projects.

16 Directive (EU) 2022/2464 of the European Parliament and of the Council of 14 December 2022 amending Regulation (EU) No. 537/2014, Directive 2004/109/EC, Directive 2006/43/EC and Directive 2013/34/EU, as regards corporate sustainability reporting.

17 Directive (EU) 2024/1760 of the European Parliament and of the Council of 13 June 2024 on corporate sustainability due diligence and amending Directive (EU) 2019/1937 and Regulation (EU) 2023/2859.

18 Regulation (EU) 2020/852 of the European Parliament and of the Council of 18 June 2020 on the establishment of a framework to facilitate sustainable investment and amending Regulation (EU) 2019/2088.

- Regulation on ESG Rating Activities[19] focus on enhancing the transparency and integrity of ESG ratings, which assess a company's or financial instrument's sustainability profile.
- Omnibus Directive (Consolidation Initiative)[20] achieves the purpose to consolidate these ESG regulations into a single "omnibus directive". In essence the goal is simplifying the regulatory landscape and reduce the burden on businesses.

The difference between the UK and EU is, fundamentally, the former, the UK, possesses a robust legal framework suitable to influence ESG practices in construction. Fundamentally, ESG arises from Bribery Act 2010 and Modern Slavery Act 2015:[21] the current legislation, indeed, stresses the importance of compliance by way of criminal prosecutions and financial crimes.[22] In a nutshell, the UK approach is based fundamentally on the idea that governance framework, that promote ethical conduct, should be integrated across the supply chain system.[23]

4. The ESG contract clause

Parties can incorporate ESG[24] and CSR[25] codes of conduct into their contracts, for example, a potential clause may be the following:

> XXX shall implement procedures that demonstrate its commitment to the YYY Supplier Code of Conduct as set out in Annex 6 ('Code of Conduct'). XXX shall use its commercially reasonable efforts to communicate these principles to its suppliers and encourage them to implement practices consistent with these principles.[26]

From this clause three consequences arise:

- The content of the document referred to the clause is incorporated into the contract: each term of the code of conduct becomes a part of the contract and forms contractual obligations that are binding on both parties. Nevertheless, a problem

19 Regulation of the European Parliament and of the Council on the transparency and integrity of Environmental, Social and Governance (ESG) rating activities, and amending Regulations (EU) 2019/2088 and (EU) 2023/2859.
20 Proposal for a Directive of the European Parliament and of the Council amending Directives 2006/43/EC, 2013/34/EU, (EU) 2022/2464 and (EU) 2024/1760 as regards certain corporate sustainability reporting and due diligence requirements.
21 (Castro and El Daouk 2025).
22 *R v Sweett Group* plc UKHL 73.
23 *Henry Brothers (Magherafelt) Ltd & others v Department of Education for Northern Ireland* [2007] NIQB 116.
24 Environment, Social and Governance.
25 Corporate Social Responsibility.
26 Woodward, Inc. (WWD) Form 10-Q, (Quarterly Report) EX-10.1, 8 August 2018.

of interpretation occurs, for instance the validity of the contractual consent, the respect of the code of conduct if parties reserve the right to modify it unilaterally.

- If the clause will be successfully incorporated, it precludes behaviour that is inconsistent with the content and the spirit of the document. According to 2016 International Institute for the Unification of Private Law's (UNIDROIT) Principles of International Commercial Contracts (PICC) and, more precisely, with Article 1.8, "a party cannot act inconsistently with an understanding it has caused the other party to have and upon which that other party reasonably has acted in reliance to its detriment". This is a well-known principle, called *venire contra factum proprium* in civil law legal system and called estoppel in common law system. To explain, a duty may arise for one or both parties of the contract; a breach of the duty may entail creation, loss, suspension and/or modification of rights.
- This clause imposes the use of the best efforts[27] to integrate one's party code of conduct in the other party's operations. The "best efforts" clause corresponds to a minimum degree of diligence; that is, to perform a contract in a manner that may be generally expected from a diligent and commercial party in the same circumstances.

From a practical perspective, tenancy agreements, this signifies, for example, that tenant

> shall use commercially reasonable efforts to ensure energy efficient operation of the Premises . . . by reasonably minimizing unnecessary use of electricity, water, heating and air conditioning. . . . For the avoidance of doubt, this Section . . . shall not require Tenant to expend any funds to meet any such sustainability targets or to minimize unnecessary use.[28]

Moreover, parties are free in establishing contractual mechanisms to monitor compliance and recovery in case of breach: it is also possible to mention the breach of sustainable development obligations as a reason to terminate the contract.

A clause on monitoring of compliance achieves the purpose to ensuring companies' compliance with binding instruments that require companies to prevent human rights breaches and environmental harm in their supply chain.[29] The underlying needs of this clause is that one of the challenging aspects of enforcement of the regulatory framework of sustainable development in supply chain is that if a breach occurs at the other stage of such chain, the privity of contract limits the possibility of enforcement to the parties of contract. Therefore, it is required

27 Article 5.1.4.(2) PICC stipulates that the duty of best efforts alludes to an obligation to "make such efforts as would be made by a reasonable person of the same kind in the same circumstance". See also (Adams 2019).

28 EXELIXIS, INC. (EXEL), Form 10-Q (Quarterly report) EX-10.2, 01 August 2018, www.sec.gov/edgar/search/#.

29 (Beckers 2023).

that all contracting parties comply with sustainable development obligations, this means, for example, to keep records of such contracts. Furthermore, from an EU perspective, the EU Corporate Sustainability Due Diligence Directive requires multinationals formed in accordance with the legislation of member state to be diligent in their global operations and to use their best endeavours to prevent foreign subsidiaries on the contractor for causing environmental damage and human rights violation.

In the event where a breach of obligations, linked with sustainable development, is discovered, liability, recovery damages and contract terminations may be suitable outcomes. Yet parties may decide to draft a clause aimed to prevent the immediate termination of a contract and focus on realising corrective actions.[30]

5. The sustainable contract

Before approaching the analysis of this specific topic, the first element to stress is the quintessential role played by consent principle in contract law,[31] which depends on the explicit consent of the parties.

A sustainable contract requires that parties pursuant both their own interests as well as the interests of the other parties and society, for example how and if actions may affect the environment and human health. Sustainable contracts are contracts based on the principles of sustainable development, general legal principles and norm of international law regulating the sphere of public relations.

More in depth, a sustainable contract is an agreement which terms are direct to reduce risks in the economic, environmental and social spheres to protect the rights and the interests of the present and future generations. Moreover, the implementation of sustainable contracts is intended to secure some interest, such as the following:

- Qualifying the contract in the framework of sustainable development can guarantee many preferences for both the contracting parties and third parties, such as investors.
- Contract efficiency associated with the compliance with ESG standards.
- Development of recommendations subject to ESG principles for future contracting.

The 2011 UN recommendations suggest a list of Principles for Sustainable Contracts turns around four main parameters: principles of justice, rationality,[32] responsibility and transparency. The principle of justice means that all parties to the contract

30 (Pannebakker 2024).

31 By contrast, consent in company law appears with a different nuance: in corporate law, more precisely, consent is a more attenuated concept. Hence, corporate law views the shareholder as having consented to the contract terms in the charter and certificate of incorporation through their choice for investing in corporation. (Farnsworth 2004).

32 It is aimed at accounting for the interest of parties and possible environment impacts.

must be equal, without discrimination or exploitation; further, all participants must have equal opportunities to represent their interests and defend their rights. The principle of responsibility implies a responsible attitude to nature and resources, both human and natural, as well as predicting the consequences of activities and accounting for negative factors. A vital role is played by transparency principle: it may be necessary to use in the conclusion of sustainable contracts, since contracts' information should be clear and accessible to all parties; the reference is to terms of the contract, the obligations of the party as well as any potential risks or problem.[33]

Finally, a problem is the cost of ESG contract, that is, an assessment of which durable problems parties face and an assessment of which private strategies or public law would best achieve the parties' goal at the lowest cost. To elaborate, the issue is whether contracting provision mandating ESG is efficient or increases the costs.[34] For example, an emerging legal risk is greenwashing: it is the "practice of misrepresenting the extent to which a financial product or investment strategy is environmentally friendly, sustainable, or ethical".[35] The concern is that greenwashing can undermine investor confidence as well as distort investor's ability to make an accurate assessment when considering their investment decisions. Investors; notion encapsulates consumers[36] too and, more precisely, consumers that have clear incentives to claim green friendly credentials. Thus, ESG concerns should no longer be ignored because both consumers and investors support climate change initiatives that have also led to environmental innovations. In other words, both consumer and investors allocate their resources towards firms that both talk about climate change initiatives and put into practice strategies that are designed for reducing carbon emissions.[37]

References

Adams, Kenneth A. 2019. "Interpreting and Drafting Efforts Provisions: From Unreason to Reason." *The Business Lawyer* 74 (3): 677–722.

Beckers, Anna. 2023. "Global Value Chains in EU Law." *Yearbook of European Law* 42 (1): 322–46.

Castro, Armando, and Mohamad El Daouk. 2025. "ESG Risks in Construction Law: Adding Teeth to the Governance of Construction Supply Chains." *SCL Journal* (online).

Ciro, Tony. 2024. "Green and ESG Derivatives: Financial Innovation in the Global Fight Against Climate Change." *Journal of International Banking Law and Regulation* 39 (1): 1–13.

Della Giustina, Camilla, and Pierre de Gioia Carabellese. 2025. "Indoor Air Quality as a Human Right." *European Energy and Environmental Law Review* 34 (2) (online).

Eberlein, Burkard, Kenneth W. Abbott, and Julia Black. 2014. "Transnational Business Governance Interactions: Conceptualization and Framework for Analysis." *Regulation & Governance* 8 (1): 1–21.

33 (Gladilina et al. 2024).

34 (Kostritsky, Fox, and Spiller 2023).

35 How to avoid greenwashing when offering or promoting sustainability-related products/ASIC.

36 For consumer protection, see Chapter 5, paragraph 5, titled "Consumer contract".

37 (Ciro 2024).

Farnsworth, E. Allan. 2004. *Contracts*. Panel Publishers.

Fimmanò, Francesco, Pierre de Gioia Carabellese, and Camilla Della Giustina. 2024. *Company Law in the UK and EU: ESG and Digitalisation*. Rome. Universitas Mercatorum

Folkesson, Emelie. 2013. "Human Rights Courts Interpreting Sustainable Development: Balancing Individual Rights and the Collective Interest." *Erasmus Law Review* 2: 142–54.

Gladilina, Irina, Hafis Hajiyev, Irina Vaslavskaya, Elena Kirillova, Olga Dymchenko, Emil Hajiyev, Olga Averina, and Rustem Shichiyakh. 2024. "Adapting ESG Principles to Contracting Practices: Towards Sustainable Business Agreements." *International Journal of Sustainable Development and Planning* 19 (7): 2627–34.

Jensen, Michael C., and William Meckling. 1967. "Theory of the Firm: Managerial Behavior, Agency Costs and Ownership Structure." *Journal of Financial Economics* 3: 305–60.

Kostritsky, Juliet P., Jillian T. Fox, and Blake Spiller. 2023. "The Hidden Cost of Contracting for ESG: A New Perspective on Private Ordering." *Case Western Reserve Law Review* 74 (1): 91–157.

Pannebakker, Ekaterina. 2024. "Sustainable Development Clauses in International Contracts Through the Lens of the UNIDROIT Principles." *Uniform Law Review* 29 (2): 352–61.

Sands, Philippe, Jacqueline Peel, and Adriana Fabra Ruth MacKenzie. 2018. *Principles of International Environmental Law*. Cambridge University Press.

19 International trade law

An introduction

Chapter Overview

1. International trade law: a definition

International trade law is an area of law focused on the regulation of international commerce, with the ensuing implications of both a public and private law nature.

The first limb, public law, is concerned with the coordination of commercial policies of States, and it falls within public international law. By contrast, the private area of international trade law refers to international commercial transactions between people belonging to different States.

International bodies, such as United Nations Commission on International Trade law, have tried to develop standard laws on different aspects of transnational transaction to achieve a harmonisation among different legal systems. The process, already mentioned, is described as unification of law.

The aim of international trade law is to foster free trade among nations: people should be free to buy and sell goods across national borders. Furthermore, trade law encompasses rules and customs governing trade between countries. The reference goes to trade remedies too: these are tools used by government to take corrective actions against imports that causing material injury to a domestic industry. The latter constitutes a consequence of unfair foreign policy and government subsidies.[1]

For a long period of time, international trade relations, among traders, have been under the *Lex Mercatoria* regulations. *Lex Mercatoria* may be defined as a set of

1 (McGillivray 2004)

DOI: 10.4324/9781003645948-19

unwritten rules, based on customs and usage, that encompassed, and to a certain extend still encompass, loyalty in the conclusion and execution of contracts, the rights of defence, the rule of the commercial transactions. Moreover, *Lex Mercatoria* is a collection of customs and practices that formed a binding rule involved in international trade law.

International trade law lies in an interdisciplinary section, because it involves multiple branches of law, such as commercial law, business law, company law, international payment law.

As far as the legal sources are concerned, the relevant ones are as follows:

- National law.
- International law, such as Vienna Convention on the International Sale of Goods (1980).
- The Rome I Regulation.
- *Lex Mercatoria.*

2. History development

From a historical perspective, international trade traces its roots in the ancient times when individuals were engaged in trade to acquire goods and resources not available in the local area. For example, Mesopotamians, Egyptians and Phoenicians established trade network. Similarly, the Code of Hammurabi provided an early documentation of trade and regulation practices. Moreover, the first trade agreement of the story was signed between Rome and Carthage from 507 BC and was concerned about the promotion and the regulation of trade that already existed. Another treaty, signed also between Rome and Carthage, contained the principle of non-discrimination: Rome and Carthage guarantee the same rights at local citizens.

With the Age of Exploration, such as 15th and 17th centuries, a significant expansion of international trade routes occurred. Thanks to these new explorations, new trade links with colonies were established. The purpose was to exchange goods, resources. More precisely, the exchange was between continent, on one hand, and colonies, on the other hand. Coherently with this trade activity is the doctrine of mercantilism[2] (from the 16th to 18th centuries) connected with colonialism. The latter played a critical role to establish market and to maintain a monopoly on trade.

Within the Industrial Revolution, international trade benefited from a sea-change: technology development, for example, mechanisation and improved transportation infrastructure, supported mass production and trade from a global perspective.

2 It was never an entire doctrine. David Hume, in *Of the Balance of Trade*, demonstrated how the real-world factors of labour and fixed assets were prime determinants of commercial expansion and wealth creation. He criticised trade restriction bred by national antagonism and argued for a mutual expansionary gain for foreign trade and domestic manufacturing accruing from free trade.

Furthermore, the telegraphy constituted a means of enhancing communication and coordination across long distances. As a result of this, trade and commerce too benefited from a significant improvement.

In 1860 the first Treaty, the Anglo-French Treaty was signed: it was a bilateral treaty, called "Tariff truce", because it was aimed to reduce mutual tariffs affecting the cross-border commercial activities between these two countries.

Within World War I, an international economic collapse occurred; because of this, at the beginning of 1920s most States adopted a protectionist economic policy aimed to shield national economies. Thus, international trade decreased in a considerable way. After the World War II the main objective was to promote international trade cooperation: the main reason for this was the limitation of bilateral approach to international trade. In this scenario, it was established the General Agreement on Tariffs and Trade[3] in 1947: GATT was considered as an *interim* solution until the establishment of an International Trade Organisation (ITO); however, this establishment failed in the 1950. Therefore, GATT was the sole framework for international trade policy for more than half a century. An important year was 1995: GATT evolved into World Trade Organization,[4] the latter plays an important role in fostering a rules-based international trading system.

A further evolution of international trade occurred because of IT revolution. The contemporary era is characterised by e-commerce, platform economy and Internet of Things; the main consequence is the revolution of both business conduct and cross-border transactions. For instance, two main examples are as follows:

- Platforms such as Alibaba Group connected to online marketplace.
- Global supply chains, that is an interconnection for production, distribution and consumption of goods.

In this scenario, globalisation[5] has also an impact on the traditional rule of trade law because it facilitates the commerce of goods and services through cross borders. Globalisation, indeed, constitutes an ongoing trend of increasing interconnectivity of nations across the globe. Moreover, globalisation refers to the growing interdependence of countries because of an integration process of trade, finance, people and ideas in the global marketplace. Additionally, globalisation possesses two main factors:

- Technology advancement.[6]
- The increasing liberalisation of trade and capital market.

3 Henceforth GATT.
4 Henceforth WTO.
5 (Potter and Biukovic 2011).
6 (Dimitropolous 2022).

3. The philosophical background

The underlying doctrine of international trade law is the Universal Economy one: it was espoused by philosopher, theologians, such as Seneca, Philo of Alexandria and Saint Theoderet of Cyrrhus. The latter in *On Divine Providence* said that

> trade between regions should be accepted as beneficial and even be permitted to run its course free from interference. . . . Providence deliberately scattered resources and goods around the world unequally to promote commerce between different regions. According to [noted economist] Jacob Viner [who identifies the Doctrine as the oldest, longest lived economic precept, and a forerunner of the factor endowments theory of trade, such as the Hecksher-Ohlin Theorem], [there are] four distinct elements [in the Doctrine]. First, it embraces the stoic-cosmopolitan belief in the universal brotherhood of man. Second, it describes the benefits to mankind arising from the trade and exchange of goods. Third, it embodies the notion that economic resources are distributed unequally around the world. Finally, it attributes this entire arrangement to the Divine intervention of a God who acted with the deliberate intention of promoting commerce and peaceful cooperation among men.[7]

The conclusion appears the same even if under a different doctrine, such as the classical liberal theory: these theorists believed that both democracy and free trade constitute suitable instruments to prevent war between countries.[8]

Moreover, international trade is an area affected by ethical theory principles too. These informed the analysis on two main directions: the level of analysis and the method of analysis. The first one touches upon the topics of transactions, transactors and the relationship between individual beings and other thing. The second one alludes to the metric for the moral assessment, named ethical theory which is based on three main pillars: utilitarianism, virtual ethics and deontological theory.

Utilitarianism states that actions are morally right if and only if they maximise the good or the bad; traditional utilitarian are Jeremy Bentham and John Stuart Mill. Acting according to utilitarianism means that a utilitarian calculation shall apply to each individual action. Virtue ethics has ancient Greek roots: the most authoritative philosopher in this area is Aristotle. On the ground of this theory, it is claimed that ethics is about agents, not actions nor consequences.

Finally, deontological theory is based on both morality and certain duties or obligations; it claims that specific actions are intrinsically right or wrong, regardless of the consequences that may follow from those actions. To elaborate, there is a duty to act in accordance with moral norm, irrespective of the potentially beneficial effects of acting otherwise. The reference goes to Kant whose famous phrase is "act

7 (Bhala 2025).
8 (Wolff 2022).

so that you treat humanity, both in your own person and in that of another, always as an end and never merely as a means".

All these principles have a practical application.[9] For example, World Trade Organisation Members (WTO) developed rules for ethical conduct in an arduous way and in any of their activities, such as negotiations, reporting, evaluation or adjudication. Only on April 2014, 20 years later the birth of WTO, the WTO Appellate Body adopted new guidelines to deal with conflicts-of-interest in cases involving former judges and member of staff.[10]

4. Principles in international trade

The main principles in international trade law does not constitute merely theoretical principles, due to their implication on global economy. These principles prompt (1) the start of negotiations of trade agreements, (2) the set-up of tariffs and, finally (3) the shaping of an economic market.

As just stressed, the exchange of goods and services across national borders represents the main pillar of the global economy.

Based on such background, the main general principles of international trade are as follows:

- The exchange of goods and services.
- Import and export activity, as a vital element for countries' economic balance.
- Trade agreements, thanks to which it is possible to define rules of trade. It encompasses tariff reduction; the establishment of trade standards; the enhancement of foreign investments.
- Non-tariff barriers, that includes quotas; embargoes and standards that restrict import and export.

From another point of observation, there are some fundamental WTO principles, such as the following:

- Non-discrimination principle aimed to ensure that all members benefit equally from economic trade and to prevent discrimination against foreign products once they have passed customs.
- Free negotiation whose purpose is to lower tariffs and facilitate the existence, as well as the maintenance, of an open international trade market.
- A predictable, transparent and clear regulation of trade market.
- The promotion of fair competition to prevent practices capable of distorting market.
- The support of economic development and reform into the global economy.

9 (Bhala 2025).
10 (Dunoff and Pollack 2017).

Although these principles constitute the main rules, some exceptions too are duly acknowledged. The first one deals with the concept of free-trade-zone. A free-trade-zone is an area wherein goods may be landed, handled, manufactured and reconfigured without the intervention of customs authorities. These zones are settled around major airports and seaports; examples are Hong Kong, Singapore, Copenhagen, Stockholm and Los Angeles. The primary purpose, pursuant by free-trade-zone, is to remove hindrances to trade.

A further exception relates to the concept of developing countries in the name of a solidarity principle. To elaborate, developing countries, before entering a global competition, shall boost and improve their supply chain capacity. Furthermore, other exceptions are concerned with the protection of public morals, human or animal or plant life and/or health,[11] to protect national heritage, such as goods of artistic, historical or archaeological value.

The underlying economic theory is that free trade is aimed to guarantee the increase in the prosperity of all countries, thus economic protectionism is not, theoretically, coherent with this purpose. However, countries, often, use "protectionist instruments", therefore tricks whereby the prohibition of a free market is circumvented in an indirect way. Among these tools we can refer to customs duties, tariff and non-tariff barriers to trade (quantitative restrictions for example). Another goal of free trade is to reward states for political allegiance.

The starting point is that world trade, as human society, at the beginning of its existence, relied on a State of anarchy. To guarantee peace and a political balancing between nations, it becomes quintessential to establish rights and duties. Thanks to the existence of WTO, international trade market is under a legal framework based on the main principle of non-discrimination free trade.[12]

This legal order is built on an international legal framework, informed by international law principles. This means that:

- Contracts under international law are concluded and ratified by legal entities involved in such international trade.
- The application of international treaties is decided by individual states to comply with the principle *pacta sunt servanda*, that is, agreements must be kept.
- Customary international law is made up of elements of long-term exercise and/or enforcement and the belief that this exercise is lawful.
- International law of treaties does not have priority over customary international law.
- Common principles are the following ones: (1) *pacta sunt servanda*; (2) *lex specialis derogat legi generali*; (3) *lex posterior derogat legi priori*; (4) *venire contra factum proprium*.

11 In this respect, the reference goes also to the protection of "exhaustible natural resources if such measures are made effective in conjunction with restrictions on domestic production or consumption", see Article XX(g) GATT.

12 (Lester, Mercurio, and Davies 2018).

- Interpretation rules come from Vienna Convention on the Law of Treaties. Article 31(1) stipulates the following: "A treaty shall be interpreted in good faith in accordance with the ordinary meaning to be given to the terms of the treaty in their context and in the light of its object and purpose". Further, Article 33(3) stipulates that in case of multilateral treaties which are aimed at a long-term cooperation, the interpretation shall be interpreted according to the common purpose of the treaty and its promotion.

5. A different approach: from free trade to managed trade

A different approach to trade comes from South-East Asian economies, defined as economies under a specific WTO categorisation. These economies differ from the classical liberal economies. Further, South-East Asian economies differ also from communist economies because:

- They are democracies.
- They are engaged in international trade market.

The main characteristic of South-East Asian economies is based on managed trade policy. The latter constitutes an international trade policy in which government plays an active role in regulating and shaping terms of trade with other countries. This approach shall be used to protect domestic industries and to promote the interest of domestic producers. Further objectives shall be achieved, such as the promotion of economic development and/or to address trade imbalances. Managed trade policies may include:

- A tariff, as a tax on imported goods used to protect domestic industries by making imported goods more expensive, thus less competitive.
- The establishment of quotas to limit the import of foreign goods.
- Subsidies, that is, financial assistance provided by government, to make domestic industries more competitive.
- Trade agreements between one or more countries to regulate the flow of both good and services between Signatories parties.

Within "managed trade policy", a government achieves multiple goals, such as the following ones: (1) the promotion of economic development in developing countries; (2) the equitable balancing in trade; (3) the protection of domestic industries from foreign competition; (4) the growing of internal economy.[13]

On the opposite side, there are also negative effects:

- Higher cost of goods and services for consumers.
- The existence of trade conflicts with other countries.
- A lack of innovation and efficiency of domestic industries.

13 (Sbragia 2010).

- Economic imbalances as well as economic distortion in the international trade system.
- A complicated situation to negotiate and manage trade agreements.

It is quintessential to highlight that free trade is a concept that does not exist in a pure meaning, because negotiations for tariff concessions require that the State use tariffs for purposes of protectionism. Moreover, the scenario is complicated by the fact that production has become even more transnational, thus mono-local product does not exist yet. An example of this comes from Apple, a US company where

- Invention and design of product are done in the US.
- Products' components come from different countries.
- All components are assembled in China.

The process just described is named "supply chain": it is an international network of production in which goods are sent from country to country to take advantage of low-wage labour and other services. The purpose is optimising performance of the chain and, at the same time, add as much value as possible for the least cost possible. In other words, all supply agents need to cooperate jointly within the firm to maximise productivity in the supply chain. A different nuance is the notion of supply chain management: it is the management, indeed, of material, money, men and information within and across the supply chain to maximise customer satisfaction and to get an edge over competitors.[14]

In this respect, WTO coined the expression "Made in the World".

Finally, the attention shall turn into the definition of main concepts relating to definition of free trade area.[15]

Free trade area means that members agree to reduce, or abolish, trade barriers such as tariffs and quotas between themselves. However, members retain their own individual tariffs and quotas against non-member of this zone. Partially different is preferential trade areas as an agreement in force of which it is required the lowest level of commitment to reducing trade barriers. It is crucial to stress that barriers do not eliminate, rather they reduce.

A different concept is customs unions: it means that countries that belong to customs unions agree to reduce and/or abolish trade barriers between themselves. Moreover, these countries agree to establish a common tariff and quotas against non-members.

Other two concepts may be confused by each other's, such as the following:[16]

- Common market, that is, a custom union in which members agree (1) to reduce restrictions on the movement of factors of productions (such as people and finance); (2) to decrease barriers on the sale of goods.

14 (Shukla, Garg, and Agarwal 2011).
15 (Lester, Mercurio, and Davies 2018).
16 (Perlkmans 2024).

- Economic union, that is a common market with a common economic policy in taxation, common currency and interest rates. The best example is European Union. Economic union differs from custom union because, in the latter, although members enjoy free movements of goods, they do not share currency or allow workers to move freely across borders. In this respect, although European Union is a genuine common market, it is not a perfect common market: there is a continuous attention and pressure to transform it into a "single market".

All these concepts are covered under the umbrella of regional trading arrangement notion. More in general, a regional trading arrangement encompasses agreements and treaties signed by two or more countries to encourage the free movement of goods and services across the borders of its members. Therefore, the first conclusion is that a regional trading arrangement is, fundamentally, a political decision: it is based on objectives pursuant by governments.[17]

References

Bhala, Raj. 2025. *International Trade Law: A Comprehensive E-Textbook*. Wheat Law Library, University of Kansas.

Dimitropolous, Georgios. 2022. "Law and Digital Globalization." *University of Pennsylvania Journal of International Law* 44 (1): 41–110.

Dunoff, Jeffrey L., and Mark A. Pollack. 2017. "The Judicial Trilemma." *American Journal of International Law* 111 (2): 225–76.

Freund, Caroline, and Emanuel Ornelas. 2010. "Regional Trade Agreements." *Annual Review of Economics* 2 (1): 139–66.

Lester, Simon, Bryan Mercurio, and Arwel Davies. 2018. *World Trade Law: Text, Materials and Commentary*. Hart Publishing.

McGillivray, Fiona. 2004. *Privileging Industry: The Comparative Politics of Trade and Industrial Policy*. Princeton University Press.

Perlkmans, Jacques. 2024. "Common markets." In *Handbook of Regional Cooperation and Integration*, edited by di Philippe De Lombaerde, 63–107. Edward Elgar Publishing.

Potter, Pitman B., and Ljiljana Biukovic. 2011. *Globalization and Local Adaptation in International Trade Law*. UBC Press.

Sbragia, Alberta. 2010. "The EU, the US, and Trade Policy: Competitive Interdependence in the Management of Globalization." *Journal of European Public Policy* 17 (3): 368–82.

Shukla, Rajendra Kumar, Dixit Garg, and Ashish Agarwal. 2011. "Understanding of Supply Chain: A Literature Review." *International Journal of Engineering Science and Technology* 3 (3): 2059–72.

Wolff, Alan. 2022. *Trade for Peace: Examining the Relationship Between Commerce and International Relations*. Peterson Institute for International Economics (online).

17 (Freund and Ornelas 2010).

20 General Agreement on Tariff and Trade (GATT)

Chapter Overview

1. Introduction

The World Trade Organization,[1] from a legal perspective, is a complex organisation with its body of law which encompasses different International Agreements. More in detail, it is possible to affirm that WTO encapsulates agreements, legal instruments and, also, annexes. It is crucial to clarify that agreements do not exhaust the potential sources of law of this organisation. The whole legal framework of the WTO is constituted by the following:

- Prior practices existing under General Agreement on Tariff and Trade (GATT).
- Reports of GATT dispute settlements panels.
- WTO practice.
- General principles of law.
- The so-called WTO-rules: international instruments aimed to improve and contribute to the rapidly growing and increasing law in this specific field.

1 Henceforth WTO.

DOI: 10.4324/9781003645948-20

In this legal scenario, the Dispute Settlement Understanding[2] handles resolution of disputes relating to substantive rights and obligations of WTO members and covered by international agreements.

It should be noted that GATT, on one hand, is successful in reducing barriers, but on the other hand, it makes international trading relationships more complex.

2. GATT

The main principles of international trade law are encapsulated into GATT: this international agreement is composed of 37 Articles, number of explanatory understandings and addenda. Although the basic legal text and the framework of GATT remain identical, there are several multilateral negotiations (called "rounds") which have further liberalised the market, with both tariff reduction and the expansion of voluntary agreements.[3]

GATT was concluded in 1948, whereas a further negotiation was signed in 1994. In that year, under the Uruguay Round:

- It was signed Marrakech Agreement.
- WTO was established.

Marrakech Agreement is crucial because its preamble changed the original GATT's preamble. To better explain, it is critical to distinguish these different preambles. Original GATT's preamble states that the signatory parties recognised that

> their relations in the field of trade and economic endeavour should be conducted with a view to raising standards of living, ensuring full employment and a large and steadily growing volume of real income and effective demand, and expanding the production of and trade in goods and services, while allowing for the optimal use of the world's resources.
>
> Marrakech preamble adds the following phrase:
>
> In accordance with the objective of sustainable development, seeking both to protect and preserve the environment and to enhance the means for doing so in a manner consistent with their respective needs and concerns at different levels of economic development.

GATT sets out the basic rules for trade in goods. By contrast, the trade in services was under the regulation of General Agreement on Trade in Services.[4]

2 Henceforth DSU.
3 (Lester, Mercurio, and Davies 2018).
4 Henceforth GATS.

GATS defines trades in services as the supply of a service among different spatial approaches, such as the following:[5]

- Cross-border supply, that is from the territory of one member into the territory of another member.
- Consumption abroad, such as in the territory of one member to a service consumer of any other member.
- Supply through commercial presence, that is, by a service supplier of one member, through a commercial presence in the territory of any other member.
- Supply through the presence of natural persons, such as by a supplier of one member, through the presence of natural persons of a member in the territory of any other member.

Articles I-III of GATT are related to the core principles, such as the following:

- The most-favoured nation rule (article I) in force of which parties shall ensure that if a special treatment is given to the goods of one country, it shall be given to all WTO members. This rule recognised two exceptions: (1) regional trade agreements; (2) developing countries.
- The national-treatment rule (article III) requires that the products of other countries be treated "no less favourably" than "like products" manufactured in the importing country. The underlying ratio is to ensure that products made abroad possess the same opportunity to compete in domestic markets.

It is critical to stress that "no less favourably" treatment rule means that domestic rules may be different for domestic and foreign product, however it is mandatory that the treatment of imported products is no less favourable in terms of opportunity to compete in market. Moreover, the law shall be the same for both domestic and foreign product but, in the case of which the imported product is, *de facto*, treated worse, this constitutes a breach of this specific rule.[6]

The concept of "like product" represents a controversial matter from which a significant case law originates. The starting point is the consideration that "like product" is defined under a case-by-case approach, due to its different meaning and the fact that a single definition does not satisfy both paragraphs of article III GATT. Moreover, the definition of "like product" is not developed to guarantee a consensus. A suitable definition states that "likeness"[7]

- Constitutes a relative concept and evokes an "accordion".
- Shall be defined under specific context and circumstances.

5 See Article 1(2) GATS.

6 (Herwig 2015).

7 *WTO Dispute Appellate Body Report on Japan – Alcoholic Beverages*, I.T.L.R. vol 1, iss. 2 at 242 (July 11, 1996).

3. External and internal trade requirement

GATT agreement does not prevent the formation of both custom union[8] or free trade area (FTA);[9] however, some requirements need to be met (Article XXIV:5(b).[10] In analysing FTAs it is necessary to distinguish between external and internal requirements.[11]

From an external perspective, and as regards as free-trade areas, Article XXIV: 5(b) establishes that

> the duties and other regulations of commerce maintained in each of the constituent territories and applicable at the formation of such free–trade area or the adoption of such interim agreement to the trade of contracting parties not included in such area or not parties to such agreement shall not be higher or more restrictive than the corresponding duties and other regulations of commerce existing in the same constituent territories prior to the formation of the free-trade area, or interim agreement as the case may.

To illustrate, a party, in entering an FTA, does not alter its external protection in such a manner as to negatively affect non-FTA members. Moreover, FTA includes complex rules about origin which may affect a significant manner of external protection.

Custom unions entailed two main obligations:

- Not to raise the overall level of external protection above a certain threshold. This signifies that customs union seeks further to liberalise trade among

8 A "customs union shall be understood to mean the substitution of a single customs territory for two or more customs territories" Article XXIV: 8(a).

9 "A free-trade area shall be understood to mean a group of two or more customs territories in which the duties and other restrictive regulations of commerce (except, where necessary, those permitted under Articles XI, XII, XIII, XIV, XV and XX) are eliminated" Article XXIV: 8(b).

10 "Accordingly, the provisions of this Agreement shall not prevent, as between the territories of contracting parties, the formation of a customs union or of a free-trade area or the adoption of an interim agreement necessary for the formation of a customs union or of a free-trade area; *Provided* that: (*a*) with respect to a customs union, or an interim agreement leading to a formation of a customs union, the duties and other regulations of commerce imposed at the institution of any such union or interim agreement in respect of trade with contracting parties not parties to such union or agreement shall not on the whole be higher or more restrictive than the general incidence of the duties and regulations of commerce applicable in the constituent territories prior to the formation of such union or the adoption of such interim agreement, as the case may be; (*b*) with respect to a free-trade area, or an interim agreement leading to the formation of a free-trade area, the duties and other regulations of commerce maintained in each of the constituent territories and applicable at the formation of such free–trade area or the adoption of such interim agreement to the trade of contracting parties not included in such area or not parties to such agreement shall not be higher or more restrictive than the corresponding duties and other regulations of commerce existing in the same constituent territories prior to the formation of the free-trade area, or interim agreement as the case may be; and (*c*) any interim agreement referred to in subparagraphs (*a*) and (*b*) shall include a plan and schedule for the formation of such a customs union or of such a free-trade area within a reasonable length of time".

11 (Lester, Mercurio, and Davies 2018).

members. Yet customs unions go beyond FTAs because they require an external protection too. In other words, members forming a custom union are under a duty vis-à-vis their external protection (tariffs) so that all members provide the same level of protection.

- To compensate external members in cases where the custom duties in some members of custom union have been raised to match the level of demand appropriate by the custom union.[12] According to Article XXIV:6 GATT custom unions have some specific obligations to compensate external members in cases where the customs duties in some members of the customs union have been raised to match the level deemed appropriate by the customs union.

From an internal perspective, for both custom union and free-trade areas, Article XXIV requires the following:

- For the customs unions to eliminate duties and other restrictive regulations of commerce "with respect to substantially all the trade between the constituent territories of the union or at least with respect to substantially all the trade in products originating in such territories" and to apply by each of the members of the union to the trade of territories not included in the union "substantially the same duties and other regulations of commerce".[13] To demonstrate the existence of a custom union both of these requirements shall be satisfied.[14]
- For free trade areas to apply "substantially the same duties and other regulations of commerce by each of the members of the union to the trade of territories not included in the union".[15]

4. The Agreement of Technical Barriers to Trade

The Agreement of Technical Barriers to Trade[16] covers standards-related measures that might be non-tariff barriers to trade. More in detail, these encompass the following:

- Technical performance standards that a product must meet to be imported or exported, such as energy and efficient standard for washing machines.

12 Article XXIV:5 (a): "with respect to a customs union, or an interim agreement leading to a formation of a customs union, the duties and other regulations of commerce imposed at the institution of any such union or interim agreement in respect of trade with contracting parties not parties to such union or agreement shall not on the whole be higher or more restrictive than the general incidence of the duties and regulations of commerce applicable in the constituent territories prior to the formation of such union or the adoption of such interim agreement, as the case may be".

13 Article XXIV (8)(a)(i)(ii).

14 Appellate Body Report, Turkey – Textiles Clothing. Products, AB-1999-5, WT/DS34/AB/R (99-4546).

15 Article XXIV (8)(b).

16 Henceforth TBT.

- Environmental, health, labour and others standard that a product meet during its lifecycle. For example, foreign products shall come from sustainable managed forests.

TBT Agreement applies fully to all government standard also to most levels of government. By contrast, non-governmental and non-mandatory standards are less strict and are covered by the Code of Good Practice. It is crucial to draw the difference between GATT and TBT. The first one, GATT, is aimed to establish a relative standard of treatment for trade in goods: to elaborate, the core principle is that foreign goods do not receive a worst treatment than domestic goods. By contrast, TBT requires the compliance, in absolute way, to certain standards of treatment.[17]

Furthermore, TBT is mainly addressed to central government bodies, yet it explicitly aims to extend its application to other bodies involved in the preparation, adoption and application of technical regulations, standards and/or conformity assessment procedures.[18] Other bodies are as follows:

- Local government bodies, such as provinces and municipalities.
- Non-governmental bodies other than central or local government bodies, such as the American National Standard Institute and the European Committee for Standardization.

5. The Agreement on the Application of Sanitary and Phytosanitary Measures

The Agreement on the Application of Sanitary and Phytosanitary Measures[19] was negotiated under the "Uruguay round". It refers to standard, defined as "necessary", to protect humans, animals and plants from certain hazards linked with the movement of these specific elements in international trade. For example, the reference goes to standard aimed to protect animals, plants, human and environment against the risk of pest, disease and disease-related organisms entering the country with these trade goods.[20] SPS agreement provides *ad hoc* standards of rules to ensure that sanitary as well as phytosanitary measures relate to each other.[21]

Additionally, SPS agreement:

- Describes what condition shall be present in trade movement, such as notification, transparency.

17 (Villarreal 2018).

18 (Van den Bossche and Zdouc 2017).

19 Henceforth SPS.

20 A further example consists of risks arising from additives, contaminants, toxins or diseasing organism in foods, beverage, *etcetera*.

21 (Rigod 2013).

- Requires that standard shall be based on scientific evidence[22] and that a risk assessment shall be undertaken. Risk assessment involves a scientific process, its purpose to identify the existence of a risk and establish the likelihood that the risk may materialise according to the measures that could be applied to address the risk. By contrast, risk management considers both scientific results of risks and the societal values, such as consumer preferences, industries interest, relative costs.[23]

Finally, GATT, Annex 1A has further multilateral agreements on trade in goods, such as the following: (1) Agreement on Agriculture; (2) the Agreement on Trade-Related Investment Measures; (3) Agreement on Reshipment Inspection; (4) the Agreement on Rules of Origin; (5) the Agreement on Import Licensing Procedures; (6) the Agreement on Subsidies and Countervailing Measures; (7) the Agreement on Safeguards. In the case where a provision of the GATT and the provision of another multilateral agreement on trade and goods are in conflict, the latter will prevail.

6. Agreement on Trade-Related Aspects of Intellectual Property Rights

This agreement, Agreement on Trade-Related Aspects of Intellectual Property Rights,[24] was negotiated in the 1986–1994 Uruguay Round, and it introduced intellectual property rules into the multilateral trade system for the first time. The basic concept of intellectual property is that it protects the products, results and rewards of the exercise of human intellectual and commercial behaviour.

In this specific area, one of the most important principles of WTO, the facilitation of world's trade and production, is noteworthy. Thus, the underlying economic theory suggests that intellectual property rights may be either to enhance or limit economic growth. Nevertheless, the evidence is that intellectual property may increase economic development due to its positive role. Consequently, there are two central economic goals of intellectual property protection:

- The investment promotion in knowledge creation of business innovation through the establishment of exclusive rights to both use and sell new technologies, goods and services.
- The widespread promotion and dissemination of new knowledge by encouraging and/or requiring right's holder to place their inventions and ideas on market.

22 It means that scientific evidence must have a rational relationship to the measure to be sufficient to demonstrate the existence of a risk which the measure is supposed to address and is necessary for a risk assessment. *Panel Report, US – Poultry (China)* (2010) para 7.200.

23 (Van den Bossche and Zdouc 2017).

24 Henceforth TRIPS.

From a different perspective, that is, under an economic approach, intellectual property right creates a negative dynamic externality since its connection with the problem of uncertainty as well as risks in competitive appropriation. The opposite side of the coin suggests that intellectual property rights rules play a central role in the promotion and encouragement of creativity and innovation, in the consumer protection by trade control of counterfeit goods, in the transfer of technology development to business enterprises.[25]

TRIPS plays a quintessential role because of the following:

- It was the first single, truly international agreement to establish minimum standards of protection for several forms of intellectual property.
- It was the first international intellectual property agreement to mandate detailed civil, criminal and border enforcement provisions.
- It was the first international intellectual property agreement subject to binding enforceable, dispute settlement.

TRIPS applies basic international trade principles to member states regarding intellectual property and most-favoured nation treatment. It establishes minimum standards for the availability, scope, use and seven forms of intellectual property (copyrights, trademarks, geographical indications, industrial designs, patents, layout designs for integrated circuits, and undisclosed information (trade secrets)).

TRIPS should be read together with further treaties, such as WIPO Copyright Treaty (WCT) and the WIPO Performances and Phonograms Treaty (WPPT).

Finally, it should be recalled the Hague System for the international deposit of industrial designs: it is an international registration system that enables owners to obtain protection for their industrial designs with a minimum of formality and expense. Currently, the Hague System has 77 contracting parties.[26]

7. Regional Trade Agreements

A regional trade agreement may be defined as a treaty signed between two or more governments that define the rules of trade for all signatories. In this respect, the reference goes to:

- North American Free Trade Agreement.[27]
- Central American Dominican Republic Free Trade Agreement.[28]
- European Union.[29]
- Asia-Pacific Economic Cooperation.[30]

25 (Correa 2020).
26 (Embley, Bamford, and Hancock 2024).
27 Henceforth NAFTA.
28 Henceforth CAFTA-DR.
29 It would be discussed in Chapter 22, paragraph 4, entitled "EU Custom law".
30 Henceforth APEC.

These agreements lay down the foundations of strategic institutional infrastructure for regional integration. Notably, their aim is to reduce costs and, at the same time, to define the main rules where economies shall operate. Furthermore, if regional trade agreements are efficiently designed, they can improve policy cooperation across countries through economic and social welfare growth.

NAFTA was inspired by the European Economic Community in the elimination of tariffs to enhance trade among its members. The proponents stressed the importance to establish a free-trade area in North America as a way to stimulate trade among its members and, therefore, prosperity. In 1988 Canadian-US free trade agreement was concluded and NAFTA was extended also to Mexico. The aim was to ensure an eventual "duty-free access" for a vast range of manufactured products, such as goods and commodities signed between Signatories. Moreover, the *status* of "national goods" was provided to products imported from other NAFTA countries. In this respect, any state, local or provincial government do not impose taxes and/or tariffs on such goods. Moreover, NAFTA set forth legal provisions whose purpose is to protect intellectual property rights. Consequently, it adopts strict measures against industrial theft.

In a further moment, NAFTA has expanded, indeed:

- In 2004 the Central America Free Trade Agreement includes five central American countries[31] in NAFTA (El Salvador; Guatemala; Honduras; Costa Rica, Nicaragua).
- Between 2006 and 2007 Colombia, Peru and Panama joined in this agreement.

CAFTA-DR constitutes a treaty aimed to abolish tariff and encourage trade between US and several Central American nations, which include El Salvador; Guatemala; Honduras; Costa Rica, Nicaragua; Dominica Republic and Caribbean. The initial intention was to boost exports and job creation in all its members.

APEC constitutes a non-binding, consensus-based forum or, better, an economic group, of 21 members[32] whose aim is to promote and facilitate trade, economic growth and the improvement of living standards for Asia-Pacific region. It was established in 1989, and it does not require its members to enter a legally binding obligation. To elaborate, this forum is based on consensus-based decision-making, and members are called "economies" because APECA is primarily based on trade and economic dealings. More in detail, cooperation is based on four main principles:

- Consensus: it means that all decisions shall be agreed upon and beneficial of the 21 Member Economies.

31 Henceforth CAFTA.

32 These members are as follows: Australia, Brunei Darussalam, Canada, Chile, China, Hong Kong-China, Indonesia, Japan, South Korea, Malaysia, Mexico, New Zealand, the Philippines, Peru, Papua New Guinea, Russia, Singapore, Chinese Taipei, Thailand, the United States and Vietnam.

- Voluntary and non-binding: it indicates that all agreements are voluntary.
- Concerted unilateralism: it refers to the fact that the implementation of decisions is made collectively in line with each economy's capabilities without all reciprocity requirements and/or expectations.
- Differentiated time frames: this means that advanced economies are expected to liberalise before.

APEC is focused on two main areas. The first one is liberalisation of trade and investment by ensuring goods, services and investments across borders. This is achieved through the import/export cost reduction and the promotion of free trade. The second objective concerned with the facilitation of economic growth in a multiple way.

Examples of this are as follows: (1) faster customs procedures; (2) aligned regulations and standards; (3) the creation of favourable business environment; (4) improving logistic; (5) accelerating economic integration among different regions.

Additionally, APEC achieves other goals, such as the following:

- Raising standard of both living and education.
- The inclusivity of these economies in decision-making process with allocation of both funds and services.
- To close the gap between developing and developed economies.
- Improve sustainability in specific sector, for instance, energy efficiency.

Finally, because of the latest weather shocks linked with climate change, APEC has launched climate change centres to investigate causes and consequences of this phenomenon. The reason for this is concern on the impact of climate change on economic development. More in depth, empirical studies demonstrate that temperature and precipitation shocks make income inequality even worse. In this context, the most problematic element is that current redistribution policies do not seem to effectively mitigate these adverse consequences.

References

Correa, Carlos Maria. 2020. *Trade Related Aspects of Intellectual Property Rights: A Commentary on the TRIPS Agreement*. Oxford University Press.

Embley, Judith, Keir Bamford, and Nick Hancock. 2024. *Commercial and Intellectual Property Law and Practice*. College of Law Publishing.

Herwig, Alexia. 2015. "Competition, Not Regulation – or Regulated Competition? No Regulatory Purpose Test Under the Less Favourable Treatment Standard of GATT Article III: 4 Following EC-Seal Products." *European Journal of Risk Regulation* 6 (3): 405–17.

Lester, Simon, Bryan Mercurio, and Arwel Davies. 2018. *World Trade Law: Text, Materials and Commentary*. Hart Publishing.

Rigod, Boris. 2013. "The Purpose of the WTO Agreement on the Application of Sanitary and Phytosanitary Measures (SPS)." *European Journal of International Law* 24 (2): 503–32.

Van den Bossche, Peter, and Werner Zdouc. 2017. *The Law and Policy of the World Trade Organization: Text, Cases and Materials*. Cambridge University Press.

Villarreal, Andrea Barrios. 2018. *International Standardization and the Agreement on Technical Barriers to Trade*. Cambridge University Press.

21 The World Trade Organization (WTO)

Chapter Overview

1. Introduction

The World Trade Organization (WTO) was established on 1st January 1995 on the GATT structure.

In principle, there was no reason for creating a new organisation; however, one country, Canada, proposed the establishment of a new international body. The underlying aim was to set up a single institutional framework for world trade. Under the auspice of Uruguay Round, three main new structures were shaped, that is:

- GATT.
- New agreements on services (GATS).
- New agreements on intellectual property rights (TRIPS).

DOI: 10.4324/9781003645948-21

In referring to "round", we need to introduce the notion of negotiation. The latter represents the driving force of a multilateral trading system. More in detail, negotiations are instruments used to agree on rules and procedures whose purpose is to reduce trade barriers.

WTO is, also, a negotiation forum where disciplines relating to trade policies may be agreed upon, against the background of the provision of the different agreement that should be concluded. Moreover, it is crucial to clarify that although WTO is a multilateral institution, it relies on bilateral and plurilateral interaction among different members. Therefore, negotiations, *de facto,* are taken by the trade giants, the few members of the WTO which really matter.

From a procedural aspect, negotiation takes place in permanent bodies and often in an informal way.

It is worth stressing the difference between WTO and GATT. The first one, WTO, is an international organisation with legal personality and, consequent, the power to sign agreement with States. By contrast, GATT is a binding international treaty promoted by the WTO. More precisely, WTO is an international organisation with full legal personality as well as all privileges and immunities necessary to exercise its functions. Moreover, it has the ability and mandate to develop relations with other international organisations.[1]

2. WTO objectives

It is difficult to understand what the main objective of WTO is. From an official perspective, WTO has three main objectives: (1) being a negotiation forum; (2) providing a set of rules; (3) helping to settle disputes among members.

First, WTO is a negotiation forum: it is a place where representatives of governments go to try to sort out the trade problems they face with each other. Further, WTO is a set of rules since the essence of WTO is based on agreements, the latter being negotiated and signed by the bulk of the world's trade nations. These documents provide the legal ground rules for international commerce: they are contracts, binding governments to keep their trade policies within agreed limits. The ultimate purpose is to help producers of goods and services; exporters and importers conduct their business while allowing governments to meet social and environmental objectives. In other words, the achieved goal is to help trade and flow as freely as possible; this means:

- Removing obstacles.
- Ensuring that individuals, companies and governments are aware of the trade rules around the world.
- Guarantee the existence of clear, transparent and predictable rules.

WTO settles disputes too: trade relations involve conflicting interests, the need to negotiate some agreements or to interprete it. Thus, neutral procedures based on

1 (Lester, Mercurio, and Davies 2018).

agreed legal foundation may represent the most harmonious solution to settle these differences.

Furthermore, world trade system promotes the following principles: non-discrimination; freer trade through reduction of barriers; fair and undistorted competition; more beneficial treatment for developing countries.[2]

Article II WTO establishes the scope of the WTO: "The WTO shall provide the common institutional framework for the conduct of trade relations among its Members in matters related to the agreements and associated legal instruments included in the Annexes to this Agreement".[3]

The subsequent Article III clarifies the functions of WTO:

- To facilitate "the implementation, administration and operation, and further the objectives" of the Agreement.
- To provide with the framework for the implementation, administration and operation of the Plurilateral Agreement.
- To be a forum: (1) for negotiations among its member within multilateral trade relations; (2) for further negotiations among Members.
- To administrate both the Understanding on Rules and Procedures Governing the Settlement of Disputes and the Trade Policy Review Mechanism.
- To cooperate with both the International Monetary Fund and the International Bank for Reconstruction and Development.

2.1 The neutrality principle

The neutrality principle represents the most ancient principle of international law, born in the state of war. Subsequently, it was developed in international relationships. The main objective achieved by neutrality principle is justice on a global scale. Furthermore, it is possible to affirm that neutrality principle constitutes a cornerstone of the rule of law: it is aimed, also, to ensure transparency, fairness and impartiality in international relations among states. From a legal theory perspective, the neutrality principle relates to resolution mechanism as a mean or promoting both fairness and justice.

In international trade law, neutrality principle plays the role to guarantee that all countries have an equal position in the formulation, as well as implementation of trade policies. Only in doing so is it possible to maintain a sensible global trade environment and strike a balance between smaller nations and bigger ones. To elaborate, in the international trade it is quintessential that, despite the existing differences, each country may have equal and standing voice in the implementation and enforcement of trade policies.

Nevertheless, there are some difficult elements of application.

The first one is linked with procedural neutrality, that is, the methods and process used in implementing international trade law. The aim of procedural neutrality

2 Ibid.

3 Agreement Establishing the World Trade Organization, Article II(1).

is that all countries are treated in equal way under the law. The reference goes to the decision-making processes, dispute settlement mechanism and enforcement of trade regulation. To ensure the application of procedural neutrality, international trade bodies are under an obligation to prevent biases and favouritism; at the same time, they shall also maintain the credibility and the effectiveness of international trade system.[4]

The other side of the coin is the substantive neutrality: rules and regulations shall be designed in a way that they do not inherently benefit certain nations due to their economic and/or political status. Moreover, substantive neutrality concerned with fulfilling legal rights as regulated by law.

As a result of this close to the neutrality principle, the principle of rule of law steps up to the place. The latter constitutes, together with the second one (neutrality principle), a foundational concept in the way both a legal system and international relations are governed and managed. To elaborate, both neutrality principle and rule of law principle share common elements, such as stability, fairness and effectiveness of legal and political systems.

Rule of law principle requires a nation to be governed by laws rather than arbitrary decisions or personal inclinations of some political personalities.

Furthermore, the rule of law encapsulates three main points:

- Principle of equality: all individuals, regardless of their status and position, shall be held accountable under the law.
- Legal certainty: the importance of clear and transparent law.
- Access to justice: all individuals have the access to both legal remedies and a fair legal system.

Through the lens of the neutrality principle, principle of equality is read and discussed for the political "soul" or side of the neutrality principles, therefore the promotion of peaceful resolutions in international relations. As far as the legal certainty is concerned, if this is read through the neutrality principle, it means that government and institutions' actions shall be impartial and without any bias.

Finally, the access to justice, if applied to neutrality principle, illustrates that impartial actors are bound by a duty to facilitate negotiations and peace process without any favour for parties.

Neutrality principle in international trade law consists of the fact that WTO has the duty to contribute to the economic growth, stability and peace on the global scale. As a result of this, both nations and citizens may benefit from this action. Moreover, neutrality in trade regulation alludes to the idea that countries should enact and enforce trade rules and regulations without favouring and/or discriminating against specific trading partners and domestic industries. To elaborate, it is quintessential that trade regulation will apply in a uniform way: the underlying idea is that all participants to the international market have equal opportunities to access

4 (Hershey 1916).

the international scenario. Thus, a critical role is played by DSU. Indeed, neutrality principle requires DSU to set out the rules and procedures for resolving trade disputes. The latter shall be decided under fairness and impartiality approach. To summarise, the neutrality principle applied into international trade disputes means:

- To prevent undue delays.
- To maintain trust among member countries.
- To prevent unilateral actions, trade wars and retaliations.
- To encourage peaceful resolution of disputes.
- To contribute to economic stability and prosperity on a global scale.

At a final stage, neutrality principle translates into non-discrimination principle, encompassing the following:

- Most-Favoured-Nation.
- National Treatment.

2.2 Non-discrimination principle

Non-discrimination principle encapsulates Most-Favoured-Nation[5] and National Treatment.[6]

The first principle, MFN, is based on the idea that every member state should treat each of its trading partners equally. For example, if the products of country X and Y are the same, a state should not give preferential treatment to the goods of one country in detriment of those of another. Article I(1) GATT stipulates that with respect

> to customs duties and charges of any kind imposed on or in connection with importation or exportation or imposed on the international transfer of payments for imports or exports, and with respect to the method of levying such duties and charges, and with respect to all rules and formalities in connection with importation and exportation, and with respect to all matters referred to in paragraphs 2 and 4 of Article III, any advantage, favour, privilege or immunity granted by any contracting party to any product originating in or destined for any other country shall be accorded immediately and unconditionally to the like product originating in or destined for the territories of all other contracting parties.

Moreover, Article I GATT has two main applications:

- If WTO members negotiate and grant trade concession to other countries, this concession shall be automatically extended to all other WTO members.

5 Henceforth MFN.
6 Henceforth NT.

- If a WTO member enacts legislation or specific trade-restrictive rules or requirements, it cannot discriminate between products from a WTO member and the correspondent product of any other country. It is based on the premise that the scenario is outside of trade negotiations.

The other side of "non-discriminatory principles" is the NT principle. Its focus is on the domestic dimension. More in depth, NT principle assumes that a country should treat imported goods as the same way on which it treats domestic products. Moreover, NT possesses two sides:

- Taxation: the reference is Article III(2) GATT, in force of which the products of the territory of any contracting party "imported into the territory of any other contracting party shall not be subject, directly or indirectly, to internal taxes or other internal charges of any kind more than those applied, directly or indirectly, to like domestic products. Moreover, no contracting party shall otherwise apply internal taxes or other internal charges to imported or domestic products in a manner contrary to the principles set forth in paragraph 1".
- Internal regulation: it means that imported products shall not be subject to more stringent rules, regulations or requirements than those applicable to domestic products.[7]

2.3 *Restrictions on trade circulation*

It is well-known that some products are subject to import taxes, or tariffs, upon being imported to another country.

From a general perspective, tariffs may be defined as import taxes, which may be:

- *Ad valorem* tariffs: these are equal to a certain percentage of the value of good.
- Specific duty tariffs: it means that tariff does not depend on the value of good since it is based on a per-unit basis.

Tariffs may constitute a form of protectionism measures which are never desirable. Therefore, one of the most critical elements of GATT is schedule of concessions, that is, a list of the result of several bilateral trade negotiations about tariff levels.

A further restriction are the quantitative restrictions: they are in the form of quotas, such as the limit imposed on the quantity of good that can be imported.

7 In this respect, see Article 3(4) GATT: "The products of the territory of any contracting party imported into the territory of any other contracting party shall be accorded treatment no less favourable than that accorded to like products of national origin in respect of all laws, regulations and requirements affecting their internal sale, offering for sale, purchase, transportation, distribution or use. The provisions of this paragraph shall not prevent the application of differential internal transportation charges which are based exclusively on the economic operation of the means of transport and not on the nationality of the product".

Quantitative restrictions spark off a greater distortive effect on the market: they impair the economy's ability to determine an efficient price and quantity. To elaborate, the effect of quantitative restrictions consists of the following:

- Impair the domestic economy ability of each economy to achieve efficient relations between price and quantity.
- Force domestic consumer to either change their preferences or purchase goods, in the domestic market, at a higher price.
- Encourage domestic producer to increase their output of low quantity goods to fill the gap between domestic demand for a good, particularly that of a high quality, and its availability.

It is worth emphasising that quantitative restriction is popular, from a political perspective, due to their immediate and direct results.

As far as quantitative restriction regulation is concerned, Article XI(1) GATT stipulates as follows:

> prohibitions or restrictions other than duties, taxes or other charges, whether made effective through quotas, import or export licences or other measures, shall be instituted or maintained by any contracting party on the importation of any product of the territory of any other contracting party or on the exportation or sale for export of any product destined for the territory of any other contracting party.

The general rule is a prohibition against quantitative restrictions. Nevertheless, some few exceptions are recognised. More in detail, export prohibitions or restriction complies with GATT rules in the following cases:

- Their aim is to prevent, or relieve critical shortage of foodstuff or other products, essential to the exporting contracting party.
- They are necessary to the application of standard or classification, granting or marketing of commodities in international trade.
- They regard agricultural or fishing product imported in any form necessary for the enforcement of governmental measures.[8]

8 As far as governmental measures are concerned, Article XI(2)(c) requires that these governmental measures operate "(i) to restrict the quantities of the like domestic product permitted to be marketed or produced, or, if there is no substantial domestic production of the like product, of a domestic product for which the imported product can be directly substituted; or (ii) to remove a temporary surplus of the like domestic product, or, if there is no substantial domestic production of the like product, of a domestic product for which the imported product can be directly substituted, by making the surplus available to certain groups of domestic consumers free of charge or at prices below the current market level; or (iii) to restrict the quantities permitted to be produced of any animal product the production of which is directly dependent, wholly or mainly, on the imported commodity, if the domestic production of that commodity is relatively negligible".

Preferential trade agreement represents an agreement in which parties offer each other more favourable treatment than that offered to third countries. Preferential trade agreement[9] is, at the same, a violation of the MFN principle and an exception recognised by GATT.

Additionally, preferential trade agreement may assume the form of free trade agreement: the latter is an agreement where parties promise to eliminate all import tariffs and to allow the free flow of goods across their borders. An example of this is the just discussed North American Free Trade Agreement (NAFTA).

Further, preferential trade agreement may have, also, the form of customs unions: a free trade agreement with an additional stipulation in force of which its member jointly set import tariffs for the products of countries not involved in this union.

2.4 Remedies against unfair practices

Trade remedies potentially adopted by GATT may be defined as tools that a country can use when it is affected by unfair trade practice of a third country.

The first remedy is the anti-dumping one. Dumping refers to a situation where a producer who sells goods in a foreign market does so at prices lower than those at which goods are usually sold in its domestic country. In other words, dumping alludes to a situation of international price discrimination involving price and cost of a product in the exporting country in relation to its price in the importing country.

The consequence of a dumping practice is challenge on a domestic industry for the control of a market: the mechanism activated is the sale of merchandise at prices much lower than the ones that the domestic industry can afford in selling its own goods. The remedy consists of anti-dumping duties (Article VI GATT): the latter are taxes imposed on dumped goods with the purpose of raising their price in the importing market.

To assess if a country is a victim of dumping, an objective examination shall be delivered. This objective examination is based on "the volume of the dumped imports and the effect of the dumped imports on prices in the domestic market for products, and the consequent impact of these imports on domestic producers of such products".[10]

An antidumping agreement is an agreement whereby a product is introduced into the commerce of another country at less than its normal value.[11] Therefore, a product is considered "dumped" where the export price of that product is less than its normal value than its comparable price in the ordinary course of trade, for the "like" product destined for the consumption in the exporting country. The assessment of a dumping practice is based on the definition of three main factors:[12]

9 See Article XXIV GATT.
10 See Article 3(2) Anti-Dumping Agreement.
11 See Appellate Body US – Zeroing Japan (2007).
12 (Van den Bossche and Zdouc 2017).

- The concept of normal value, it is the price of the like product in the home market of the exporter of producer. Article 2(1) of the Anti-Dumping Agreement imposes four conditions on domestic sales transactions: (1) the sale must be in the ordinary course of trade; (2) the sale must be of the like product; (3) the product must be destined for consumption in the exporting country; (4) the price must be comparable.[13]
- The assessment of export price is ordinarily based on the transaction price at which the producer in the exporting country sells the product to an importer in the importing country. According to Article 2(3) Anti-Dumping Agreement,

  - the export price may be constructed on the basis of the price at which the imported products are first resold to an independent buyer, or if the products are not resold to an independent buyer, or not resold in the condition as imported, on such reasonable basis as the authorities may determine.

- In essence the constructed export price is based on the price at which the product is first sold to an independent buyer.
- The methodology for assessing dumping, it alludes to a mechanism based on which the export price is compared with the normal price. It is based on two stages:[14]

  1) A fair comparison between the export price and the normal value according to the same level of trading.
  2) An adjustment which encompasses differences in terms of conditions and terms of sale, taxation, levels of trade, quantities, physical characteristics and any other differences.

- The assessment of dumping margin, that is the difference between the export price and the normal value generally based on the "W-W or T-T" comparison methodology. The "W-W methodology" (weighted average to weighted average) compares the weight average normal value of goods in the exporting country with the weighted average export price of those goods in the importing country. It considers all transactions. The second one "T-T" (transaction to transaction) compares the price of each individual transaction in the exporting country with the corresponding export price of the same transaction in the importing country. It is more sensitive to the variation in price between transaction and appears more complex to administer.

Another un-trade practice is subsidy: it constitutes into a sum of money provided to a private party by the government or public body.[15] The purpose of the subsidy is

13 Appellate Body US – Hot-Rolled Steel United States – Anti-Dumping Measures on Certain Hot-Rolled Steel Products from Japan, WT/DS184.

14 See Article 2(4) Anti-Dumping Agreement.

15 (Van den Bossche and Zdouc 2017).

to lower the price of goods of a specific producer, therefore, to help an industry to become competitive. According to Article 1 of Agreement on Subsidies and Countervailing Measures, a subsidy exists if

> there is a financial contribution by a government or any public body within the territory of a Member (referred to in this Agreement as "government"), i.e., where: (i) a government practice involves a direct transfer of funds (e.g. grants, loans, and equity infusion), potential direct transfers of funds or liabilities (e.g. loan guarantees); (ii) government revenue that is otherwise due is foregone or not collected (e.g. fiscal incentives such as tax credits); (iii) a government provides goods or services other than general infrastructure, or purchases goods; (iv) a government makes payments to a funding mechanism, or entrusts or directs a private body to carry out one or more of the type of functions illustrated in (i) to (iii) above which would normally be vested in the government and the practice, in no real sense, differs from practices normally followed by governments; or (a)(2) there is any form of income or price support in the sense of Article XVI of GATT 1994.

Moreover, there are three forms of subsidies:

- Green light subsidies relating to specific forms of assistance for research activities or to disadvantaged regions of a country. These are explicitly permitted.
- Orange light subsidies are forbidden only when they are specific and able to cause adverse effects to a country's trading partners.
- Red light subsidies are tailored to increase exports and those contingent on an industry's use of domestic goods. They are always forbidden.

The *ad hoc* remedy is countervailing duties: they are special duties aimed to "offsetting any bounty or subsidy bestowed, directly, or indirectly, upon the manufacture, production or export of any merchandise".[16]

3. WTO

As far as WTO is concerned, the main pillar is the minister conference: between meetings of minister conferences, WTO is managed by General Council. The latter operates through three subsidiaries:

- The Council for Trade in Goods.
- The Council for Trade in Services.
- The Council for Trade-Related Aspects of Intellectual Property Rights.

As a result of this, WTO is a network organisation.

16 See Article VI(3) GATT.

The Ministerial Conference has the duty to adopt important decisions about existing trade agreements. The conference, more in detail, includes representatives from all members of the WTO: these members are in equal representation to all its members regardless of the size of their economy or share in international trade. The Ministerial Conference's daily activities are carried out by three administrative bodies:

- General Council.
- Dispute Settlement Body.
- Trade Policy Review Body.

The General Council comprises the representatives of all member countries and acts as the representative of the Ministerial Conference. Furthermore, the General Council encompasses multiple councils and committee that focus on specific topics. For example, the reference goes to Council on Goods, the Councils on Services, the Committee on Textiles under the Council on Goods, etc.[17]

Dispute Settlement Body constitutes part of General Council, and it is responsible for settling trade disputes that arise between member states. Further, there is also an Appellate Body whose function is to decide appeals.

Finally, the Trade Policy Review Body has the duty of ensuring the trade policies of member states comply with WTO goals.

To better clarify WTO structure, it is possible to affirm that it is a hierarchy model based on four levels:

- The highest level, the first one, encompassed Ministerial Conference.
- The second level concerns the daily work handled by three bodies: (1) the General Council; (2) the Dispute Settlement Body; (3) the Trade Policy Review Body.
- The third level refers to three councils whose duty is to report to General Council. These three councils are (1) Goods Council; (2) Services Council; (3) TRIPS Council, that is, the Council for Trade-Related Aspects of Intellectual Property Rights.
- The fourth level is the level of the subsidiaries body. Indeed, every council possesses subsidiaries bodies named committee.

Moreover, another important structure is WTO Secretariat, located in Geneva, whose role is to provide members with technical and logistic support. The reference goes to the organisation of meeting of governing bodies as well as the arrangement of the background documentation. More in detail, WTO Secretariat responsibilities are the following:

- Administrative and technical support for WTO delegate bodies aimed to support negotiations as well as the implementation of agreements.

17 (Lester, Mercurio, and Davies 2018).

- Technical support for developing countries.
- Delivery of the analysis of trade performance and trade policy.
- Assistance from legal staff in the resolution of trade disputes relating to both WTO rules and precedents.

Moreover, the Secretariat plays a quintessential role to reducing transaction costs by distributing information and enhancing transparency by undertaking periodic reviews of member trades policies.

4. Decision-making process

Most decision-making process in the WTO is based on bargaining and consultation. Further, consensus constitutes the *modus operandi* of this institution. The WTO does not have an executive body, rather it does have a board comprising of a subset of members. Thus, consensus is facilitated by different GATT traditions, more specifically:

- The search for consensus before the formal vote is cast.
- The lack of progression on a potential vote, if one party was again (so-called one party's obstinacy).

As far as the decisions' rules are concerned, it is possible to summarise them as follows:

- Unanimity is required to amend general principles, such as non-discrimination principles.
- Three-quarters majority is required in relation to interpretations of the provision of WTO and waivers of WTO disciplines for members.
- Two-thirds majority occurs where amendments are linked with issues relating to general principles, such as accession.[18]
- Consensus in other case, where it is not otherwise specified.

Based on such a background, it appears clear and obvious that the dominant practice is *consensus*: it means that, if one member is absent at the meeting when the decision is taken, that member may formally object to the proposed decision.

Moreover, based on Article 40 of the Vienna Convention, an amendment does not require the consent of all parties; however, no party is bound by the amendment unless it gives its consent. In this respect, Article X of WTO Agreement prescribes stricter rules, such as:

18 It is the rule also of the Vienna Convention on the Law of Treaties. Thus, Article 9(2) stipulates that the "adoption of the text of a treaty at an international conference takes place by the vote of two-thirds of the States present and voting, unless by the same majority they shall decide to apply a different rule".

- The Ministerial Conference shall approve an amendment proposal with a two-thirds majority of the members, if it cannot reach consensus within 90 days.
- Further, two thirds of members shall ratify the amendment, in the opposite case this amendment does not become effective.
- As far as the most-favoured-nation treatment rules are concerned, every member's consent is mandatory.

Nevertheless, and based on Article X(1), the main rule is the following one:

> Laws, regulations, judicial decisions and administrative rulings of general application, made effective by any contracting party, pertaining to the classification or the valuation of products for customs purposes, or to rates of duty, taxes or other charges, or to requirements, restrictions or prohibitions on imports or exports or on the transfer of payments therefor, or affecting their sale, distribution, transportation, insurance, warehousing, inspection, exhibition, processing, mixing or other use, shall be published promptly in such a manner as to enable governments and traders to become acquainted with them.

It is important to clarify that amendment encompasses accession and withdrawal.

Accession[19] means the accession of a new member to the WTO: in other words, an amendment to the WTO agreement. The reason for that is simple: with accession this agreement is modified since the Accession Protocol is an agreement signed between the new member, on one side, and the WTO, on the other side.

In cases where a member intends to modify, or withdraw from, a GATT concession, for instance tariff concession, this possibility is given by Article XXVIII of the GATT 1994. In this respect, member should reach an agreement with the other members and with members having an interest in it. Further, should no agreement be reached, the member can proceed, albeit unilaterally, with either the modification or withdrawal of its concession. Consequently, other members can withdraw the equivalent concession.

Upon the occurrence of exceptional circumstances, the Ministerial Conference and the General Council can waive specific WTO obligations. Waivers shall be temporary and under an annual review. Duc to its exceptional nature, a waiver must be reported to the relevant council for consideration. The Ministerial Council, when adopting a decision to grant a waiver, must state the exceptional circumstances

19 Article XXI, titled "Accession", stipulates that "1. Any State or separate customs territory possessing full autonomy in the conduct of its external commercial relations and of the other matters provided for in this Agreement and the Multilateral Trade Agreements may accede to this Agreement, on terms to be agreed between it and the WTO. Such accession shall apply to this Agreement and the Multilateral Trade Agreements annexed thereto. 2. Decisions on accession shall be taken by the Ministerial Conference. The Ministerial Conference shall approve the agreement on the terms of accession by a two-thirds majority of the Members of the WTO. 3. Accession to a Plurilateral Trade Agreement shall be governed by the provisions of that Agreement".

justifying the decision, the terms, the conditions governing the application of the waiver, the termination date.[20]

Finally, authoritative interpretation represents a special instrument suitable to refine or revise multilateral trade rules in the interpretation provided for in Article IX:2.[21] This instrument was adopted under Uruguay Round; the responsibility to adopt such interpretation is on the Ministerial Conference and General Council side. Once given, such interpretation would bind all members. As far as the relevant effects are concerned, an authoritative interpretation may add to or diminish rights and obligations of members under the WTO Agreement: this means that the political bodies of the WTO are able to refine existing trade rules.

5. Multilateral trade negotiations

The first round of multilateral negotiations was in Geneva (1947) which led to the creation of the General Agreement. The most important "rounds" are these three:

- Tokyo round.
- Uruguay round.
- Doha round.

Tokyo Round, 1973–1979, led to the adoption of specific disciplines, such as the legalisation of preferential tariff and non-tariff treatment in favour of developing countries and among developing countries. Further, codes were negotiated on subsidies and countervailing measures, technical barriers to trade, government procurement *etcetera*. The use of code was driven by the fact that developing countries objected to the expansion of GATT.

20 Article IX (3) states that "In exceptional circumstances, the Ministerial Conference may decide to waive an obligation imposed on a Member by this Agreement or any of the Multilateral Trade Agreements, provided that any such decision shall be taken by three fourths4 of the Members unless otherwise provided for in this paragraph. (a) A request for a waiver concerning this Agreement shall be submitted to the Ministerial Conference for consideration pursuant to the practice of decision-making by consensus. The Ministerial Conference shall establish a time-period, which shall not exceed 90 days, to consider the request. If consensus is not reached during the time-period, any decision to grant a waiver shall be taken by three fourths4 of the Members. (b) A request for a waiver concerning the Multilateral Trade Agreements in Annexes 1A or 1B or 1C and their annexes shall be submitted initially to the Council for Trade in Goods, the Council for Trade in Services or the Council for TRIPS, respectively, for consideration during a time-period which shall not exceed 90 days. At the end of the time-period, the relevant Council shall submit a report to the Ministerial Conference".

21 Literally "The Ministerial Conference and the General Council shall have the exclusive authority to adopt interpretations of this Agreement and of the Multilateral Trade Agreements. In the case of an interpretation of a Multilateral Trade Agreement in Annex 1, they shall exercise their authority on the basis of a recommendation by the Council overseeing the functioning of that Agreement. The decision to adopt an interpretation shall be taken by a three-fourths majority of the Members. This paragraph shall not be used in a manner that would undermine the amendment provisions in Article X".

The Uruguay Round, 1986–1994, was focused on the following:

- Trade policies measures.
- Further liberalisation of international trade.
- The reintegration of agricultural trade, textiles and clothing into the trading system.

The last one is Doha Round, which was launched in 2001. Its purpose is to conclude a broad deal to facilitate the development through trade and better integration in the global economy. Based on such a programme, 20 areas would be covered, such as agriculture, services trade, market access for non-agricultural products and specific intellectual property issues. It represents the most ambitious round of WTO negotiations: the "strange" element is that, now, the Doha Round has not been formally completed due to the difficulties found during its negotiations.

It is wort highlighting that developing nations may have some potential benefits in the Doha Agenda, due to its focus on the improvement of access to rich country markets in specific areas, agriculture, for example.

This means that a success or breakthrough in agricultural matter leads to the development of many nations whose business is mainly based on agriculture. Despite this, Doha round, again, is not regarded a successful negotiation. During this round, the debate has been "politicised" and polarised between two main groups: industrialised countries versus developing ones.

Moreover, during Doha Round, the Trade Ministers opened the possibility of discussing the "Singapore issues" in the future. In other words, the question was if Singapore issues should be included in this round as one of the major sources of disagreement among WTO members. Nevertheless, the possibility of starting to discuss this topic should have had some benefits: among these, the opportunity, and the benefit, for WTO to establish rules in this developed area.

As far as the "Singapore issue" is concerned, it should be observed that it had been constituted a hot topic since 1995, that is, the establishment of WTO. More in detail, "Singapore issues" encapsulates different sectors:

- Investment and its focus on the idea to create rules for the investor's rights against any interference of the host country.
- Competition policy and, more in detail, the creation of rules to ensure fair competition without discrimination between foreign and domestic countries.
- Government procurement focused on transparency to allow foreign companies to participate in a non-discriminatory competition.
- Trade facilitation that means the creation of new rules aimed to simplify and reduce the cost of transactions.

Admittedly, the Doha Agenda has also some positive aspects, for example:

- The clarification of the flexibility available in Intellectual Property Agreements for developing countries to address public health crises.

- A major liberalisation in specific sectors.
- The improvement of antidumping measures.
- To help developing countries to participate in an effective way in the new round of negotiations.

Finally, a short comment shall be delivered in relation to the methodological approach. The experience has showed the failure to deliver negotiation on a multilateral approach, therefore, the possibility to adopt plurilateral negotiations. The latter may involve subsets of WTO members and often are focused on a particular sector. Potentially, plurilateral negotiations can produce agreements more quickly. At the same time, they may reduce the risk of "hostage-taking" phenomenon, that is, the pressure of some countries on a particular agenda. Moreover, there are two main approaches to plurilateral negotiations:

- An open approach that shall guarantee benefits of an agreement extended to all other WTO members. However, this may have a "dark-side": the risk of "free-riding" problem. To elaborate, non-participants receive benefits even though they do not commit to trade liberalisation measures.
- Via a "club-approach": benefits are extended by participants only to other participants rather than to all WTO members. This approach is called, also, "conditional most favoured nation plurilateral": it may originate the risk of policy fragmentation between signatories and non-signatories.[22]

The scenario is complicated by the fact that some plurilateral initiatives take place outside the WTO framework. An example of this is negotiations for Trade in Services Agreement[23] launched in 2013 between 23 WTO members, including EU and US. The EU asked to adopt a "flexible multilateralism" in the WTO: this expression means that EU:

- Actively supports full multilateral negotiations where possible.
- Actively supports and pursues negotiations for open plurilateral agreements in areas where multilateral consensus is not possible.

6. World trade law in between international law and domestic law

The nature of world trade law is controversial: fundamentally, it is not perspicuous if world trade law may be defined as part of international trade law. To commence, international law, different from domestic law, is decentralised because it has no central legislator that creates its rules: the creators of international law are, fundamentally, the main subjects of international law, that is, States. Moreover, international law is the law of cooperation: its creation depends on the consent of States;

22 (Lester, Mercurio, and Davies 2018).
23 Henceforth TiSA.

its rules are, generally, binding for all States. International trade law focuses, first and foremost, on the sale and purchase of goods and services across international borders. Consequently, international trade law is governed by a set of rules codified in treaties and trade agreements. To better understand the aim of this discipline, it is quintessential to recall three main theories.

The first one is named the "absolute advantage": a country may have an absolute advantage in the production of a good when it is able to produce more of that specific good than any other another country. Some countries have an absolute advantage in the production of certain goods: in this case, these countries have a specialisation in the production of certain goods while recording, at the same time, an excess of production.

A second theory, named "comparative advantage", stresses the fact that a comparative advantage exists even if a country has "a greater margin of superiority or a smaller margin of inferiority"[24] in the production of a certain good. In other words, a country does not have an absolute advantage in the production of a good, although it does have a comparative advantage if it is relatively better suited to produce a certain good.

Finally, the third theory ("free trade") emphasises that free trade, that is, a trade without barriers, promotes and enhances peace.[25] In this respect, there is a "virtuous cycle",[26] due to the promotion of democratic values and ideas of society thanks to economic integration.

Based on such background, international trade law holds some fundamental principles, such as democracy, that shall be discussed and read later. Bearing this in mind, world trade law is perceived as a part of public international law: WTO rules are part of international law and constitute *lex specialis* of some rules of general international law. WTO regulates the trade relations between States.[27] An opposite position highlights that world trade law is not part of international law: while the latter is relevant for the former, world trade law is not a species of the genus international law.[28] One of the main reasons is that international trade law is a fragmented law due to its bilateral and multilateral agreements. This is corroborated by the perception that WTO is perceived as a member-driven organisation focused on negotiation.[29] An additional question is about the domestic legal status of WTO agreements, that is, if WTO law has a direct effect or not. From a general perspective, direct effect means that a private person in a State may base a claim in, and be granted relief from, the domestic court of that State against another private person or State on the basis of the State's obligation under international treaty.[30]

This topic may be approached in between the US, the UK and the EU.

24 (Bhala 2012, 149–51).
25 (Lester 2012).
26 (Griswold 2007).
27 (Pauwelyn 2001).
28 (Trachtman 2004),
29 (Cottier 2015).
30 (Cottier and Schefer 1998).

6.1 The US approach

Article VI of US Constitution stipulates as follows: "All Treaties made, or which shall be made, under the Authority of the United States, shall be the supreme Law of the Land".[31] Thus, treaties are placed on the same level as statutes in the US legal system. Consequently, a conflict between treaties and statutes may arise; often it is resolved according to the rule *lex posterior derogat priori*, adopted by the US Supreme Court in Head Money Cases.[32]

Moreover, the governing rule is the self-executing one: a treaty is self-executing when it "operates of itself without the aid of any legislative provision" and "whenever its provisions prescribe a rule by which the rights of the private citizen or subject may be determined".[33] Further, the treaties may not deal with matters which have been expressly and exclusively delegated to Congress.[34]

As far as GATT applicability is concerned, one group of federal cases argued that GATT does not have treaty status; thus, the issue of self-execution is avoided.[35] By contrast, in *United States v Star Industries*[36] there is an assumption about both the binding authority and self-executing status for GATT. More precisely, the court assumed that GATT has a legal status in such dispute: this implies self-execution force of Article I of the GATT. Nevertheless, in the Trade Agreements Act of 1979,[37] Congress clarified that the implementation of Tokyo round agreements would not allow any provision of those agreements to prevail over a US statute.[38]

As a result of this, direct effect of WTO law is excluded; indirect effect represents a theoretical possibility which has not improved in its legal position.[39] To better explain, indirect effect becomes relevant when the domestic statute at issue is ambiguous and incapable of being interpretated consistently and inconsistently with WTO law. In the US the most important case is *Murray v The Charming Betsy*,[40] later known as *Charming Betsy* doctrine. It began with *Murray v The*

31 U.S. CONST. art. VI, cl. 2.

32 112 U.S. 580,598-99 (1884): "But even [though a treaty is the law of the land as an act of Congress is] • * there is nothing in [a treaty] which makes it irrepealable or unchangeable. The Constitution gives it no superiority over an act of Congress in this respect, which may be repealed or modified by an act of a later date. . . . In short, we are of the opinion that, so far as a treaty made by the United States with any foreign nation can become the subject of judicial cognizance in the courts of this country, it is subject to such acts as Congress may pass for its enforcement, modification, or repeal".

33 See Head Money Cases, 112 U.S. at 598–99; (Riesenfeld 1980).

34 (Brand 1997).

35 *United States v Yoshida Int'l, Inc.*, 526 F.2d 560 (C.C.P.A. 1975); *Sneaker Circus, Inc. v Carter*, 457 F. Supp. 771 (E.D.N.Y. 1978).

36 *United States v Star Indus.*, 462 F.2d 557 (C.C.P.A. 1972).

37 Trade Agreements Act of 1974, Pub. L. No. 96-39, § 3(0, 93 Stat. 144, 148 (codified at 19 U.S.C. § 2504(0(1980)).

38 It was clarified that Tokyo round agreements were not to be "construed as creating any private right of action or remedy for which provision is not specifically made in the implementing legislation".

39 (Lester, Mercurio, and Davies 2018).

40 *Murray v Schooner Charming Betsy*, 6 U.S. (2 Cranch) 64, 118 (1804).

Schooner Charming Betsy,[41] when the Supreme Court confronted the seizure of the *Charming Betsy*, a privately owned schooner that was sailing on the open seas, by a US military vessel. The captain of the Navy vessel seized the schooner under the Authority of the Federal Nonintercourse Act, a statute that prohibited any form of trade between France and American citizens. Between the time that the act was passed and the time the schooner was seized by the US Navy, the vessel was sold from an American to a Danish citizen that had been born in America. The captain of the US Navy vessel seized the schooner believing that it was still American vessel, therefore in violation of the act prohibiting to engage in trade with France. The Danish citizen had papers that demonstrated that ship was Danish; the US Navy captain seized the ship anyway. The Danish government contested the legality of the seizure, claiming that the ship was not American, therefore, seizing the ship violated a recognised principle of international law. The issue before the US Supreme Court was whether the "Charming Betsy [was] subject to seizure and condemnation for having violated a law of the United States". The Supreme Court agreed with Danish government: the seizure of the schooner was unlawful because there was no reason to believe that schooner was an American vessel within the meaning of the statute. Justice Marshall stated that "an act of Congress ought never to be construed to violate the law of nations if any other possible construction remains".[42] Consequently, statutes which are capable of being interpreted consistently with international obligations should be so interpreted.[43]

Charming Betsy doctrine has been applied in further cases; the most important are, at least, three. The first one is *Weinberger v Rossi*[44] where the word "treaty" was ambiguous: Congress enacted a statute that prohibited employment discrimination against US citizens "unless such discrimination [was] permitted by a 'treaty' between the United States and the host country".[45] In this respect, the doubt was if the term "treaty" referred only to treaties found in Art. II, § 2, cl. 2 of the Constitution, which are "concluded by the President with the advice and consent of the Senate", or if it also included executive agreements like the one entered into between the president and the Filipino government, without the advice and consent of the Senate. The court applied *Charming Betsy* doctrine: the statute was interpreted in a way that avoided the conflict with the executive agreement.

In *Trans World Airlines, Inc. v Franklin Mint Corp*[46] there was a contrast between a 1929 international air carriage treaty and the 1978 repeal of the gold standard in the United States adopted by Congress.[47] The court held that the Congress's intent was ambiguous because "there was no direct conflict between the treaty and the

41 6 U.S. (2 Cranch) 64 (1804).

42 Schooner Charming Betsy, 6 U.S. (2 Cranch) at 118.

43 (Bean 2015).

44 *Weinberger v Rossi*, 456 U.S. 25, 27 n.2 (1982). This 1968 agreement was known as the Base Labor Agreement, U.S.-Phil., May 27, 1968, 19 U.S.T. 5892.

45 Military Selective Service Act § 106 of 1971, Pub. L. No. 92–129, § 106, 85 Stat. 348, 355.

46 *Trans World Airlines, Inc. v Franklin Mint Corp.*, 466 U.S. 243, 245 (1984).

47 (Bean 2015).

statute, so the court refused to find abrogation given that the statute did not speak to the question at issue".[48]

Ultimately, in *Roeder v Islamic Republic of Iran (Roeder I)* it was demonstrated that *Charming Betsy* cannon applied on textual ambiguity.[49]

6.2 The United Kingdom approach

From a UK perspective, international treaties may have effect in a domestic legal system, if they are written into, or incorporated by, the relevant legislation. As a result of this, if legal provisions of a treaty were not incorporated into UK legislation, they do not constitute part of the UK law.

This approach to international law is called dualistic approach to international law: it means that international law and domestic law are separate legal systems.

By contrast, the monism approach to international law stipulates that international law and national law constitute two sides of the same coin, therefore beyond the metaphor of the same legal system. In this respect, international law is at the very top of the legislative hierarchy.

The first British case to refer to in this respect is *R (S G) v Secretary of State for Work and Pensions*.[50] Lord Kerr affirmed that two main, dominant principles

> have traditionally restricted the use of international treaties in British domestic law. The first is that domestic courts have no jurisdiction to construe or apply treaties which have not been incorporated into national law; that they are effectively non-justiciable. The second is that such treaties, unless incorporated into domestic law, are not part of that law and therefore cannot be given direct effect to create rights and obligations under national or municipal law.

The UK approach is clarified also in *Miller & Anor, R (on the application of) v Secretary of State for Exiting the European Union*,[51] where the UK Supreme Court dealt with these main principles: the dualist approach to international law, on one hand, and the parliamentary sovereignty, on the other hand. In this respect, it was stressed by the court that "international law and domestic law operate in independent spheres". The majority opinion[52] emphasised that:

48 See *Owner-Operator Indep. Drivers Ass'n v U.S. Dep't of Transp.* (OOIDA), 724 F.3d 230, 241 (D.C. Cir. 2013) (Sentelle, J., dissenting).

49 333 F.3d 228, 237–38 (D.C. Cir. 2003).

50 [2015] UKSC 16, at 235.

51 [2017] UKSC 5. In the 2017, after the 2016 Brexit referendum, the UK government announced its intention to trigger Article 50 of the Treaty of European Union to withdraw from the EU. Miller and others claimed that government did not have the right to give notice under Article 50 without a vote in Parliament permitting it.

52 By contrast, the minority highlighted that ECA was a constitutional statute.

- European Union does not become a source of the UK law; however, it takes precedence over all domestic sources of UK law, including statutes.
- The European Communities Act 1972[53] does not constitute the source of EU law itself: more correctly, it established various EU institutions as sources of UK law.
- The ECA constitutes a "conduit pipe" for EU to enter the UK law.

In a nutshell, the UK Parliament can, theoretically, make any law it wishes domestically relevant; nevertheless, the effect of domestic law remains unchanged. By contrast, if it breaches an international obligation, it might be lawful in domestic law, but it would be unlawful in international law.

Additionally, Lord Sumption, in *Belhaj v Straw*[54] stressed that

> international law may none the less affect the interpretation of ambiguous statutory provisions, guide the exercise of judicial or executive discretions and influence the development of the common law. Although the courts are not bound, even in these contexts, to take account of international law, they are entitled to do so if it is appropriate and relevant.

Bearing this in mind, the main question relates to the management and handling of potential frictions between countries. From the international trade point of observation, the reference goes to Dispute Settlement Body.[55]

Based on Article 3(2) of Dispute Settlement Understanding,[56] the role of DSB is to "preserve the rights and obligations of Members under the covered agreements". More in detail, DSB shall encourage amiable resolution of disputes and secure the preservation of a member's rights when an amicable solution cannot be reached.

6.3 European Union

In the European Union the direct effect doctrine was developed in cases concerning the application of community law before national court. The landmark case is *Van Gend en Loos v Nederlandse Administratie der Belastingen*[57]: a Dutch importer challenged the transfer of *ure-aformaldehyde* (a resin) from one tariff class to another by the Netherlands government on the ground that it increased the import duties contrary to Article 12 of the Treaty Establishing the European Economic Community. The court stated that Article 12 "must be interpreted as producing

53 Henceforth ECA.
54 [2017] UKSC 3 at 252.
55 Henceforth DSB.
56 Henceforth DSU.
57 *NV Algemene Transport- en Expeditie Onderneming van Gend & Loos v Netherlands Inland Revenue Administration. Reference for a preliminary ruling: Tariefcommissie – Netherlands.* Case 26-62.

direct effects and creating individual rights which national courts must protect".[58] The conclusion is that direct effect means the communities law takes precedence over national law of a member state even if national law measure is adopted after the effective date of the community law measure.[59]

As far as the General Agreement on Tariffs and Trade, the Court of Justice applied the direct effect doctrine for the first time in International Fruit case.[60] The first question was if General Agreement was biding upon the community: the court found that there was a clear intention on the part of the member states that the community assume the functions inherent on tariff and trade policy and be bound by the obligations entered into under the General Agreement. The reference was to Article 110 of EC Treaty Agreement, which prescribed "the adherence of the Community to the same aims as those sought by the General Agreement". The court concluded that "Article XI of the General Agreement is not capable of conferring on citizens of the Community rights which they can invoke before the courts". The reason was dual: (1) the General Agreement is characterised by great flexibility of its provisions, and it confers the possibility of derogation; (2) GATT is based on "the principle of negotiations undertaken based on 'reciprocal and mutually advantageous arrangements".

This general approach should be read together with two exceptions, the so-called Nakajmia[61]/Fediol[62] exceptions. Based on such exceptions, the legality of EU law can be reviewed considering WTO law when an EU measure explicitly refers to a particular WTO obligation that is implemented by that measure. Moreover, such exceptions operate when interpreting EU legislative measures consistently with WTO law is not possible.[63]

7. Game theory in trade agreement

From a legal theory perspective, multilateral trade negotiations can be analysed under the game theory and game theoretic concept.

International trade represents an area endowed with the concept of free trade: based on this, the golden rule is that countries can gain more benefit from this approach. By contrast, international trade produces winners and losers. Game theory helps understand situations where decision-makers interact. The reason is quite simple: a game is, fundamentally, an activity affected by the following characteristics:

58 1963 E.C.R. at 13.

59 *Amministrazione delle Finanze dello Stato v Simmenthal SpA*. Case 106/77.

60 *International Fruit Company NV and others v Produktschap voor Groenten en Fruit*. Joined cases 21 to 24-72.

61 *Nakajima All Precision Co. Ltd v Council of the European Communities*. Case C-69/89.

62 *Fédération de l'industrie de l'huilerie de la CEE (Fediol) v Commission of the European Communities*. Case 70/87.

63 (Brand 1997).

- Competitive aim between participants.
- The existence of a set of rules which informs competition.

7.1 Game theory

In a general idea "game" is that which we are familiar in context of *parol* game: the reference goes to a sequence of personal moves, at each of which one of the players chooses from among several possibilities, interspersed among these there may be the chance, or random, moves such as throwing a die or shuffling a deck of cards. A game, also from a general perspective, is based on three main elements: (1) alternation of moves, either personal or random; (2) a possible lack of knowledge; (3) a payoff function.

Game theory is the branch of mathematics that analyses situations where actions by players are interdependent. Additionally, game theory is the study of how and why players, which encompass both individual and entities, make decisions about their situations. The underlying intention is to produce optimal decision-making of independent and competing actors in a strategic setting. From a historical perspective, game theory can be traced to the 18th century, the major development began in 1920 thanks to John von Neumann (1903–1957). The most important event is the publication of the book *Theory of Games and Economic Behaviour* by von Neumann and Oskar Morgenstern.

The outcome is based on three main pillars:

- The structure of the player, that is, the interaction.
- The information available to the players.
- The expectations of the player about the actions of other players.

Furthermore, games may, alternatively, be the following:

- Cooperative. It means that the outcomes of the game are efficient in the sense that gains from the trade are maximised.
- Non-cooperative. It emerges in scenarios where there is a lack of central enforcement mechanism and there is not any presumption that the outcome will be pareto-optimal.[64]

Additionally, there are two main models in the game theory:[65]

- Strategic game (or) is focused on the action of individuals, and it considers situations in which actions are chosen once for all. This is the model of interacting decision-makers, called players, where each player has a set of possible actions.

64 Pareto-optimal situation occurs when no party can be made better off without another party being made worse off.

65 (Osborne 2000).

- Extensive game is focused on action of individuals, but the attention is on situations in which there is the possibility that plans may be revised as they are carried out.
- Coalition game is focused on the outcomes that can be achieved by groups of individuals.

One of the key principles is the theory of rational choices: it stipulates that the action chosen by a decision-maker is at least as good, according to their preferences, as every other available action. To elaborate, for any action, it is possible to design some preferences that no other action is preferred; if the assumption is that we have a lack of information about a decision-maker's preferences, and make no assumption about their character, any single action fits in the theory. By contrast, if the assumption is that a decision-maker, who is indifferent between two actions, sometimes choses one action and sometimes the other, not every collection of choices for different sets of available actions is consistent with the theory.

An additional crucial principle is "Nash equilibrium": it is built on the idea of a set of strategies – one for each player – would be stable if nobody has a unilateral incentive to deviate from their own strategy. In other words, Nash equilibrium means a set of strategies, one for each of the players of game, that has the property that each player's choice is his best response to the choice of the n-1 other players. For example, if the goal is to provide with advice (the prescription of a behaviour) all the players of the game (what strategy to adopt), any advice that was an equilibrium to each player is the best response to the advice given to the other players. If the goal is prediction, and not prescription, "Nash equilibrium" assumes a different nuance. Hence, it can be interpreted as a potential stable point of a dynamic adjustment process in which individuals adjust their behaviour to that of the other players in the game, searching for strategic choices that will give them better results. Finally, another interpretation is linked with self-enforcing agreement: an implicit or explicit agreement that, once signed by players, does not need any external means of enforcement. The reason is the self-interest of each player to follow the agreement if the others do, thus the concept of cooperative and non-cooperative game. In the former, agreement can be enforced (e.g., through the courts); the second enforcement mechanism does not exist.[66]

Prisoner's Dilemma is a strategic game coming from a story involving suspects in a crime; its importance comes from situations where participants face incentives like those faced by the suspects in the story.

This example explains strategies used in international trade under static game with incomplete information. The concept describes a situation where two suspects are arrested by the police and charged with a crime, but members of police lack sufficient evidence. These suspects are in two different cells, and each is explained the consequences that could happen based on the action and responses that he/she gives in this interrogation. The prisoners do not have the possibility to interact. The scenarios are the following:

66 (Holt and Roth 2004).

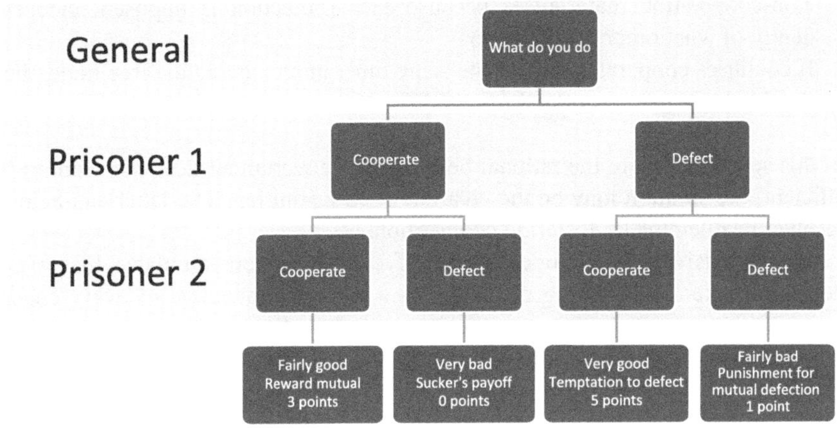

Figure 21.1 Prisoner's Dilemma

- If only one prisoner, either prisoner 1 or prisoner 2, confesses and the other one does not confess, who confessed is free and used as witness against the other, who will be imprisoned.
- If both prisoners confess, both are imprisoned.

The decision of the game is to "confess" or to "not confess". The equilibrium is obtained when one player's strategy is optimal for a given strategy of another player and vice versa. According to strategic game scheme, the structure is:[67]

- Players: the two prisoners or suspects.
- Actions: each player's set of action is (quiet, fink).
- Preferences according to the different positions.

To elucidate, the Prisoner's Dilemma shapes a scenario in which:

- There are gains from cooperation: each players prefers that both players choose "Quiet" than they both choose "Fink".
- Each player has an incentive to choose "Fink", thus, to free ride, whatever the other player does.

Under this approach, there is a single possible outcome that makes both players better off. More in detail, Prisoner's Dilemma in trade policy means that:

- If pay-off is inferior to pareto-optimal, free trade is the solution.

67 (Osborne 2000).

- Non-cooperation materialises because each protection is imposed, independently of what other countries do.
- If countries cooperated and, at the same time, implemented the free trade, they would obtain pareto-optimal results.

In this scenario, where the rational behaviour of government does not seem to be efficient, the solution may be the creation of an institution. The latter can help to resolve the dilemma by fostering cooperation.

The extensive game model with perfect information stipulates that every decision-maker in assuming decision has a perfect knowledge of every consequence of events as well as the previous actions adopted. The extensive game fits with situations where, after some consequences of events, these scenarios unfold:[68]

- The members of a group of decision-makers choose their actions simultaneously.
- Each member knows every decision-maker's previous actions.
- The contemporaneous actions of the other members of the group are unknown.

Finally, the coalition game is a model of interacting decision-makers that focuses on the behaviour of groups of players. It alludes to a set of actions with every group of players, not only individual players. Each group is called coalition, and the coalition of all players is the "grand coalition". One outcome is a partition of the set of players into groups together with an action for each group in the partition. To elucidate, a coalition game consists of the following:

- Set of players.
- Set of actions for each coalition.
- Preferences for each player over the set of all actions of all coalitions of which he/she is a member.

The nitty-gritty of coalition game is the set of actions of the grand coalition so that no coalition has an action that all its members prefer to a set of actions. Therefore, it is quintessential to find the set of actions of the grand coalition upon which no coalition improve.[69]

7.2 Game theory in international trade law

A multilateral trade negotiation consists of a set of rules of non-cooperative international trade game where the outcome of negotiations is rarely pareto-optimal. This problem arises where the government has no incentive to diverge from free trade. In the opposite situation, a dominant country may exist because it alters/diverges

68 Ibid.
69 Ibid.

from cooperation: to elaborate, to pursue national objectives, a country may reduce the welfare of other countries by imposing negative externalities to them.

More appropriate seems to be the pattern of the Prisoner's Dilemma (discussed previously) where players, in choosing individually rational strategies, end up in an equilibrium that is not efficient. In a nutshell, game theory represents a suitable methodology because it is, fundamentally, a strategy on the optimal decision-making of independent and competing actors in a strategic setting. Further, it is a part of microeconomics used in different economic fields, such as international trade, macroeconomics, financial economics, etc.

Moreover, game theory may be applied to tariff/trade wars and trade negotiations. In tariff/trade wars one of the most applied concepts is non-cooperative negotiations.[70] To elaborate, the scenario is the following:

- Players are nations.
- Strategies are choices of tariffs.
- The maximisation of social welfare is a function of aggregate consumption quantities.

The assumption of the example is that there are only two countries: Australia and China having comparative advantages and exporting good-1 and good-2 prince in foreign market. A further assumption is that tariff does not affect the pattern of trade. Pc is the domestic price of good-2 in China and Pc' is the foreign price of good-2 in foreign market. In the same way, Pc and Pc' is the price of good-1 in Australia, the domestic market, and the foreign market, respectively. If both countries impose import tax, each country seeks to maximise its own utility function (a function of domestic price, price of other countries and disposable income of the native country).

This example demonstrates that if a large country imposes either a relatively small tariff or an optimal tariff in a perfectly competitive market, the domestic national welfare will rise. Yet foreign national welfare will fail.[71]

If we translate this in our examples, if (1) Australia imposes a set of products from China, and (2) China imports a different set of products from Australia, and (3) each country chooses two distinct trade policies (free trade and optimal tariff), the result is that each policy choice represents a game strategy.

To determine which strategy the two governments would choose in this game, it is necessary to identify the objectives of the players as well as the degree of cooperation. A cooperative approach alludes to a set of strategies that would maximise the sum of the benefit accruing to the player, that is, trade policy game about a set of strategies based on free trade for both nations. By contrast, a non-cooperative solution alludes to a set of strategies aimed to guarantee the maximisation for the

70 (Owen, Guillermo. 2013).
71 Ibid.

welfare of each country subject to the strategy chosen by the other countries. This mechanism is based on Prisoner's Dilemma.

As it was said previously, game theory helps also for trade negotiations and, more specifically, to analyse the outcomes of trade negotiations between two countries. WTO may be read as a dynamic game and, more appropriate, as a set of sequential game where players play their strategies in a sequence that is successive in time and is with incomplete information. This signifies that one player does not know one or more of the winning functions of the other player. It is titled Bayesian Game or Harsanyi Games with Incomplete Information: a game used to described situations by assigning to players additional components (types and beliefs). In a nutshell, Bayesian Game is suitable for describing situations affected by uncertainties.[72] A perfect balance is struck when both a lot of strategies and assumptions are satisfied. For example, player A has three choices of actions: support for agriculture; use of barriers; give up. There are different scenarios:[73]

- A chooses the latter – give up – the game ends without player B choosing his own actions.
- A chooses one of the other strategies (support for agriculture; use of barriers) but B has not chosen, but choosing between two actions, the game terminates after this decision.
- The equilibrium derives from two choices: support for agriculture–support for agriculture; or use of barriers–use of barriers.

Ultimately, international trade liberalisation is often based on Prisoner's Dilemma: all countries have a common interest in the economic gains from free trade. Nevertheless, countries face incentives to protect sensitive domestic industries at the same time.[74]

References

Bean, Andrew H. 2015. "Constraining Charming Betsy: Textual Ambiguity as a Predicate to Applying the Charming Betsy Doctrine." *BYU Law Review* 13 (6): 1801–24.

Bhala, Raj. 2012. *Dictionary of International Trade Law*. LexisNexis.

Brand, Ronald A. 1997. "Direct Effect of International Economic Law in the United States and the European Union." *Northwestern Journal of International Law & Business* 17 (1): 556–608.

Cottier, Thomas. 2015. "The Common Law of International Trade and the Future of the World Trade Organization." *Journal of International Economic Law* 18 (1): 3–20.

Cottier, Thomas, and Krista Nadakavukaren Schefer. 1998. "The Relationship Between World Trade Organization Law, National and Regional Law." *Journal of International Economic Law* 1: 91–101.

72 (Wu et al. 2021).

73 (Khurana 2022).

74 (Krapohl, Ocelík, and Walentek 2021).

Griswold, Daniel. 2007. *Trade, Democracy and Peace: The Virtuous Cycle*. Peace Through Trade World Trade Centers Association.

Hershey, Amos S. 1916. "Neutrality and International Law." *The International Journal of Ethics* 26 (2): 168–76.

Holt, Charles A, and Alvin E. Roth. 2004. "The Nash Equilibrium: A Perspective." *Proceedings of the National Academy of Sciences* 12 (101): 3999–4002.

Khurana, Chaitanya. 2022. "Review of Game Theory Applications in International Trade." *International Journal of English Literature and Social Sciences* 7 (1): 196–206.

Krapohl, Sebastian, Václav Ocelík, and Dawid M. Walentek. 2021. "The Instability of Globalization: Applying Evolutionary Game Theory to Gloabl Trade Cooperation." *Public Choice* 188: 31–51.

Lester, Simon, Bryan Mercurio, and Arwel Davies. 2012. *World Trade Law: Text, Materials, and Commentary*. Hart Publishing.

Lester, Simon, Bryan Mercurio, and Arwel Davies. 2018. *World Trade Law: Text, Materials and Commentary*. Hart Publishing.

Osborne, Martin J. 2000. *An Introduction to Game Theory*. Oxford University Press.

Owen, Guillermo. 2013. *Game Theory*. Emerald.

Pauwelyn, Joost. 2001. "The Role of Public International Law in the WTO: How Far Can We Go?" *American Journal of International Law* 95 (3): 535–52.

Riesenfeld, Stefan A. 1980. "The Doctrine of Self-Executing Treaties and US v. Postal: Win at Any Price?" *American Journal of International Law* 74 (4): 892–904.

Trachtman, Joel P. 2004. "Conflict of Norms in Public International Law: How WTO Law Relates to Other Rules of International Law." *The American Journal of International Law* 98 (4): 855–61.

Van den Bossche, Peter, and Werner Zdouc. 2017. *The Law and Policy of the World Trade Organization: Text, Cases and Materials*. Cambridge University Press.

Wu, Yuhu, Shuting Le, Kuize Zhang, and Xi-Ming Sun. 2021. "Agent Transformation of Bayesian Games." *EEE Transactions on Automatic Control* 67 (11): 5793–808.

22 Trade in goods

Chapter Overview

1. Physical movement of goods

International trade law is focused on the physical movement and electronic transfer of goods and services across national borders. More in detail, it encompasses the movement of commodities, such as natural resources, manufactured goods and transfer of services. Among services, it includes commercial data, banking and financial transactions and other kind of professional and business-related activities.

The globalisation process refers to an interdependence of the world's economies, culture and populations brought about by cross-border trade in goods and services. From a general perspective, countries usually rely on selected "points of entry and release", normally seaports, airports or land borders, through which imported goods transit.

In some cases, businesses are located inland and prefer clearing imported goods at inland locations, in places usually called "dry ports". The latter acts as a logistics centre where goods are duly released or cleared. More in detail, a dry port provides services for the handling and temporary storage of containers, general and/or bulk cargoes that enters or leaves the dry port by any mode of transport, such as road, railways, inland waterways or airports.

DOI: 10.4324/9781003645948-22

Furthermore, it is worth stressing that dry ports constitute a notion under closer scrutiny among scholars. The most important reason for that is the fact that the concept of dry port encapsules a wide range of phenomena. More in detail, inland terminals are, *de facto*, "wet", because they have direct access to inland waterway systems. Furthermore, the inland location can effectively be a port if a barrage of service is concerned.[1] A definition of dry port may be: "an inland intermodal terminal directly connected to a seaport, with high-capacity traffic modes, preferably rail, where customers can leave and/or collect their goods in intermodal loading units, as if directly to the seaport."[2]

An intermodal inland terminal, to be defined a dry port, shall satisfy two main parameters:[3]

- An extension of a seaport offering services that are usually available at the seaport. This extension will serve as an interface inland of the seaport.
- A connection to a seaport, thanks to a higher capacity of transportation, such as rail rather than barge or inland waterway transportation.

Dry port constitutes an integral part of a large transportation network involving numerous stakeholders with different interests and ambitions. The reason is quite simple: dry port is an essential node of the production based with seaport. The surge in containerisation has led to congestion at seaports promoting the integration of dry ports as a strategic measure to relieve congestion at seaports. Thus, dry port ensures a higher level of connectivity, cut demurrage costs, reduce congestion and avoiding delays in trade supply chain networks. Consequently, one of the main challenges is it creates an effective trade supply chain sustainability.[4]

In this scenario, before goods may be imported, it is quintessential that a few regulations shall be satisfied. To elaborate, when a good is imported from a third country, it acquires the status of "good in temporary storage": the importer is under an obligation to declare how this good shall be treated or used as well as the usage under customs procedures. In this respect, a procedure is named "release for free circulation": the goods may acquire the status of "Community goods" and may circulate freely in the EU single market.

Based on such background, the just mentioned procedure refers to goods in circulation among countries where there is not a common market, without barriers. Therefore, the focus is on customs regulation. The underlying historical and juridical reference is dual: the EU regulation, on one hand, and the regulation of goods circulation after Brexit, on the other hand. Before approaching this topic, it is quintessential to analyse the freeports concept too.

1 (Rodrigue and Notteboom 2022).
2 (Roso, Woxenius, and Lumsden 2009).
3 (Khaslavskaya and Roso 2020).
4 (Beyene et al. 2023).

2. Freeport notion

Freeports constitute a fundamental aspect in international business: they allow importers and exporters to move goods from one place to another without having to pay duties on their goods unless the goods leave the freeport and enter a nation's customs territory.[5] From a metaphorical perspective, freeports are a quasi "no man's land"[6] yet are not a wholly regulation-free zone.[7]

The idea of freeport originated in the exemption of specific seaports and cities from having to pay taxes on incoming goods to a central authority. Sea-facing cities, such as Livorno, Genoa and Venice were the first declared to be freeports, and it was from Italy that the idea spread to other parts of Europe. In essence, freeports represent special economic zones of modern area started as provisional arrangements with the aim to kickstart economic development in particular areas. For example, the US FTZ No. 1 was established in 1937 at t Brooklyn Navy Yard to provide temporal relief due to the sudden shortfall in investment during the global economic crisis of the early of 1930s.[8]

One of the most significant issues alludes to level of regulation about the development of freeports: in both England and Wales the level of legislation is poor.[9] Furthermore, although the UK left the European Union, it possesses more freedom to deregulate the matter. Despite this, it is quintessential to ensure a respect of World Trade Organisation rules as well as the UK-EU trade agreements.[10]

UK's freeports are a new hub of business and enterprise created with the aim to regenerate communities and turbocharge after Brexit.[11] A freeport, known also as a free zone, constitutes a secure, enclosed customs zone in which some normal tax and customs' rules do not apply. In the UK there are the following freeports:

- East Midlands Freeport.
- Freeport East.
- Humber Freeport.
- Liverpool City Region Freeport.
- Plymouth and South Devon Freeport.
- Solent Freeport.
- Teesside Freeport.
- Thames Freeport.
- Forth Green Freeport.
- Inverness and Cromarty Firth Green Freeport.
- Anglesey Freeport.
- Celtic Freeport.

5 (Tiefenbrun 2013).
6 Ibid., 153–54.
7 (Saleeby 2023).
8 (Schwarzkopf and Backsell 2021).
9 (Nowak-Far, de Gioia Carabellese, and Della Giustina 2025).
10 In this respect, see (Slater and Claydon 2020).
11 (Holden and Harmer 2025).

Freeports are special economic zones which offer customs and tariffs flexibility as well as other tax benefits to businesses. Yet after the exit of UK from the European Union, freeport has become quintessential to ensure free circulation of goods. Moreover, after the public consultation, and more precisely, from 2022 freeports became operative. In this respect, there are three main pillars established by the government:

- The establishment of freeport as national hubs for global trade and investment across the UK.
- The promotion of regeneration and job creation.
- The creation of hotbeds for innovation.

In this scenario, a unique factor is the circumstance in force of which new English freeports are heterogeneous entities. To better explain, the Teesside Freeport involves the regeneration of a large area; the Midlands Freeport is based around an airport, thus it does not constitute a genuine freeport. Furthermore, the Liverpool City Region Freeport achieves the growth of public community, and Plymouth carries out the improvement of the city economic growth based on marine innovation. As a result of this, freeports may be defined, properly, as the mechanism for regional development rather than a transformative trade initiative.[12]

3. Custom procedure

A good from a third country, to be admitted into national borders, shall pass custom controls: each exit from a customs territory and each entry into a customs territory gives rise to export and import formalities.

From a general perspective, each country constitutes a customary territory. The exception of this general rule is the case of customs unions: in the latter, indeed, formalities are harmonised. This means that goods can move freely withing the countries of the customs union area.

In this respect, there are two fundamental rules: the identification of products classification and the identification of the origin of the product.

The first one issue, the identification of products classifications, imposes different rules from export and import. As far as the export is concerned, it is required a complete trade description of goods which shall encompass, also, the tariff classification for the exporting country. By contrast, for import activities, when goods enter custom, these goods shall be classified into the customs nomenclature of the importing country. The custom classification number, named also custom tariffs, is linked with either the import controls or tariffs.

The second topic is the identification of the origin of the product. This activity means that, on the export, the value declared shall correspond to the value of

12 Patrick Holden and Nichola Harmer, "Post-Neoliberalism? The Strange Case of the New English Freeports", *New Political Economy* (August 2, 2024), https://doi.org/10.1080/13563467.2024.2373069.

the goods at the point of exit from the national territory plus further parameters: transports cost to the national or customs borders. This value is quintessential to establish the basis for certain export duties as well as for compiling external trade statistics. Further, the value of the exported goods shall correspond to the price that foreign buyer pays for the goods. On the other side, that s, the import, the customs value consists of the price paid or payable by the importer for the imported good.

This value is formed by the following elements: the price, paid or payable; the costs of packaging; transport; insurance, handling and loading to the place where goods enter the import territory.

It is well-known that European Union, now, encompasses 27 member states after the UK exit from the EU territory. In January 2020, the European Parliament and the UK Parliament ratified the Withdrawal Agreement. Consequently, the UK officially left EU on 31st January.

As a result of this, the UK entered a transition period from the 1st February until 31st December 2020. During this period the UK was treated, for the purposes of the movement of goods, services and people, as if it were a full EU member state.

Moreover, provisions relating to Northern Ireland are covered by the revised protocol to the Withdrawal Agreement, effective from 1st January 2021. The effect of this protocol allows for goods originating in Northern Ireland to be treated as Union goods when trading with the EU, and vice versa. Additionally, the EU-UK Trade and Cooperation Agreement[13] deleted tariff duties for trade between EU and the UK in case in which the relevant rules on origin are met.

4. EU Custom law

4.1 An overview

First and foremost, European Union customs union signifies that all member states are working together to ensure and guarantee the same tariffs to goods imported into their territory from the rest of the world. Because of this, no tariff would apply internally. Furthermore, another meaning of this concept under discussion is that there are no customs duties to be paid, when goods are transported from one member state to another. Consequently, it appears clear that customs union constitutes one of the few exclusive competences of the European Union: the EU Commission proposes legislation on EU customs affairs and makes sure that it will be implemented.

EU's customs law is focused on four main areas:

- To make sure that all member states work together effectively and efficiently within the customs unions.

13 Henceforth TCA.

- To propose both legislation and procedures to ensure a better security and safety for citizens and, at the same time, to facilitate legitimate trade.
- To help EU countries to exchange information that could be used for customs agencies.
- To guarantee the free movement of goods from one member state to another in the EU; single market.

From a historical perspective, the EU customs Union was established in 1968 with the aim that customs authorities of all EU countries work together. In this respect, a further consequence of customs Union is that all authorities apply the same tariffs to goods imported into their territory from the rest of the world and do not apply tariffs internally. From a different point of observation, customs' controls at the EU's external borders protect consumers from goods and products which could be dangerous, or bad, for their health. These controls are aimed, also, to protect animals and environment by fighting illicit trade in endangered species as well as to prevent plant and animal diseases. Another objective pursuant by custom authorities is to fight against organised crime and terrorism: more in detail, the reference is to traffic of people, drugs, weapons and counterfeited goods.

The role of customs has changed in the last years to adapt and respond to the evolution of international trade. The principal function of customs under the international trade law is to collect duties and taxes on both the exportation and importation of goods. Nevertheless, its role has changed to deal with multifarious changes in international supply chain.

According to this line of reasoning, also the EU custom has evolved. While at the beginning EU custom was focused on checking cargos at the border, now the focus is the supervision of the Union's international trade.[14]

Based on such background, it is possible to affirm that European law constitutes the most important source of law for the Custom Code. Since 1957, the objective of the creation of a common market was declared. Thus, Article 2 of Treaty Establishing the European Economic Community stipulates that one of the community goal is the creation of a "common market" and to "progressively approximate the economic policies of Members States".

In force of the Treaty of Rome, and more precisely pursuant to its Article 9, Custom Union was required to cover all trade in goods. It also introduced the necessary tools to achieve these goals. The final aim was the "adoption of a common customs tariff in their relations with third countries".

In this respect, a third country was defined as a country that was not member of the EU. As a result of this, the products of a third country are subject to import duties: once these products/goods have been subject to appropriate duties on crossing the external border of the union, they are qualified as "good in free circulation". In other words, a good under the free circulation status is treated like any other

14 Communication to the council and the European Parliament towards an integrated management of the external borders of the member states of the European Union COM (2002)233 final.

goods produced in the EU. It is worth stressing that free circulation constitutes one of the fundamental freedoms of the free movement of goods.

Based on the EU principles, it is possible to state that these three are the most important principles:

- The prohibition of customs duties on imports and exports.
- The prohibition of quantitative restrictions.
- The prohibition of measures having equivalent effects.

As far as the first one is concerned, the legal source is EC Treaty and, more in depth, Articles 9 and 12. This was confirmed in *Van Gend en Loos*,[15] the European Court of Justice found as follows: "Member States shall refrain from introducing between themselves any new customs duties on imports and exports or any charges having equivalent effect, and from increasing those which they already apply in their trade with each other".

Moreover, in *Sociaal Fonds voor de Diamantarbeiders*,[16] it was established that a customs duty should not be protectionist.

The prohibition of quantitative restrictions on imports and exports refer to measures imposed by member states whose purpose is to limit the quantity of imports and exports.[17] Strictly connected with this prohibition is the prohibition of measures having equivalent effects. The latter was discussed in *Dassonville*[18]: it was held that a "distinctly applicable measure of equivalent effect" to a quantitative restriction on trade in EU existed on a Scotch whisky imported from France.

Moreover, some exceptions are recognised. To elaborate, quantitative restrictions and measures having equivalent effect may be justified under specific circumstances:

- Public morality.
- Public policy.
- Public security.
- The protection of health and life of humans, animals or plants.
- The protection of national treasures, possessing artistic, historic or archaeological value.
- The protection of industrial or commercial property.

15 *NV Algemene Transport- en Expeditie Onderneming van Gend & Loos v Netherlands Inland Revenue Administration*. Case 26-62. The claimant, Van Gen den Loos, imported chemicals from Western Germany to the Netherlands where they were asked to pay imported taxes at Dutch customs. The defendant argued that it did not comply with Article 12 of the Treaty of Rome.

16 *Sociaal Fonds voor de Diamantarbeiders v S.A. Ch. Brachfeld & Sons and Chougol Diamond* Co. Joined cases 2 and 3-69.

17 See *Geddo v Ente Nazionale Risi* Case 2–73: 1973 ECR 865 and *R v Henn & Darby* (1979) ECR 3795.

18 *NV Algemene Transport- en Expeditie Onderneming van Gend & Loos v Netherlands Inland Procureur du Roi v Benoît and Gustave Dassonville*. Case 8-74.

All of these are now encompassed with the Union Customs Code. The Council Regulation (ECC) 2913/91[19] established that the Community Custom Code[20] constitutes the primary legislative act in charge of the regulation of EU customs procedures. It entered into force in 1991, and it became applicable no earlier than 1st January 1994 as a legally binding act. Furthermore, it was directly applicable in all member states: it meant that the Union Customs Code took precedence over any conflict national law.

Moreover, the Union Customs Code was aimed at promoting the uniformity of construction and application of the EU customs regulation across the EU.

In the next years, the original Community Customs Code was amended in the following way:

- Between 1995 and 2005 the Community Customs Code was amended several times and in the last version it introduced the concept of Authorised Economic Operator.[21] The AEO is a business that, because of an audit of their internal processes, becomes accredited by customs.
- In 2005 the Commission proposed the Modernised Customs Code,[22] whse objective was to move to paperless customs transactions. In a nutshell, the MCC achieved the implementation of the IT solutions in customs operations. MCC entered into force on 24th June 2008.

4.2 The Union Customs Code (UCC)

The Union Customs Code[23] constitutes the "modern" version of the MCC. The UCC legal basis is Articles 33, 144 and 207 of the Treaty on the Functioning of the European Union. UCC was adopted on 9th October 2013[24] and entered into force on 30th October 2013. The main characteristic of UCC may be summarised as follows:

- UCC applies to EU customs territory: it includes Denmark but not Faroe Islands and Greenland. Moreover, EU territory encompasses territorial waters and airspace of the member states.
- UCC is based on the use of the electronic data processing.
- UCC does not extend to trade in services or capital buy because its objective is international trade in goods.

19 Council Regulation (EEC) No. 2913/92 of October 12, 1992 establishing the Community Customs Code

20 Also, CCC.

21 Henceforth AEO.

22 Also, MCC. Regulation (EC) No. 450/2008 of the European Parliament and of the Council of 23 April 2008 laying down the Community Customs Code (Modernised Customs Code).

23 Henceforth UCC.

24 Regulation (EU) No. 952/2013 of the European Parliament and of the Council of October 9, 2013 laying down the Union Customs Code (recast).

In this respect, "goods" means "products which can be valued in money, and which are capable as such of forming the subject of commercial transactions";[25] thus "good" encapsulates, also, gas and electricity. Moreover, it is possible to distinguish between the following:

- Union goods, that is, goods with EU origin as well as those that originate from foreign customs territories but are into free regulation.
- Non-Union goods, that is, goods other than Union goods or, alternatively, goods which have lost their Union goods *status*.

The UCC was amended on 1st May 2016 and some transitional arrangements operated not earlier than 2020. The UCC was implemented through secondary legislation: Delegated Act and the Implementing Act.

Additionally, although UCC substantives amendments provisions became applicable, the European Commission has recognised that an increasing number of customs provisions are no longer fit with the original aim. More in detail, the reference goes to e-commerce, shifting of political scenario and crises, such as Covid-19.[26]

Therefore, the Commission proposes reforms to implement EU custom legislation, reforms based on three main pillars:

- New partnership with business.
- A smarter approach to custom checks.
- A modern approach to e-commerce.

The first pillar – new partnership with business – refers to the establishment of a single window to reduce the administrative burden for businesses when interacting with the EU customs authorities. As a result of this new approach or, better, within "EU Customs Data Hub", businesses will only have to submit data once for multiple consignment. A further implementation concerned with AEO programme: the latter shall be extended, also, to "Trust & Check" category. The latter shall benefit from the reduction of both physical and document-based controls.

The aim of the new system is based on digitalisation; consequently, customs authorities may control goods movement thanks to a real-time data and artificial intelligence program. The latter shall predict potential problems, risks before the shipping of the goods from third countries. To summarise, thanks to digitalisation: (1) EU customs authorities may operate more effectively; (2) proper collection of both duties and taxes will facilitate; (3) EU customs authorities may fight against illegal or unsafe goods more efficiently.

The reference is to e-commerce: the intention of the Commission is to make the online platform as key actors to ensure that goods sold in the EU market respect all

25 This definition was shaped in *Commission of the European Communities v Italian Republic*. Case 7-68.

26 See Proposal for a Regulation of the European Parliament and of the Council establishing the Union Customs Code and the European Union Customs Authority and repealing Regulation (EU) No. 952/2013 COM/2023/258 final.

customs obligations. More in depth, it is quintessential to ensure that custom duties and VAT will be paid when the customer makes a purchase on platform.

Additionally, the proposal encapsulates some further little changes, such as the folllowing:

- The notion of "importer" shall replace the existing notion of "declarant".
- The introduction of common provisions on customs infringements and non-criminal sanctions for those infringements.
- The enhancement of international cooperation between national customs authorities.

Finally, as far as the timeline is concerned, the EU Commission purpose is to open the "EU- Customs Data Hub" for e-commerce in 2028 and for all other importers in 2032; it will become mandatory in 2038. This hub should be managed by a new organisation, named EU Customs Authority; the main function of this authority will be "to pool expertise and competence that are currently scattered across the EU to steer, coordinate and support national customs authorities in the EU". Moreover, the centralised clearance for imports of "Trust & Check" traders will be implemented for 2028.

To summarise, the proposal is aimed to shift the EU's approach to the enforcement of non-customs legislation by concentrating controls at the border in "one-stop-shops". Consequently, national customs authorities will play a quintessential role to protect the single market.

By contrast, the creation of the EU Customs Authority achieves the goal of the establishment of a centralised EU customs authority. The latter will be in charge to ensure the coordination function. Thus, the ultimate objective will be the uniform application of customs legislation.

Additionally, the EU Parliament adopted on 13th March 2024 its position on this reform.[27] In this respect, it was highlighted the importance to revise the EU customs system based on the following considerations:

- The importance to guarantee safety and compliance of goods entering in the EU.
- The need to improve utmost efficiency for businesses.
- The quintessential role of the Customs Data Hub.

4.3 EU Customs procedure

In the EU custom law, the existing Automated Entry Processing[28] was replaced by the Automated Import System.[29] The latter, AIS, was introduced since 23rd November 2023 to comply with the Union Customs Code.[30]

27 Parliament adopts its position on major reform of EU Customs Code | News | European Parliament (europa.eu).

28 Henceforth AEP.

29 Henceforth AIS.

30 Henceforth UCC.

Moreover, the introduction of AIS achieved three main goals: (1) to replace the AEP; (2) to introduce changes to the import procedure impacting on those involved in the import supply chain; (3) to change the structure and the content of import declaration.

As far as the import declaration is concerned, the AIS, now, requires that goods imported into the EU shall be declared to Revenue[31] electronically via Revenue's Automated Import System. Based on electronical declaration, two pieces of information are required: (1) the commodity code and (2) the customs procedure code.

With the AIS introduction some benefits are available. In other words, the AIS is required when goods are imported from non-EU nations. The AIS overseas data processing, validation, customs declaration and duty accounting. The main objective is to ensure that products are imported legally. Furthermore, AIS is an electronic system aimed to increase efficiency and, consequently, to minimise mistake. To elaborate, AIS replaces the requirement for paper-based customs declaration with an automated system. As a result of this, thanks to AIS, data is validated before the submission; consequently both transparency and cost optimisation are guaranteed.

4.4 The digitalisation of customs

Based on the EU Commission proposal, the customs' future is based on digitalisation as well as artificial intelligence.

In this respect, the Single Window has been proposed an ambitious objective to unifying and simplifying the customs formalities process.[32] The Single Window suggestion is based on the introduction of a single portal for the information exchanged between all actors involved, for instance, customs authorities, traders, IT system providers, etc.

According to this approach, the Single Window refers to different platforms, for example:

- The European Union Customs Single Window Certificates Exchange System[33] which initially should be relating to cover EU non-customs formalities digitalised at the EU level. The EU CSW-CERTEX is an electronic system managed and developed by the Commission in collaboration with member states.
- The National Single Window Environments for Customs constitute a set of services and systems owned, managed and developed by the member states. Initially, it will focus on intergovernmental exchanges, and at the latter, it shall provide a business-to-government channel. This means that economic operators submit all border data required for goods clearance directly to the national single window environment for customs.

31 Revenue is responsible for controlling imports into Ireland for custom purposes and on behalf of government departments.

32 The EU Single Window Environment for Customs – European Commission (europa.eu).

33 Henceforth EU CSW-CERTEX.

- The Union Non-Customs Services will be introduced to manage specific non-customs formalities required in international trade in goods.

From a comparative perspective, in 2023 the UK government passed the Electronic Trade Documents Act: the bill grants digital documents the same legal status as paper trade documents. Moreover, it achieves the objective to reduce processing time and increase sustainability for businesses engaged in international trade. On 20th July 2023 the Electronic Trade Documents Act 2023[34] received Royal Assent and became law.

The EDTA was aimed to rectify deficiencies in the treatment of electronic trade documents under English law. Before the EDTA, under English law, electronic document did not possess the same legal status as the paper document. With EDTA, electronic documents possess the equivalent legal value of the paper trade documents.

Based on Article 2(2) an "electronic trade document" is based on a reliable system used to

> (a) identify the document so that it can be distinguished from any copies, (b) protect the document against unauthorised alteration, (c) secure that it is not possible for more than one person to exercise control of the document at any one time, (d) allow any person who is able to exercise control of the document to demonstrate that the person is able to do so, and (e) secure that a transfer of the document has effect to deprive any person who was able to exercise control of the document immediately before the transfer of the ability to do so (unless the person is able to exercise control by virtue of being a transferee).

Furthermore, a paper trade document may be converted into an electronic trade document and an electronic trade document may be converted into a paper trade document.[35] This change of form is possible only if

- The new form encompasses a statement with certify that the document converted is included in the new form.
- The compliance of any contractual or other requirements relating to the conversion process are met.

Finally, as far as the effect of the conversion is concerned, when a document is converted, the old document ceases to have effect. Additionally, all rights and liabilities linked with the document continue to have effect. These effects are relating to the relevant document in its new format.

34 Henceforth ETDA.
35 See Article 4.

5. The EU-UK relations in the aftermath of Brexit

On 23rd June 2016 the United Kingdom voted to leave the European Union: because of this Brexit represents one of the most important political events in Europe.[36] According to Article 50(1) TUE "Any Member State may decide to withdraw from the Union in accordance with its own constitutional requirements". While the UK government planned to initiate autonomously the process of withdrawal from EU, a litigation started on the need to obtain parliamentary approval before doing so. In *R (Miller) v Secretary of State for Exiting the European Union*,[37] the UK Supreme Court established that

> Parliamentary sovereignty is a fundamental principle of the UK Constitution . . . the Royal Prerogative encompasses the residue powers which remain vested in the Crown, and they are exercisable by Ministers, provided by that the exercise is consistent with Parliamentary legislation.[38]

In other words, the issue was focused on whether the government could use the royal prerogative to give notice of the United Kingdom's intention to leave the EU according to Article 50 TUE or whether Parliamentary authorisation via primary legislation was enquired. Moreover, it was clarified that if "ministers cannot give Notice by the exercise of the prerogative powers, only legislation which is embodied in a statute will do it. A resolution of the House of Common is not legislation".[39] After this, the UK government adopted the European Union (Notification of Withdrawal) Act 2017[40] which gave the UK Prime minister the legal power to notify the European Council the UK's intention to withdraw from the EU, in compliance to Article 50 TUE. The notification of Article 50 TEU required that the European Commission and European Parliament appointed their shifted negotiations for Brexit and the European Council had to agree that the Commission would undertake the negotiation with the UK on behalf of the EU.

Consequently, the UK withdrawal process from the EU was shaped according to Article 50 TUE, which encompasses three main stages:

- The first one alludes to decision of a member state to withdraw according to its own constitutional requirements. It includes the first sentence of Article 50 TUE, the notification of that intention to European Council.

36 (Fabbrini 2017).

37 [2017] UKSC 5. It should be noted that *R (Miller) v Secretary of State for Exiting the European Union* saw an unusual convocation of 11-member Supreme Court bench: by a majority of 8:3, the court ruled that primary legislation was required to authorise the government to give notice under Article 50 TEU. See (Webb 2023).

38 [2017] UKSC 5 para 43, 47.

39 Ibid., para 123.

40 Government Bill Originated in the House of Commons, Session 2016–17.

- The second one is based on negotiation, the reference goes to Article 50(2) TUE, which stipulates,

> A Member State which decides to withdraw shall notify the European Council of its intention. In the light of the guidelines provided by the European Council, the Union shall negotiate and conclude an agreement with that State, setting out the arrangements for its withdrawal, taking account of the framework for its future relationship with the Union. That agreement shall be negotiated in accordance with Article 218(3) of the Treaty on the Functioning of the European Union. It shall be concluded on behalf of the Union by the Council, acting by a qualified majority, after obtaining the consent of the European Parliament.

- The third stage is the outcome of the negotiations: treaty rights and obligations apply to the state until the withdrawal agreement is concluded or until two years from the date of notification, unless the European Council unanimously agree to extend that period. It is encapsulated into Article 50(3)(4).[41]

One of the main cores of negotiations was free trade agreement (FTA):[42] in its first version (January 2020) it was, fundamentally, a zero-tariff trade agreement because of "the first negotiation in history where both parties started off with free trade and discussed what barriers to erect".[43] During the withdrawal negotiations, the EU insisted on the UK's binary choice between existing models against the UK government's preference for a model as a "a middle option that is neither Norway nor Canada".[44] From a definitory perspective, TCA appears as an international agreement without a legal homogeneity but aimed to respect equality and autonomy of each side.[45]

The EU-UK Trade and Cooperation Agreement (TCA)[46] covers only trade in goods; the respect of goods is divided into thematic chapters:

- National treatment and market access for goods.
- Rules of origin.
- Sanitary and phytosanitary measures.

41 "3. The Treaties shall cease to apply to the State in question from the date of entry into force of the withdrawal agreement or, failing that, two years after the notification referred to in paragraph 2, unless the European Council, in agreement with the Member State concerned, unanimously decides to extend this period. 4. For the purposes of paragraphs 2 and 3, the member of the European Council or of the Council representing the withdrawing Member State shall not participate in the discussions of the European Council or Council or in decisions concerning it".

42 (Bennett and Vines 2022).

43 Pascal Lamy, interviewed by The Week in Westminster, BBC, 1st February 2020.

44 (Owen, Stojanovic, and Rutter 2017).

45 (Kahraman 2023).

46 See (Eckes and Leino-Sandberg 2022).

- Technical barriers to trade.
- Customs and trade facilitation.

The main pillar of the TCA is based on a limitation of the principle of national treatment: indeed, the TCA does not eliminate non-discriminatory measures, nor does it establish the principle of mutual recognition; it does not implement the market access principle. Furthermore, the TCA prohibits customs duties both on imports and exports for goods originating in, and provided by, the UK and EU. The zero tariff treatment on all products under the TCA distinguishes the TCA from other trade agreements. Although it is true, TCA requires the collection of data on preference utilisation.

Another pillar is the application of zero quotas. In this respect, Articles 26 TCA stipulates as follows:

> A Party shall not adopt or maintain any prohibition or restriction on the importation of any good of the other Party or on the exportation or sale for export of any good destined for the territory of the other Party, except in accordance with Article XI of GATT 1994, including its Notes and Supplementary Provisions. To that end, Article XI of GATT 1994 and its Notes and Supplementary Provisions are incorporated into and made part of this Agreement, mutatis mutandis.

In a nutshell, the TCA provides both zero tariff and zero quota trade in goods. Nevertheless, it does not eliminate other significant obstacle to interstate trade regulation: the reference goes to technical barriers relating to trade[47] and sanitary and phytosanitary standards.[48] It should be noted that, according to an EU perspective, TCA "goes well beyond traditional free trade agreements and provides a solid basis for preserving our longstanding friendship and cooperation".[49]

First and foremost, it is vital to highlight the differences existing between TBT and SPS. The second one, SPS measures, are limited to measures aimed to protect human, animal and plant life as well as health. However, both TBT and SPS pose problems on trade liberalisation and domestic safety standard.

To elaborate, before the UK's withdrawal from the EU, the burden of complying with diverging technical regulations was avoided either through EU harmonisation or through the principle of mutual recognition. The latter ensured that, normally, procedure would need to meet only one set of regulations. Thus, the combination of two main principles, mutual recognition and harmonisation, was that, in most cases, manufacturers were obliged to meet only technical requirements.

47 Henceforth TBT.

48 Henceforth SPS.

49 European Commission, "EU-UK Trade and Cooperation Agreement: Protecting European Interests, Ensuring Fair Competition, and Continued Cooperation in Areas of Mutual Interest", https://ec.europa.eu/commission/presscorner/detail/en/ip_20_2531.

By contrast, under TCA, it is required for the UK producers to comply with both TBT and SPS of each member states of the EU, and vice-versa.

As far as SPS agreement is concerned, it is not covered by the TBT agreement; the SPS agreement refers to requirements aimed to protect humans, or animals or plants carrying diseases. Additionally, SPS agreement is shaped on the WTO framework: Article 72 TCA recalls rights and obligations existed under the WTO's SPS agreement.[50]

More in detail, TBT was incorporated into TCA: it means that EU-UK trade will be subject to domestic product requirements. According to this line of reasoning, the principle of non-discrimination will be focused on the negative effects of technical barriers in the UK and EU. To better explain, domestic product requirements are allowed with the result that exported products will need to meet the technical requirements of each host State market. This is true under the parameter on conditional on equal treatment and necessity.

The CE marking[51] was introduced to eliminate regulatory obstacles. This marking is required for a wide range of products, such as medical devices, machinery, radio equipment. It constitutes as proof of the fact that the product complies with all the EU requirements and has undergone conformity assessment.

From a UK perspective, it adopted the UKCA mark[52] from 1st January 2021 which attested the quality and safety after Brexit. UKCA stands for "UK Conformity Assessed", and it represents the UK version of the CE. It constitutes a conformity marking used for products to be placed on the market on Great Britain.

Based on the UK government official documents,[53] it is possible to infer that the UK government wants to lay legislation to enable business to continue to place CE mark in the Great Britain for a range of goods.

Moreover, the government will recognise, indefinitely, the current EU requirements, including the CE marking. At the same time, businesses have also the opportunity to use the UKCA marking to place relevant product on GB market. In a nutshell, businesses have the flexibility to use either UKCA or CE marking. Finally, the UKCA marking applies to most products for which the CE marking can also be used. For example, it applies to aerosol dispensers and measuring container bottles.

It is critical to stress that, if a business wants to use the recognised EU marking to place products on GB market, it shall ensure that it complies with all the necessary conformity processes.[54] Furthermore, it is also quintessential that business provides a Declaration of Conformity that has been translated into English.

50 (Barnard and Leinarte 2022).

51 It means Conformité Européene, or European Conformity marking.

52 It means UK Conformity Assessed.

53 UK Department for Business & Trade, Policy Update: Placing Products on the Market in Great Britain Using UK or EU Product Markings, January 2024.

54 This process includes, also, the use of an EU notified body where it is required to apply the relevant EU conformity marking.

Additionally, the business is under an obligation to declare that all the relevant EU product regulations have been met.

Based on such UK document, "Policy Update: Placing products on the market in Great Britain using UK or EU product markings", a fast-track UKCA process will be introduced.

The fast-track UKCA (again, the UK conformity Assessed), albeit non-mandatory, achieves the objective to create more flexibility on how manufacturers can use the UKCA making to place products on the GB market. In other words, thanks to fast-track UKCA manufacturers can use the UKCA to demonstrate that they have met either the UK or the EU recognised essential requirements. The latter, again, constitutes a proof of the conformity assessment procedures for each regulation applicable to product.

Fast-track UKCA possesses a further meaning: a product falls within multiple regulations. More in detail, it means that a product may comply with both EU and UK conformity assessment procedures. In this specific case, the fast-track UKCA shall be used to demonstrate the compliance with the UK requirements: the outcome of this compliance is that the "UKCA marking" can be applied to that specific product. In a nutshell, under fast-track UKCA, a manufacturer ensures that:

- The EU essential requirements are met.
- Relevant EU conformity assessment procedures have been carried out.

There is availability of a draft of the Product Safety and Metrology etc (Amendment) Regulations 2024 that come into force on 1st October 2024. This UK legislation continues recognising the EU requirements, including the CE marking. Moreover, this legislation shall apply indefinitely for a range of products. To elaborate, businesses will have the flexibility to use either UKCA or CE marking to sell products in Great Britain.

It is worth highlighting that the UKCA marking is not recognised on the EU market. Consequently, many products need a CE marking to show that they comply with the EU rules before they can be supplied in the EU market. This sparks off a further consequence: the UKCA marking does not apply to Northern Ireland: products that can use UKCA marking in Great Britain shall meet EU rules in Northern Ireland. The latter encapsulates, among others, CE marking.

It should be noted that on 28th April 2025 there was the first UK-EU Arbitration Ruling under the Trade and Cooperation Agreement: the sandeel fishing ban. It offers an interpretation of the TCA substantive provisions. The dispute is about fisheries, which is an area that not only exercised the TCA negotiators considerably but is also still a source of controversy in the UK-EU relations. In essence, the rules on fisheries are set out in Heading Five of Part 2 TCA. Article 493 TCA acknowledges the sovereign rights of coastal states and requires that the parties exercise them in accordance with international law.[55]

55 The Parties affirm that sovereign rights of coastal States exercised by the Parties for the purpose of exploring, exploiting, conserving and managing the living resources in their waters should be

The objectives of the TCA Fisheries provisions are set out in Article 494(1)-(2) TCA:

> The Parties shall cooperate with a view to ensuring that fishing activities for shared stocks in their waters are environmentally sustainable in the long term and contribute to achieving economic and social benefits, while fully respecting the rights and obligations of independent coastal States as exercised by the Parties.

The dispute was about sandeel fishing in the North Sea. Sandeel are small eel fish that feed on plankton. As they constitute a substantial proportion of the diet of several marine mammals, seabirds and fish, they are important for the marine ecosystem in the North Sea. Sandeel are a shared stock within the meaning of Article 495(1) TCA; they are found in waters where the EU and UK agree on shares of total fishing quotas per year. In accordance with Annex 35 TCA, sandeel fisheries have been managed based on a strategy whereby the annual maximum quantity that may be caught is set so that the stock may replenish the following year. When agreeing the above quantity, the UK and the EU rely on scientific advice provided by an intergovernmental marine science organisation known as the International Council for the Exploration of the Sea. While Norway, Sweden, Germany and Denmark participate in the sandeel fishing in the North Sea, it is the latter that is the primary holder of the EU-allocated sandeel quotas. On 26 March 2024, following public consultation, the UK imposed a ban on sandeel fishing in the English waters of the North Sea and in all Scottish waters. The former was imposed, in accordance with the Fisheries Act 2020, under Statutory guidance setting out variations to licences granted to fishing vessels by the Marine Management Organisation; the latter was imposed under the Sandeel (Prohibition of Fishing) (Scotland) Order 2024, which was adopted under Section 5(1)(a) of the Sea Fish (Conservation) Act 1967. The objective of the ban was to increase sandeel stocks to increase the food availability for seabirds, marine mammals and other fish species and, therefore, bring about wider environmental and ecosystem benefits. On 16 April 2024, the EU requested consultations with the UK under Article 738 TCA. On 25 October, the EU served on the UK a request to establish an arbitration tribunal under Article 739 TCA.

The EU claimed that the previous ban violated the TCA on three grounds: (1) best available scientific advice obligation; (2) proportionality and non-discrimination; (3) ban was contrary to the obligation to grant full access to its waters to fish.

The ruling of the Arbitration Tribunal may be summarised as follows:

- The first claim was rejected because the EU had failed to demonstrate that the sandeel fishing ban had been imposed without having regard to the best available scientific advice.

---

conducted pursuant to and in accordance with the principles of international law, including the United Nations Convention on the Law of the Sea.

- As far as proportionality, the Tribunal pointed out the failure of the UK to take account of the adverse effects of the ban on the rights of interests of the EU. This was not the case with the ban in Scottish waters which was adopted after the decision-maker had considered not only the benefits of the sandeel prohibition but also the economic cost to the UK and EU fishing and processing industries and the impairment of the rights of the EU during the adjustment period. By failing to consider the principle of proportionality in banning sandeel fishing in the English waters of the North Sea, the UK also failed to grant access to EU vessels in accordance with Article 2(1)(a) of Annex 38 to the TCA.
- The discrimination claim was rejected: a clear nexus between the differential treatment and the legitimate objective of the ban was founded. Finally, the third claim was upheld without analysis.

6. UK Customs procedure after Brexit

On 29th August 2023, the UK government published the final Border Target Operating Model in which it was confirmed the UK approach to border controls for goods imported into Great Britain. These controls were introduced progressively, from January 2024, to better protect UK against biosecurity threats. The last goal to achieve is to create a world-class border system. The Border Target Operating Model will be implementing controls based on three main pillars:[56]

- On 31st January 2024 health certification on imports of medium-risk animal products, plants, plant products and high-risk food (and feed) of non-animal origin from the EU was introduced.
- On 20th April 2024 a documentary and risk-based identity and physical checks on medium risk animal products, plants, plant products and high-risk food (and feed) of non-animal origin from the EU was introduced.
- On 31st October 2024, the date on which Safety and Security declarations for EU imports will come into force.

Furthermore, since 7th September 2023, "New customs rules for trade with the EU" have been applicable. It means that goods moving between the UK and EU shall meet the rules of origin[57] requirements. RoO constitutes a parameter thanks to which it is possible to determine the "economic nationality" of a good, based on where the products or materials used in their production come from.

This constitutes a part of the customs process which aim is to ensure that duties are paid on goods moving across the border as well as goods comply with safety, health and environmental requires. This control was introduced since 1st January 2021. In this respect, the legal source is the government's Border Operating Model.[58]

56 See The Border Target Operating Model, 4th September 2023, Statement UIN HCWS998.

57 Henceforth RoO.

58 HM Government UK Transition, The Border with the European Union. Importing and Exporting Goods, June 2022.

Based on this document, the core process encompasses the following elements: custom declaration that means exports and imports, custom duties, VAT and Safety and Security Declaration.

As far as customs declaration is concerned, it is required, on the one hand, that importers and exporters have complied with UK and EU customs declarations after the end of the transition period. On the other hand, customs duties require importers to ensure that any customs duties applicable to their goods, and originating from the new UK Global Tariff, are paid. In this respect, importers will need to determine the origin, the classification and customs value of their goods.[59]

In this scenario, a very strategic activity consists of the classification of goods: businesses are responsible for the correct classification of goods and recording of origin of goods.[60]

Finally, on 29th May 2025 there was a Summit between the UK and EU in which parties agreed on a substantial package covered different areas: agri-food, energy, emissions and trading systems, steel, law enforcement and judicial cooperation, irregular immigration, defence and security development, youth and education mobility, fisheries and business mobility.[61]

Commencing with agri-food market, EU represents, for the UK, one of the largest agri-food market, however, since Brexit exports are down 21 percent and imports down 7 percent. Therefore, the agreement establishes a "UK-EU Sanitary and Phytosanitary Zone"; this signifies the following:

- The removal of Export Health Certificates, plant health certificates, Certificates of Inspection for organic products, marketing standards certification requirements.
- To stop routine border checks on UK agri-food products and some EU products, such as milk, dairy, eggs, red meat, plants for planting, potatoes.
- British products that were banned (e.g., fresh sausages and burgers, certain shellfish from domestic waters, and seed potatoes) will be able to resume trade to EU.
- To adopt a multiuse pet passport valid for travel to EU.

A topic connected with this is fishing: under the existing Trade and Cooperation Agreement parties, the UK and EU are in an adjustment period until June 2026, during which a reciprocal access to water is guaranteed. After this, parties agreed for a new twelve access arrangement that means as follows:

- Reciprocal access to each other water.
- UK exercises the control over its water to achieve sustainable fishing policies, but UK remains outside EU's fishing rules.

59 Furthermore, there are also some goods that are qualified as prohibited: these goods cannot be imported. However, in some cases, little derogations are recognised.

60 Therefore, the commodity codes.

61 Policy Paper, "UK-EU Summit – Explainer", 19th May 2025, https://www.gov.uk/government/publications/ukeu-summit-key-documentation/uk-eu-summit-explainer-html.

- To remove Export Health Certificates as well as reopening shellfish trade since shellfish from certain type of GB domestic waters are banned in the EU.

On the side of energy cooperation, the purpose is strengthening energy security to achieve net zero goals. Not only does it signify participation in EU electricity trading platforms (and developing new renewables in North Sea), but also, energy cooperation is instrumental in maximising cooperation on clean energy technology (such as hydrogen, carbon capture use and storage, and decarbonised gases). Strictly linked with this topic is the UK-EU agreement on link emissions trading system (ETS) to decarbonise industry and, consequently, achieve net zero goals.

An additional pillar is law enforcement and judicial cooperation about the improvement of the cooperation with Europol and to exchange criminal records through IT development, such as biometric data exchange (e.g., facial recognition). A corner of this is tackling irregular immigration thanks to an enhancement of EU's border and Coast Guard Agency cooperation.

At the end there is the agreement of persons movement, that is business travel and youth educational mobility.

References

Barnard, Catherine, and Emiliaja Leinarte. 2022. "Movement of Goods Under the TCA." *Global Policy* 13 (2): 106–18.

Bennett, Adam, and David Vines. 2022. "The EU-UK Trade and Cooperation Agreement: Lessons Learnt." *Oxford Review of Economic Policy* 38 (1): 68–81.

Beyene, Zellalem Tadesse, Simon Peter Nadeem, Matiwos Ensermu Jaleta, and Andre Kreie. 2023. "Research Trends in Dry Port Sustainability: A Bibliometric Analysis." *Sustainability* 16 (1): 263–84.

Eckes, Christina, and Päivi Leino-Sandberg. 2022. "The EU-UK Trade and Cooperation Agreement – Exceptional Circumstances or a New Paradigm for EU External Relations?" *Modern Law Review* 85 (1): 164–97.

Fabbrini, Federico. 2017. *The Law & Politics of Brexit*. Oxford University Press.

Holden, Patrick, and Nichola Harmer. 2025. "Post-Neoliberalism? The Strange Case of the New English Freeports." *New Political Economy* 30 (1): 19–33.

Kahraman, Sevilay. 2023. "Brexit and the EU-UK Trade and Cooperation Agreement in Comparison: EU Principles and Practices of Governing the Neighbourhood." *Journal of Contemporary European Studies* 31 (3): 659–944.

Khaslavskaya, Alena, and Violeta Roso. 2020. "Dry Ports: Research Outcomes, Trends, and Future Implications." *Maritime Economics & Logistics* 22 (2): 265–92.

Nowak-Far, Arthur, Pierre de Gioia Carabellese, and Camilla Della Giustina. 2025. "Mass Regulation in Nordic And Baltic Sea Countries: A Comparative Analysis." *Journal of Transportation Law, Logistics & Policy* 92 (1): 21–53.

Owen, Joe, Alex Stojanovic, and Jill Rutter. 2017. "Trade After Brexit: Options for the UK's Relationship with the EU." *Journal of Contemporary European Studies* 1–54.

Rodrigue, Jean-Paul, and Theo Notteboom. 2022. "Dry Ports." In *Port Economics. Management and Policy*, edited by Theo Notteboom, Athanasios Pallis, and Jean-Paul Ro, 140–67. Routledge.

Roso, Violeta, Johan Woxenius, and Kenth Lumsden. 2009. "The Dry Port Concept: Connecting Container Seaports with the Hinterland." *Journal of Transport Geography* 17 (5): 338–45.

Saleeby, Cates Grier. 2023. "How Free Should a Freeport Be? Reducing Money Laundering in the Art Market Through Freeport Regulation." *Vanderbilt Journal of Entertainment and Technology Law* 25 (1): 239–66.
Schwarzkopf, Stefan, and Jessica Inez Backsell. 2021. "The Nomos of the Freeport." *Society and Space* 39 (2): 328–46.
Slater, Anne-Michelle, and Jim Claydon. 2020. "Marine Spatial Planning in the UK: A Review of the Progress and Effectiveness of the Plans and Their Policies." *Environmental Law Review* 22 (2): 85–105.
Tiefenbrun, Susan. 2013. "US Foreign Trade Zones, Tax-Free Trade Zones of the World, and Their Impact on the US Economy." *Hofstra International Law & Business* 13 (12): 149–90.
Webb, Thomas E. 2023. "R (on the Application of Miller) v Secretary of State for Exiting the European Union [2017] UKSC 5, Supreme Court." *Essential Cases: Public Law* (online).

23 Trade in services

Chapter Overview

1. Introduction

International trade in services and investments has become a quintessential element of the global commerce. The evolution in both informational and telecommunications technologies expand the scope of services and their impact in the cross-border relations. Moreover, countries use foreign investment in new private and competitive markets established in crucial infrastructure services. References go to telecommunications, education, consume tourism and medical services. Indeed, services constitute one of the fastest-growing components of the global economy. Furthermore, trade and foreign direct investment in services are expanding at a pace that is more accelerated than goods.

Nevertheless, liberalisation[1] in services does not represent an automatic phenomenon due to the significant challenges entailed to the introduction of a genuine competition. A proof of this is that services in Doha round have received little attention because the public policies are now focused on protectionist policies in agriculture. In this respect, for the future, three main elements shall be considered:

- International agreements aimed to increase competition in services shall advantage developing countries.
- Openness of cross-border trade in service sector constitutes one of the most dynamic dimensions of international trade.

1 (McGuire 2002).

DOI: 10.4324/9781003645948-23

- In practice, some regional cooperation in service is presented; these are focused on the elimination of explicit barriers to the entry for services providers.

In a nutshell, trade in services shapes welfare gains for society since trade in services promotes a more efficient allocation of resources and greater economies of scale. Moreover, trade in services lead to an increase in the variety of services available to both consumers and produces, for example, transport, telecommunications, finance, water and electricity distribution. These are known as infrastructural and/or producer services.

2. The notion of service

The word "service" covers a multifarious and heterogeneous range of intangible products and activities, therefore, making it difficult to give a simple and, at the same time, comprehensive, definition.

More in general, services are the outcome, the result of a production activity: the latter plays a critical role because, via its activity, it changes the consuming units and/or facilitates the exchange of the products or financial assets. Additionally, services possess the tendency to be intangible, nonscorable and they require simultaneous production and consumption. Moreover, a service may be defined as a "an economic activity that adds value either directly to another economic unit or to a good belonging to another economic unit". Thus, services have a defining feature: the requirement for direct interaction between producers and consumers or at least a consumer's assets, before the service can be rendered.[2]

It is also worth stressing that services, often, intermediate inputs: consequently, they play a key role in the efficiency of the manufacturing sector and the entire economy. As a result of this, public policy and regulation are more pervasive: the underlying reason lies on the asymmetry of information between providers and consumers. A further reason is the fact that most of these services shall be defined as universal services.

Services may be divided into the following:

- Change-effecting services.
- Margin services.

Change-effecting services consist of changes in the conditions of the consuming units realised by activities produced at the demand of consumers. Change-effecting services encompass, also, transformation services. The latter refers to (1) changes in the condition of the consumers' goods; (2) changes in the physical condition of persons; (3) changes in the mental condition of persons. Moreover, changes may be either temporary or permanent.

Margin services are the result of the change of ownership of goods, knowledge-capturing of products. Additionally, some services or financial assets

2 (Findlay and Warren 2005).

are exchanged between two different institutional units. Further, these kinds of services resemble change-effecting services where the entities are not separate.

A further classification of services is distinguished among the following:

- Distributive services, such as wholesale and retails, transportation and communications.
- Producer services, for example advisory, legal services, banking and finance.
- Social services, for instance hotels and catering.

Differences that exist between trade in services and trade in goods are critical. Service trade is different from goods trade because the second one, goods trade, involves shipping goods from one country to another. In this respect, cross-border trade is a feature worthy of analysis. By contrast, service in trade does not require a personal contact to be in place between producers and consumers or between customers and clients. Thus, trade in the services sector is possible through affiliates, for example.

Furthermore, services tend to be subject to higher regulation: many typologies of services are publicly provided to, or are produced by, regulated monopolies. Therefore, barriers to trade in services stem from domestic regulation. The latter achieves a dual goal: (1) to respond to market failure; (2) to protect local suppliers from foreign competition. As a result of this, the identification of trade barriers in services sector constitutes a complex activity. Under GATT regulation, services are the following: business; communications; construction; distribution; educational; environmental; financial; related to health and social sector; tourism and travel activity; recreational, cultural and sporting based; transports.

Finally, international service transactions take place in different ways:

- Cross-border. In this case services supplied from the territory of one country into the territory of another one.
- Consumption abroad where services supplied in the territory of one country to the consumer of another.
- Commercial presence or foreign direct investment if services are supplied through any type of business, or professional establishment, of one country in the territory of another.
- Presence of natural persons, or labour movement. Under this circumstance, services are supplied by nationals of one country in the territory of another.

3. The importance of trade in services

Trade between countries in services has multiple advantages in international relations between countries. Fundamentally, advantages may be explained based on two main approaches:

- The existing differences among countries to generate trade.
- Gains from specialisation because of increasing return to scale agglomeration.

To elaborate, the differences existing among different countries constitute an incentive to trade; more in detail, differences may be relating to technology, natural resources, government policies, institutions, etc.

Thus, one of the major sources of differences existing among countries is constituted by factor supplies. The latter encompass, fundamentally, the availability of skilled labour and capital. For instance, a country with an abundance of forested land will export goods and services that are intensive in such sector; if a country possesses an abundance of skilled workers, it will export goods and services where those skilled workers show their major skills.

Moreover, differences among countries can also arise from other sources, such as the following:

- Technological source, in this case a country with sophisticated medical technology will export medical services.
- Legal systems as well as institutions: insurance services, for example, require the trust of client in the fact that the contract will be honoured if a claim is made. Consequently, differences in legal and regulatory system may affect, on one hand, both trust and confidence and, on the other hand, the flexibility of these services.

All these differences may have a positive effect on the trade of services.

First and foremost, producers gain from access to a larger market and higher prices; similarly, consumers have access to a wider variety of goods and services to lower-priced imported both goods and services. However, this explanation assumes that markets are perfectly competitive. Consequently, markets may maximise their profits.

Nevertheless, a problem may be the following one: factors that have strong ties to import-competing industries will tend to lose from trade, while factors with strong ties to export industries will tend to gain.

In other words, it is unlikely that there will ever be unanimity on the benefits on liberalisation trade services. From a purely theoretical perspective, the opposition between the interest of the single individual and the interest relating to groups can be overcome by taxing the gainers to compensate the losses. Yet this occurs rarely, due to the underlying complexity of this mechanism.

Therefore, to assess the impact of trade liberalisation, a typical evaluation is the one relating to the impact on income distribution. More in detail, this assessment is even more important when a country does not have a social insurance mechanism. In fact, the latter may help those who lose their job or whose incomes suffer major reductions during the adjustment of free trade.[3] It is also worth emphasising that trade constitutes only one of many elements that affect the distribution of income. A further element is technological change: it represents one main driver in increasing inequality.

3 (Jensen 2011).

Although differences existing among countries constitute one explanation of the benefits of the trade, by contrast it is also true that, in similar countries, trade possesses a great volume. A possible explanation of this lies on the so-called "market-niche effect": it means that variety in service sector is tailored to individual customer needs.[4] Consequently, if trade is driven by market-niche effect, three advantages are generated:

- The total variety of products available to consumer in any given market will increase consumers gain access to both domestic and foreign varieties of products.
- Each individual produce will access the larger market.
- Specialised services that should not be economically viable in a small country, by contrast, may be viable because of the market expansion.

The just described mechanism is less significant where trade occurs among differences between countries because of the following:

- Product variety is valued.
- Trade can increase import and export in the same sector.
- Both opportunities and competition increasing in any sector.

Furthermore, "market-niche effects" is focused on a set of people or business whose purpose is to "purchase" a specific section of the market, by focusing on a small audience. Consumers in a niche market have specific preferences, wants and/or needs. Within niche markets a business can achieve, also, a social strategy since:

- Many niche costumers may become repeat buyers.
- Fewer brands may compete in a specific sector.
- A better marketing strategy shall be defined.

4. Trade in services and monopoly

In services, sectors often are characterised by the existence of natural monopoly situations where costs of provision are minimised with only one supplier market. Nevertheless, the problem is that a single producer may take advantage of its monopoly power by restricting the quality and the quantity output. Thus, the costs arise. Therefore, the opening to trade creates the opportunity for introducing alternative supplier. At the same time, a further challenge may arise, namely, how to arrange the transition to a new provider and regulating it in an appropriate way.

In a nutshell, while a natural monopoly constitutes a common feature in the sector of some services, for example infrastructure and telecommunications, in other and different circumstances this problem shall not materialise. Furthermore, natural

4 (Whalley 2004).

monopoly can also play a critical role to distinguish the part of the chain of supply from other elements where competition shall develop. It is critical to stress that the concept of natural monopoly is linked with the borders of a particular market. Additionally, in some cases, natural monopoly is increased by policy: an example comes from markets characterised by the importance of networks effects. In the latter, policy may exclude a segment of domestic market from the international network: that is, transport services may be excluded from international network. Small economies may be advantaged because restrictions on foreign entry may increase a natural monopoly problem. Although it is true, by contrast, markets open to trade converts this element into a component of larger market in which competition can be sustained.

A potential solution may come from the concept of economies of scale. For example, a rail network may constitute a natural monopoly in a technical cost of sense. However, a sufficient competition in transport sector is present; this can provide a valid substitute service. The result is that the ability of a single operator is limited to engage in monopoly market or the rail transport market. In this specific case the problem is concerned with the definition of market. A strict issue is the importance of a response from policy. To elaborate, once all firms involved have had sufficient time to choose their scale of plant to minimise costs per unit of service delivered, a single provider with an inefficient scale of plant may face sufficient competent discipline from a rival with a more appropriate scale of plan. For example, the telecommunications sector represents a field of market where technology has been changing for a while in a rapid way. Thus, the economy of scale failed rapidly.

Finally, a natural monopoly may provide an effective discipline by threat of competition: this is even more true for smaller developing economies. The size of market where developing economies operate may be small in relation to the prevailing technologies. This means that lowest unit cost is better achieved from one producer. Nonetheless, if this producer is subject to credible threat of replacement by a rival, the latter may provide enough discipline for the monopolist to align prices to costs. A threat, to be credible, requires multifarious conditions to be met:

- The absence of legislative or regulatory barriers to such entry.
- The rival does not incur in any costs that they could not recoup if they were unsuccessful.
- The lack of sunk costs:[5] these are all costs that cannot be recovered once committed.

It is worth highlighting that, in some cases relating to infrastructure services, investments are lumpy and location specific: this ensures that their costs may be

5 If sunk costs work, it means that market shall be contestable. For example, sunk costs encompass the costs of market research and advertising. These costs may be significant.

defined as sunk.[6] Where sunk costs are prevalent, rivals are likely to be reluctant to commit resources; thus, the incumbent may have a strong incentive to lower prices if necessary to deter entry.

Under GATT regulations, it is required that monopolists are bound by specific commitments whilst applying the monopoly service. Article VIII GATT stipulates as follows:

- Each member is under an obligation to ensure that "any monopoly supplier of a service in its territory does not, in the supply of the monopoly service in the relevant market, act in a manner inconsistent" with Member's GATT obligations.
- Member must ensure that a supplier does not abuse its monopoly position to act in its territory in a manner inconsistent with such commitments.[7]
- Member is guarantor of the fact that the supplier does not abuse its monopoly position to act in a manner inconsistent with such commitments.

5. Trade in services in the IT era

The contemporary era is characterised by *e-commerce* and the networking revolution. E-commerce constitutes an impactful element at an international level as a factor able to shape international regulatory framework. To elaborate, *e-commerce* constitutes an opportunity to transform the existing trade network and, at the same time, to reduce the geographical isolation issue. *E-commerce* is a term used to describe both contracts between business parties (B2B) and between business and consumer (B2C).[8]

From an international trade perspective, *e-commerce* impacts on four main pillars:

- Competition policy due to the impact of *e-commerce* on telecommunication sector. Traditionally, telecommunication industry was characterised either by a monopolistic approach or by a private enterprise. Moreover, Microsoft based in both US and EU showed dominance in PC operating system and consumer behaviour. To elaborate, Microsoft demonstrated its ability to exercise market power into complementary parts of the network in view of the importance interoperability of software system in a networked environment.

6 Sunk cost is a cost or payment that has already occurred and cannot be refunded. It means that something has already been paid for, and these costs cannot be covered. Moreover, sunk cost is independent from any event and should be considered when an investment and/or a project decision is assumed. Furthermore, sunk cost is also considered a fixed cost, but not all fixed costs may be defined sunk costs. Finally, sunk cost is a past cost. From a different perspective, sunk cost epitomises a tendency to continue and endeavour once an investment in money, effort or time has been made.

7 The premise is that if "a Member's monopoly supplier competes, either directly or through an affiliated company, in the supply of a service outside the scope of its monopoly rights and which is subject to that Member's specific commitments", Article VIII(2) GATT.

8 (Embley, Bamford, and Hancock 2024).

- Intellectual property rights because trademarks and copyrights play a vital role in the era of cyberspace. It is alluded to piracy, illegal downloading of music. Furthermore, another challenge has recently emerged: the opportunity to consider goods in cyberspace as "commons".
- Taxation under different aspects: (1) the definition of digital products; (2) the treatment of indirect taxes, such as value added taxes; (3) the definition of "place of permanent establishment" for *e-commerce* firms.
- Consumer protection because online transactions are characterised, in some cases, by a lack of transparency and legal uncertainty.

One of the main problems is the law applicable to *e-commerce* contracts: unlike physical barriers, *e-commerce* is borderless nature of online transactions. Thus, digital transactions occur across the border making it difficult to apply traditional regulatory frameworks. Consequently, it becomes vital to provide with a definition of cyberspace as international venue in which a billion transactions occur every half hour. Linked with this topic is the customs procedures and taxation duties. For the latter it is vital to determine the appropriate tax treatment for digital goods and services, due to the lack of physical barriers. Furthermore, *e-commerce* represents a heterogeneous topic which encapsulates intellectual property rights; banking and financial law; tax law; international and public; data protection; consumer law (more in general contract law)[9] labour law and platform economy.

From a practical perspective, platforms such as Amazon, Alibaba and eBay are influential intermediaries able to connect buyers and sellers in the digital marketplace; these platforms offer a wide range of services at a competitive price and provide streamlined shopping experiences.

Upon the underpinning scenario the WTO plays a central role in shaping international trade rules including *e-commerce*. Several existing trade agreements address aspects of digital trade and *e-commerce*. For example, the United States-Mexico-Canada Agreement (USMCA) encompasses provisions relating to cross-border data flows, non-discrimination of digital products and prohibition on data localiation requirements. In a similar way, the Comprehensive and Progressive Agreement for Trans-Pacific Partnership (CPTPP) contains a set of provisions on data localisation, digital customs procedures and intellectual property rights.[10]

Finally, *e-commerce* issue may be summarised according to two main pillars: (1) issue and (2) how different nations approach it. Concerns are fundamentally the following ones:[11]

- Cross-border data and information flows: about this topic both US and EU adopt the same approach, that is, the idea that data should flow freely with exceptions. China has a sceptical approach to free data flows, and Japan endorses trade restrictive measures that would fully legitimate public policy objectives.

9 In this respect see Chapter 5, paragraph 5, entitled "consumer contract".
10 (Prasad 2023).
11 (Abendin and Pingfang 2021).

- Consumer protection and privacy: the US stresses that members should apply only restrictive measures necessary and proportionate to privacy risks existing. The EU emphasises the importance of restrictive measures to protect privacy; similarly for China restrictive measures should be to protect consumer privacy and ensure security. Finally, Japan focuses the attention on privacy protection.
- Customs duties: both US, EU and Japan are on the same page, that is a proposal to zero custom duties. By contrast, China, proposes zero custom duties only until the next WTO Ministerial Conference.
- Data localisation, it is clearly prohibited by US, EU and Japan; China has a sceptical approach about banning it.
- Intellectual property: both EU and US want a ban on source code transfer/access; Japan proposed one based on source code transfer/access and China does not address this issue.
- Internet taxes are banned by US; the China position is unknown; EU endorses internet taxes and Japan endorses ban on internet taxes.
- Market access for telecommunication, in this case US proposed an open access to the internet; the EU bans restrictions of access to the internet by members; Japan endorses barring members from the restriction of access to the internet; and China endorses firm state control.

A practical example is "Scherm case"[12] which involves Facebook (Meta), and the topic is the transfer of personal data from countries in the European Union to third countries. This term – third countries – means, in this specific context, "United States of America". The outcome was that the US European Commission's US "Safe Harbour" decision of 26 July 2000 is invalid.[13] This first case started because Scherm lodged a complaint on 25th June 2013 with the Irish data transfer from Facebook's European headquarters in Ireland to its server in the US over concerns relating to NSA's data collection process.[14]

After the invalidation of the Safe Harbour mechanism, the EU Commission and US Department of Commerce began a data transfer mechanism that would follow EU data protection requirements when transferring personal data from the EU to US. This second corner is known as "Scherm II"[15] in which the EU-US Privacy Shield Decision was declared invalid. Privacy Shield was a legal framework to legitimate transfers of personal data from the EU to US to ensure adequate protection and safeguard in transferring these data(s). It was based on seven principles: (1) the right to know; (2) the choice principle; (3) the limitation of the scope of how personal data is handled when transferred to a third-party organisation; (4)

12 *Maximillian Schrems v Data Protection Commissioner*. Case C-362/14.

13 2000/520/EC: Commission Decision of 26 July 2000 pursuant to Directive 95/46/EC of the European Parliament and of the Council on the adequacy of the protection provided by the safe harbour privacy principles and related frequently asked questions issued by the US Department of Commerce (notified under document number C(2000) 2441).

14 (Ojanen 2016).

15 *Maximillian Schrems v Data Protection Commissioner*. Case C-311/18, (the Schrems II case).

security principle; (5) data integrity and purpose limitation; (6) access principles (individual cannot prevented from accessing data that was collected); (7) recourse; enforcement and liability principles.[16]

The reason for this decision was, fundamentally, that the protection of personal data had limitations due to the US domestic law; thus, US laws do not satisfy requirements that are essentially equivalent to those required under the EU law. More precisely, two main elements were stressed by the Court of Justice of European Union:[17]

- US public authorities' use, and access of EU data, were not restricted by the principle of proportionality.
- The Ombudsperson mechanism does not provide data subjects with any cause of action before a body. In other words, US does not offer guarantees substantially equivalent to those required by EU law.

From a different perspective, the UK and US signed the well-known "data bridge",[18] an expression used to describe the decision to permit flow of data from the UK to the other country without any need for further safeguards. It replaces the previous Privacy Shield framework, established in 2016 to provide a legal basis for companies to comply with EU data protection requirements when transferring personal data to the US. Consequently, thanks to data bridge the UK has established, indeed, a bridge for the UK Extension to the Data Privacy Framework that allows certified US companies to sign-up to be able to receive UK personal data through the framework. In essence, the data bridge ensures higher protection for UK individuals when their data is transferred to another country.

References

Abendin, S., and D. Pingfang. 2021. "Global E-Commerce Talks at the WTO; Positions on Selected Issues of the United States, European Union, China, and Japan." *World Trade Review* 12 (5): 707–24.

Baldock, K., and A. Smyth. 2024. "UK-US Data Bridge." *Privacy Laws & Business United Kingdom Newsletter* 135: 18–19.

Barczentewicz, M. 2025. "Schrems III: Gauging the Validity of the GDPR Adequacy Decision for the United States." International Center for Law & Economics Issue Brief 2023-09-25 (online).

Connolly, M. 2024. "Will the EU-US Data Privacy Framework Survive Scherms III?" *Trinity College Law Review* 124: 87–124.

Embley, J., K. Bamford, and N. Hancock. 2024. *Commercial and Intellectual Property Law and Practice*. College of Law Publishing.

Findlay, C., and T. Warren. 2005. *Impediments to Trade in Services*. Routledge Studies.

Jensen, J. 2011. *Global Trade in Services: Fear, Facts, and Offshoring*. Peterson Institute for International Economics.

16 See (Massey 2019; Ustaran 2016; Connolly 2024).

17 (Barczentewicz 2025).

18 (Baldock and Smyth 2024).

Massey, R. 2019. "European Commission Completes Second Annual Review of the EU-US Privacy Shield." *Computer and Telecommunications Law Review* 25 (4): 93–95.
McGuire, G. 2002. *Trade in Services: Market Access Opportunities and the Benefits of Liberalization for Developing Economies*. University of California Press.
Ojanen, T. 2016. "Making the Essence of Fundamental Rights Real: The Court of Justice of the European Union Clarifies the Structure of Fundamental Rights Under the Charter: ECJ October 6, 2015, Case C-362/14, Maximillian Schrems v Data Protection Commissioner." *European Constitutional Law Review* 12 (2): 318–29.
Prasad, R. 2023. "Cyber Borderlines: Exploring the Interplay Between E-Commerce and International Trade Law." *Studies in Law and Justice* 2 (4): 1–9.
Ustaran, E. 2016. "The Privacy Shield explained: Part 3." *Privacy & Data Protection* 16 (7): 3–4.
Whalley, J. 2004. "Assessing the Benefits to Developing Countries of Liberalisation in Services Trade." *World Economy* 27 (8): 1223–53.

24 International contract law and its harmonisation

Chapter Overview

1. Introduction

The harmonisations process relating to international trade law straddles two opposite poles: public and private. The second one is focused, also, on the contract law matter. Promoting harmonisation of international private law constitutes a means

DOI: 10.4324/9781003645948-24

of harmonising measures within private law, since the latter has blossomed on the two pillars: obligations and contract.

Therefore, harmonisation has a further significance: increasing economic transactions and, thus, the relevant economic volume. To better explain, WTO, as well as GATT, cannot implement free world trade in goods and services without a prejudice for contractual relationships. This concept is true even if those relations do affect, directly, free trade and services.

In a nutshell, the commercial policy of foresting free international trade constitutes the underlying *ratio* for harmonising contract law. To elaborate, free international trade works better in a legally harmonised environment than in the opposite situation, because economic integration requires a legal framework as a support. By contrast, a lack, or an absence, of uniform commercial rules makes the outcome of litigation unpredictable.

Based on such background, it becomes clear the importance of international commercial contracts in a global economy based on free trade market. Moreover, harmonisation constitutes the outcome of multifarious factors, such as the following:

- Internal agreement.
- Legal framework.
- Commercial policies.
- Political and cultural needs.

Consequently, the rationale behind harmonisation is given by both legal and practical reasons. An example of this is the European Community, in more recent times, European Union as well as the principle in force of which an entity will function under the principle of free market. Subsequently, it became necessary to discuss about the legal conundrum of the borders that may have theoretically affected this freedom.

The result was a complex "dialogue" and friction between commercial needs, on one hand, and social regulation of commercial agreements, that is, contracts, on the other hand. Finally, from the EU experience, one principle may be inferred: commercial and contractual harmonisation is more relaxed in the case of regional harmonisation.

2. International contract law: a definition

One of the ancillary notions to discuss is the concept of "international contract law", a notion interpreted in several ways.[1] From a general perspective, international contract law was defined as an international activity linked with contractual relations, in which the parties of agreement:

1 (DiMatteo 2021).

- Being habitually resident in different countries.
- Having place their business in different countries.
- Agreed that the contract signed will take place in more countries than one.
- Choosing international rules and principles.

Furthermore, international contract law represents a substantive part of the law of contracts, however it encapsulates, also, the law of negotiable instruments, for example.

In this respect, Article 1 of Principles of International Commercial Contracts[2] stipulates as follows:

> The international character of a contract may be defined in a great variety of ways. The solutions adopted in both national and international legislation range from a reference to the place of business or habitual residence of the parties in different countries to the adoption of more general criteria such as the contract having "significant connections with more than one State", involving a choice between the laws of different States, or "affecting interests of international trade".

Additionally, the term "international" alludes to the connection between two States or among more States or, better, all cases involving a choice between the laws of two States. Thus, the expression conflict of laws identifies the set of rules and criteria among the two or more applicable national laws.

The opposite notion of international contract is national contract: the latter refers to a contract in which all its significant elements are connected only with one State.

It is worth stressing that, if and when one or more significant elements of a contract will result in being connected with different territorial units within the same territory, the contract should not be qualified as international but as national contract. The reference goes to, by example: (1) England (with Wales) and Scotland in the UK; (2) Quebec and Labrador in Canada; (3) Queensland and Victoria in Australia; (4) Massachusetts and California with the reference to United States. Each of these countries, a sovereign State, is made up of three or more jurisdictions.

International contract encapsulates, also, the concept of international trade contract.

The latter represents either a contract signed to achieve a commercial transaction, or a contract made by trader for the purpose of his own business. To summarise, international trade contracts are contracts through which each party intends to act in the exercise of its trade or profession. Moreover, under the umbrella term of international trade contracts, both commercial activities of merchant and commercial activities of professional are covered. According to this line of reasoning, insurance contracts and contracts transferring licensing intellectual property rights constitute international trade contracts.

2 Knowns, also, as Unidroit Principles, International Institute for the Unification of Private Law 1994.

Agency as well as franchising contract may qualified as international trade contracts; whether a party is acting in the exercise of its trade or profession is an element linked with the circumstances of the contract. Therefore, it does not constitute a mere status of the parties. For instance, an individual may act, at the same time, as a trader or professional in relation to a specific transaction and as a consumer for others.

International contract law constitutes part of private international law: when parties signed an international contract, it is quintessential to understand which law will rule their relationship. Legal provisions that govern contractual obligations can differ among countries. These differences may have an impact on the outcome of a dispute. Bearing this in mind, private international law refers to procedural rules suitable to identify the national law applicable to an international specific case. Because of this, private international law may be defined as the procedural technique aimed to recognise the appropriate and applicable national law.[3]

Finally, an additional clarification is required: the categorisation of contract according to civil law and common law systems. The first one – civil law system – has three main categories of contract:

- Public contract, regulating the relationship between the State and the individual or private bodies.
- Private contract (or also civil contract), regulating the relationship between private individuals.
- Commercial contract in between civil contract and business relationships.

The second one – common law systems – approaches contract as one category.

3. Legal sources: international conventions and agreements

Trade creates wealth, an essential element for the health of the world. Within the expansion of world trade, it becomes necessary realising a new set of standards and rules to harmonise and modernise the worldwide assortment of both nationals and regional regulations.

The United Nations Commission on International Trade Law (UNCITRAL) 1966 recognised the need for playing a more active role in removing legal obstacles; UNCITRAL became the core legal framework for the United Nations system in international trade law.[4] UNCITRAL produces one of the most significant international conventions; the United Nations Convention on Contracts for the International Sale of Goods (called, also, the "Vienna Convention" or CISG).

UNIDROIT is an independent intergovernmental organisation, established in 1940 based on multinational agreement. It has 63 member states from five

3 By contrast, international civil procedural law is focused on the applicable jurisdiction to a specific international private controversy.

4 (Twigg-Flesner 2022).

continents, including both the UK and the US. The purpose is to modernise and harmonise private international law and the commercial law between States as well as to draft international conventions to address the needs. The first edition was the UNIDROIT Principles of International Commercial Contracts (PICC), produced in 1994.

From the European Union perspective, the most important legal framework is the Lando Commission (1989): a resolution of the European Parliament, the European Commission on European Contract law.

3.1 United Nations Convention on Contracts for the International Sale of Goods (CISG)

The CISG was adopted on 11th April 1980; it is a multinational accord which establishes a comprehensive set of civil code provisions, applicable to the transactions for the sale of goods in international commerce.

According to Article 1, CISG will apply if the following conditions are met; these are as follows:

- The contract is for the sale of goods (commercial rather than personal).
- Both parties are in different Contracting States.
- The parties have agreed that their contract will be subject to the law of a Contracting State.
- The parties agree that the CISG will govern their contract.
- The court of a country where a dispute has broken out finds that the applicable law is the law of a Contracting State.
- The parties have not opted out of the CISG.

In this case, the nationality or residence of parties is not relevant.

CISG, if applicable to a transaction, provides with default or gap filling rules that govern sale of goods contract: contract formation; rights of the buyer and seller; obligations of the buyer and seller; passing of risk; remedies; however, it does not cover mistake, misrepresentation or agency. Furthermore, it should be noted that CISG recognises the principle of contract autonomy: it provides with express contract provisions take precedence over the default provisions of the Convention. Thus, contracting parties remain free to specify the applicable law and/or terms they wish to apply to the transaction, and similarly, they may exclude others.

Ultimately, the rules encompassed into CISG work together with international trade usages.

3.2 The UNIDROIT Principles of International Commercial Contracts (PICC)

The last edition of PICC is the 2016 one: it is a setting of non-binding rules applicable to international commercial contracts. The PICC purpose is establishing a balanced set of rules designed for use throughout the world irrespective of the legal traditions and the economic and political conditions of the countries in which there are to be applied.

The preamble defines the application of PICC; it will apply to an international commercial contract[5] when the parties have incorporated them; furthermore, PICC may:

- Apply to an international commercial contract when the parties have agreed that the contract be governed by general principles of law, the *lex mercatoria*,[6] or "the like", or if the parties have not chosen any law to govern their contract.
- Be used to interpret or supplement other international law instruments or domestic law.

The PICC covers the following topics: contract formation, authority of agents, validity (including illegality), interpretation, contents, performance, non-performance (breach) and remedies, set-off, assignment and plurality of parties.

3.3 Principles of European Contract Law (PECL)

As PICC, PECL is non-binding and PECL achieves the harmonisation of European contract law. Article 1:101 stipulates that PECL is intended to be applied as a general rule of contract law in the EU. It will apply if the parties have agreed to incorporate them. Further, PECL may:

- Be applied when the parties have agreed that the contract be governed by general principles of law, the *lex mercatoria*, or "the like", or if the parties have not chosen any law to govern their contract.
- Be used as a "solution to the issue raised" where the applicable law does not provide one.

As far as the topics are concerned, PECL encapsulates the following:

- Rules of contract formation, authority of agents, validity (including mistake and "incorrect information"), interpretation, contents, performance, non-performance (breach) and remedies.
- Plurality of parties, assignment of claims, substitution of new debt, transfer of contract, set-off, prescription, illegality, conditions and capitalisation of interest.

3.4 The Uniform Commercial Code (UCC)

The UCC constitutes one of the uniform acts that has been promulgated in the US to harmonise the law of sales and other commercial transactions in all 50 States. It

5 (Chuah 2023).

6 The PICC can be used, also, to interpret or fill gaps where either there is uncertainty, or the domestic or international law does not provide with a solution.

covers the main important types of commercial transactions, such as sales, leases, bank deposits, fund transfers and securities. UCC is relevant in an international contract if parties either choose to incorporate it or choose the law of US as the law of the contract.

Article 2 encompasses seven sections about scope and definitions; form, formation and variation of the contract, including assignment; obligations and construction, including delivery and quality; title, including retention of title; performance; breach and repudiation; remedies.

4. Harmonisation under legal sources

Harmonisation of private international law is based, from a legal perspective, on the Hague Conference of Private International Law[7]: an international organisation comprising 83 members, that is, 82 plus the European Union. The HCCH led to the adoption of Principles on Choice of Law in International Commercial Contracts (2015).

These principles are international instruments to apply to interpret and supplement domestic private international law rules as well as regional, supranational and intercharacter of the Rome Convention. A further legal source is Rome Convention, replaced by Rome I Regulation[8]: the latter constitutes the legal sources in all European Union States except for Denmark. Rome I Regulation constitutes a piece of legislation adopted at EU level.

Rome I Regulation:[9]

- Shall apply to contractual obligations in civil and commercial matters, in situation where a conflict of law materialises.
- Does not apply to revenue, customs or administrative matters.
- Does not apply to questions relating to status or legal capacity of natural obligations.
- Does not apply to contractual obligations relating to the following:

  1) Will and succession.
  2) Company law.
  3) Evidence and procedure.
  4) If an agent can bind a principal to a third party.

Finally, a critical concept is the "disconnection clause": this clause refers to source of law concerned and other legal instruments. Based on Article 25, Rome I Regulation, a regulation shall not prejudice the application of international conventions to which one, or more member states, are parties at the time when the regulation was adopted.

7 Henceforth HCCH.

8 Regulation (EC) No. 593/2008 of the European Parliament and of the Council of 17 June 2008 on the law applicable to contractual obligations (Rome I).

9 See Article 1(1)(2).

4.1 The applicable law

Based on Rome I Regulation, the general principle is the contractual freedom. This principle stipulates as follows: "A contract shall be governed by the law chosen by the parties".[10] Parties of a contract are best placed to decide which set of legal provisions is more appropriate for their transaction.

Moreover, the choice of law, or any modification of choice of law, shall be, alternatively, made:

- Expressly or explicit.[11]
- Tacit or implied, that is, appear clear in the provision of the contract or in the circumstances detailed in the agreement. It can be inferred from the provisions of the contract based on the language used by parties, currency payment, set of the arbitral tribunal choose.[12]

"*Depeçage*" means that parties have chosen that other laws are applicable to different parts of the contract. In other words, *depeçage* has effect if the contract is governed by more than one national law. By contrast, parties may also designate that a specific law governed the entire contract. Furthermore, parties may also decide that their agreement will be governed by *lex mercatoria*, the law of merchants or by general principles of law. It should be noted that parties, when deciding what law will govern their agreement, shall be aware of the consequences of their choice.

Consequently, parties need to consider the following:

- The effectiveness of the national law.
- The existence of different legal systems in a single nation.
- The existence of the "*renvoi*"[13]: the application of law of a third country designated pursuant to the private international law provision of that country. From a

10 Article 3(1).

11 In *Vita Food Products Inc v Unus Shipping Co Ltd* [1939] UKPC 7 the Judicial Committee of the Privy Council stated that the proper law of a contract is the law which parties intended to apply. Consequently, this intention should be objectively ascertained; further if this intention did not express, it would be presumed from the terms of the contract and the relevant surrounding circumstances. To summarise, this case is significant since it expanded the ability of parties to choose the jurisdiction of the contract.

12 For example, if the contract does not contain any definition of the governing law, but parties refer to the court of a country, the law of that court constitutes an implicit choice of the applicable law. In this respect, Preamble 12, Rome I Regulation, stipulates as follows: "An agreement between the parties to confer on one or more courts or tribunals of a Member State exclusive jurisdiction to determine disputes under the contract should be one of the factors to be taken into account in determining whether a choice of law has been clearly demonstrated". A further example is the connection with other contracts. For instance, a guarantee connected with an underlying contract: if the contract is governed by English law but the guarantee is not explicitly governed by a specific law, the implied choice is the English law. The latter, more in detail, constitutes the applicable law to both the contract and the guarantee connected with the contract.

13 The *renvoi* refers to the possibility for the judge of the forum is to take account of the rules of private international law prevailing in the country to which the *lex fori* refers. Moreover, under a strict

practical perspective, the contract contains the expression "substantive law of" or "excluding its conflict of law provisions".

Parties' freedom is limited by two kinds of rules:

- Rules of public law, such as import and export restrictions, tax provisions, anti-trust law. These are applicable directly to the contractual relations as well as cannot be replaced by foreign law. According to Article 9 the choice of foreign law by the parties will not prejudice the application of mandatory rules of home country to the contract.
- Public policy law, it means that fundamental values of the *lex fori* which shall not be jeopardised by the application of a foreign law.

Finally, if parties do not choose the applicable law, there are two solutions:

- The applicability of international or national rules on conflict of laws: these are rules established at international level, by convention, or at national level, shaped by private international law provisions.
- The applicability of substantive law of the forum when such application is required either by international convention or domestic law.
- Article 4, Rome I Regulation, which establishes a default rules.

According to Article 4, Rome I Regulation establishes default rules. The latter refers, first, to the typology of contract. For instance, "a contract for the sale of goods shall be governed by the law of the country where the seller has his habitual residence"[14] or a "contract relating to a right in rem in immovable property or to a tenancy of immovable property shall be governed by the law of the country where the property is situated".[15] In cases where contract does not fall within the typologies described in Article 4(1), the rules are the following ones: this contract will be governed "by the law of the country where the party required to effect the characteristic performance of the contract has his habitual residence".[16]

If the applicable law shall not be defined according to previous criteria, the contract must be governed by the law of the country with which it is most closely connected.[17]

To summarise, it is possible to affirm that international contract law constitutes the suitable "instrument" to govern a contract with an international impact. In this respect, one of the most important issues is concerned with the applicable law. The

---

interpretation *renvoi* means the foreign law, having jurisdiction in the matter, had referred the case back to the *lex fori*.

14 Article 4(1)(a).

15 Article 4(1)(c).

16 Article 4(2).

17 Article 4(3)(4).

latter depends on the choice of the parties of the contract. As to the latter, it is possible to elucidate as follows:

- The choice can be either express or implied.
- If the choice cannot be inferred, Article 4, Rome I Regulation, contains supplementary criteria.
- In international contract law some rules cannot be derogated by parties.

4.2 The applicable law to specific contract

Consumer contracts, individual employment contracts and insurance contracts have *ad hoc* rules.[18]

Consumer contracts, based on Article 6, Rome I Regulation, are contracts whose object is the supply of goods or services to a person for a purpose which may be regarded as being outside his trade or profession or a contract for the provision of credit for that object. The general rule is that the applicable law is the law

> of the country where the consumer has his habitual residence, provided that the professional: (a) (b) pursues his commercial or professional activities in the country where the consumer has his habitual residence, or by any means, directs such activities to that country or to several countries including that country, and the contract falls within the scope of such activities.[19]

Yet parties can also choose another law to apply to the contract they are negotiating. In this specific case, the choice of the law should not prejudice the consumer. Consequently, the consumer will benefit, also, from the protection afforded to him by the mandatory rules of the law of the country in which he has the habitual residence.

Finally, all these rules do not apply to the following contracts:[20]

- For the supply of services in cases where "services are to be supplied to the consumer exclusively in a country other than that in which he has his habitual residence".
- Of carriage.
- Relating to a right *in rem* in immovable property and/or a tenancy immovable property.
- Where "rights and obligations which constitute a financial instrument and rights and obligations constituting the terms and conditions governing the issuance or offer to the public and public take-over bids of transferable securities, and the subscription and redemption of units in collective investment undertakings in so far as these activities do not constitute provision of a financial service".

18 (Cordero-Moss 2014).
19 Article (1).
20 Article 6(4).

As far as individual employment contracts are concerned, Article 8(1) stipulates that these contracts are under the law chosen by parties. However, this choice should not deprive an employee of the protection afforded to him by provision that cannot be derogated. If parties do not choose the applicable law, Article 8(2) prescribes that "the contract shall be governed by the law of the country in which or, failing that, from which the employee habitually carries out his work in performance of the contract". Moreover, if the law applicable shall not be determined based on Article 8(2), Article 8(3) stipulates as follows: "The contract shall be governed by the law of the country where the place of business through which the employee was engaged is situated".

Insurance contracts now fall under Rome I Regulation; however, the Rome Convention had excluded these contracts from its scope. To elaborate, under Rome Convention, if the risk was situated outside the EU, the Convention was applicable. The reason for this choice was based on two directives: (1) Directive 88/357 for Non-Life Insurance; (2) Directive 90/619 for Life Insurance. Nevertheless, if the risk was not located in one of the member states or the contract was a re-insurance contract, the Convention was applicable. In *American Motorists Insurance v Cellstar*[21] the crucial issue was to determine the governing law of the insurance contract. The court concluded that parties made a real choice to have an insurance contract governed by Texas law because not only was the contract issued in Texas, but also, the factors did not demonstrate a different choice. Consequently, Texas law was regarded to be the applicable law.

Additionally, under Article 4, Rome I Regulation, the applicable law for the contract should be determined by the country in which it is most closely connected. In the specific case, the insurance policy covered risks in different countries but only three of the countries were EU member states. Thus, the risks were predominantly allocated outside the UK and the EU: Texas law is determined to be the governing law.

Under Article 7, Rome I Regulation, this Convention shall apply to insurance contracts "whether or not the risk covered is situated in a Member State, and to all other insurance contracts covering risks situated inside the territory of the Member States. It shall not apply to reinsurance contracts".

In this respect, it is critical to distinguish between:

- Insurance contracts that cover large risks. In this case parties can freely settle, by agreement, the law of any State relevant to the contract in force of the principle of autonomy. If a choice of parties is missed or this choice is not valid, subsidiary criteria will be applicable.
- Insurance contracts that cover mass risk. The principle of autonomy does not apply in this case, due to the application of a list of criteria for deciding the applicable law, in derogation from the law of the parties.

21 [2003] EWCA Civ 206. The claimant was a US insurance company that operates under a trading name. The claimant seeks declaratory relief to establish that he had not liability under a contract of insurance regarding the loss of two shipments of mobile phones made by the second defendant.

To summarise all, the matter may be explained through different questions:

- Is the matter excluded? à "Yes": regulation does not apply.
  ↓ "No"
- Have parties chosen applicable law? "Yes": Choice prevails
  ↓ "No"
- Law governing contract: country of seller's habitual residence
  ↓ Unless
- Contract more closely connected with another country.

Subject to: 1) mandatory rules; 2) consumer contracts; 3) insurance contracts; 4) employment contracts.

5. The content of international contract law

Parties to an international contract generally opt for fixing in writing the agreement to reach throughout negotiation. In some cases, the law applicable to the contract requires that contract to be in writing form, in compliance with certain formalities.

In this respect, one of the most important stages is the drafting. More in detail, in drawing up a contract, parties state both the substance and terms of their respective obligations. Therefore, the contract constitutes the "law" of the parties and, the latter act as a "legislator", albeit for purposes of the limited perimeter. Thus, parties shall be defining the following elements:

- Rights and obligations.
- The designation of either a court or arbitration.
- Terms and conditions.

More in general, during the negotiation stage, a pivotal role is played by lawyers or legal counsels, whose purpose is to provide legal assistance. More in-depth, lawyers work together with banks and financial advisors to structure and implement large international transaction.

If parties use the expression "subject to contract", this signifies that parties do not intend to be bound by the terms of any informal agreement or pre-contractual negotiations. This qualification is often used to confirm the usual presumption that in commercial contracts the parties do not intend to be bound. Nevertheless, courts will look at the conduct of the parties during negotiations; consequently, parties should also include an express statement to the effect that they do not intend to be legally bound.

5.1 Clauses of a contract

It is possible that parties seek to impose their own terms on the other, and it would not be totally clear whose standard terms apply. The expression "battle of the forms" alludes to situations where, for example, the seller provides the buyer with an invitation to treat, encompassing seller's terms and conditions, and the buyer makes an offer introducing its own terms. Where the seller does not accept the buyer's terms and insists on reinstating its own terms, the seller has made a counteroffer. Moreover, if negotiations are protracted there may be several sets of terms and conditions put forward; where a dispute may arise, the court will consider whose terms and conditions were on the table at the time of acceptance. In doing so, the court applies the "the last shot wins doctrine".[22] From an international perspective,[23] the "battle of the forms" is called "knock-out doctrine".

Finally, the notion of boilerplate clause should be introduced. Such clauses, boilerplate, are adopted in many international contracts. Boilerplates clauses are standardised clauses in contracts which are often agreed with little or no negotiation. Common boilerplate clauses are entire agreement; no representation or no reliance clause; no waiver clause; confidentiality, force majeure; governing law; and variation clause.

5.1.1 Prevail clause

A "prevail clause" applies when there is a battle of the forms: the seller's terms will prevail. From a legal perspective, this clause is ineffective as any later set of terms which are introduced will act as a counteroffer and override an earlier set. Yet a prevail clause is frequently included for bluff value.

5.1.2 Entire or whole agreement clause

An entire or whole agreement clause may be inserted by the seller to prevent any statements made by sales representatives or statements included in sales literature, brochures and forming terms of contracts. In essence, this clause means that the seller's terms and conditions form the whole agreement between the seller and the buyer and cannot be varied in any way. Often, it also prescribed that no other express terms, written or oral, shall be included as a part of the contract. The purpose is avoiding difficulties associated with oral presentation and discussion.

The entire or whole agreements clause has some problems:

- It is open to the same objections of the prevail clause.
- It might be excluding other documents which parties do wish to have considered, for instance a price list.

5.1.3 No authority clause

No authority clauses are attempts by the seller to:

- Put a limit on the extent to which its sales representatives or other employees are permitted to negotiate individual terms with the buyer.

22 *Tekdata Interconnections Ltd v Amphenol Ltd* [2009] EWCA Civ 1209: it was confirmed that it is required to courts to apply the traditional offer and acceptance analysis to decide on a battle of forms dispute.

23 (Klee 2018).

- Exclude any extra claims made by the sales representatives to induce buyer to enter the contract.

5.1.4 Jurisdiction clause

One of the most important clauses in negotiation phases is the choice of jurisdiction, that is the governing law of contract signed by parties. Cross-border contracts may involve different international organisations which operate in different legal systems.

Consequently, it becomes quintessential to determine which legal system will govern the contract. Jurisdiction represents a critical clause, due to the geographical and juridical limitation of a court's power if a controversy will arise. Further, a jurisdiction clause specifies which court has the power to decide controversy under the contract signed between parties.

Jurisdiction clauses may be as follows:

- Exclusively: it means that parties agree to a specific court's exclusively jurisdiction.
- Non-exclusively: it signifies that parties agree that dispute may be determined in a specific jurisdiction. Yet parties may also decide to refer the case to the court of another jurisdiction. Therefore, this clause gives more flexibility to parties.
- Unilateral: it shows that one party may chose a specific jurisdiction, but the other party has the power to file litigation against the first party in the jurisdiction of its choice.

Moreover, jurisdiction clause may be:

- Express jurisdiction agreement where parties clearly demonstrate consent to submit to the jurisdiction on a specific court.
- Implicit jurisdiction agreement where parties establishing through trade usages or an established course of dealing that a specific jurisdiction agreement has always governed their transaction. Further, a specific agreement to submit to the jurisdiction of a particular court may infer from parties' conduct.

Also, it is worth stressing that there are international conventions in place whose purpose is to ascertain if an implied jurisdiction agreement shall be valid in its form and substance.

Thus, an implied jurisdiction agreement needs to possess an adequate formal validity. To elaborate, this agreement shall be in writing form, evidence of this form shall be provided, and it also requires the signature. Additionally, the substantive validity of an implied jurisdiction agreement is also linked with further factors, such as the following one: the existence of consent; the absence of fraud or mistake; and the absence of the lack of capacity. A further critical topic is that an implied jurisdiction agreement shall not contain an explicit applicable law that governs such agreement. The reason for that is that it will be paradoxical to have an express applicable law to the jurisdiction agreement in absence of an express jurisdiction agreement.

To assess the validity of an implied jurisdiction agreement, there are both international and national instruments. The first one, international instruments, encapsulates the following:

- The Hague Choice of Court Convention 2005 aims to regulate the exclusive choice of courts in global sphere. This Convention suggests that implied jurisdiction agreement is potentially enforceable if the chosen court decides that these agreements are valid under its law.[24] In this respect, Article 3(c) stipulates that "an exclusive choice of court agreement must be concluded or documented – *i)* in writing; or *ii)* by any other means of communication which renders information accessible so as to be usable for subsequent reference".
- The Hague Judgments Convention 2019 says that a court shall be "designated in an agreement concluded or documented in writing or by any other means of communication which renders information accessible so as to be usable for subsequent reference".[25] Therefore, only the requirement of formal validity is addressed.
- From an EU perspective, the reference goes to the "Convention on jurisdiction and the recognition and enforcement of judgments in civil and commercial matters". Article 23(1) prescribes that a jurisdiction agreement is formally valid if it is:
    - (a) in writing or evidenced in writing; or (b) in a form which accords with practices which the parties have established between themselves; or (c) in international trade or commerce, in a form which accords with a usage of which the parties are or ought to have been aware and which in such trade or commerce is widely known to, and regularly observed by, parties to contracts of the type involved in the particular trade or commerce concerned.

It is possible to affirm that this legal provision presupposes the existence of a consensus between parties.

As far as national regulations are concerned, it is vital to distinguish between civil law and common law jurisdictions. The first one, civil law countries, complies with the just mentioned "Convention on jurisdiction and the recognition and enforcement of judgments in civil and commercial matters". However, for non-EU civil law jurisdiction the national law shall be scrutinised. For example, Article 63(1),

24 Article 5(1) states as follows: "The court or courts of a Contracting State designated in an exclusive choice of court agreement shall have jurisdiction to decide a dispute to which the agreement applies, unless the agreement is null and void under the law of that State".

25 See Article 5(1)(m).

Brazil Code, stipulates that Brazilian courts are able to enforce a jurisdiction agreement only if "it is stated in a written document and is expressly stated in relation to a specific legal transaction". Moreover, the Dubai International Financial Courts emphasised that:

- Parties may elect in writing that Dubai International Financial Courts may hear any civil and/or commercial dispute.
- It is crucial that agreements encompass specific, clear and express provisions.

As regards common law jurisdictions, it seems that the approach is like the position adopted by English courts. Therefore, it seems to be a favour to the proper law of the main/host contract as the governing law. The latter will determine the validity and the existence of a choice of court agreement within the contract. Consequently, under common law, there is not a difference between formal and substantive validity. Despite this, in *Enka Insaat ve Sanayi AS v OOO Insurance Company Chubb*,[26] it was held that the law of the main contract, if chosen by parties, governs an arbitration agreement. However, if the law of the main contract was not chosen by parties, the arbitration agreement was governed by the law of the seat of arbitration. From this, it is possible to infer the following principles:

- The governing law of the main contract also applies to jurisdiction agreements.
- If a specific choice of law is not made, the law of the chosen court governs matters relating to validity.

As far as implied jurisdiction agreement is concerned, there are multifarious approaches under English common law. To summarise, the *modus operandi* shall be based on the contractual terms. To elaborate, jurisdiction agreements under English common law constitute a contractual term, consequently in principle it will be oral, written, express and implied.

Furthermore, in *Vizcaya Partners*[27] Lord Collins stressed that the general take to implied terms should be the traditional one. Thus, the reference to both "business efficacy" and "officious bystander" tests. These two tests pursue the objective to ascertain the presumed intention of the parties or, alternatively, to give the efficacy on a transaction. In other words, courts must apply the implied term only if the implied term is necessary, or if it is obvious that the term should be included without explicitly stating.

More in detail, the business efficacy test is aimed to ascertain if the term was necessary to give the contract business efficacy; in other words if the contract makes business sense without it. Consequently, the court must apply the term only if this implied term is necessary to do so.[28]

26 [2020] UKSC 38.
27 *Vizcaya Partners Ltd. v Picard* [2016] UKPC 5.
28 See *The Moorcock* (1889) 14 PD 64.

By contrast, based on the officious bystander test,[29] it was held that:

- An officious bystander shall be present at the time the contract was made.
- A term shall be included if it appears obvious that both parties have agreed on it.

A recent court decision, *J.P. Morgan International Finance Limited v Werealize.com Limited*,[30] deals with exclusive jurisdiction agreement in favour of the English courts and a "no liability clause". The Viva Wallet Holdings Software Development SA was a Greek fintech company; the terms of the shareholders relationship ware governed by an agreement (the SHA) between JPM, WEREALIZE.COM ("WRL") and Viva Wallet. Based on the Greek proceedings, JPM sued a co-founder of Viva Wallet and three individual directors of Viva Wallet appointed as directors to the board of the Viva Wallet. JPM argued that its shareholding rights in Viva Wallet had been rendered worthless by the conduct of the Directors; therefore, he sued them for 1 million euro in damages.

The general rule is that the governing law of a contract determines to what extent the parties can limit their contractual liability. Despite this, often, the aim of exclusion clauses is to exclude tort liability. This raises the question of whether the governing law of the contract or the law applicable to the non-contractual obligation determines if the parties can limit their liability. The most accepted view is that the law applicable – determined in adherence with Rome II Regulation – takes precedence.[31] This route has been followed by the English court in such case. The main problem was that the shareholders' agreement was governed by English law. At the same time, the potential non-contractual liability of some of the directors was shaped according to Article 4, Rome II Regulation. Thus, the governing law might have been the Greek one. Moreover, English law: (1) prohibited the parties from excluding liability for their own fraud; (2) this exception applied only to claims where fraud was a necessary ingredient. By contrast, Greek law stipulated that any agreement made in advance to exclude or limit liability for intentional conduct or gross negligence should be null and void. The outcome was an anti-suit injunction in favour of the Greek directors who had been sued by some shareholders in Greece. This was based on an alleged implied term of the shareholders agreement. The latter prevented the shareholders from bringing proceedings to assert such liability. This final point did not consider that the jurisdiction agreement in the shareholders' agreement in favour of the English courts did not extend to them.

5.1.5 Arbitration clause

Arbitration clause is an area adjacent to the jurisdiction clause. First and foremost, it is pivotal to draw the differences between these two clauses. Arbitration clause

29 *Shirlaw v Southern Foundries* [1939] 2 KB 206.
30 [2025] EWHC 1842 (Comm).
31 See Article 15(b), Rome Regulation II.

is a private dispute resolution scheme. Parties agree to avoid proceedings before national courts. Furthermore, parties refer that any potential dispute may arise from and/or in connection with their contract to an arbitrator.

On the other side, a jurisdiction clause is aimed to determine the national court that will have exclusive jurisdiction to adjudicate any disputes that may arise in connection with parties' contract.[32] Nevertheless, to understand if parties want to adopt an arbitration clause or an exclusive jurisdiction clause, it is necessary to analyse how the contract is construed. To elaborate, the key is the interpretation that a reasonable person gives to the meaning of the contract. In this respect, in *Melford Capital Partners (Holdings) LLP and Others v Digby*[33] the court stated that the arbitration clause determined that disputes shall be resolved by arbitration. By contrast, the exclusively jurisdiction clause defined that the courts should have supervisory power on the arbitral process.

This conclusion was adopted by the Singapore Court of Appeal in *BXH v BXI*[34]: if parties signed a contract which encompassed both an arbitration clause and an exclusive jurisdiction clauses, court should give effect to both clauses. Thus, if a contractual dispute arises, it shall be resolved in accordance with the arbitration clause. Additionally, the Singaporean courts shall exercise its supervisory jurisdiction under the exclusive jurisdiction clause.

The first one, that is, the arbitration clause means that a future and potential controversy between parties shall be refer to arbitration agreement. To be enforceable, an arbitration clause shall possess:

- The scope of the arbitration agreement.
- An ambiguous statement in force of which all disputes covered under the agreement shall be referred only through arbitration.
- A clear endorsement of arbitration to resolve and define in a binding and final manner the controversy.

Additionally, arbitration clause shall also encapsulate:

- The number of arbitrators and the method of their appointment.
- The place of the arbitration or arbitral seat.
- The language of the arbitration.

Arbitration shall be either *ad hoc* arbitration or administered arbitration. The first one, *ad hoc* arbitration, means that there is not any arbitral institution in charge of administering the proceeding from the beginning to the end. Consequently, parties do not pay administrative fees. Administered arbitration refers to a situation in which parties opt for institutional or administered arbitration. The arbitration

32 (Andenas and Heidemann 2024).
33 [2021] EWHC 872 (Ch).
34 [2020] SGCA 28.

agreement shall clearly indicate if parties have chosen an institution to act as the administrator.

From a legal perspective, the international source of law is the New York Convention which applies to recognise and enforce foreign arbitral awards. In a nutshell, New York Convention achieves two main goals:

- This Conventions provides that every contracting State "shall recognize an agreement in writing under which the parties undertake to submit to arbitration all or any differences which have arisen, or which may arise between them in respect of a defined legal relationship, whether contractual or not, concerning a subject matter capable of settlement by arbitration".[35]
- New York Convention is aimed to ensure that every contracting State "shall recognize arbitral awards as binding and enforce them in accordance with the rules of procedure of the territory where the award is relied upon" save for limited circumstances where recognition and enforcement may be refused".[36]

5.2 The formation of a contract

Contracts may be defined as binding agreements signed by parties; they are enforceable agreements from which arise obligations between parties. Business practice recognises a wide range of contract with a different level complexity.[37] Therefore, among Scholars, it is usual to adopt the concept of graduated complexity of a contractual type. The latter shall be illustrated based on the "stairway" methodology:

- The first step is represented by the contract of sale where the complexity will increase if some of its elements deviate from the standard.
- A contract of supply constitutes a more complex agreement due the repetition of performance over a determinate period.
- Manufacturing and supply contract in which goods are provided in instalments withing a determinate timeframe. This contract encompasses both typical clauses of supply contract and new clauses linked with intellectual property, for example.
- The most complicate structures refer to cross-border corporate deals.

Negotiation constitutes the first phase in the process of formation of a contract, a phase where the definition of contractual terms is progressive. Further, the preparatory activity is named, also, pre-contractual phase. Finally, it is critical to highlight that in business negotiation one of the parties enjoys more bargaining power: it means that one party has an advantageous negotiation position for many reasons.

35 Article II(1).
36 Article III and V.
37 (Uff 2025).

For example, the advantage shall derive from technological level, financial strength, the money invests in negotiations, or the resources employed in the negotiations.

5.2.1 Pre-contractual agreements

Linked with pre-contractual bargaining is the concept of pre-contractual agreements.

Within the latter, contracting parties may wish to outline the progress of the negotiation by drafting and exchanging notes in the State of the negotiation process. These notes may assume the forms of letters, memoranda, or terms of agreements. One of the most common instruments is the letter of intent[38]: the latter may have different structures, such as a business letter or a merely contract which encapsulates parties' intentions and, consequently, binding them to set their signature on the final text.

A LOI is, generally, not a legally binding document but has a strong moral value for parties and engages their business reputation. LOI purpose is to ensure that both parties have understood the most important terms of the transaction. Nevertheless, it is also possible that some pre-contractual documents may encompass biding provisions, for example timing for conclusion of the contract, confidentiality information or exclusivity in the negotiation.

A recent case is in Logix Aero Ireland Limited v Siam Aero Repair Company Limited[39]: it deals with no face-to-face negotiation and the exchange of a LOI. The critical issue is ascertaining the identity of a counterparty when a contract has been agreed through technological tools. From a factual perspective, Logix and Siam Aero agreed a LOI regarding the sale and purchase agreements (SPAs). After the conclusion of these agreements, invoices were issued, and Logix had transferred US$ 825,000. A fraud was discovered because, despite the existence of a proof of payment, Siam Aero did not receive any payment and the fraudster has been unidentifiable. The SPAs were negotiated via email: during the negotiations, a fraudster was able to interject themselves into the parties' email: because of this, neither party knew they were actually dealing with other. Logix issued a claim seeking declaration, damages and delivery up of the engines. The court found that no binding contract was formed between Logix and Siam Aero on the terms of SPAs. To better explain, the following Logix's claim failed: (1) the enforceability of SPAs; (2) a breach of confidentiality clause encompassed into the original LOI.

Furthermore, a court could not enforce an "agreement to agree": an agreement to enter a contract later, or an agreement that a certain provision will be agreed between the parties after the commencement of the contract would be void for uncertainty. More appropriate, an agreement to agree is a fact of the commercial life; for example, in *Morris v Swanton Care & Community Ltd*[40] the Court of Appeal clarifies the distinction between:

38 Henceforth LOI.
39 [2025] EWHC 1283 (KB).
40 [2018] EWCA Civ 2763.

- Unenforceable agreements: parties have deferred their agreement on contractual terms.
- Enforceable agreements: parties have reached agreement but left gaps which can be resolved by reference to objective criteria which are capable of assessment by the court.

The demarcation line depends on the wording used in each specific contract.

As far as confidentiality is concerned, often parties include a specific clause, named confidentiality clause, known also as nondisclosure provision. The goal of this clause is to prohibit or restrict the ability of parties to disclose confidential information to third parties. More in detail, a confidentiality clause is a clause in force in which parties agree to accept that specific information, clearly specified, in the contract will be confidential. By contrast, it means that this specific information cannot be accessed by third parties due to the potential harm for the company competitiveness. Further, confidential information shall cover: (1) communications and documentations relating to contract; (2) ideas; (3) technology and invention. If this clause is missed, the law protects specific confidential information.

5.2.2 Preliminary agreements

A preliminary agreement differs from both letter of intention and memorandum of understanding. Preliminary agreement constitutes a suitable legal instrument applicable in situations where parties have not convened on all detail, but they are aimed to conclude the main contract in the future. Moreover, if one party breaches the preliminary agreement to conclude the main contract, the other party may claim a compensation for both damages and expensing of negotiations. Furthermore, the injured party is also entitled to claim the enforcement of specific performance of the obligations.

5.2.3 Lock-out and lock-in agreements

A lock-out agreement is an agreement where A, the manufacturer, agrees with B, the distributor, not to negotiate with anyone other than B; it constitutes a negative promise. Moreover, this agreement gives to B consideration for the promise not to negotiate with anyone else. In other words, A agrees not to negotiate with anyone else outside of B, but A is not obliged to negotiate with B.

By contrast, a lock-in agreement occurs when one party agrees to negotiate with another party and in between these parties there is an obligation to negotiate. In *Walford v Miles* such agreements have been defined as "unworkable in practice".[41]

Finally, parties may also include a cancellation clause: both the buyer and the seller might want to have a let-out clause. The latter allows them to withdraw from the contract without liability in some cases.

41 [1992] 1 All ER 453, HL, Lord Ackner.

References

Andenas, Mas, and Maren Heidemann. 2024. *Commercial Contract Law and Arbitration: From Assignments to Unfair Terms*. Routledge.

Chuah, Jason. 2023. *Law of International Trade*. Sweet & Maxwell.

Cordero-Moss, Giuditta. 2014. *International Commercial Contracts: Applicable Sources and Enforceability*. Cambridge University Press.

DiMatteo, Larry A. 2021. *International Contracting: Law and Practice*. Wolters Kluwer.

Klee, Lukas. 2018. *International Construction Contract Law*. Wiley-Blackwell.

Twigg-Flesner, Christian. 2022. *Foundations of International Commercial Law*. Routledge.

Uff, John. 2025. *Construction Law*. Sweet & Maxwell.

25 Negotiation in international law

Chapter Overview

1. Introduction

Parties to an international contract generally opt for fixing in writing the agreement to reach throughout negotiation. In some cases, the law applicable to the contract requires that contract to be in writing form, in compliance with certain formalities.

In this respect, one of the most important stages is the drafting. More in detail, in drawing up a contract, parties state both the substance and terms of their respective obligations. Therefore, the contract constitutes the "law" of the parties and the latter act as a "legislator", albeit for purposes of the limited perimeter. Thus, parties shall be defining the following elements:

- Rights and obligations.
- The designation of either a court or arbitration.
- Terms and conditions.

More in general, during the negotiation stage, a pivotal role is played by lawyers or legal counsels, whose purpose is to provide legal assistance. More in depth, lawyers work together with banks and financial advisors to structure and implement large international transactions.

It should be recalled the English Arbitration Act 2025 which has recently modernised and amended the existing Arbitration Act 1996. There are three main

DOI: 10.4324/9781003645948-25

areas of interventions. The first one deals with the introduction of a new Section, 39A, which prescribes that the tribunal may make an award on the summary basis in relation to a claim if the tribunal considers that: a party has no real's prospect for succeeding either in the claim or in the defence of such claim. The second alludes to the "emergency arbitrators": it modernises the arbitral framework by including express references to emergency arbitrators and ensuring that where parties have agreed on the application of arbitral rules that provide for the appointment of an emergency arbitrator. The third major intervention is the permission to parties to make application to the competent courts for interim or conservatory measures subject to obtaining the consent of the tribunal after it has been constituted.

2. Jurisdiction clause

One of the most important clauses in negotiation phase is the choice of jurisdiction, that is the governing law of contract signed by parties. Cross-border contracts may involve different international organisations which operate in different legal systems. Consequently, it becomes quintessential to determine which legal system will govern the contract. Jurisdiction represents a critical clause, due to the geographical and juridical limitation of a court's power if a controversy will arise. Further, a jurisdiction clause specifies which court has the power to decide controversy under the contract signed between parties.[1]

Jurisdiction clauses may be as follows:

- Exclusively: it means that parties agree to a specific court's exclusive jurisdiction.
- Non-exclusively: it signifies that parties agree that dispute may be determined in a specific jurisdiction. Yet parties may also decide to refer the case to the court of another jurisdiction. Therefore, this clause gives more flexibility to parties.
- Unilateral: it shows that one party may chose a specific jurisdiction, but the other party has the power to file litigation against the first party in the jurisdiction of its choice.

Moreover, jurisdiction clause may be as follows:

- Express jurisdiction agreements where parties clearly demonstrate consent to submit to the jurisdiction on a specific court.
- Implicit jurisdiction agreements where parties establish, through either trade usages or an established course of dealing, that a specific jurisdiction agreement has always governed their transaction. Furthermore, an implicit agreement to submit the controversy to the jurisdiction of a particular court may be inferred from parties' conduct.

1 (Gee 2020).

Also, there are international conventions whose purpose is to ascertain if an implied jurisdiction agreement shall be valid in its form and substance.[2]

Thus, an implied jurisdiction agreement needs to possess an adequate formal validity. To elaborate, this agreement shall be in writing form, evidence of this form shall be provided, and it also requires the signature. Additionally, the substantive validity of an implied jurisdiction agreement also relates to further factors, such as the following ones: the existence of consent, the absence of fraud or mistake and the absence of the lack of capacity.

A further critical topic is that an implied jurisdiction agreement shall not contain an explicit applicable law that governs such agreement. The reason for that is that it will be paradoxical to have an express applicable law to the jurisdiction agreement in absence of an express jurisdiction agreement. To assess the validity of an implied jurisdiction agreements, there are both international and national instruments.

The first one, international instruments, encapsulates the following:

- The Hague Choice of Court Convention 2005 aims to regulate the exclusive choice of courts in global sphere. This convention suggests that implied jurisdiction agreement is potentially enforceable if the chosen court decides that these agreements are valid under its law.[3] In this respect, Article 3(c) stipulates as follows: "an exclusive choice of court agreement must be concluded or documented – *i)* in writing; or *ii)* by any other means of communication which renders information accessible so as to be usable for subsequent reference".
- The Hague Judgments Convention 2019 stipulates that a court shall be "designated in an agreement concluded or documented in writing or by any other means of communication which renders information accessible to be usable for subsequent reference".[4] Therefore, only the requirement of formal validity is addressed.
- From an EU perspective, the reference goes to the "Convention on jurisdiction and the recognition and enforcement of judgments in civil and commercial matters". Article 23(1) prescribes that as jurisdiction agreement is formally valid if it is

    - (a) in writing or evidenced in writing; or (b) in a form which accords with practices which the parties have established between themselves; or (c) in international trade or commerce, in a form which accords with a usage of which the parties are or ought to have been aware and which in such trade or commerce is widely known to, and regularly observed by, parties to contracts of the type involved in the particular trade or commerce concerned.

2 (Avraham-Giller 2022).

3 Article 5(1) states as follows: "The court or courts of a Contracting State designated in an exclusive choice of court agreement shall have jurisdiction to decide a dispute to which the agreement applies, unless the agreement is null and void under the law of that State".

4 See Article 5(1)(m).

It is possible to say that this legal provision presupposes the existence of a consensus between parties.

As far as national regulations are concerned, it is vital to distinguish between civil law and common law jurisdictions.

The first ones – civil law jurisdictions – comply with the just mentioned "Convention on jurisdiction and the recognition and enforcement of judgments in civil and commercial matters". However, for non-EU civil law jurisdiction the national law shall be scrutinised. For example, Article 63(1), Brazil Code, stipulates that Brazilian courts can enforce a jurisdiction agreement only if "it is stated in a written document and is expressly stated in relation to a specific legal transaction".

Moreover, the Dubai International Financial Courts emphasised as follows:

- Parties may elect in writing that Dubai International Financial Courts may hear any civil and/or commercial dispute.
- The importance that such agreements encompass specific, clear and express provisions.

As regards common law jurisdictions, it seems that the approach is epitomised by the *modus operandi* of English courts. Therefore, it seems to be a favour to the proper law of the main/host contract as the governing law. The latter will determine the validity and the existence of a choice of court agreement within the contract.

Consequently, under common law, there is not a difference between formal and substantive validity. Despite this, in *Enka Insaat ve Sanayi AS v OOO Insurance Company Chubb*,[5] it was held that the law of the main contract, if chosen by parties, governs an arbitration agreement. However, if the law of the main contract was not chosen by parties, the arbitration agreement was governed by the law of the seat of arbitration. From this, it is possible to infer the following principles:

- The governing law of the main contract also applies to jurisdiction agreements.
- If a specific choice of law is not made, the law of the chosen court governs matters relating to validity.

As far as implied jurisdiction agreement is concerned, there are multifarious ways English common law categorise this area.

To summarise, the contractual terms are paramount since jurisdiction agreements under English common law constitute a contractual term. Consequently, in principle they will be oral or written, express or implied too.

As regards the implied terms, in *Vizcaya Partners*[6] Lord Collins stressed that these terms are inferable thanks from the "business efficacy" and "officious bystander" tests. These two tests pursue the objective to ascertain the presumed

5 [2020] UKSC 38.

6 *Vizcaya Partners Ltd. v Picard* [2016] UKPC 5.

intention of the parties or, alternatively, to give the efficacy on a transaction. In other words, courts must apply the implied term only if the implied term is necessary, or if it is obvious that the term should be included without explicitly stating.

More in detail, the business efficacy test is aimed to ascertain if the term was necessary to give the contract business efficacy, that is, if the contract make business sense without it. Consequently, the court must apply the term only if this implied term is necessary to do so.[7]

By contrast, based on the officious bystander test,[8] it was held that:

- An officious bystander shall be present at the time the contract was made.
- A term shall be included if it appears obvious that both parties have agreed on it.

3. Arbitration clause

Arbitration clause is an area adjacent to the jurisdiction clause. First and foremost, it is pivotal to draw a demarcation line between these two clauses. Arbitration clause is a private dispute resolution scheme: parties agree to avoid proceedings before national courts.[9] Furthermore, parties submit any potential dispute – that may arise from and/or in connection with their contract – to an arbitrator. On the other side, a jurisdiction clause is aimed to determine the national court that will have exclusively jurisdiction to adjudicate any disputes that may arise in connection with parties' contract.[10]

Nevertheless, to understand if parties want to adopt an arbitration clause or an exclusive jurisdiction clause, it is necessary to analyse how the contract is construed. The key is the interpretation that a reasonable person given to the mean of the contract: in *Melford Capital Partners (Holdings) LLP and Others v Digby*[11] the court stated that the arbitration clause determined that disputes shall be resolved by arbitration. By contrast, the exclusively jurisdiction clause defined that the courts should have supervisory power on the arbitral process.

This conclusion was adopted by the Singapore Court of Appeal in *BXH v BXI*[12]: if parties signed a contract which encompassed both an arbitration clause and an exclusively jurisdiction clauses, court should give effect to both clauses. Thus, if a contractual dispute arises, it shall be resolved in accordance with the arbitration clause. Additionally, the Singaporean courts shall exercise its supervisory jurisdiction under the exclusively jurisdiction clause.

The first one, that is, the arbitration clause means that a future and potential controversy between parties shall refer to arbitration agreement.

7 See *The Moorcock* (1889) 14 PD 64.
8 *Shirlaw v Southern Foundries* [1939] 2 KB 206.
9 (Garnett 2013).
10 (Blake, Browne, and Sime 2016).
11 [2021] EWHC 872 (Ch).
12 [2020] SGCA 28.

To be enforceable, an arbitration clause shall possess the following:

- The scope of the arbitration agreement.
- An unambiguous statement in force of which all disputes covered under the agreement shall be referred only through arbitration.
- A clear endorsement of arbitration to resolve and define in a binding and final manner the controversy.

Additionally, arbitration clause shall also encapsulate the following:

- The number of arbitrators and the method of their appointment.
- The place of the arbitration or arbitral seat.
- The language of the arbitration.

Arbitration shall be either *ad hoc* arbitration or administered arbitration.

The first one, *ad hoc* arbitration, means that there is no arbitral institution in charge of administering the proceeding from the beginning to the end. Consequently, parties do not pay administrative fees. Administered arbitration refers to a situation in which parties opt for institutional or administered arbitration. The arbitration agreement shall clearly indicate if parties have chosen an institution to act as the administrator.[13]

Furthermore, arbitration clauses may also be unilateral or optional: it signifies that one party to an agreement has the exclusive right to decide between arbitration or litigation as the forum to resolve a dispute. In some jurisdictions these clauses are enforceable, according to the Latin expression *pacta sunt servanda* (England and Wales and Hong Kong); other jurisdictions do not consider these clauses enforceable due to the significant violation to principles of equality and mutual agreement between parties (for example Poland).

In a recent decision, it was said that optional arbitration clauses are enforceable: once party opts for arbitration, the agreement becomes binding. Furthermore, it is not required complete procedural detail, as well as the failure to specify seat, arbitrators or rules does not invalidate the clause, as the act provides default mechanisms. In this decision it has been established a favour approach to arbitration: even if ambiguous, arbitration agreements should be upheld to give effect to party autonomy.[14]

From a legal perspective, the international source of law is the New York Convention which applies to recognise and enforce foreign arbitral awards.

In a nutshell, New York Convention achieves two main goals:

- This Conventions provides that every contracting State

> shall recognize an agreement in writing under which the parties undertake to submit to arbitration all or any differences which have arisen, or which

13 (Blake, Browne, and Sime 2016).

14 Dalam Mahkamah Rayuan Malaysia (Bidang Kuasa Rayuan) Rayuan Sivil No: A-02(Im)(C)-1587-09/2024 Antara Setia Awan Management Sdn Bhd (No. Syarikat: 201001014879 (899115-D) . . . Perayu Dan Spnb Aspirasi Sdn Bhd (No. Syarikat: 490479-V).

may arise between them in respect of a defined legal relationship, whether contractual or not, concerning a subject matter capable of settlement by arbitration.[15]

- New York Convention is aimed to ensure that every contracting State "shall recognize arbitral awards as binding and enforce them in accordance with the rules of procedure of the territory where the award is relied upon" save for limited circumstances where recognition and enforcement may be refused.[16]

4. International Commercial Arbitration

Arbitration constitutes one form of alternative dispute resolution (ADR)[17] which encompasses the following:

- Conciliation.
- Mediation.
- Arbitration.

Conciliation is a form of ADR in which a neutral third party acts to bring disputing parties together for the purpose of the settlement of the dispute in an informal process. Mediation represents a form of ADR in which a mediator follows a structured process to facilitate an agreed settlement between parties to a dispute. Arbitration is a form of ADR in which parties to a dispute submit to a binding decision of a sole arbitrator/arbitral tribunal, rather than a court of law. It should be noted that modern arbitration has been developed under English law; while arbitration in England dates to the 15th century, it was formally recognised under Arbitration Act of 1967.

4.1 Legal framework

The legal framework of international commercial arbitration (ICA) is, fundamentally, the New York Convention and arbitration agreement. The latter is related to procedural rules or institutional or *ad hoc* rules and with procedural rules.

According to Article 16(1) UNCITRAL Model Law the arbitral tribunal may rule on its own jurisdiction, including any objections with respect to the existence or validity of the arbitration agreement. This is the competence of the tribunal, thus the competence-competence rule. According to English Arbitration Act

> (1) Unless otherwise agreed by the parties, the arbitral tribunal may rule on its own substantive jurisdiction, that is, as to – (a)whether there is a valid arbitration agreement, (b)whether the tribunal is properly constituted, and

15 Article II(1).
16 Article III and V.
17 (Barrett and Barrett 2004).

> (c)what matters have been submitted to arbitration in accordance with the arbitration agreement. (2) Any such ruling may be challenged by any available arbitral process of appeal or review or in accordance with the provisions of this Part.[18]

A different perspective is encompassed into Scotland Arbitration Act 2010, in force of which

> The tribunal may rule on – (a)whether there is a valid arbitration agreement (or, in the case of a statutory arbitration, whether the enactment providing for arbitration applies to the dispute), (b)whether the tribunal is properly constituted, and (c)what matters have been submitted to arbitration in accordance with the arbitration agreement.[19]

The effect of the competence-competence principle is, at the same time:

- Positive: only arbitral tribunal can decide on its own jurisdiction.
- Negative: courts, in general, do not have jurisdiction to decide on procedural challenges.

Another quintessential rule is the separability doctrine. Based on Article 16(1), UNCITRAL Model Law, for that specific purpose,[20]

> an arbitration clause which forms part of a contract shall be treated as an agreement independent of the other terms of the contract. A decision by the arbitral tribunal that the contract is null and void shall not entail ipso jure the invalidity of the arbitration clause.

Separability doctrine on English Arbitration Act means that

> Unless otherwise agreed by the parties, an arbitration agreement which forms or was intended to form part of another agreement (whether or not in writing) shall not be regarded as invalid, non-existent or ineffective because that other agreement is invalid, or did not come into existence or has become ineffective, and it shall for that purpose be treated as a distinct agreement.[21]

To be valid, an International Arbitration Agreement needs two elements: (1) formal validity; (2) substantial validity.

18 Section 30.

19 Section 19, Scottish Arbitration Rules, Schedule 1, Scotland Arbitration Act 2010.

20 Reference is to competence-competence.

21 Section 7.

To understand the formal validity, the reference goes to Article II of New York Convention and Article 7, UNCITRAL Model Law.

The first one – Article II of New York Convention – requires that

> Each Contracting State shall recognize an agreement in writing under which the parties undertake to submit to arbitration all or any differences which have arisen or which may arise between them in respect of a defined legal relationship, whether contractual or not, concerning a subject matter capable of settlement by arbitration.

The expression "agreement in writing" alludes to arbitral in a contract or an arbitration agreement which is either signed by parties or contained in an exchange of letter or telegrams.

The second one – UNCITRAL Model Law – Article 7 includes two different options. The first one is that arbitration agreement is an agreement by which parties submit to arbitration all or certain disputes which have arisen or may arise between them. These disputes may be related to a defined legal relationship, whether contractual or not. It is important that the arbitration agreement is in writing form and its content is recorded in any form, whether the arbitration agreement or contract has been concluded orally, by conduct or by other means. Writing requirements alludes to the following ones: electronic communication, exchange of statement of claim and defence, reference in a contract to any document containing an arbitration clause.[22]

The second option of Article 7 defines an arbitration agreement an agreement by the parties to submit to arbitration all or certain disputes which have arisen, or which may arise between them in respect of a defined legal relationship, whether contractual or not, based on the agreement signed.

As regards substantive validity, there are three specific issues: party intent and consent to arbitrate; incapacity of a party concluding the arbitration agreement; fraud, mistake, duress and similar concepts.

4.2 The applicable law

In an international agreement, the rules, based on a hierarchical process, are the following: arbitration agreement, *lex arbitri* and the New York Convention.

An arbitration agreement is binding on tribunal, and any deviation from the rules may affect the final award. More precisely, an arbitration agreement defines the personal subject matter and temporal jurisdiction of the tribunal. It incorporates arbitration rules that define procedural framework. Finally, an arbitration agreement selects the seat of arbitration that defines the procedural framework and the relationship with the courts.

22 (Berger 2023).

If parties do not adopt a choice, then the default rules to determine the seat will apply. They are concerned about the formal validity, the procedure and the awards. The procedure includes fundamental principles, the constitution of the tribunal and the power of the tribunal. The award needs to follow specific rules, such as criteria for them to be enforceable.

Article II and V, New York Convention:

- Establish treaty obligations to enforce valid arbitration agreements.
- Define formal validity of an arbitration agreement.
- Define grounds for non-recognition and enforcement of foreign arbitral awards.

4.3 Appointing and removing arbitrators

The constitution of an arbitral tribunal is shaped according to party's autonomy[23]; however there are some limitations. The first step when a dispute commences is to establish the tribunal; this means: (1) selection and nomination of tribunal; (2) compliance with both the arbitration agreement and the *lex arbitri*; (3) decision about either a sole arbitrator or members of tribunal.

The first element is the definition of the person of arbitrator; in this respect parties' autonomy may have some limitations, for example the UNCITRAL Model Law establishes that no person shall be precluded by reason of his nationality from acting as an arbitrator, unless otherwise agreed by the parties. The Scotland Arbitration Act 2010 stipulates that only an individual (not an entity) may act as arbitrator, unless they are under 16 or an incapable adult. Furthermore, parties are free to determine the number of arbitrators; however, both institutional rules and *lex arbitri* have default rules in the absence of an agreement. For example, the UNCITRAL Model Law prescribes three-member panel as default rule; the English Arbitration Act 1996 and Scotland Arbitration Act 2010 have as default rule the sole arbitrator.

The selection of an arbitrator constitutes a strategic decision that shall be delivered according to various criteria; these are relating for the dispute, the technical and legal expertise, the availability, the experience as a sole arbitrator and the overall reputation. Regarding the appointment, the rule differs depending on whether there is a sole arbitrator. In the latter case parties must agree on the individual jointly. By contrast, if the panel shall be made up of three members, each party appoints an arbitrator, and both parties appoint a third arbitrator acting as chairman. In the case in which parties do not agree on the sole arbitrator, the *lex arbitri* refers the matter to the court or another authority designated by parties.

An arbitrator may be removed in the following circumstances:

- Death.
- Incapacity to serve as an arbitrator.

23 (Kosta-Foti and Del Carmen Ibrahim 2025).

- Timeframe elapsed.
- Challenged and removed.

Challenging an arbitrator occurs when there is a lack of independence and impartiality.[24] These two requirements are essential for the legitimacy of ICA as an adjudicatory process requiring a neutral and objective tribunal. Similarly, independence and impartiality constitute two different qualities;[25] however, it should be highlighted that between independence and impartiality an overlap may arise.

Independence alludes to relationship of arbitrator, if they are professional or personal related to one of the parties or has a familiar[26] or business connection[27] to or with that party. The independence depends also on the degree of such relationship and the separation between the arbitrator and a party to an arbitrator. Furthermore, the measure of independence is conceived in an objective manner, because it is based on what a reasonable person concludes in the light of the relationship in issue. Slightly different is impartiality because it deals with a state of mind; an arbitrator may be defined as partial if he displays preference for one party and against another or if a third person reasonably may apprehend such partiality. Partiality does not depend on factors relating to independence simply because impartiality is concerned with a bias. Therefore, the test applicable to impartiality is subjective because it goes to the actual state of mind where applicable, ensuing conduct of the arbitrator.[28]

Article 12(1), UNCITRAL Model Law, states the following one:

> When a person is approached in connection with his possible appointment as an arbitrator, he shall disclose any circumstances likely to give rise to justifiable doubts as to his impartiality or independence. An arbitrator, from the time of his appointment and throughout the arbitral proceedings, shall without delay disclose any such circumstances to the parties unless they have already been informed of them by him.

The IBA Guidelines adopt a general definition of impartiality and independence; Article 2(1) stipulates that an arbitrator "may be challenged only if circumstances exist that give rise to justifiable doubts as to his impartiality or independence, or if he does not possess qualifications agreed to by the parties". Moreover, the IBA

24 (Camillacci, Takeshita, and Barysheva 2025).

25 (Timmer 2012).

26 For example, a professional relationship may include a relationship where the arbitrator or partner as acted or is acting as counsel, an employee, an adviser or consultant on behalf of one party. See Commonwealth *Coatings Corp v Continental Casualty Co* (1968) 393 U.S. 145; *Laker Airways Inc v FLS Aerospace Ltd* [2000] 1 W.L.R. 113.

27 It includes business venture where the arbitrator or partner holds an executive or non-executive position or is a party to a business transaction. *AT&T Corp v Saudi Cable Co* [2000] 2 All E.R. (Comm) 625.

28 (Trakman 2007).

Guidelines adopt a categorisation of situations where arbitral impartiality and independence may be divided, and more precisely, there are three lists[29]:

- Red. It alludes to situations in which give rise to per se doubt as to an arbitrator's impartiality and independence.
- Orange. It refers to specific situations where the party might reasonably have doubts about the arbitrator's impartiality and independence and the arbitrator, on its side, has a duty to disclose it.
- Green. It occurs when there is no appearance of a lack of impartiality and independence.

A recent court decision of the Norwegian Supreme Court approaches the concept of independence and impartiality.[30] In this case, one of the arbitrators was a partner in a law firm that assisted one of the parties in a matter unrelated to the arbitration. The law firm had billed approximately NOK 1.9 million on the matter, while the firm's total revenue was more than NOK 1 billion. The arbitrator was not involved in the other matter but had failed to disclose the case when he was asked to serve as arbitrator since the arbitrator was formerly a member of the board in the law firm and later become managing partner. The Supreme Court found that the arbitrator had failed to meet his duty of disclosure, yet it was held that there was no legitimate reason to doubt his impartiality and independence in the arbitration. To summarise, the key points are as follows:

- There is no basis for establishing that there are general differences in the threshold for disqualification for judges and arbitrators.
- Whether a lawyer is disqualified from being an arbitrator because of a client relationship with a party to the arbitration will depend on an overall assessment of the nature, scope and duration of the client relationship.
- An essential factor is if the arbitrator or a colleague who has managed the client relationship. In doing so, the size and organisation of the firm constitute relevant factors.

The decision of the court touched upon three salient features. The first one is that the firm had a significant assignment for one of the parties in the arbitration. Furthermore, the Supreme Court emphasised that the matter was insignificant in relation to the law firm's other activities and that the assignment was concerned with assistance in a specialised field, and not strategic advice. Finally, albeit more importantly, the arbitrator had no connection to the other matter: the circumstance in force of which the arbitrator was a key figure in the firm was not sufficient to outweigh the mentioned factors.

29 Ibid.

30 HR-2025-921-A (Case No. 24-159248SIV-HRET) Appeal against the Hålogaland Court of Appeal's judgment of July 3, 2024.

References

Avraham-Giller, Shahar. 2022. "The Court's Discretionary Power to Enforce Valid Jurisdiction Clauses: Time for a Change?" *Journal of Private International Law* 18 (2): 209–37.

Barrett, Jerome T., and Joseph Barrett. 2004. *A History of Alternative Dispute Resolution: The Story of a Political, Social, and Cultural Movement*. Wiley.

Berger, Klaus Peter. 2023. "Contractual Arbitration Clauses and Non-Contractual Claims." *Journal of International Arbitration* 40 (2): 105–24.

Blake, Susan, Julie Browne, and Stuart Sime. 2016. *Alternative Dispute Resolution*. Oxford University Press.

Camillacci, Arianna, Yoshie Concha Takeshita, and Nataliya Barysheva. 2025. "International Arbitration and Alternative Dispute Resolution." *International Business Law Journal* 1: 95–103.

Garnett, Richard. 2013. "Coexisting and Conflicting Jurisdiction and Arbitration Clauses." *Journal of Private International Law* 17 (9): 361–86.

Gee, Steven. 2020. "Jurisdiction and Arbitration Clauses." In *The Evolving Law and Practice of Voyage Charterparties*, edited by Thomas Rhidian, 35–52. Informa Law from Routledge.

Kosta-Foti, Alexandra, and Mariam Del Carmen Ibrahim. 2025. "Party Autonomy, Comity and the RusChemAlliance Saga." *Journal of International Arbitration* 42 (2): 251–84.

Timmer, Laurens J.E. 2012. "The Quality, Independence and Impartiality of the Arbitrator in International Commercial Arbitration." *Arbitration: The International Journal of Arbitration, Mediation and Dispite Management* 78 (4): 348–58.

Trakman, Leo. 2007. "The Impartiality and Independence of Arbitrators Reconsidered." *International Arbitration Law Review* 10 (4): 124–35.

26 Documentary credits

Chapter Overview

1. Introduction

Letter of credits are legal instruments developed through customs. More in detail, many operational rules come from the banking customs in the context of importers and exporters activities. The other counterparty is/was, traditionally, shipping and insurance companies.

To elaborate, trading across international borders is riskier than trading within national borders. Trading partners, indeed, are in different countries that may be separated by a large distance which results in long shipping times as well as different laws and speaking languages.

A letter of credit[1] constitutes a legal instrument whereby the risk to pay, which is usually borne by one of the trading partners, is shifted into a bank, since the letter receives a fee to do so. From a broader perspective, in international trade, it is quite

1 Henceforth LC.

DOI: 10.4324/9781003645948-26

common to affirm that buyer and seller are engaged into a "hate-love" relationship. The first one, the buyer, achieves the objective to remove any degree of uncertainty potentially affecting the transaction. By contrast, the seller wants to see the capital tied with the sale of the good "assured" and guaranteed – therefore paid – at the time of delivery of good. To elaborate, the seller, ideally, would like to be paid when the goods are dispatched. The buyer, on their hand, would want to be paid only when they have received the goods and have the chance to inspect them. The seller's perspective is justified by the need for paying suppliers, employees, etc: this constitutes a cash-flows in all businesses, although it is exacerbated in international sale contracts due to the distances over which goods are shipped.

In this relationship, a bank, a third party, with the instrument of letter of credit or the documentary credit, may resolve a potential conflictual relationship. More in detail, with a documentary credit, the seller sees its risk stemming from specific international transaction neutralised. The intervention of a third party, the bank, means that the latter undertakes the negative consequences of the buyer's failure in paying off. Furthermore, the buyer does not significantly benefit from using a documentary credit: the buyer can raise funds from a bank on the strength of the documents. Therefore, he/she alleviates the need to have enough funds to pay the seller.

In a nutshell, it is possible to affirm that, thanks to a letter of credit, the buyer agrees to pay the seller using a reliable paymaster. The latter is a bank located in the seller's country. This bank pays when a document, stipulating in compliance with the terms of the credit, is presented.

In other words, documentary credits are fundamental in international transaction because, thanks to documentary credits:

- Transactions operate in a safe context.
- Transactions are not affected by claims, particularly from the side of the buyer.
- Issues linked with the underlying contract are postponed after the performance of the transaction.

In the contemporary era, the International Chamber of Commerce embodied these customs in the Uniform Customs and Practice for Documentary Credits.[2] Moreover, often, banks subject their letter of credit to the UCP as a primary source of letter of credit but not the only one. Additionally, the law of documentary letters of credit has also been influenced by other regulations, national legislation and case laws.

The key documents are (1) the bill of landing; (2) the commercial invoice; (3) the policy of marine – or air – insurance; (4) documents relating to trade finance (such as documentary credits); (5) documents relating to border clearance (such as export/import licences and certificate of origins).[3]

2 Henceforth UCP.
3 (Embley, Bamford, and Hancock 2024).

2. The documents involved with international sale of goods transactions

As said previously, in international transactions there are five main documents, used by parties. Before analysing each of them, the concept of shipping "paper trail" should be clarified. Shipping "paper trail" starts when the arrangements are made for a cargo to be shipped and terminates with payment. Meanwhile, very large numbers of documents should be filled and checked before a ship can either enter or leave a port.

It should be noted that such traditional "paper trail" has become an "IT tail" for two main reasons. The first one is linked with Covid-19 pandemic: one problem coupled with coronavirus was that paper documents could be a source of infections. The second one is that new technologies, such as blockchain, smart contracts, have the potential to simplify the documentation and finance in international trade.

3. The bill of lading

The bill of lading (BoL or B/L) is given by the carrier of the goods to the consignor of the goods at the time of the goods being loaded. BoL is governed in the UK by the Carriage of Goods by Sea Act 1992.

It serves three main purposes:

- To provide a receipt for the goods and provide evidence that they are in good condition at the loading.
- To encompass the terms of contract of carriage.
- To be evidence of the title to the good and a right to possess them.

At the destination, the goods will be handed over to the person holding the bill of lading. The bill is given to the carrier in exchange for the goods: it should be arrived before the goods as the goods travel by sea, but the bill is sent by airmail.

The most important consequence of the bill of lading is given to the holder the title to the goods, as only the original bill is required. From this, two consequences arise:

- A photocopy faxed or email is not good.
- If a bill of lading is used together with a documentary credit, the BoL must be conforming, that is conforming with the terms of the documentary credit.

There are three main kinds of bill of lading: (1) inland; (2) ocean; (3) through bill of lading. The first one – inland bill of lading – constitutes a contract between a shipper and transportation company used when transporting goods overland to an exporter's international carrier. The second one – the ocean bill of lading – is a contract between an exporter and an international carrier for transport of merchandise to a specified foreign market overseas. The last one – bill of lading – is a document encompassing the terms between a shipper and transportation company covering both domestic and international transport of export goods, between specified points for a specified charge.

It should be emphasised that bills of lading have some disadvantages:

- They are expensive to arrange and administer.
- They were intended for the sale of bulk commodities which were shipped slowly a considerable distance by sea.
- Traditionally, they are set of three but only one copy needs to be presented for claiming goods from the carrier.[4]
- If goods arrived before the bill of lading or have discrepancies, the carrier will usually deliver the goods to the buyer in return for a letter of indemnity (LOI) from the seller.

The use of bills of lading has decreased, and waybills are preferred. From a definitory perspective, waybill is a receipt for the goods and evidence of the carriage contract, but it is not a document of title to the goods. A waybill has been used for sea freight but now are also used for the sea freight with increasing frequency.

Finally, there is no equivalent to the bill of lading in air transport. Traditionally, an "air waybill" is adopted based on "FOB airport contract". The seller's duties end when goods are delivered at the destination airport to the carrier of the buyer's agent. As regards as road and rail transport, the contract is made with a firm that undertakes the whole transport chain normally using container transport for the goods.

4. Legal sources

As far as the legal sources are concerned, the reference is to both common law and the just mentioned UCP.

From a historical perspective, due to the growth of international commerce, one of the first need for overseas transactions was to reduce conflicts withing national laws; hence, the adoption of a unified approach to documentary letter of transactions. In 1920 the New American Commercial Credit Conference drafted a set of rules in relation to letters of credit addressed to banks operating the US. The same approach was adopted in Germany, France, Norway, Czechoslovakia, Italy and Sweden, among the major countries/jurisdictions. In 1930, it became commercially necessary to verge towards international harmonisation in respect to documentary credit transactions.

4 A general principle is that the delivery by the carrier to someone who is not the lawful holder of the bill of lading represents a breach of contract of carriage. In this respect, see *Glyn Mills Currie & Co v East and West India Dock Co* (1882) 7 App Cas 591. This principle has been established in *Unicredit Bank AG v Euronav NV* [2023] EWCA Civ 471. In the latter, the essential issue was whether a shipowner, Euronav, was liable to the bill of lading holder, UniCredit, for delivering a cargo of oil from the vessel Sienna without production of the bill of lading.

Bankers had already cooperated on a regional basis to create uniform rules for these transactions. The most important support came from the International Chamber of Commerce,[5] which supported the UCP. The main objective was to guarantee a worldwide application and to stabilise elements and features in international trade.

The first version of UCP was adopted during the 7th Congress held in Vienna in 1933: it was taken on by bankers in several European Countries and on individual basis by some banks in the US. A second version was adopted in 1951 at Lisbon Conference to amend it, considering changes occurred in international trade. It is worth emphasising though that the United Kingdom, together with other Commonwealth countries, rejected it.

In 1962 a new version of UCP was adopted, and one of the major purposes was to shape a system suitable, also, for common law countries. In this year, again 1962, this goal was eventually achieved.

During the following years, further versions were adopted, the last one being in 2007. The reasons for this successful feast are multiple; they may be summarised as follows:

- UCP prescribes everyday international banking practice.
- UCPO reflects the banks practice worldwide.
- UCP helps banks to stay away from courts, and it does not permit desuetude.

The UCP 600 came into force on 1st July 2007. UCP 2006 stands for "Uniform Customs & Practice for Documentary Credits". It constitutes the official publication which is issued by ICC, and it consists of a set of 39 articles on issuing and using Letters of Credit. Moreover, the UCP 600 replaced the UCP 5 as from the 1st July 2007. The latest version, again UCP 600 was created by industry experts and mandated by Banking Commission.

5. Uniform Customs and Practice for Documentary Credits (UCP)

The UCP 600 rules are voluntarily incorporated into contracts and must be outlined in trade finance contracts to apply.

The UCP 2006 coupled with the International Standard Banking Practice for the Examination of Documents under Documentary Credits.[6]

UCP 600 is built on some main elements:

- Definition of key terms prevalent in international trade.
- The way international trade documents can be signed.
- The differences between documents, such as goods and services.
- The parts of a letter of credits that are negotiable and those which are not.

5 Henceforth ICC.
6 Henceforth ISBP.

- The way credit works and payment is made.
- The way banks can communicate the confirmation of goods.
- Transportation of goods, modes of transports and who bears responsibility.
- The way to deal with discrepancies, waivers and notices to be given.
- The provision of original documents or electronic copies.
- Bills of lading.
- Insurance and covering the cost of goods.
- Loss of shipping documents in transit.

In 2019 the ICC released an updated supplement for electronic rules, named e-Rules of the Uniform Customs and Practice for Documentary Credits. More precisely, two years before, that is, during 2017, the ICC Banking Commission launched a Digitalisation Working Group to anticipate and accompany the digitalisation of trade finance. In this respect, the aim was double: on one hand to update the existing version of the e-UCP to ensure continued digital compatibility, and on the other hand, a draft of eURC was made. The purpose of this secondo goal was to ensure continued digital compatibility for presentation of electronic records under Collections.

It was recognised the impact of IT development among different sectors: to Internet of Things, smart contracts, distributed ledger technology and machine learning. Based on such background, the final decision was to continue monitoring these eRules to ensure the applicability. It was stressed the importance that these new rules will be recognised by the market due to benefits that may arise from digitalisation on traditional trade.

Based on such background, Article e1 clarifies that the purpose of eUCP is to both supplements the UCP 2007 as well as "accommodate presentation of electronic records alone or in combination with paper document".[7]

Based on Article e1, it is possible to affirm that an eUCP credit shall encompass specific elements, such as the following:

- The physical location of the issuing bank.
- The physical location of any nominated bank and, if different, the physical location of the confirming bank.

Moreover, it becomes quintessential to understand how eUCP and UCP work together. Article 2, titled "Relationship of the eUCP to the UCP", stipulates as follows:

- An eUCP credit is also subject to the UCP without express incorporation of the UCP.
- If the eUCP applies, its provision shall prevail to the extent that they would produce a result different from the application of the UCP.

7 See Article e1(a).

- In case in which

> an eUCP credit allows the beneficiary to choose between presentation of paper documents or electronic records and it chooses to present only paper documents, the UCP alone shall apply to that presentation. If only paper documents are permitted under an eUCP credit, the UCP alone shall apply.

Furthermore, based on UCP 600, a credit is "any arrangement, however named or described, that is irrevocable and thereby constitutes a definite undertaking of the issuing bank to honour a complying presentation" (Article 2). By contrast, based on Article e6 eUCP, it is established that:

- "An eUCP credit must indicate a place for presentation of electronic records".
- "An eUCP credit requiring or allowing presentation for both electronic records and paper documents must, in addition to the place for presentation of the electronic records, also indicate a place for presentation of the paper documents".

Additionally, an "honour", always based on Article 2,

> means a. to pay at sight if the credit is available by sight payment. b. to incur a deferred payment undertaking and pay at maturity if the credit is available by deferred payment. c. to accept a bill of exchange ("draft") drawn by the beneficiary and pay at maturity if the credit is available by acceptance.

By contrast, the most important definition included in the eUCP is "electronic record". It alludes to

> data created, generated, sent, communicated, received or stored by electronic means, including, where appropriate, all information logically associated with or otherwise linked together so as to become part of the record, whether generated contemporaneously or not, that is: capable of being authenticated as to the apparent identity of a sender and the apparent source of the data contained in it, and as to whether it has remained complete and unaltered, and capable of being examined for compliance with the terms and conditions of the eUCP credit.[8]

Moreover, a further difference refers to the presentation of the document. Based on UCP 600, a presentation

> consisting of more than one set of transport documents evidencing shipment commencing on the same means of conveyance and for the same journey, provided they indicate the same destination, will not be regarded as covering

8 See Article e3(b)(iii).

> a partial shipment, even if they indicate different dates of shipment or different ports of loading, places of taking in charge or dispatch. If the presentation consists of more than one set of transport documents, the latest date of shipment as evidenced on any of the sets of transport documents will be regarded as the date of shipment.

In addition, it is stressed that presentation

> consisting of one or more sets of transport documents evidencing shipment on more than one means of conveyance within the same mode of transport will be regarded as covering a partial shipment, even if the means of conveyance leave on the same day for the same destination.[9]

Article 15, titled "Complying Presentation", states that, if a bank "determines that a presentation is complying, it must honour" or negotiate. Additionally, in cases where "a nominated bank determines that a presentation is complying and honours or negotiates, it must forward the documents to the confirming bank or issuing bank".[10]

When a presentation does not comply, this may refuse to honour or negotiate. In this respect, if "an issuing bank determines that a presentation does not comply, it may in its sole judgement approach the applicant for a waiver of the discrepancies".[11]

As far as eUCP is concerned, the main rules are encompassed with Article e6. This legal provision clarifies that a credit shall indicate a place for presentation of electronic records. Further, the eUCP credit, to comply with presentation rules:

- Contains both electronic records and paper document.
- Indicates a place for presentation of the paper documents as well as the place for presentation of electronic records.

Ad hoc rules are defined for electronic records. These may be presented separately and need not be presented at the same time. In case in which one or more electronic records are presented alone or in combination with paper documents, the presenter shall provide a notice of completeness to three different banks: (1) nominated bank; (2) confirming bank; (3) issuing bank. This procedure applies if a presentation is made directly. In this respect, the notice of completeness:

- Acts as notification that the presentation is complete.
- Means that a period of examination[12] of the presentation has commenced.

9 See Article 31(b)(c).

10 Article 15 (a)(b)(c).

11 See Article 16(b).

12 Article e7(a)(i) stipulates as follows: "The period for the examination of documents commences on the banking day following the day on which the notice of completeness is received by the nominated bank, confirming bank, if any, or by the issuing bank, where a presentation is made directly".

- May be given as an electronic record or paper document.
- Shall identify the eUCP credit to which it relates.

It is worth stressing that every presentation of an electronic record under an eUCP credit shall identify the eUCP credit under which it is presented. This element is specified through the following "paths": (1) the reference into electronic record; (2) metadata attached or superimposed; (3) identification in the covering letter.

6. Autonomy principle

One of the most important principles of letters of credit is that the undertaking of the issuing of a bank, or confirming bank, to pay against document represents a primary obligation.

This obligation should not be affected by any dispute existing between seller and buyer as to the contract of the sale or as to the validity of the same.

In *Hanzeh Malas and Sons v British Imex Industries Ltd*[13] it was stressed that a letter of credit possesses autonomy and does not affect the obligations of the bank in respect of such letter. To elaborate, principle of autonomy does not include reference of the bank with the contractual relationship. More in detail, it includes only the verification process of the document. Therefore, payment must be made upon examination and ascertainment that documents conform with the terms of the credit as they appear.

This is summarised by the principle: "pay now, litigate later". That means that only a specific, exceptional reason, can restraint payment. The aim of the principle of autonomy is to enhance the utility and marketability of commercial letters of credit. Nevertheless, the principle of autonomy does not constitute an absolute principle, due to the existence of two exceptions: (1) fraud; (2) illegality. A controversial topic is the exception of nullity: based on English common law, it is possible to affirm that a nullity exception shall not be distinguished from fraud.[14]

By contrast, Singaporean court states that a bank is not obliged to make payment where it is established that a material document required under the credit is forged, null and void.

The exception of nullity is based on the implicit requirement in force of which a conforming document constitutes the assumption that the document provided to the bank is true and genuine.[15]

The difference shall be explained as follows:

- English court emphasised that nullity does not constitute a separate exception and does not belong to the documentary credit law.

13 [1957] EWCA Civ J1210-3.

14 See *Montrod Ltd v Grumdkotter Fleischvertriebs-GmbH* [2001] EWCA Civ 1954 where the court ruled that there was not a general nullity exception based upon the concept of a document being fraudulent in itself or devoid of commercial value.

15 *The Beam Technology (Mfg) Pte Ltd v Standard Chartered Bank* [2002] SGCA 53.

- Singaporean court stressed nullity is a separate exception to the principle of autonomy.

As far as illegality is concerned, under English common law the leading case is *Group Jose v Walbrook Insurance Co Ltd and Others*.[16] In this the concept of illegality was considered as a separate ground of non-payment under a letter of credit.

Furthermore, in *Mahonia Ltd v JP Morgan Chase Bank and West LB*[17] the conclusion was that the autonomy principle does not stop a letter of credit from being tainted with illegality in the underlying transaction.

More in general, illegality shall refer to the following:

- The documentary letter of credit, since it is issued contrary to a governmental prohibition.
- The case, in which before the payment of obligation or reimbursement obligation arises, the issuing bank is banned from carrying out its business.
- The situation, in which illegality affects both letter of credit and underlying transaction.

In these cases, the letter of credit is illegal, but illegality should not be invoked as exception of the principle of autonomy.

Only, in *Group Josi Re v Walbrook Insurance Co. Ltd. and Others*,[18] it was said that, if illegality refers to underlying transaction, it constitutes an exception of the principle of autonomy. Therefore, it affects the letter of credit in general and provides a separate ground upon which the autonomy principle can be breached.

As far as fraud is concerned, it is recognised in English common law, although statute never regulated it. More in detail, fraud shall be demonstrated, since a mere allegation is not enough for this purpose.

Therefore, it is possible to conclude that fraud:

- Constitutes a procedural mechanism, it means that the request from the buyer shall be aimed to stop the bank to pay the seller.
- Requires a material representation of the fact that is untrue.
- Involves the knowledge of the beneficiary.
- Shall be "documentary fraud", not a fraud affecting the underlying contract.

Finally, the fraud exception shall come from the party, not from the bank.[19] By contrast, in the US, the fraud encapsulates both the underlying contract and the documents.

16 [1996] 1 WLR 1152.

17 [2003] EWHC 1927 (Comm).

18 (QBD) [1995] 1 Lloyd's Rep 153.

19 See *United City Merchants (Investments) Ltd v Royal Bank of Canada (The American Accord)*, [1982] 2 QB 208.

7. Letter of credits

One of the most important rules in the letter of credits area is the fact that these letters of credit are transactions autonomous or independent of the underlying contract on which they are based, usually an international sale and purchase agreement. To elaborate, the general rule is that a letter of credits is a contract signed between the issuer (the bank) and the beneficiary (the seller).

In this respect, the letter of a credit constitutes an independent transaction of the underlying contract between the applicant (the buyer) and the beneficiary (the seller).

The principle of independence is encompassed with two Articles: Article 3 and 4 UCP. The first one, Article 3, stipulates as follows: "Credits, by their nature, are separated transactions from the sales or other contract(s), even if any reference whatsoever to such contract(s) is included in the Credit". The second one, that is, Article 4, stipulates: "In credit operations all parties concerned deal with documents and not with goods, services and/or other performances to which the documents may relate".

By contrast, the US approach to independence is achieved via a different point of observation. More precisely, in the US the independence principle is shaped as follows:

> Rights and obligations of an issuer to a beneficiary or a nominated person under a letter of credit are independent of the existence, performance, or non-performance of a contract or arrangement out which the letter of credit arises or which underlies it, including contracts or arrangements between the issuer and the applicant and between the applicant and the beneficiary.[20]

Nevertheless, the independence principle is the most important principle that governs letter of credit transactions. Again, under the principle of independence: credits are by their nature agreements separate from their underlying transactions. Furthermore, the issuer's payment shall be based only on a determination of the conformity of the documents presented with the terms and conditions. In a nutshell, it shall not be possible to refer to beneficiary's performance under the contract. As a result of this, a bank is a under duty to accept the tender of conforming documents and shall not be involved in the underlying controversy between buyer and seller.

Based on such background, the strict compliance principle shall be also interpreted under an IT approach. In other words, FinTech may constitute an appropriate technological means of protect and ensuring the respect of strict compliance.

7.1 Letter of credit structure

Letters of credit, in their traditional structure, involve two parties: a party promises to another party to pay a certain amount of money through a letter.

20 See Uniform Commercial Code § 5-108, entitled "Issuer's Rights and Obligations".

The other party would ship goods to the agent of the aforesaid party.

As a result of the growing scale of business, the network of merchants was not sufficient to guarantee the credit of an individual buyer. Therefore, merchants need the help of a third party, that is a bank, to secure payment between the seller and their unknown buyer. Thus, a third party, again a bank, was adjoined to modern letters of credit. It is possible to affirm that a letter of credit constitutes a kind of documentary transaction that involves credit from the bank, which payment obligation is triggered once the letter of credit is delivered. A letter of credit may also be defined as a written promise of the bank to a seller in which the bank states that the tendered documents will be honoured if a condition is met: the document complies with the terms and conditions defined in the letter of credit.

To achieve this result, it is quintessential that:

- The buyer clearly instructs its bank about the preconditions of the letter of credit.
- The bank promises to pay the seller an agreed amount of money if the beneficiary presents documents of compliance.

7.2 Strict compliance principle

A letter of credit constitutes a written undertaking by a bank to pay a beneficiary when a beneficiary delivers the documents agreed. Moreover, the buyer knows that the letter of credit amount will be released only upon delivery of the conforming documents based on terms and conditions of the credit. In this context, documents are the key elements in the functioning of the letter of credit transaction. Their availability, jointly with the conditions agreed parties, determines the enactment of the letter of credits. It means, in other words, the payment of the amount promised. Consequently, credit function is possible where and if all documents complied with the credit conditions.

Moreover, as emphasised among scholars "the implicit obligation of the bank is to pay against 'genuine' conforming documents; otherwise, credits would be a sham and open to all sorts of chicanery".[21] From a legal point of observation, Article 13(a) UCP stipulates as follows:

> Banks must examine all documents stipulated in the Credit with reasonable care to ascertain whether or not they appear, on their face, to be in compliance with the terms and conditions of the Credit. Compliance of the stipulated documents on their face with the terms and conditions of the Credit, shall be determined by international standard banking practice as reflected in these Articles. Documents which appear on their face to be inconsistent with one another will be considered as not appearing on their face to follow the terms and conditions of the Credit.

21 (Megrah 1982).

Based on this provision, a clear standard of care exercisable by bank is not defined.

By contrast, Uniform Commercial Code stipulates as follows: "An issuer's obligation to his applicant includes good faith and observance of a general banking usage . . . honesty in fact in the conduct of the transaction concerned".[22] Under English common law, the leading case is *Moralice (London) Ltd v E.D. and F Man*,[23] where it was held that documents evidencing a short shipment, in this case 0.06 percent, could be rejected due to the lack of compliance with the terms of the credit. More in depth, in this specific case, the date of shipment, as stated in the bill of lading, was not consistent with the contractual shipment date. Based on this circumstance, the issuing bank was deemed entitled to reject the documents and withhold the payment. Furthermore, another British case law is *Hamzeh Malas & Sons v British Imex Industries Ltd*,[24] where the principle was the following one: a confirmed letter of credit constitutes a contract between the bank and the seller.

This contract imposes upon bank an absolute duty to pay, irrespective of any dispute among parties. The only exception is the existence of a fraudulent transaction. A partially different approach is to consider letter of credit as a payment method, not a payment itself.[25] Therefore, the bank duty arises only from the beneficiary's fulfilment of its obligation by providing conforming documents before the expiry of the credit: a letter of credit represents a means to obtain payment. Ultimately, efficacy may not constitute an excuse for a bank to proceed to payment irrespective of conformity of the documents.

Bearing this in mind, the conclusion is that strict compliance principle requires that:

- Beneficiaries submit the complying documents.
- Bank fulfils its payment obligations once the presented documents conform to the standards in the letter of credit.

Furthermore, the buyer needs to precisely specify what kinds of documents he needs, to prove the possession of the goods from the seller. It is important to stress that this negotiation does not involve the bank and puts the applicant in a strong position, since the beneficiary might find himself stuck in a situation in which he has to submit unavailable documents or accepts non-documentary conditions, if he does not pay attention to the requirements defined in the letter of credit. Yet the buyer, that is the bank's customer, needs to pay for goods that he is unable to examine before the money in transferred.

Moreover, under the strict compliance principle, the agreement between parties may not be restructured. This means that the beneficiary cannot argue that he cannot fulfil his duty in the letter of credit because one of the documents he needs to

22 §5-102(a)(7).
23 [1954] 2 Lloyd's Rep 526.
24 [1958] 2 QB 127.
25 (Van Houten 1984).

submit to the bank shall be taken from the buyer. The underlying reason is that the beneficiary has accepted such requirement under the letter of credit. Thus, once the terms have been accepted, these terms shall be followed.

7.3 Substantial compliance

Substantial compliance standard is based on equity principle. It means that the conditions of the letter of credit are deemed to be met when a document is presented, even if this document does not conform in every formal aspect. This arises because, on some occasions, most courts understand the strictly compliance principle as an absolute standard. For instance, it was required that documents had to comply – words by words – with requirements which were stipulated in the credit. Moreover, strict compliance requires the issuer to verify that all presented documents are according to the literal and exact form. To elaborate, the documents should respect the preconditions of the credit letter, even though the customer had required certification proving payment.

By contrast, in *US Industries v Second New Haven Bank,*[26] the court stated that a strict compliance principle should apply only if a fatal difference was found in the documents. Practically, substantial compliance consists of the fact that the bank is allowed to overlook minor technical differences in documents. However, substantial compliance shall "open the door" to constitute a threat to certainty of the letter of credit. In other words, under the substantial compliance standard, the effectiveness of the letter of credit decreased and, by contrast, the time to examine the documents by banks increased. Despite this, the custom of trade accepts, only, the strict compliance principle, as the essential rule in letters of credits. However, it is also true that in some circumstances, courts combine this rule with other principles of contract law, such as equity law, banking law, etc.

It is also critical to be aware of the fact that letters of credit do not constitute a contract, thus, from a theoretical perspective, the application of the law of contracts to letters of credits should not be encouraged. In a nutshell, to appreciate the importance of letters of credits functions, it is worth focusing the attention on the role of these commercial instruments. Thus, letters of credit are expected to perform several functions: to protect the interests of the issuer and provide applicants with protection that other kinds of payment may lack.

In addition to this, parties in the letter of credit are informed that documents will be honoured if the comply. All these functions may be ensured only under the strictly compliance principle. By contrast, the application of the substantial compliance frustrates the main purpose of letter of credit, that is, to guarantee that the beneficiary guest paid without any uncertainties. Again, the substantial compliance standard has, therefore, discretion of the issuer since the latter acts as judge to evaluate documents presented by the beneficiary in a short time.

26 Civ. No. N-75-305.

8. FinTech in commercial credit

Based on the latest consideration, that is, the progressive transition from the strict compliance principle to substantial compliance concept, one of the challenges that the financial industry faces is how to interpret the former. This uncertainty may lead to disputes and, ultimately, to an inefficient use of letter of credits.

In this scenario, a solution may come from the potential link between IT and customs' needs: FinTech. It is well-known that contemporary era is characterised by the influence of new technologies in a wider range of activities.

FinTech represents an expression which encompasses the use of new technologies to offer products in the financial sector. However, FinTech encapsulates, also, big-tech companies with an interest in the financial sector. Moreover, FinTech constitutes a method, based on IT and offered by big-tech, for both financial and non-financial businesses.[27]

In this respect, IT encompasses different kinds of technologies' applications, that are as follows:

- Blockchain.[28]
- Smart-contracts.[29]
- Internets of Things (IoT).
- Internet of Everything (IoE).

IoT may be defined as any device suitable to realise an Internet connection in real time with devices or their surrounding environment. IoE represents an evolution of IoT: IoE involves more than linking devices on the Internet because it is constituted by four elements: people, processes, data, things. Moreover, IoE constitutes a concept which includes, also, machine-to-machine (M2M) communications, machine-to-people (M2P) technology and technology-assisted people-to-people (P2P) technology.

Further, FinTech in the international trade sector has, at least, two main advantages:

- To guarantee digital payment and it means a reduction of transaction costs, exchange rate risks for import and export enterprises, enhance attractiveness of a country for foreign investors.
- To enhance authentication measures and, consequently, mitigate risks associated with fraud and compliance. To summarise, it means a secure environment for buyers and sellers.

All in all, blockchain and smart contracts diverge from the traditional letter of credit in two main ways:

27 See (de Gioia Carabellese and Della Giustina 2024).

28 Blockchain technology is known, also, as a distributed ledger technology (DLT) or consensus ledger technology. Based on this technology, transactions are based on the block and each block is verified by a network.

29 This term was adopted, for the first time, by Nick Szabo in 2016.

- The applicant no longer fills in the preliminary application that the issuer would use to draft the letter of credit. In other words, the applicant drafts the letter of credit using a standard template provided by the bank and enters it on the blockchain.
- The applicant may include IoT terms in the letter of credit, and the IoT system may track the transaction. In this respect, the applicant would have the primary control and responsibility of drafting the letter of credits. After, the applicant uploads the documents on the blockchain for the issuer to approve, deny or suggest changes. Once the letter of credit is finalised, the issuer adds the parties to the permissioned blockchain: the issuer can control and limit the information available to third parties.

The management of information for the third parties is important, because international transactions involve, often, third parties such as customs, ports and the *ad hoc* departments, for example the Department of Agriculture.

As far as blockchain is concerned, this technology eliminates the need for physical presentment due to the possibility that the blockchain system generates itself the documents. In other words, blockchain may pre-generate documents to ensure that the information reflects the reality of the goods. This mitigates the risk that the document is fraudulent.

Thanks to blockchain technology it is possible to achieve the objective named "tokenisation of letters of credits".

It means a digitalisation of letter of credits to guarantee transparency, security and efficiency in global trade transactions. In this respect, it is guaranteed that every transaction is recorded. Tokenisation is aimed to transform physical asserts, or rights, into digital token within a blockchain framework. It means that thanks to this procedure, letters of credits are converted from the traditional paperwork to a digital token recorded into a blockchain network. These tokens encapsulate all terms, conditions and obligations linked with the letter of credits. In this way, each transaction is secure and efficient. Further, a digital representation of a letter of credits:

- Enhances the security and transparent of trade.
- Makes more responsive and responsive the trade process.

An even better result comes from a combination between tokenisation and blockchain technology: the cryptographic nature of blockchain technology ensures a high level of integrity and security for tokenised letter of credits.

Additionally, the incorporation of letters of credit into smart contracts allows both to comply with predetermined terms and to reduce the risk of fraud or errors. However, a recent international case does not corroborate such approach. In *COSCO Shipping Heavy Industry (Dalian) Co Ltd & Anor v Osta Fleet Sdn Bhd*[30] the dispute was around the manipulation of digital document. More precisely, this case dealt

30 [2024] MLJU 2250.

with the authenticity of a Builder's Certificate: the plaintiff alleged that the submitted certificate for the vessel's registration had been digitally forged. In assessing such matter, the court adapted traditional forensic methods to the digital context. Thanks to this, forensic evidence demonstrated that both the signature and the Commissioner for Oath's stamp were not wet-ink signed by inkjet-printed toner images. Moreover, both the signature and the stamp were identical in design, size, spacing and alignment across different documents. Therefore, it was established that it was vital to ascertain that digital documents are true and not manipulated.

Ultimately, this new *modus operandi* suggested by "*COSCO Shipping Heavy Industry (Dalian) Co Ltd*" guarantees trust, reliability in the system, by ultimately reducing the cost of both global and domestic trade.

Not secondarily, blockchain reduces, also the issuer's role in determining documentary compliance: the issuer only gets involved if something is wrong.

The mechanism under blockchain technology works in the following ways:

- Blockchain verifies the information of the document with the terms of the letter of credit.
- If there are no discrepancies, the blockchain notes that the document is complying. Consequently, the smart contract may authorise the goods to proceed to the next step.
- The issuer makes the final assessment relating to the documentation compliance.

It is clear why the principle of strict compliance is a form of guarantee. Data from the blockchain are encompassed with the documents. Consequently, banks are able to adhere to the rule only dealing with documentary conditions. Moreover, the issuer should not impose its own subjective opinions on the underlying contract. This is possible because the documents that are produced based on blockchain technology constitute objective facts. In other words, blockchain technology:

- Helps the issuer to adhere to the strict compliance principle because are more objective.
- Help parties to detect potential documentary discrepancies.

Finally, it is possible to affirm that blockchain, smart contracts and IoT are means of ensuring that letters of credit remain a commercial credit mechanism also in the future and in the IT era. The underlying reason is the fact that these technologies facilitate the documentary compliance.[31]

Consequently, thanks to FinTech letter of credits, on one hand, become even more IT oriented and, on the other hand, it is possible to bind one of the most ancient principles, the principle of strict compliance.

31 (Larson 2018).

References

de Gioia Carabellese, Pierre, and Camilla Della Giustina. 2024. *Banking Law and Financial Regulation in the UK and EU: Technology, Human Rights and Crises*. Routledge.

Embley, Judith, Keir Bamford, and Nick Hancock. 2024. *Commercial and Intellectual Property Law and Practice*. College of Law Publishing.

Larson, Dakota A. 2018. "Mitigating Risky Business: Modernizing Letters of Credit with Blockchain, Smart contracts, and the Internet of Things." *Michigan State Law Review* 930–85.

Megrah, Maurice. 1982. "Risk Aspects of the Irrevocable Documentary Credit." *Arizona Law Review* 24: 255.

Van Houten, Stephen H. 1984. "Letters of Credit and Fraud: A Revisionist View." *The Canadian Bar Review* 62: 371–88.

27 Marine insurance

Chapter Overview

1. Introduction

The insurance of a ship constitutes an old practice. From a linguistic perspective, insurance, more in detail the insurance policy (as the contract of insurance is traditionally defined), comes from Italian, and it derives from "*polizza*" as promise or undertaking.[1]

In *The Sadlers Company v Badcock*,[2] the concept of insurance was linked with the aversion *periculi*, *periculum* meaning danger in Latin: it indicates the intention of all insurances being to avert any damages or loss the insured might sustain.

As regards English law, the most entrenched forms of policies were three: marine, life and fire. Among these, marine insurance was the most ancient, as well as one of the most uncertain from the legal point of view.

The customs and practices of merchants to be insured were encompassed into *lex mercatoria*. Moreover, from "Continental law" has derived the influence to adopt clauses called "interest or no interest".

These were aimed to flag up those policies contained clauses named "wager policies" in force of which the insured did not need to prove his interest. The insured was able to receive protection for the ships and/or cargos, but he did not have any interest as a means of gaining profit. If a loss occurred, the insured would be able

1 (de Gioia Carabellese 2024).
2 (1743).

DOI: 10.4324/9781003645948-27

to claim the insured value, even if he had not suffered any loss for the lack of insurable interest. By contrast, if the loss did not occur, he lost the premium.[3]

Based on *Pole v Fitzgerald*,[4] marine insurance was defined as a contract where there is a potential indemnity relating to things transported by sea from one country to another country.

More in general, it is critical to construe marine insurance through the economic lens of international trade law. In this respect, this contract, marine insurance, plays a quintessential role for businesses engaged in cross-border trade. The reason for that is quite simple: marine insurance provides financial protection against various risks associated with the transportation of goods by sea.[5]

In this respect, marine insurance covers a range of perils: fire; theft; collision; sinking; and damages caused by rough sea. Furthermore, it is possible to affirm that marine insurance[6] achieves different objectives for businesses:

- Risk mitigation, since it provides a safety net that allows business to recover financially after unforeseen mishaps.
- Financial protection.
- The reputation and customer relationship to be maintained and guaranteed.
- Compliance with trade contracts: some of these agreements impose that buyer or seller obtain marine insurance to protect the interest of both parties during transportation process.
- Contribution to the overall resilience of global supply chain.

2. The contract of marine insurance

The Marine Insurance Act 1906[7] constitutes the main legal source that governs the relationship between parties to a contract of marine insurance in common law.

A contract of marine insurance is aimed to cover marine losses: based on Section 1, MIA 1906, a contract of marine insurance may be defined as "a contract whereby the insurer undertakes to indemnify the assured, in manner and to the extent thereby agreed, against marine losses, that is to say, the losses incident to marine adventure".

For marine adventure, Section 3, MIA, refers to a situation where:

- Ships' goods or other movables are exposed to marine perils.
- "The earning or acquisition of any freight, passage money, commission, profit, or other pecuniary benefit, or the security for any advances, loan, or disbursements, is endangered by the exposure of insurable property to maritime perils".[8]

3 These policies were prohibited under Marine Insurance Act 1745, henceforth MIA 1745.
4 (1750) Wiles 641.
5 (de Gioia Carabellese 2024).
6 (Gürses 2023).
7 Henceforth MIA 1906.
8 Section 3(1)(b), MIA 1906.

- Any liability of a third party in which the owner, or other person (i.e., a person interested in or responsible for), may be incurred for insurable property by reason of maritime perils.

Further, Section 3(2) provides a definition of "Maritime perils": it refers to

> the perils consequent on, or incidental to, the navigation of the sea, that is to say, perils of the seas, fire, war perils, pirates, rovers, thieves, captures, seizures, restraints, and detainments of princes and peoples, jettisons, barratry, and any other perils, either of the like kind or which may be designated by the policy.

It is critical to stress that a ship shall be insured also if she is under construction. In this case the policy assumes the form of marine policy.

In this respect, the reference foes to Section 2(2), MIA 1906, which states as follows:

> Where a ship in course of building, or the launch of a ship, or any adventure analogous to a marine adventure, is covered by a policy in the form of a marine policy, the provisions of this Act, in so far as applicable, shall apply thereto; but, except as by this section provided, nothing in this Act shall alter or affect any rule of law applicable to any contract of insurance other than a contract of marine insurance as by this Act defined".

A marine policy may also refer to land risk that may occur before and after the marine risk. In this respect, in *Leon v Casey*[9] the policy encompassed a warehouse-to-warehouse clause. The latter covered the ancillary journey by rail from Cairo to the port as well as the sea voyage. The court held that this policy was in the form of marine policy; additionally, the land risks were covered by the warehouse-to-warehouse clause.

Finally, a critical point is concerned with the definition of "sea". Indeed, MIA 1906 does not provide a definition. However, under the Institute Time Clauses Hull 1983 clause 6.1.1 and International Hull Clauses clause 2.1.1. the expression "perils of the seas" encompasses rivers, lakes and, more in general, "other navigable waters".

Although under English common law this matter is not disputed, nor controversial, a different approach comes from the Australian common law. For example, in *Gibbs v Mercantile Mutual Insurance (Australia) Ltd*,[10] the accident occurred

9 [1932] 2 KB 576.

10 P48/2001 [2002] HCATrans 259. Mr Gibbs was insured on a "Marine Pleasure craft Policy" which covered third party liabilities. This policy was extended: (1) to any persons navigating or in charge of the vessel; (2) to cover commercial paraflying; (3) contained a navigation warranty of "Protected waters of WA as per permit". Mr Gibb conducted a commercial paraflying operation in the estuarine

when the boat was too close to land, whilst being driven, and eventually crashed into trees. It was emphasised that "marine insurance" meant that the insurance concerned risks arising from sea voyages. Thus, a river should not be defined as sea, consequently it exceeded the perimeter of MIA 1906.

By contrast, the major opinion stressed that the concept of "sea" was not limited to the open ocean, and the most important element consisted into the kind of risk that would be insured. In this respect, it is highlighted that MIA 1906:

- Was aimed to codify the law regulating dealing with commercial markets.
- Did not preclude the expansion of the marine insurance markets, such as marine technology development.
- The expression "marine perils" encapsulates more that the merely "perils of the seas".
- "Perils of the sea" refers, also, to risk that should not be occurs at sea.

3. Main contractual principles

As said previously, marine insurance constitutes a contract in which one person, named insurers, is legally bound to pay a sum of money, or its equivalent, to another person, the insured, if a specific event will occur.

Bearing this in mind, there are three main principles within marine insurance:[11]

- The principle of indemnity.
- The principle of utmost good faith.
- The principle of insurable interest.

The first one, the principle of indemnity, pursues two main objectives:

- To ensure that the amount compensated or reimbursed shall not increase the assets of the insured in any way. In other words, it is quintessential to guarantee that an insurance policy does not become a source of benefit and/or profit for the insured.
- To guarantee that the amount of compensation, or reimbursement, should not exceed the value of the policy taken. The amount agreed constitutes the upper limit of the compensation shall be paid.

The utmost good faith principle[12] is linked with the nature of the marine insurance contract. Section 17, MIA 1906 stipulates that "Insurance is *uberrimae fidei*. A contract of marine insurance is a contract based upon the utmost good faith and, if the

waters of the Swan River in Perth (Western Australia). In doing so, Mrs Morell was injured whilst paraflying and Mr Gibbs claimed on the e Marine Pleasurecraft Policy.

11 (Thomas 2023).

12 This principle was shaped in *Carter v Bohem* [(1766)] 3 Burr 1905.

utmost good faith be not observed by either party, the contract may be avoided by the other party".

The third principle is the principle linked with the insurable interest. In this respect, it is quintessential to distinguish contracts where relationship between the assured and the subject matter is sufficiently close as to justify that a sum of money shall be paid in the event of its loss or damages, from the case where the linkage is not close.

Based on Section 5(1), MIA 1906, every person "has an insurable interest who is interested in a marine adventure". Furthermore, it is possible to affirm that an insurable risk shall present three main characteristics:[13]

- The insured may benefit by the safety or due arrival of insurable property or be prejudiced by its loss or damage or detention or in respect of which he may incur liability.
- The insured stands in a legal or equitable relation to the adventure or to any insurable property at risk in such adventure.
- The benefit shall arise in consequence of the legal or equitable relation.

In *Lucena v Craufurd*[14] the court stated as follows:

> A man is interested in a thing to whom advantage may arise or prejudice happen from circumstances which may attend it. Interest does not necessarily imply a right to the whole or part of a thing, nor necessarily and exclusively that part which may be the subject of privation but having some relation to or concern in the subject of the insurance which relation or concern may be so affected as to produce a damage, detriment or prejudice to the person insuring.

As far as the types of interest are concerned,[15] the following shall be insured:

- Ownership of property carries.
- The mortgage of a ship for the amount for which the ship was its security. In this respect, Section 14(1), MIA 1906, stipulates as follows: "Where the subject-matter insured is mortgaged, the mortgagor has an insurable interest in the full value thereof, and the mortgagee has an insurable interest in respect of any sum due or to become due under the mortgage".
- Profit on the ground that it forms an additional part of the value of the goods in which the party has already an interest.
- Pervasive interest that may found in commercial contracts as a matter of commercial convenience.
- Defeasible interest as well as partial interest.

13 (de Gioia Carabellese 2024).
14 (1806) 2 BOS & PNR 269.
15 (Rainey, Blackwood, and Walsh 2019).

As a result of this, it is even more clear that insurable interests are multiform and numerous.[16]

A critical element is the date of loss: "The insured assured must be interested in the subject-matter insured at the time of the loss though he need not be interested when the insurance is effected". Therefore, if the insured effects the insurance, believes that he will acquire an interest, and he acquires it before the loss, he can recover. In *Sutherland v Pratt*,[17] the court held that a policy represents a clearly contract of indemnity against all past as well as all future: losses sustained by the assured in the respect of the interest insured. Additionally, it operates in the same way as if the defendant had agreed for a premium. If the goods had at the time of the purchase sustained any damage by perils of the sea, he would make it good.

4. The structure of marine insurance policy

The contract of marine insurance shall be in a policy in which it is specified: the name of the insured; the subject-matter; the risks, the voyage or period covered by the insurance; the sum insured, the name of the insurer. This contract shall be also signed by the insurer and/or his/her representative.

A policy is voided if there is:

- Any implied conditions to the commencement of the risk because the adventure shall be commenced within a reasonable time.
- Alteration of port of departure.
- Sailing to different destination.
- Change of voyage.
- Deviation.
- Delay.

5. The impact of IT evolution: the insurance of remote-controlled and autonomous ship

In the contemporary era, one of the most controversial issues concerned with the liability relating to remote control vessel[18] and autonomous vessel.[19] To elaborate, these kinds of vessels may be able to operate in a legal way only if maritime laws

16 From a comparative perspective, in the US an in *Hooper v Robinson*, 98 U.S. 528 (1879), it was stated as follows: "A right of property in a thing is not always indispensable to an insurable interest. Injury from its loss or benefit from its preservation to accrue to the assured may be sufficient, and a contingent interest thus arising may be made the subject of a policy. In the law of marine insurance, insurable interests are multiform and very numerous".

17 (1843) 11 M &. W 296.

18 Also, ROV. Traditionally, it should not be qualified as a vessel, due to the lack of the autonomy from the "main" vessel. Additionally, a ROV cannot face the risk and dangers.

19 Also, AV: it possesses a more advanced IT support and may have, also, a high-speed and precision motion performance.

shall be applicable. Consequently, the main question concerns the amended of these rules.

More in detail, the controversial aspects refer to the following:[20]

- The liability of manufacturer and if the latter will respond to a causality report that alludes to any software-related issues.
- The fact that maritime conventions will be updated.
- Insurance warranty may impose an obligation on the part of the assured based on two main pillars: (1) "take all reasonable steps"; (2) to maintain and update software and hardware required for autonomous navigation.

In this respect, International Maritime Organization[21] is going to develop its regulatory framework for autonomous ships.

Additionally, European Boat Association[22] suggests the adoption of a regulation based on different levels of automation, as well as the specific sector in which the AV shall be used.

Based on such a background, the best approach seems to be case-by-case regulation, focused on a specific economic sector.

Furthermore, for every level of automation, the following elements shall be discussed: human element, technology and operational procedures.[23]

US Regulation encourages Coast Guard to ensure that experimentation will be delivered systematically and at a lower cost: the aim is to identify beneficial uses of this new technology.[24] It is also important to put the attention on the fact that the Maritime Safety Committee (MSC) approved Interim guidelines for MASS trials.[25] Based on such guidelines, the most important thing is that trials should be conducted in a manner that provides the same degree of safety, security and protection of the environment as provided by the relevant instruments.

According to this line of reasoning, it is vital that risk associated with the trials should be identified in an appropriate manner. Therefore, all measures necessary to reduce risks should be adopted. Furthermore, it is also crucial that personnel involved in MASS trial possesses an appropriately qualified and experienced to safety conduct MASS trials. Finally, it is also recommended that the area of trials should be determined, marked and communicated to all relevant parties. In this

20 (de Gioia Carabellese and Della Giustina 2024).

21 Henceforth IMO.

22 Henceforth EBA.

23 EBA Position Statement Autonomous Shipping, October 19, 2019.

24 U.S. Coastal Guard supports testing of autonomous shipping under certain conditions. Based on *Guidelines for Human-Supervised Testing of Remote Controlled and Autonomous Systems on Vessels* some guidance to Captains of the Port for testing autonomous ship technologies are provided. These guidelines stress that tests shall not delivery in a way that reduce the number of crew on a vessel. This system consists into a case-by-case process on a local level: the applicant shall work directly with local level, i.e., Coast Guard Captains of Port.

25 See MSC.1-Circ.1604.

respect, the area of trials involves both coordination and cooperation of coastal States, flag States and port States.

From an EU perspective, it is worth emphasising the adoption, on 1st October 2020, of "Eu Operational Guidelines for Safe, Secure and Sustainable Trials of Maritime Autonomous Surface Ships (MASS)", defined as non-mandatory, to support a uniform application of the operational process for allowing trials.

The latter should be delivered in designated testing environments, such as: test areas and/or ships safety zone. The goal is to guarantee the protection of human life, maritime safety, security and the environment.

These guidelines define the power of the competent authority where it authorises trials. More in detail, the authority, named Relevant Administration, is the organisation(s) responsible for designation of test areas and/or ships zones. Furthermore, the Relevant Administration is the Competent Authority or National Authority in charge to authorise or approvals trials in such areas. The most important element is concerned with the Applicant's duties.

An applicant is the relevant stakeholder that formally apply for trials and, therefore, it assumes both responsibility and liability for trials. In addition, the applicant submits all necessary information to the relevant administration.[26]

Finally, a potential new "player" shall become quintessential: the Remote Operation Centres.[27] The latter constitutes the centre in charge of the control of the Maritime Autonomous Surface Ships.[28]

More in detail, ROC constitutes the "human" factor inside the remote-control centres.[29] The latter is the IT control system, therefore, one of the main questions is if RCC shall be interpreted as a part or, better, as an extension of the remote-controlled vessel.[30]

If the answer is "yes", it will play a significant role in determining vessel's seaworthiness. Furthermore, the RCO shall be defined as the "ship manager" under the following duties:

- To monitor the location and movement of vessel.
- To instruct the operator to direct the vessel to a location.
- To define the performance of the maritime adventure.

Technically,[31] it should be distinguished between two different situations if a collision arises. The first one refers to the negligence of RCO. The question is if the shipowner will be liable for the negligence of RCO even if the RCC is an

26 https://transport.ec.europa.eu/system/files/2020-11/guidelines_for_safe_mass.pdf.

27 Henceforth RCC. See European Maritime Safety Agency, *CMOROC Identification of Competences for MASS Operators in Remote Operation Centres* (Lisbon: EMSA, 2023).

28 Henceforth MASS.

29 Henceforth RCC.

30 (Della Giustina and de Gioia Carabellese 2025).

31 (Della Giustina and de Gioia Carabellese 2024).

independent contractor. It seems that the owner should not be liable, unless it will show that the owner acted negligently in delegating responsibility to specific contractor.

By contrast, a second scenario refers to software/hardware error. Potentially, in this case, liable may be considered the shipowner.

References

de Gioia Carabellese, Pierre. 2024. *From Utmost Good Faith to Algorithmic Faith in Marine Insurance: A 'Blue IT' Perspective*. Studium.

de Gioia Carabellese, Pierre, and Camilla Della Giustina. 2024. "Legal Categorisation of Autonomous Vessels Before the Court: A Recent Dictum from South Africa." *Diritto del Mercato Assicurativo e Finanziario* 1 (1): 1–10.

Della Giustina, Camilla, and Pierre de Gioia Carabellese. 2024. "Drone Technology in Green Transition from Sky to Sea." *Journal of Transportation Law, Logistics & Policy* 2: 173–89.

Della Giustina, Camilla, and Pierre de Gioia Carabellese. 2025. "A Holistic Approach to Esg Transition Through 'Drones' Technology." *Revista de Derecho del Transporte* 121–43.

Gürses, Özlem. 2023. *Marine Insurance Law*. Routledge.

Rainey, Simon, Guy Blackwood, and David Walsh. 2019. *Chalmers' Marine Insurance Act 1906*. Bloomsbury Publishing.

Thomas, D. Rhidian. 2023. *The Modern Law of Marine Insurance*. Routledge.

28 Finance and security in international sale of goods

Chapter Overview

1. Introduction

An international contract of sale of goods usually sets out the payment provisions agreed between the parties.

In this respect, a vital role is played by bills of exchange and documentary credits: these have developed over centuries; they involve complex networks of contractual relationships between the seller, buyer and the parties' respective banks.

It should be noted that there are three main methods of payment available in international transactions:

- Cash in advance: the seller may insist on payment in advance, particularly where they have not dealt with the buyer before or lack confidence in the buyer's creditworthiness. In practice, this is unusual, and insistence on cash in advance may cause the buyer to seek the goods from other suppliers.
- Payment on "open account": parties deal with each other on a regular basis, and the seller has complete faith in the creditworthiness of the buyer, the seller may agree to "open account" terms. This is more favourable to the buyer than insistence on cash in advance. There are advantages for both parties; payment on open account is cheaper than the use of a bill of exchange, since bank charges are lower. Once the seller has delivered the goods to the buyer, they will invoice the buyer. The invoice may provide for a credit period, depending on what has

DOI: 10.4324/9781003645948-28

been agreed between the parties. There is a variety of actual payment methods, for example, cheque, banker's draft, interbank transfer or international direct debit. Payment on "open account" is more usual where the sale is within Europe.

- Bill of exchange: if the seller is unsure of the buyer's creditworthiness, the parties may agree for payment to be made under a bill of exchange, which is a form of 16.1.2 16.1.3 (a) negotiable instrument. This method of payment is more likely to be used if the sale is outside of the EU, as it will be more difficult to enforce payment or reclaim the goods. Payment is arranged through the international banking system.

The advantage of a documentary credit is that the seller can be guaranteed in the payment before it ships the goods.[1]

2. The relationship between bills of exchange and documentary credits

Documentary credits and bills of exchange have very different uses and functions; they are very different legal instruments, aimed at solving very different problems. The primary function of the bill of exchange is as a means of providing payment to the seller, by way of an easy transferable document rather than the straightforward payment of cash. By contrast, the main function of a documentary credit is to help guarantee that the seller will be paid. It is a promise provided by a third-party bank, or financial institution, that the seller will be paid, even if the buyer defaults.

The provision of a documentary credit will be required where the seller is unwilling to contract with the buyer without one, for example, because it has no knowledge of the credit history of the buyer, and where it is powerful enough to get its own way. Where a documentary credit has been agreed, the sale contract will oblige the buyer to open the credit within a specified time from the date of the contract. A documentary credit creates separate contractual obligations on the part of the bank additional to and independent of the sale contract and the buyer's obligation to pay for the goods.

3. The bill of exchange

A bill of exchange or "draft" is defined in Section 3(1), Bills of Exchange Act 1882 (BEA 1882), the British piece of legislation in this area. According to this section, a bill of exchange is "an unconditional order in writing, addressed by one person to another, signed by the person giving it, requiring the person to whom it is addressed to pay on demand or at a fixed or determinable future time, a sum certain in money to or to the order of a specified person, or to a bearer". A bill of exchange is a document under the drawer orders to drawee, usually a bank or financier pay a specified sum of money to a payee, the third part. The main characteristics of a

1 (Ellinger and Neo 2010).

bill of exchange are as follows: (1) every obligation in the bill must be expressed in writing; (2) the order to pay must be unconditional; (3) it is addressed by one person to another.

Furthermore, there are different typologies of bill of exchange, such as the following:

- "Sight" bills, payable on demand, that means on presentation to the drawee, usually a bank, so payment is immediate. A cheque is an example of a sight bill: it is payable when it is presented to the drawer's bank.
- Bearer bills may be transferred merely by delivery, like a bank note. The drawee is simply obliged to pay out to whoever happens to possess the bill at the relevant time. There is no obligation on the drawee to check how the holder has obtained the bill. Bearer bills are clearly very insecure and are not used much in practice. A bearer bill cannot be "closed down": cheques used to be widely negotiable, but as a fraud prevention measure, most cheques are now printed with crossing lines and "a/c payee". This prevents them being transferable by endorsement.
- Order bills specify payment to a particular person or to their order, like a cheque. To make a bill non-transferable, it is essential to state this, specifically. In addition, an order bill may be "opened up" into a bearer bill by the present holder indorsing it in blank, and then "closed down" again by indorsing it to a particular person.

4. How bill of exchanges work

One significant advantage of a bill of exchange is that the document itself, the bill, is transferable, so that payment may be demanded not only by the original payee. Furthermore, anyone who has possession of it at the relevant time for payment. Thus, a bill of exchange may be bought and sold like any other commodity. The way in which a bill is transferred is by the holder "indorsing" it (i.e., signing their name on the back of the bill).[2]

An important concept is discounting. It alludes to the ability to transfer a bill of exchange for the seller to raise money before payment becomes due. In other words, the bill is sold to a third party. The buyer will pay less than the face value of the bill to consider the delay in receiving payment. For discounting to work, it is important that the buyer knows that the drawee of the bill (usually a bank) will pay up when the payment date is due. Term bills are therefore presented to the drawee which will indorse its "acceptance" on the face of the bill, thus guaranteeing payment of the bill in the future. When payment is due, the bill is re-presented to the drawee for payment: a term bill must be presented twice to the bank, and payment is due on the second occasion.[3]

One of the main problems is that the bill might have been stolen, or one of the previous holders of the bill might have had some other defect in their title to the

2 (Sang Man 2021).
3 (Yurdagül 2019).

bill. Thus, some rules have been developed to protect the "holder in due course". Under Section 29(1), Bill of Exchange Act 1882 (BEA), a holder in due course is anyone who gives value for a bill which is still current and which appears to be perfectly regular on the face of it. Provided that a holder in due course has taken the bill in good faith, and without knowledge of any defects in the title to the bill, they will take the bill "free from equities". This means that they can ignore any defects in the title of anyone who had held the bill before them. There is a presumption in favour of a holder that they are a holder in due course.

5. Parties to the bill of exchange

There are three original parties to a bill of exchange: drawer, drawee and payee.

The expression "collection arrangements" or "documentary collection" describes the mechanics by which the seller collects payment under a documentary bill. A bill of exchange is normally drawn either against (or guaranteed by) a documentary credit, or alternatively against the documents themselves, when it will be known as a "documentary bill".

A documentary bill is used where the seller wishes to guard against the possibility of not getting paid but is not in a strong enough bargaining position to be able to demand a documentary credit. The advantage of a documentary bill is that it uses the banking system to safeguard the seller's position so it can be reducing the risk of non-payment. Given the analogy of a cheque, it would be logical to assume that the basic position would be that the drawer is the buyer, the drawee is the buyer's bank, and the payee is the seller of the goods. However, with a bill of exchange, the position is as follows: the seller is the drawer, the buyer or their bank is the drawee and the seller is the payee, that is, the drawer and the payee are the same.

The obligation to pay on a bill of exchange is unconditional and will not be affected by any defect or breach of the underlying sales contract on the part of the seller. Thus, the obligation to pay under the bill of exchange is the result of a separate contract and remains unaffected, even if the goods are defective. In other words, a bill of exchange has an autonomy of its own, and the only real exception to this is if there is complete or partial failure of consideration by the seller. If the seller sues for payment, the buyer can raise the breach as a defence to a claim for refusal to pay the bill.

The claim is a claim on the bill of exchange: on a promise that the paper could be turned into cash. It is not a claim for breach of the payment obligations under the underlying sales contract.

6. The function of the bill of exchange in international trade

The bill of exchange performs many functions in international trade,[4] such as to facilitate the granting of trade credit in a legal format by permitting payments on agreed future dates.[5] This means it provides the following:

4 (Srivastava 2020).

5 (Putu Sudini, Wayan Sitiari, and Putu Pertamawati 2017).

- Formal evidence of the demand for payment from a seller to a buyer.
- The seller with access to finance by permitting them to transfer their debts to a bank or other financier by merely indorsing the bill of exchange to that bank or financier.

Moreover, the bill of exchange permits the banker or financier to retain a valid legal claim on both the buyer and the seller. In certain circumstances, a bank or financier may have a stronger legal claim under a bill than the party that sold them the debt. It permits a seller to obtain greater security over the payment by enabling a bank to guarantee a drawee's acceptance (guarantee to pay on the due date) by signing or endorsing the bill. It allows a seller to protect their access to the legal system in the event of problems, while providing easier access to that legal system.

The relationships of the parties with the banks involved depends on which type of credit is used. With an unconfirmed letter of credit, the Advising Bank is simply an agent of the Issuing Bank, and its only function is to notify the seller and receive the documents. Other banking arrangements may be entered, authorised by the Issuing Bank to pay, negotiate, issue a different payment undertaking or accept drafts under the documentary credit. This facilitates collection and payment in the seller's country.

With a confirmed letter of credit, the Confirming Bank is adding its own guarantee of payment. It is, in effect, entering a separate banking contract (as principal, not as an agent) with the seller to pay, provided that the seller provides the documents stipulated in the letter of credit. If the Confirming Bank fails to pay, the seller can sue it direct without needing to claim against the Issuing Bank. Thus, the setting up of a documentary credit gives rise to a complex network of contractual relationships.

References

Ellinger, Peter, and Dora Neo. 2010. *The Law and Practice of Documentary Letters of Credit*. Hart Publishing.

Putu Sudini, Luh, Ni Wayan Sitiari, and Ni Putu Pertamawati. 2017. "Bill's of Lading Implication in International Trade." *Journal of Law, Policy and Globalization* 60: 21–27.

Sang Man, Kim. 2021. *Payment Methods and Finance for International Trade*. Singapore: Springer.

Srivastava, Ajendra. 2020. *Modern Law of International Trade*. Singapore: Springer.

Yurdagül, Meral. 2019. "Strategic Management of Finance and Role of Documentary Credit." In *Handbook of Research on Global Issues in Financial Communication and Investment Decision Making*, edited by Hasan Dinçer and Serhat Yüksel, 395–416. IGI Global.

Index

For Product Safety Concerns and Information please contact our EU representative GPSR@taylorandfrancis.com Taylor & Francis Verlag GmbH, Kaufingerstraße 24, 80331 München, Germany